Why V ... ant Guide?

Traditionally, Visual Basic ha ... for friendly, easy-to-grasp programming techniques. The ... ands of Visual Basic programmers of all skill levels reach a sta ... snazzy, something to show off to their friends—something *speci* ... you how to do just that.

Like previous Instant Guides, our aim is to produce a comprehensive yet fast-paced guide to a fascinating culmination of technologies. All the major topics, concepts and constructs are dealt with in detail through commercial and publicly available examples. We have assumed that you have a solid understanding of Visual Basic and simply need a direct approach to implementing polished graphics in your code.

What is Wrox Press?

Wrox Press is a computer book publisher which promotes a brand new concept—clear, jargon-free programming and database titles that fulfill your real demands. We publish for everyone, from the novice through to the experienced programmer. To ensure our books meet your needs, we carry out continuous research on all our titles. Through our dialog with you we can craft the book you really need.

We welcome suggestions and take all of them to heart—your input is paramount in creating the next great Wrox title. Use the reply card inside this book or contact us at:

feedback@wrox.com

Compuserve 100063, 2152

http://www.wrox.com/

Wrox Press Ltd.
2710 W. Touhy
Chicago
IL 60645
USA

Tel: +1 (312) 465 3559

Fax:+1 (312) 465 4063

Instant VB Animation

Michele Leroux

Wrox Press Ltd.®

Instant
VB Animation

WROX

Published by Wrox Press Ltd. 30 Lincoln Road, Olton, Birmingham, B27 6PA.
Printed in Canada
Library of Congress Catalog no. 96-60774

ISBN 1-874416-78-8

Trademark Acknowledgements

Credits

Author
Michele Leroux

Foreword
Carl Franklin

Lead Editor
Graham Butler

Contributing Editors
Adrian M Sill
Darren Gill
Alex Stockton

Managing Editor
John Franklin

Technical Reviewers
Carl Franklin
Mike Sussman
Peter Wright
Alex Homer
Nigel Thompson
Stefan Albrecht

Production Manager
Joanne Sawyer

Design/Layout
Neil Gallagher
Andrew Guillaume
Hetendra Parekh

CD Book Authoring
Andrew Guillaume

Proof Readers
Pam Brand
Melanie Orgee
Simon Gilks
Robin Morris

Indexers
Simon Gilks
Robin Morris

Cover Design
Third Wave

Author Photo
Roger Carlsen
(Toronto, Canada
905-294-2722)

For more information on Third Wave, contact Ross Alderson on 44-121 236 6616
Cover photo supplied by The Image Bank

Dedication

Dedicated to my brother Paul,
with encouragement
and to Andres,
with great respect and adoration.

Author Biography

Michele Leroux is a programmer at ImageWare Software Inc. (based in San Diego, CA), and is part of the R&D team who specialize in digital imaging software, primarily for law enforcement. Michele also teaches beginner and advanced level VB programming at the University of California, San Diego (UCSD) and has written many technical articles for the Visual Basic Developer magazine.

Special Thanks

Special thanks to Bill Ibbetson and John Canepa at ImageWare.

```
Private Declare Function GlobalFree Lib "kernel32" (ByVal h
Private Declare Function GlobalLock Lib "kernel32" (ByVal h
Private Declare Function GlobalUnlock Lib "kernel32" (ByVa
'--copying bitmap bits
' copies a global block of data into global memory
Private Declare Sub CopyMemory Lib "kernel32" Alias "RtlM

'--copies global block of data into DIB
Private Declare Function SetDIB    "gdi32" (ByVal m_hd
  ByVal hBitmap As Long, ByVal nStartS    As Long, ByV
  ByVal lpBits As Any, lpBI As BITMAPI    ByVal wUsa

'--blits DC to DC
Private Declare Function BitBlt Lib "gdi32" (ByVal hDestDC
Private Declare Function StretchBlt Lib "gdi32" (ByVal hDes

'--palette methods
Private Declare Function CreatePalett    "gdi32" (lpLogPal
Private Declare Function SelectPalette    "gdi32" (ByVal m
Private Declare Function RealizePalette Lib "gdi32" (ByVal m
Private Declare Sub AnimatePalette Lib "gdi32" (ByVal hPal

'--device context methods
Private Declare Function SelectObject Lib "gdi32" (ByVal m_

Private Declare Function CreateCompatibleBitmap Lib "gdi32
Private Declare Function DeleteObject Lib "gdi32" (ByVal hC

Private Declare Function CreateCompatibleDC Lib "gdi32" (
```

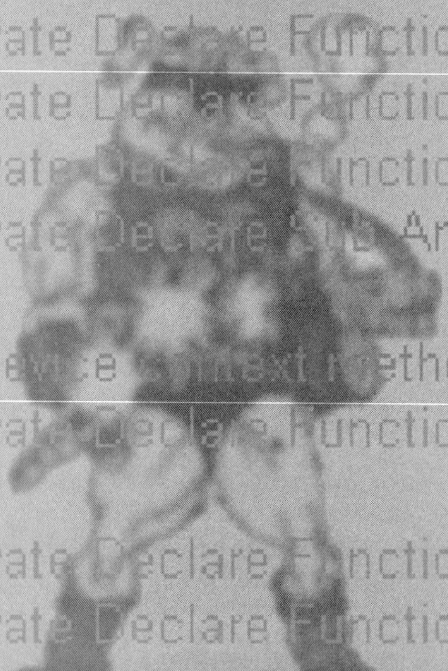

VB Animation

Foreword

I'm green with envy. When I started my journey into the heart of Windows, I dove head first into graphics programming. I was working at Crescent Software back in the days when it was just a few programmers in the basement of Ethan Winer's house in CT. Between tech support calls I was figuring out how to load, display and otherwise mangle bitmaps in VB using the API. After mastering the basics of bitmaps: loading, displaying, capturing, printing and the like, I ventured on to animation.

Although I had lots of help from the Zen Masters of Windows Graphics on the fundamentals of bitmaps, palettes and devices, animation techniques were not that widely known to Windows programmers. Needless to say, I had to take that journey alone. It was a dark and murky path, but the light at the end of that tunnel was glorious. Unfortunately, I stopped working on the animation project after I got it working, so that it never got polished up and the documentation never got written. As with most quests for knowledge, the journey is much more interesting than the destination.

So why am I green with envy? I am envious not for some small reason, such as wishing I had written this book. I am envious of you, dear reader. For you are about to embark on the most rewarding quest a programmer can take. Do not read this book merely to supply means to an end. Savor it page by page and chapter by chapter. Graphics programming is a truly spiritual topic, a constant stimulus to the ego, fueled by facts that sometimes make all the sense in the world, and sometimes make you look at your monitor like the little dog on the RCA Victor label. You may need a chiropractor.

This book goes way beyond my simple sprite animation project. Let me try and describe the experience of it to you. First of all, Michele leaves no stone unturned. She covers stuff you didn't even want to know. You will not want for knowledge. Second of all, she writes like she talks to you, as if she were sitting right next to you as you code, helping you to understand what's going on. The book starts with a good general look at all the pieces of the puzzle. There is enough information so that you can understand, but not so much as to give you a headache right off the bat. The topics are presented in precisely the right order, so you don't have to worry about not understanding what a DC is or what GDI stands for (hey, that's funny. Here I am using the first acronym in the book without first defining it ... what a lame-o).

Also, don't mistake Michele's candor for dancing around the facts. This book is technically solid. In fact, I would recommend it as an educational text. However, this is a book about graphics and animation. In that spirit, it's fun to read! Which brings me to an interesting fact. In this book, you will discover (or maybe rediscover) a Windows API called BitBlt (pronounced Bit-Blit). Well, when I was doing my bitmap code I ran across an undocumented Windows API called SplitBlt (pronounced Split-Blit). SplitBlt returns the uneaten portion of a bacon, lettuce and tomato sandwich.

Also in this book, you will learn about an API called GetDC, which is when you pass a handle to a window and it returns a handle to that window's Device Context—don't worry, Michele will explain it to you. Well, on that same day, I discovered another undocumented Windows API call, GetWashingtonDC, which you pass a million dollars and it returns a pointer to a seat in congress.

I can't emphasize enough that this is fascinating stuff. In fact, you may want to tell someone where you are when you sit down at the computer, or they might call the bureau of missing persons by mistake. You may as well get used to the fact that after you digest this book and put it to use, people will look down at your feet when you walk through the halls. You will be looked upon with the same strange fascination that befalls psychopathic artists who build scale model replicas of classic automobiles using only silly putty and buttons. It's as if your intrinsic satisfaction actually exceeds the 'oohs' and 'ahhs' of your counterparts. And it will. This is pure joy! Can I be any clearer on this point?

I have never seen a book on Windows graphics and animation that comes close to providing as much good information, insight, creativity, awesome sample code and downright wholesomeness as this book does. So, read, think, be creative, get inspired and go write some code!

Carl Franklin

```
rivate Declare Function GlobalFree Lib "kernel32" (ByVal h
rivate Declare Function GlobalLock Lib "kernel32" (ByVal h
rivate Declare Function GlobalUnlock Lib "kernel32" (ByVal
--copying bitmap bits
 copies a global block of data into global memory
rivate Declare Sub CopyMemory Lib "kernel32" Alias "RtlM

--copies global block of data in  IB
rivate Declare Function SetDIB     "gdi32" (ByVal m_hdc
  ByVal hBitmap As Long, ByVal nStartS     As Long, ByV
  ByVal lpBits As Any, lpBI As BITMAPI     ByVal wUsag

--blits DC to DC
rivate Declare Function BitBlt Lib "gdi32" (ByVal hDestDC
rivate Declare Function StretchBlt Lib "gdi32" (ByVal hDest

--palette methods
rivate Declare Function CreatePalett     "gdi32" (lpLogPal
rivate Declare Function SelectPalette     "gdi32" (ByVal m_
rivate Declare Function RealizePalette Lib "gdi32" (ByVal m
rivate Declare Sub AnimatePalette Lib "gdi32" (ByVal hPale

--device context methods
rivate Declare Function SelectObject Lib "gdi32" (ByVal m_

rivate Declare Function CreateCompatibleBitmap Lib "gdi32
rivate Declare Function DeleteObject Lib "gdi32" (ByVal hO

rivate Declare Function CreateCompatibleDC Lib "gdi32" (B
```

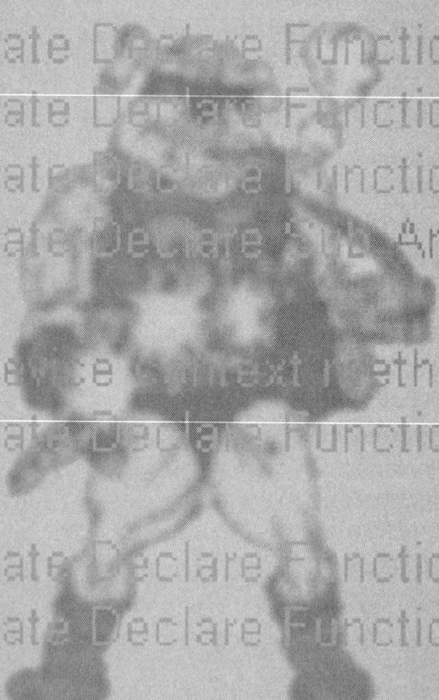

INSTANT

VB Animation

Summary of Contents

```
rivate Declare Function GlobalFree Lib "kernel32" (ByVal h
'rivate Declare Function GlobalLock Lib "kernel32" (ByVal h
'rivate Declare Function GlobalUnlock Lib "kernel32" (ByVal
--copying bitmap bits
 copies a global block of data into global memory
'rivate Declare Sub CopyMemory Lib "kernel32" Alias "RtlM

--copies global block of data into DIB
'rivate Declare Function SetDIBits Lib "gdi32" (ByVal m_hdc
  ByVal hBitmap As Long, ByVal nStartScan As Long, ByV
  ByVal lpBits As Any, lpBI As BITMAPINFO, ByVal wUsag

--blits DC to DC
rivate Declare Function BitBlt Lib "gdi32" (ByVal hDestDC A
rivate Declare Function StretchBlt Lib "gdi32" (ByVal hDest

--palette methods
rivate Declare Function CreatePalette Lib "gdi32" (lpLogPal
rivate Declare Function SelectPalette Lib "gdi32" (ByVal m_
rivate Declare Function RealizePalette Lib "gdi32" (ByVal m
rivate Declare Sub AnimatePalette Lib "gdi32" (ByVal hPale

-device context methods
rivate Declare Function SelectObject Lib "gdi32" (ByVal m_

rivate Declare Function CreateCompatibleBitmap Lib "gdi32
rivate Declare Function DeleteObject Lib "gdi32" (ByVal hO

rivate Declare Function CreateCompatibleDC Lib "gdi32" (B
```

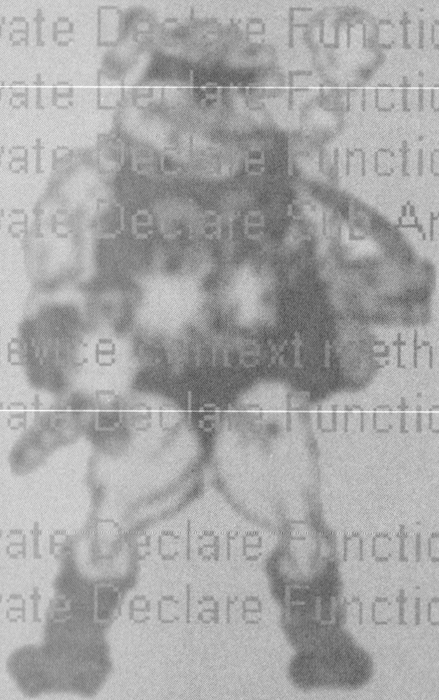

INSTANT

VB Animation

Table of Contents

```
rivate Declare Function GlobalFree Lib "kernel32" (ByVal h
rivate Declare Function GlobalLock Lib "kernel32" (ByVal h
rivate Declare Function GlobalUnlock Lib "kernel32" (ByVal
-copying bitmap bits
 copies a global block of data into global memory
rivate Declare Sub CopyMemory Lib "kernel32" Alias "RtlM

-copies global block of data in      B
rivate Declare Function SetDIB       "gdi32" (ByVal m_hdc
  ByVal hBitmap As Long, ByVal nStart     As Long, ByV
  ByVal lpBits As Any, lpBI As BITMAPI      ByVal wUsag

-blits DC to DC
rivate Declare Function BitBlt Lib "gdi32" (ByVal hDestDC A
rivate Declare Function StretchBlt Lib "gdi32" (ByVal hDest

-palette methods
rivate Declare Function CreatePalett      "gdi32" (lpLogPal
rivate Declare Function SelectPalette     "gdi32" (ByVal m_
rivate Declare Function RealizePalette Lib "gdi32" (ByVal m
rivate Declare Sub AnimatePalette Lib "gdi32" (ByVal hPale

-device context methods
rivate Declare Function SelectObject Lib "gdi32" (ByVal m_

rivate Declare Function CreateCompatibleBitmap Lib "gdi32"
rivate Declare Function DeleteObject Lib "gdi32" (ByVal hO

rivate Declare Function CreateCompatibleDC Lib "gdi32" (By
```

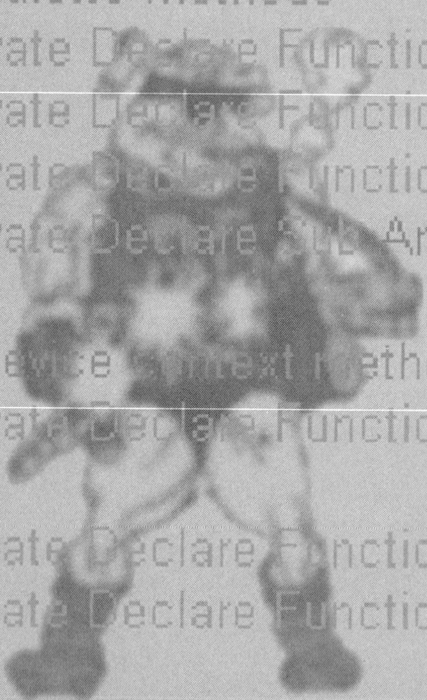

INSTANT

VB Animation

A Word from the Author

Have you ever had a bigger-than-life C programmer refer to VB as merely a handy dialog editor? Now THAT'S funny!

It's my guess that Visual Basic's visual design environment is the basis for delusions such as these that fester in unsuspecting C programmers. Personally, I can't remember the last time I said "Hey! I have a great idea! Why don't I build you some nice little dialogs, using VB, for your robust and all-powerful C program?" Maybe in some other lifetime. At any rate, this erroneous, somewhat fanciful idea is common among some 'all-knowing' C programmers and any 'stud-like' VB programmer can successfully defend these misconceptions. Gone are the days when using the lowest-level language makes you a better programmer.

It's true that VB on a good day can't do *everything*. However, let's not forget that its intent is to enable programmers to create robust Windows programs from a more 'approachable' development environment. Building a Windows program with a low-level tool like C, C++ or Pascal is a cumbersome undertaking with a daunting learning curve in either case.

When a VB programmer encounters limitations, this usually means that they've graduated to the 'stud-like' VB programmer category and have gone beyond its primary capabilities. That's when it's time to take the seat covers off and go on a little 'off-road' programming adventure with VB. When you include the right Windows API functions and can't-live-without-em custom controls in your projects, you'll be stylin'.

In this book, we'll combine custom controls, Windows API calls and a few necessary DLL calls to make a world of animation come alive on screen from VB. You can take all of the animation concepts demonstrated in this book with you to any application that requires animation, from titles and screen savers, to games and miscellaneous fun stuff you can put into any application interface to dress it up! Enjoy!

```
ivate Declare Function GlobalFree Lib "kernel32" (ByVal hM
rivate Declare Function GlobalLock Lib "kernel32" (ByVal hM
rivate Declare Function GlobalUnlock Lib "kernel32" (ByVal
-copying bitmap bits
 copies a global block of data into global memory
rivate Declare Sub CopyMemory Lib "kernel32" Alias "RtlMo

-copies global block of data into DIB
rivate Declare Function SetDIB    "gdi32" (ByVal m_hdc
 ByVal hBitmap As Long, ByVal nStartS    As Long, ByV
 ByVal lpBits As Any, lpBI As BITMAPI    ByVal wUsag

-blits DC to DC
rivate Declare Function BitBlt Lib "gdi32" (ByVal hDestDC A
rivate Declare Function StretchBlt Lib "gdi32" (ByVal hDest

-palette methods
rivate Declare Function CreatePalett    "gdi32" (lpLogPale
rivate Declare Function SelectPalette    "gdi32" (ByVal m_
rivate Declare Function RealizePalette Lib "gdi32" (ByVal m
rivate Declare Sub AnimatePalette Lib "gdi32" (ByVal hPale

-device context methods
rivate Declare Function SelectObject Lib "gdi32" (ByVal m_

rivate Declare Function CreateCompatibleBitmap Lib "gdi32"
rivate Declare Function DeleteObject Lib "gdi32" (ByVal hO

rivate Declare Function CreateCompatibleDC Lib "gdi32" (By
```

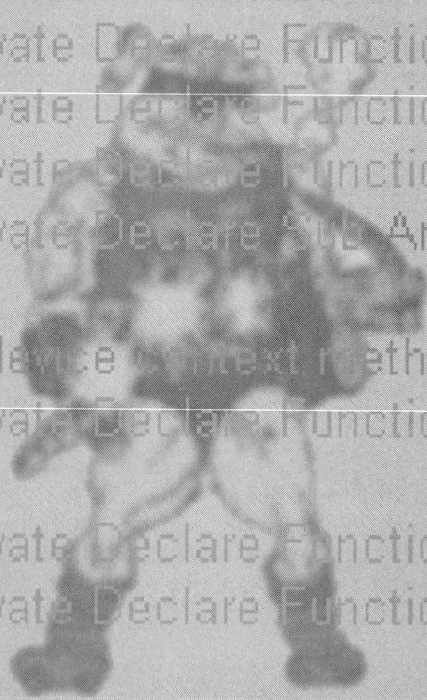

INSTANT

VB Animation

Introduction

Welcome to Instant VB Animation—your non-stop guide to learning all about animation and multimedia techniques in Microsoft Visual Basic. From here on in, we'll be taking you on a roller coaster ride of bitmap graphics, blitting, scrolling, games, screen savers and applications from which even the most novice of Visual Basic users will be able to get up to speed in an astonishingly short space of time. First of all, though, here are a few tips on how to get the most out of this package.

Who is Instant VB Animation For?

Okay, so you've written programs in Visual Basic and they were good, but now you want to make them snazzy and show off what wonders you can do in Visual Basic. Despite having a reputation for being quite a sour puss when it comes to having fun, VB can be *very* entertaining and, with a little bit of practice, you can create some quite unbelievable effects. This book is a guide for all you Visual Basic programmers who want to squeeze every last drop of fun out of Visual Basic and who are hungry for Windows programming knowledge.

What Will I Learn?

As a proficient computer user already, you'll understand the importance that graphics have on any application, especially those you write yourself. If you've used Visual Basic for a while, you'll be no stranger to the concept that Visual Basic makes smart programs for Windows very, very easily. But making the leap between 'smart' and 'exciting' is not an elementary one in Visual Basic. With Michele's help, you'll be able to endow your much-loved applications with powerfully exciting techniques and effects. No longer will you have to rely on different borders and colors to brighten up your masterpieces. You'll learn to use the Windows API, to perform clean display activity, without flicker, not just by learning how to casually throw API function calls into your applications, but also by gaining a true understanding of what's happening behind the scenes as graphics functions are put to work. That goes for all the animation theories unraveled throughout the book.

What Does Instant VB Animation Cover?

Using Microsoft Visual Basic 4 as a starting point, this book will take you on a ride through how to use the Windows API with this very popular programming language, enabling you to have complete control over display activity.

What Do I Need?

You will need a copy of Microsoft Visual Basic (4 or upwards) and, ideally, you will have grasped at least the basics of the language. Everything else you need is included in this book and on the accompanying CD. Oh, and a hot cup of java (the black juice, not the programming environment) because you won't be able to put the book down!

We'll be assuming that you have an understanding of Visual Basic programming, because we'll be up and running through aspects of VB coding which may seem a little daunting to the uninitiated. Having said that, we do include a quick guide to these concepts in Appendix A, which will also serve as a very useful revision aid for all those of us who have short attention spans. We also feature a quick and dirty guide to computer mathematics, which we'll be using throughout this book, because computer graphics just can't live without it.

What's on the CD?

As well as being a great read and a practical tutorial, this book comes with a CD packed to the brim with great code, programs and information that complement the content of the book beautifully.

As well as featuring *all* the source code and executables for every example discussed, the CD also ships with a hypermedia version of this whole book. This basically means that you can open the piece of code listed in one of the chapters on your desktop and then open up the actual text of the chapter in question in a window beside it. You can even cut and paste code between them! Another advantage of having an electronic version of this book on your screen is that you can do a text search of any topic in the whole book in just a few clicks—a huge bonus.

As well as featuring over 50MB of code from this book, we've also managed to include for your convenience a host of very useful third-party tools that can help you create stunning VB animation and multimedia presentations. Here's the rogues gallery:

- ImageWizard: an ImageWare application that is a full-blown image-editing software package, including an online manual, the Multimedia Wizard Guide.
- Bitedit and Paledit: two Microsoft applications that are standard for converting graphics into 256 colors or less and editing their palettes. Appendix C contains a tutorial on how to use these for the book's graphics.
- BadDog Screensaver: a fun and crazy ImageWare application, created with VB3, which includes some zany dogs doing some really bad things to your desktop. We'll recreate one of those bad dog examples with VB4 in Chapter 6.... can you guess which one?

- C.R.I.M.E.S. Demo Disk: an ImageWare demonstration disk for their C.R.I.M.E.S. software, in its full splendor. Chapter 4 describes how to create demonstration-like effects using a portion of this demo as the sample code.
- Powermedia by Powersoft: a 60 day evaluation copy of their incredibly popular storyboard animation system. You can find a quick introductory guide to using it in Appendix E.
- SpriteLib: a free sprite graphics library for all multimedia developers. Containing well over 700 professionally drawn images in over a dozen sizes and themes, SpriteLib is the ideal tool for developing the latest generation of games, educational programs and multimedia applications.
- Steve Neeley's Games: a collection of nine of the finest demonstrations of Visual Basic games programming. High quality graphics, music and sound effects are sewn together seamlessly to evoke the theme of each game. Visual Basic code as you've never seen it before.
- A-Quarium: a fish tank simulator based on an artificial life program called 'Boids' by Craig W. Reynolds. Each fish is modeled individually with a simple algorithm, allowing you to watch their behavior as they encounter other fish. We also supply a screen saver version.

Read the associated text file in the respective directory (listed on the inside front cover) for information on usage, the author, registration details, installation and further help.

How Do I Use this Book?

The styles used in this book are the results of feedback from all those software developers, like yourself, who have read our previous titles and who want to read the best information and tutorials in a style of prose that they can feel comfortable with. We won't assume that you can make impossibly long leaps between logical concepts and neither will we patronize you with details of exactly where to shove the disk. If you have any comments on the style, let us know by writing to us, or by filling out the reply card at the back of the book. Here's a guide to all the text styles, boxes and icons that we'll be using:

All code and programs will be highlighted with a gray background, so that you can locate them easily:

```
Dim sBytes(1 to 10000) as String * 1

sBytes(1) => palette index for pixel 1 in row 1
sBytes(2) => palette index for pixel 2 in row 2
...
sBytes(10000) =>palette index for pixel 100 in row 100
```

When an important piece of information needs to be really emphasized, we'll place it in a stand-alone box like this.

When we need to provide you with a useful, but not essential piece of background information, we'll use this style.

Where Do I Go for More Information?

Even we acknowledge that although we try to include everything you'll ever need in this book and CD package, there will always be something new around the corner. For this reason, our VB Animation Resource section will guide you to a host of the best resources related to Visual Basic and animation, especially VB Animation. If you ever need to find the latest information, though, always check out the Wrox web site, which you can find at:

http://www.wrox.com/

Here, you'll find not only all the information regarding the latest updates to this book, but also the latest support, news, web links and resources. If you want to show the world your latest VB animated creation that you coded with the help of this book, why not submit it to us and we'll put the best demonstrations up on The Best-of Instant VB Animation page. We'll reward the best creators with free copies of other Wrox books of their choice.

Bookmark the site now.

Why Should I Return the Reply Card?

Why not? If you return the reply card in the back of the book, you'll register this copy of Instant VB Animation with Wrox Press, which effectively means that you'll receive free information about updates as soon as they happen. You'll also receive errata sheets when they become available or are updated (they will constantly be updated on our web page, too).

As well as having the satisfaction of having contributed to the future line of Wrox books via your much valued comments and suggestions, you will, as a reward, be given a free subscription to the hugely popular Developer's Journal. This bi-monthly magazine, read by all the software development industry, is invaluable to every programmer who wants to keep up with the cutting edge techniques used by the best developers.

```
rivate Declare Function GlobalFree Lib "kernel32" (ByVal h
rivate Declare Function GlobalLock Lib "kernel32" (ByVal h
rivate Declare Function GlobalUnlock Lib "kernel32" (ByVal
-copying bitmap bits
 copies a global block of data into global memory
rivate Declare Sub CopyMemory Lib "kernel32" Alias "RtlM

-copies global block of data into DIB
rivate Declare Function SetDIB    "gdi32" (ByVal m_hdc
 ByVal hBitmap As Long, ByVal nStartS    As Long, ByV
 ByVal lpBits As Any, lpBI As BITMAPI     ByVal wUsag

-blits DC to DC
rivate Declare Function BitBlt Lib "gdi32" (ByVal hDestDC
rivate Declare Function StretchBlt Lib "gdi32" (ByVal hDest

-palette methods
rivate Declare Function CreatePalett    "gdi32" (lpLogPal
rivate Declare Function SelectPalette    "gdi32" (ByVal m_
rivate Declare Function RealizePalette Lib "gdi32" (ByVal m
rivate Declare Sub AnimatePalette Lib "gdi32" (ByVal hPale

-device context methods
rivate Declare Function SelectObject Lib "gdi32" (ByVal m_

rivate Declare Function CreateCompatibleBitmap Lib "gdi32
rivate Declare Function DeleteObject Lib "gdi32" (ByVal hO

rivate Declare Function CreateCompatibleDC Lib "gdi32" (B
```

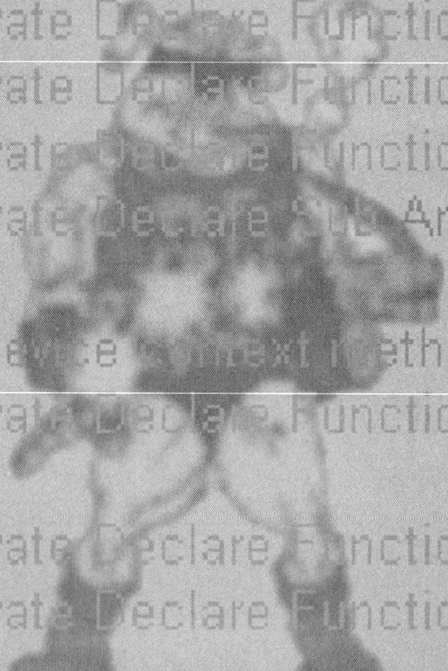

Chapter

1

Introducing Animation to VB

This book takes what I consider to be a unique approach to exploring the concept of animation programming. You see, animation goes far beyond what people usually first think of, merely characters and objects acting out parts in a scene of a game, or digital video production. If this is your view of animation, prepare to be converted.

This chapter will give you the foundation for the animation concepts built on throughout the book. By the end of the chapter, you should be clear on what kinds of animations you can program, what applications can use them and their coding methods. You should be *very* clear on VB's limitations when it comes to animation (there are many), but don't throw away the big white box, stay-tuned. As you work through the book, you'll learn how to get over VB caveats, while still using the development environment we all know and love (sort of). The samples in this chapter use straight VB to implement all animation techniques, but, as the book develops, we'll expand and improve on these techniques, and move on to progressively more complex and interesting applications. Throughout, we'll see animations as simple interface add-ins or as an entire application, like you would see in a full-blown demo, game or screensaver. By the end of the book, all you'll be missing is time to do it all.

Animation Scenarios

When many people think about Visual Basic, they think about database front-ends, utility programs and prototypes. Well, that's enough of that. It's time to have a bit more fun. C'mon, we all know that no matter what the programming project is, extra time is required to finish it. So why not go home, grab a beverage and spend some time programming cool new stuff? At the midnight hour, you can be introducing those extra niceties that every application deserves and many don't get. Or, you can even use your new skills for programming some new and exciting applications!

While the C programmers are writing all that extra start-up code, we VB programmers can be spicing things up. The recipe, of course, is animation. But what is animation? If you haven't used animation techniques in your applications before now, you may be surprised how easily it integrates into the most sober project. Heck, even database entry can be made interesting by adding a little animated pizzazz (okay, maybe not, but it's worth a try). From charming new cursors to life-like characters, we'll talk about animation in terms of:

- Adding interface pizzazz
- Captivating your audience
- Just having fun

To make any application interesting, and easy to use (uhm...not to mention...fun?) visual aids are essential. Believe me, it takes a lot more than a nicely laid out graphical interface to pull that off. We can't fool users with pretty stuff any more. They want *real* content, usefulness and a purpose for everything they see on the screen, animated or otherwise. There's lots of competition in software, especially now with all the freeware going over the Internet, so you need to measure up at any cost. Let's see where animation fits into different application scenarios.

Adding Interface Pizzazz

Animated buttons and cursors are just a few examples that can liven up an otherwise ho-hum application. These small niceties, sometimes accompanied by sounds, can do wonders for the user's attention and interest. Small attempts at entertaining the user do not go unnoticed. Even egotistical programmers (as few and far between as they are, right?) notice them and crack a smile, at least the first time. As long as an animation has a point to it and is not too long, it's a welcome reminder that programmers actually *do* have a sense of humor.

Imagine the mouse cursor passing innocently over a button or hot spot. Suddenly, the cursor changes and is animated. Then, as the user presses the mouse button, the cursor changes to signify contact. How much do you bet that this simple feature grabs the user's attention almost every time. Why? Because it catches their eye. Now, following that theory, make the cursor change over an area on the screen that isn't obviously a button but appears to be a feature on the background. Then make that part of the background animate when the user presses the mouse button over it. Now do we have their attention? You bet we do, but there's more. How about a game scenario where a skeleton hand points to an eerie and dismal looking door, beckoning you to click...do you dare?

The sample program **`\Code\Chapter1\Intface\Intface.vbp`** brings together a nice collection of interface concepts. It's a single-form application with a screenshot from an application that uses a bitmap as the interface background. This sample, shown below, is taken from the interview portion of ImageWare's **`C.R.I.M.E.S.`** program, which takes a witness through a series of questions to identify a suspect, hence the face in the upper right corner of the screen. The wood-grain background also has a series of buttons along the right-hand side, used for navigation and there's a notepad to the left, used to display different pages of questions for the interview process.

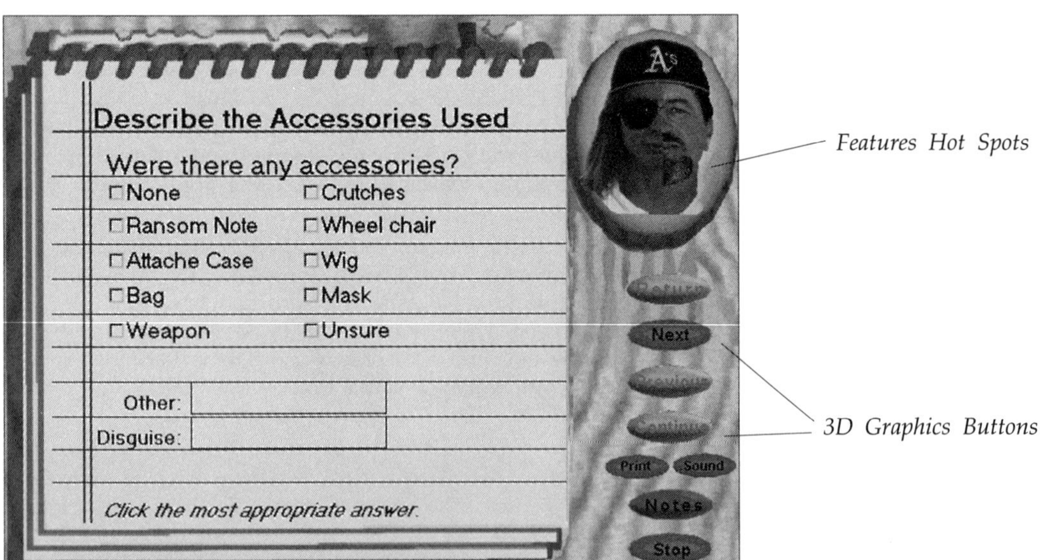

This sample program does little, but it does demonstrate how an interface like this can work. The buttons on the right are oval-shaped 3D graphics containing text to show what they do. As the mouse passes over the area, the cursor changes to an animated pointing hand, drawing the user's attention to the fact that they should click. When the user clicks, the cursor changes to a hand click and the graphic changes to a glowing version of the same button. An interesting thing to note about these buttons is that they are an integral part of the background. The 3D part of the button had to be placed on the original background image, then 'cut out' to be used later in a specific *x,y* coordinate on the interface.

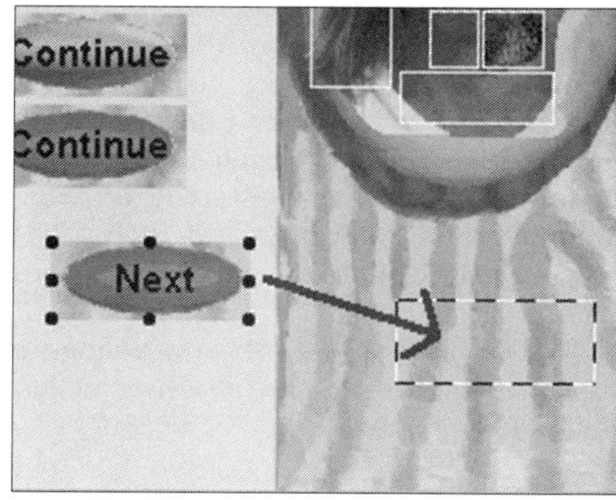

This is a good way to incorporate more interesting looking buttons into an otherwise ordinary interface. Each button has three states (normal, depressed and disabled) and each oval 3D version had to be 'cut' from the same exact position of the wood-grain, to prevent shifting when the other version of the button is displayed on the interface.

In the upper right-hand corner of the interface is a rather interesting looking face on a raised circular area. This too is an image selected from an area of the background image. Now this area looks much less like a button, or something you would click, but each component of the face takes you to a page in the interview that asks questions about that feature. To let the user know that they can click here, the cursor changes to a magnifying glass. Changing the cursor over a hot spot, is particularly useful. When the user clicks this area, the coordinates are checked against the dimensions of a control array of shape controls. Each is located over a designated feature of the face inside the picture control. This is used to break the hot spot down into smaller pieces, so that the appropriate text can be shown. Since this sample doesn't actually take you to the page inside the interview, while the mouse button is pressed a label is shown describing that item of the face.

Another interesting technique to use on your interface is to animate your buttons. Though there are custom controls that make this possible, if your buttons are graphical parts of the interface (**Intface.vbp** and **\Code\Chapter1\Vbanim\Vbanim.vbp** both use buttons as graphics rather than button controls), you have to write the animation code yourself. This isn't a problem, since when the **MouseDown** event is detected over a button graphic, code can be implemented to animate the button by changing the graphic until the user releases the mouse button. In **Vbanim.vbp**, there are five animated buttons. The first four appear on the opening form, **frmEyes**, the last on each of the other three forms, **frmLetters**, **frmBall** and **frmDragon**. These graphics work like buttons, but are actually images that are part of the background display. They animate when the user presses the mouse button over them.

Go to letter animation

Go to ball animation

Go to dragon animation

Exit

Return to eye animation

These are just a few examples of possible scenarios involving customized cursors and graphical buttons. If you take a look at the code inside **Intface.vbp** and **Vbanim.vbp**, you'll see how it all works. Don't worry, in later code descriptions we'll be stepping through how the animations work. It's important to note here that the use of these methods is more than just fun and games. Interfaces need to be interesting, appropriate and intuitive, but they also need to keep the user from wondering what's going on. For instance, when a lengthy process is about to take place, a user can be kept interested with a short burst of animation or an interesting cursor or button. If you need justification for animation, there you have it!

Thanks to VB4, we can now change our cursors effortlessly, without help from the Windows API functions. Just in case you haven't had the pleasure, here are the steps:

1 Set the MouseIcon property of the control to a **.cur** or **.ico** file of your choice.

2 Set the MousePointer property of the control to 99, for custom.

Aside from buttons and cursors being stroked into fun interface elements, we can also add other interface niceties to our applications. How about animating an area of the interface for a specific function? Take a look at the next example. In this graphical interface, the objects on the background display are more than they appear to be. The character holding the chain pulls it or lets go when the user clicks the scroll arrows. You can hear the sound of a chain as the text scrolls. This is a good, creative example of how animation can be tightly integrated into a program interface, and we haven't even got to the really juicy stuff yet!

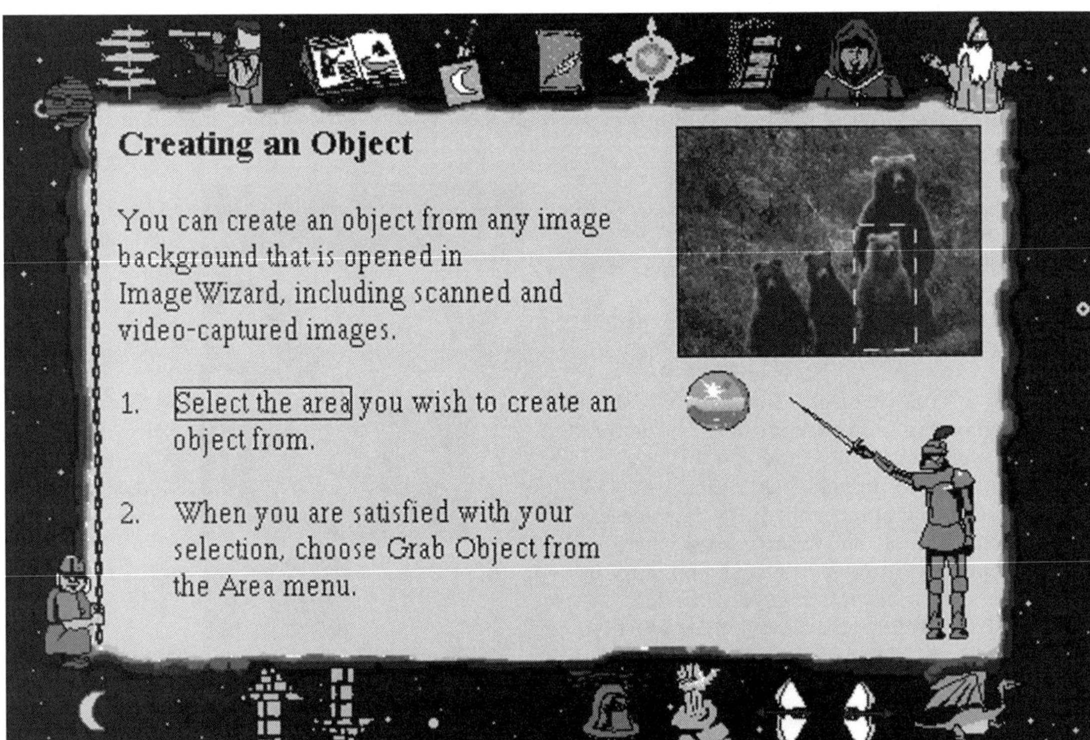

> **You can see the character from the previous figure in action if you install the ImageWizard program from the CD. This includes the Multimedia Wizard Guide, which also instructs you on how to use the program. It can be found at `D:\Apps\IWizard`.**

Captivating Your Audience

Animation is also a vehicle for presentation. As well as including interesting interface animations, your application content may also require pizzazz just to do its job. Demonstration disks and tutorials are good examples of applications that incorporate various animation techniques to present their content. Each of these applications requires the user's full attention, which can be a fairly tall order. Killer graphics and slick marketing combined with skillful programming techniques is what makes these applications a hit. As with all programs, the type of animation implemented largely depends on what's on the menu.

Demo disks are very useful in-house projects that marketing agents find invaluable to accomplish their job. The content can be general company information for prospective investors or customers, or information about specific products the company produces. If you're self-employed, you can zip one up and put it on the Internet for the world to see. If the disk is made properly (for instance, it doesn't crash on install) and it looks hot with descriptive content, you're smokin' and you'll probably generate sales. Slick transitions and movement using PowerPoint-like presentation help make the grade, and it can all be done from VB (that is, with just a little help). Have I got some ideas for you in Chapter 4's demo-disk sample!

Tutorials help teach the user to use a product and are usually interactive. They can be interactive through preplanned code (see the example on double-buffering in Chapter 2), or using OLE Automation to drive the product in question (providing, of course, that it's an OLE server application). Usually, some interactive animations, sounds and so forth, help to keep the tutorial alive, but, depending on the content requirements, anything goes. In case you haven't seen any educational or tutorial software, I'll tell you that they make heavy use of visual aids to be entertaining and informative. Some of the examples throughout the book may give you some creative ideas and a head start on the code!

Just for Fun!

Now for the really fun stuff: games, screensavers and stand-alone animation. Their sole purpose? To amuse, entertain and take you away from your work. In each case, some central theme with a cast of characters is maneuvered according to a script of sorts. Games, of course, can take on any theme, from point-and-shoot to cards. Screensavers are now using lots of juicy imaging techniques to distort the display, as well as to animate characters. Stand-alone animations really means any sort of graphics animation that is not specifically tied to a game or screensaver application. These can be implemented as splash screens that introduce a program, or really for anything you like. I'm trying not to be too vague, but you'll see that they really can fit in anywhere your creative mind wants to put them!

Usually, when it comes to these applications, animations are more complex. Many things are happening at once, interaction between players is inevitable, etc. This is where the complicated coding measures come into play, which is why you should steal the sample code as a foundation, rather than trying to develop it from scratch. Also, Windows graphics support has certainly taken a turn for the better with improved graphics methods (more on that as the book unravels), which gives it a much more receptive audience.

So far, this has been a rather general overview of the plethora of possibilities for using animation. However, I know what you're *really* here for—some hard-core, skillfully coded animation techniques that you can reuse—so I'll stop talking in general terms and get into the guts of programming animation, in preparation for the rest of the book. First, I'll describe some of the concepts and standardized methods with which they can be implemented.

Computer Animation Methods

You may have noticed that I've used the term *audience* instead of *user*. As far as I'm concerned, when you're creating *any* application, that's who you are targeting—an audience. Just like paying theatre-goers, your audience wants you to put on a good show. They want to be entertained, informed and interested in what's going on. If I've done my job properly, that's how you'll feel when you load up each and every animation sample throughout this book (hmmm... that's a tall order, but the intent is there) and, hopefully, it's what you'll pass on to the audiences of your future applications.

In TV, animation is usually stereotyped as a Charlie Brown or Scooby-Doo cartoon. What both have in common is that they are drawn characters, put together on film, each motion represented by its own frame. This is the tedium that puts together each acted scene in the cartoon. Creating animation on a computer involves drawing frames of the same characters which are input as individual digitized frames and programmed to play one after another, (regardless of the engine that plays them). This is the same as any other set of frames from a video clip, be it a newscast or an episode from your favorite sitcom.

There are two main categories for animation on the computer: digital video and coded animation. Within these categories, there are different methods for each to be implemented, but, essentially, the audience sees one or the other. In many cases, depending on how the interface is presented, the audience can't even tell the difference between the two. Though this book covers only coded animation techniques, I'll briefly summarize the differences between the two and the advantages and disadvantages of each. This should at least serve as a reference, so that you'll know what you want to use when you're planning your own applications.

Digital Video

Seeing digital video on a computer is not unlike watching a VCR tape. Movie film strips are comprised of a series of frames, one after another. Sequential frames are usually very similar, possibly containing a movement of an actor so small that you can't even see it when you compare the frames side-by-side. The specifications on realistic, lifelike motion is 32 frames-per-second (fps). That means that the naked eye sees 32 fps as real-life motion. Actually, the eye can't keep up with 32 fps. You see, the eye converts information in the form of light into signals which are decoded by the brain into an image. This process can only occur so fast, approximately 30 times per second. Yeah... whatever. At any rate, faster changes become difficult for the human eye to keep up with. This is why the benchmark for digital videos of 25 fps is not unacceptable. We can barely notice the difference, so it looks almost as good as video footage!

So what's a digital video then? It's a series of frames, where each frame is a digital image (like a `.bmp` file), displayed sequentially. If it were a digital video of the same VCR recording, it would be created by taking each frame, or a subset of them, in order and digitizing them individually as graphics, then showing them sequentially in their digitized format. As I've said, digital video can be created from actual film footage, or by grouping a series of images created from a graphics program. Once the sequential digital images are grouped together in the order they would appear in the digital movie, a special file is created to group them together as such. The prevailing file formats for digital video are AVI (Audio Video Interleaved) and MOV (QuickTime Video). AVI rules the PC platform, where MOV is mostly used on the Macintosh (though MOV can be used on either platform). I'll stick with AVI, since that's what you'd use from VB, unless you know of a Mac version of VB?

Here you can see four sequential frames (42 to 45) from **D:\Code\Rockclmb.avi** on the CD that comes with the book.

Notice that 42 and 43 are very similar, demonstrating that the each frame shows just a small change in the entire scene so that the video looks more realistic. Frame 44 and 45 also show little change between them, but frame 44 marks a new scene in the video, so is very different from frame 43. The point is that a video can have several junctures such as this, where the scene changes. There may be program instructions that decide to show the rock climber (okay, he's a snow boarder) jump, starting at frame 44, or maybe a new sequence added to the and of this AVI file, where the snow boarder falls miserably. This decision making is as easy as instructing 'go to frame 44' from anywhere in video play.

Let's talk some more on how the AVI file can be created. I've already mentioned two ways to get the digital frames, but here's a list of other sources:

- Television
- A video recording
- A series of images
- Scripted animation

The end result for any of these is the same. A series of digital still images will be compiled into a single file in the order they will appear when the resulting AVI is played. The first two choices require some form of analog-to-digital conversion to get each frame into digital format understood by any AVI-building application. This means that you must use special video capture boards or external capture devices. (This is a technology in itself that we won't be addressing in this book.) Using Video for Windows (VFW), you can build an AVI from a series of digital images, as suggested in the third option. No matter where the sequence of images came from (captured, scanned or created in a digital imaging program), VFW compiles the resulting AVI from already digitized images.

With the same concept in mind, you can also create digital video from other applications that let you move a cast of image objects, or perform special effects on an image, by scripted instructions. MorphWizard (part of the same family of products as ImageWizard which is on the book CD and is described later), for example, lets you write a script for image objects, like an animation character, to create movement, transition and other neat tricks all by script. You select the number of frames-per-second you want and, as the script is followed, individual image frames are created, then saved to a new frame in the AVI file. The animation script and the AVI settings you choose are what determines the flow and transition as the video plays back each frame (or how big is the animation jump between two frames).

The idea of creating digital video may sound nice and easy to code, since the script is already canned inside the AVI, but there are restrictions that limit what you can do with digital video. First of all, each frame has to be the same size. If only a small portion of the scene is changing, this can lead to wasted space and files can end up huge. Also, if the resolution of this frame size is larger than 320x240 (the accepted standard for AVI formats in 32-bit Windows environments), the video's performance can really suck, depending on the computer's performance capabilities and video card. Video is also canned, which means that the animation is charted, making interactive applications difficult to create on a dynamic basis. To lighten up a little, one nice thing about AVI versus true video is that you can jump from frame 0 to frame 45 in a single bound. Not so easy on a video tape that must physically move to that frame. So you can write scripts that make decisions on the next frame based on a condition in the application. This is only a problem when you want to see the background from frames 5 through 10, with the character from frames 45 through 60, which means separating components of the display into characters and scenes. This is where coded animation techniques come in to save the day. They are more versatile for programming games, screensavers and anything else that requires some interactive capability.

Coded Animation

The content of any animation plays out much like a scene in a play or movie. There's a scene or backdrop, before which actors, props and miscellaneous elements play out their role. That role can be just to sit there and look pretty, or to perform an act as the scene progresses. Though digital video can be created from this concept, programming animations using separate components rules! This means having a background image (the backdrop for the scene) to instruct your characters (a cast of graphical images performing over the backdrop).

Using coded animation, we no longer have the restriction on frame-size for each character. As a matter of fact, the background image should be separate from the characters, so that they can freely roam around the scene, randomly if you want, without disrupting the look and feel. Take the dragon animation as an example. The figure below shows the dragon frames used in the scene where the dragon flies at night. It would be easy for us to include several other animation characters in this scene, each with a varying frame-count and different acts to play out. Compared to precreated digital video, this is where the extra flexibility comes in. There is, however, a catch here too. If they are bitmap graphics, the graphics used for the animation require some special considerations to ensure that they look good as they play out the scene. You'll see more on that when we discuss the bitmaps used for animation.

DRG_N1.BMP DRG_N2.BMP DRG_N3.BMP

Since this is coded animation and a series of frames-per-second are not actually being generated, compromises are usually made regarding the number of animation frames that are required to get the point of the animation across. For instance, in the case of the flying dragon animation, there are only three frames. The middle frame is repeated on the way up and down for smoothness, but wouldn't the flight look more graceful if there were ten frames instead of three? The compromise depends on the circumstance. This is a simple demonstration of animation, but if it were a game, I may opt for ten frames. Issues, like disk space available for the installation of the application or hard disk space you expect your users to have, can sometimes also cause compromises in this area. Perhaps six frames becomes the happy medium in these instances. Get the idea?

Now let's talk a little about those repeated frames. Though there are three frames in the animation of the dragon flying at night, there are actually four frames in the run-cycle of this animation.

Dragon Frames

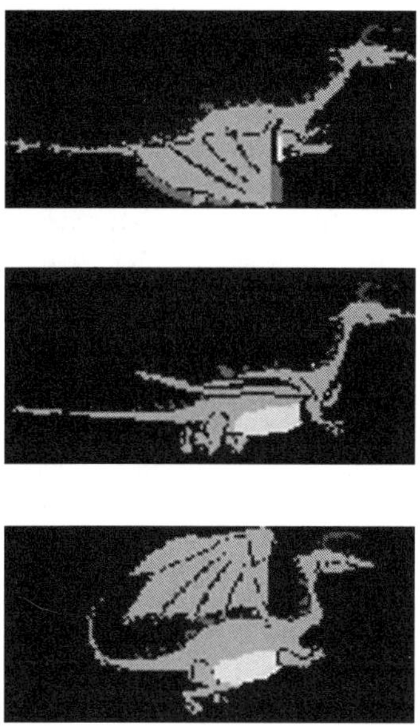

Dragon Run Cycle

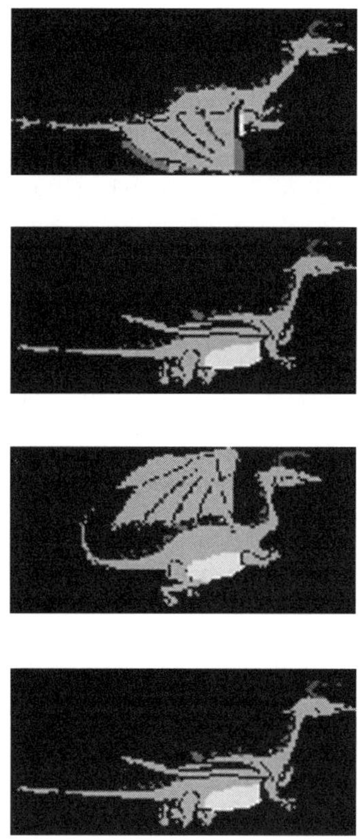

The **run-cycle** is the series of frames that, if played over and over again in a cycle, would look like a smooth animation. If just the three frames were played complete without repeating the middle frame, the dragon would appear to be always lifting its wings. A run-cycle for this animation must include the repeated middle frame. Now, the animation of these four frames can be recycled and the dragon will appear to be both lifting and lowering its wings in a realistic flying motion. We'll be using the term *run-cycle* in several areas throughout the book, so it's important to understand the difference between run-cycle and animation frames for the same character.

A Prelude to an Animation

Before you're ready to create well thought-out animations using VB, you'll need a little background information. To put together a complete application, you have to follow a series of steps. In this section, we'll talk about how to plan your attack on an application, which is paramount when you're making decisions about coding methods and graphics for animations. We'll also talk about the capabilities of VB, how to prepare your graphics and how VB handles them.

Planning Your Application

To build your application, regardless of animation content, you need a plan. Yup, every application needs theme, content and then, last of all, code. You must develop all three components to a complete application together, and be flexible as you go. Hitting a brick wall when the theme and content demand unrealistic feats of coding, possibly on an unrealistic deadline (What! *unrealistic* and *deadline* in the same sentence?), sometimes requires you to revamp the other two components. For that very reason, everyone, from designer to programmer, must be involved in the planning process.

Theme is the first thing that your application must have. What is the application? A game? A demo disk? A data-entry program? The answer to this question marks the onset of an interface design. From this, you'll know where, when and if animation even fits into the picture. Every application needs a theme, even if that theme is simply a color scheme, or a consistency of fonts and button graphics. Earlier on in this chapter we showed you a screenshot from the Multimedia Wizard Guide that comes with ImageWizard on the book's CD. Notice that the medieval theme is a distinct part of the interface. This includes the background of the interface, the foreground animations that take place and the look and feel of the buttons and text area.

Content must always accomplish what the application was created to do and should also be implemented to fit the theme. That means, what happens when the button is clicked, if anything, should follow suit with the theme, along with any other animation or executed event that is part of the application. For instance, if Charlie Brown were to appear in a dialog that provides an informative help message in my medieval interface, he wouldn't really fit in (remember Sesame Street's "One of these things is not like the other"?), but a dragon flying by, pulling a message by its tail would be somewhat more appropriate.

Code can be planned out only once you've decided on the interface issues, what the buttons should do when they are clicked and what all the other aspects of the application need to do. Part of planning the code, especially when you're working with animation, is deciding the type of graphics to use, how they must be implemented to get the results that you're looking for, and so forth. You'll see several different examples for implementing different animation techniques and their components throughout the book. Though this is not a book about designing theme and content, hopefully you'll see the tie-in here when we step through the code samples in each chapter.

What Can VB4 Do?

You should already know that one of the main benefits of VB programming is that much of the preliminary work that goes into a Windows program written in a language like C is already there. That's why you can get right down to designing and programming the interface, including any animation. You can animate with graphics, text, buttons, cursors and almost anything else you want to. The application will generally govern what is appropriate. **Vbanim.vbp** demonstrates several different animations that rely on VB alone. It shows more than just graphics animation, using different VB controls and altering their properties to gain certain effects. You'll probably notice that VB doesn't handle the display of some animations in the best way possible, but the idea for each of the animations is different, so each sample has something new to offer. As far as those areas that need improvement are concerned, that's what the rest of the book is for, so we'll get on to that.

You can create animations from any number of situations, depending on the theme of the interface and its purpose. Since **Vbanim.vbp** is a compilation of several different animation techniques using VB, I'll talk about those things that I used VB for with respect to this sample. We'll get to the underlying coding methods a little later, but, in a general summary, some of the things that VB can do for animation are:

- Movement and sizing
- Changing appearances
- Displaying graphics
- Program timing

Movement and Sizing

I'm sure it's no news that VB can be used to move and size controls, so it's no surprise that these methods would be part of animation applications. Any control, depending on the circumstances, can contribute to an animation. For instance, the first thing you see when you run **Vbanim.vbp** is a set of eyes following your cursor around the form. In this instance, two picture boxes and a couple of shape controls make the animation possible. Each picture box holds a Windows bitmap that works on the black background to give the image of two white circles, then two black circle shapes are moved within their respective picture box, acting as the pupil.

EYEWHITE.BMP

When the shape controls are moved within the boundaries of the picture boxes, you see something like this:

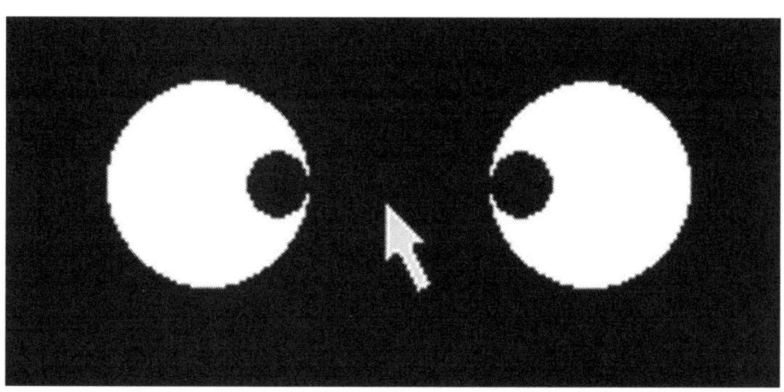

So, using a combination of controls, this animation was possible. The only downside to it is the flicker associated with the movement of the shape control.

The scripted letter animation, selected when you click on the word ANIMATION on the main interface for **Vbanim.vbp**, uses movement in a different scenario. A scripted animation moves the letters (label controls that spell ANIMATION) to the center of the screen, then bounces a red ball (shape control) over each letter, making them disappear. Once again, there's plenty of flicker with the movement of each of these controls, making a person wonder if VB can really be used to move objects for animation.

Actually, moving graphics controls, like image and picture box, doesn't illicit the same response. There's a slight flicker in the dragon example because, before a new dragon frame is displayed, the previous frame is erased. In Chapter 2, we'll discuss how to handle that type of flicker using double-buffering techniques. If you run the sample **\Code\Chapter1\Movesize\Movesize.vbp**, though, you won't see the flicker associated with moving the image control or picture control across the screen. When you're using the same control to implement the animation, there's no flicker because there's no need to erase a previous frame for the animation to proceed.

In the same example, **Movesize.vbp**, you can test out the results of sizing an image control while a sequence of frames is displayed inside of it. This doesn't flicker either, but if we were sizing the label or shape controls from the other animation examples in **Vbanim.vbp**, you would see that there would still be plenty of flicker.

Changing Appearances

Aside from moving controls to create an animation, changing certain properties of a control can also be an attention grabber. In the same letter animation sample, a color animation follows the movement of the letters to the center of the display. The color of each letter is changed randomly in a loop by setting the ForeColor property of the label controls to random color values. Something we *can* do with VB, without that movement flicker, is to change the color value of a control.

Another animation that we can get without leaving the VB environment is performed in the bouncing ball example. The ball is being animated in three ways, each of which can be deselected by the check boxes on the interface. The ball is moved and its DrawMode and FillStyle properties (it's a shape control) are changed. Ignoring how the ball moves, the other two properties affect more than meets the eye, which will be described in a little more detail when we discuss raster operations in Chapter 2. If you pay close attention, since the animation of these properties happens pretty fast, you can see that the ball gets combined somehow with the background image and its pattern changes as it is moved. This is just another example of altering the properties of a VB object to create an interesting display.

You can alter other properties to create animations of different kinds; for example, hiding and showing controls with the visible property. This is really specific to the application. It's amazing how, once the interface has been put together, you can figure out things that would make it a little more fun.

Displaying Graphics

The most popular way to animate is to use graphics. You can see this with the dragon animation in **Vbanim.vbp**, where the dragon flies across the screen. The image, picture box and form all support graphics in their picture properties, but *where* the graphics are loaded and with *what* control/form they are displayed must be decided before the animation is planned out. The form would obviously be best used to display a background graphic for the entire interface, since it's different to a moveable control. We can create further animation using image or picture box controls to load smaller graphics into the display.

Displaying graphics in a VB application can be a useful way to put across the interface concept, to implement components of the interface or to animate graphics that are part of the interface. Using graphics for interface components is shown in **Intface.vbp** with the use of graphic buttons. Animating graphics is a special topic that requires more consideration as to how it should be implemented. Examples of this are both the animated buttons on the main display of **Vbanim.vbp**, or the dragon flying across the night and day scene of the same project.

Program Timing

All of the animation examples use either a timer control, or an ongoing **DoEvents** loop to iterate through each animation sequence. This doesn't require going outside of VB either, which is convenient. We'll be comparing some different uses for the timer in a later discussion. The timer is a convenient control provided by VB for us to time our animations easily.

Creating Your Graphics

You've noticed that, unless a graphic is used, each time we've discussed an animation so far, we've mentioned flicker. Many VB controls can't be moved, sized or manipulated without introducing some flicker to what you see. Bitmap images don't present the same problem. Most of the animations in this book use graphics, so here, we'll discuss some of the considerations you need to think about when you're preparing them.

Camouflaging for Display

If you moved a circle shape across a complex background image (as in the animated ball example from **Vbanim.vbp**), you would see a circle moving over a complex background. Right, but what if that circle were replaced with the dragon frame? What then? Apparently, you'd see a dragon in a black box, flying across the room. In the daytime dragon flying scene, though, there's clearly a complex background with the castle image. So, why don't we see the black rectangle surrounding the dragon frames there? Guess what, the frames are different for the dragon flying by night and the dragon flying by day. We had to put some extra work into the daytime dragon graphics, which I'll explain.

You can rest assured that behind *every* bitmap image you see is a rectangular graphic. The rectangle is the basis for how Windows determines the area on screen in which to draw an image. Everything has to have a top left corner and a width and height or bottom right corner. Shape controls even have a rectangular bounding box when the shape is not rectangular. Image controls have the same, even when a cursor or icon file is loaded with clearly transparent areas. The bottom line is that, if what you see isn't rectangular, it's either camouflaged by the area behind it, certain pixels were told not to display when it was copied to the screen, or it's not a bitmap graphic.

The dragon at night scene shows the easiest way to effect this camouflage. By using the same *exact* color (black) for the rectangular area surrounding each frame of the actual dragon and the background color of the picture control, you can hide the rectangle of the image. No matter where the dragon is moved, you only see the shape of the green dragon flying over a black background. Whenever your background image is a solid color (i.e. not a complex background image), you can pretty much move and animate anything on the foreground, as long as it's transparent (the shape control or a Windows metafile inside an image control), or is part of a rectangle of the same solid color.

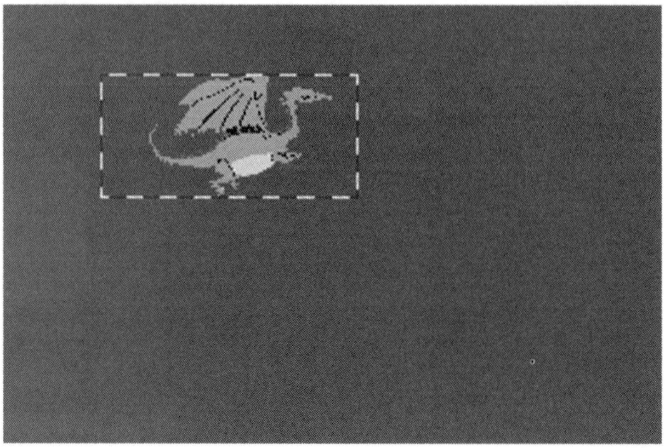

It's much harder to create a camouflage like this in a scene of the dragon flying over the castle. The simplest way to do this would be to fly the dragon in one place, then you would only need three frames, as in the night scene. Of course, in this case, the dragon could not be part of a rectangle with a black background, but placed over that area of the castle background, exactly where the animation is going to be displayed at run time. Each frame should be created from the same location on the background, just like in the button example of **`Intface.vbp`**. Then, the same three frames could be looped, with the audience never the wiser that there's a rectangle there, since it just looks like a dragon. That's the idea, right?

Since the dragon is being moved in the daytime scene, 31 frames were created to keep this illusion for the duration of the animation. It appears that the same three dragon images are being used, but they are placed strategically in different positions across the background, to give the impression that the dragon is flying and moving. Not being an artist, I'm not sure what products are out there to help you create this kind of bitmap, where you essentially need a separate graphic of the dragon, without a rectangle, to move into different positions, and to paste and create a small bitmap from it. I've always used ImageWizard, our in-house product, supplied on the CD. With it, I create three dragon objects (these are proprietary files with the extension **`.imi`**), that have transparent pixels where the dragon isn't. I paste each object, then create a new frame, each time using the same background image of the castle. I won't go any further into the product, but that should give you the idea. The rest is in the documentation.

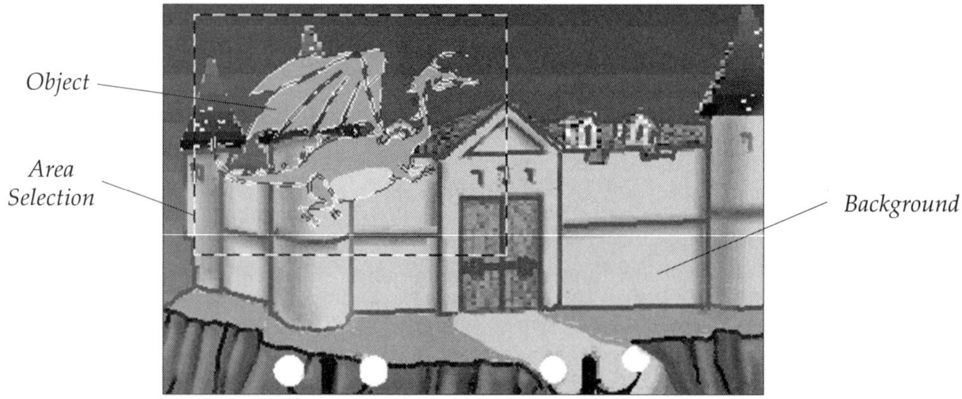

Since these bitmaps are 'hard-coded' as it were, you can't really turn the dragon around to fly backwards, thinking that it will still look okay on the display. Go ahead and give it a shot from the direction option. This is what makes this approach inflexible and definitely not helpful in a dynamic scenario of any kind. The alternative? Use bitmasking techniques. These are covered in Chapter 2, so I won't spoil it for you by going into them here. Actually, there are several other steps in preparing the graphics, ones that we'll cover in bite-size morsels throughout the book. Ugly things like disk space and palettes are among the favorite headings.

Sizing Graphics

The example **`Movesize.vbp`** includes code that sizes one of the dragon frames in two different ways. It's apparent that if this were the dragon flying and moving about the night scene in **`Vbanim.vbp`**, the changing of frame rectangle size would not affect the camouflaged outcome on the screen. It would, however, affect the appearance of the graphic. Since bitmaps are made up of individual pixels, sizing the graphic no longer accurately reflects the image. Since the background scene is a solid color, the fact that the dragon is being resized would not be an issue that would disrupt the scene. Black pixels are still black pixels, even when resized. However, when you resize it, you may want to consider the general appearance of the dragon image. In this case, the dragon is a simple graphic, without much detail, so it doesn't look *too* bad when it's sized. In most other cases, where the character carries more detail, it may not appear acceptable when sized.

Of course, you can see by comparing the next two figures that sizing doesn't do us much good when the dragon is flying over the castle scene, since the bitmaps are hard-coded.

Note the clash after enlargement

Actually, there are two coding techniques that would improve this movement code, specifically when the dragon is flying backwards. The concept of double buffering your animation and bitmasking techniques that enable you to implement transparent graphics (i.e. the dragon frames for night, moved over the daytime scene without seeing the black frame). The picture box and its **`PaintPicture`** method can be used to implement both of these improved animation techniques, but we'll be covering these topics in Chapter 2, including more details on raster operations and Boolean logic. Just so you know, all is not lost without the Windows API.

Images, Picture Boxes and PaintPicture

Since the focus of animation in this book is the animation of graphics, it's important to understand the capabilities of VB, specifically with relation to the use of graphics. Much of VB programming hides the behind-the-scenes Windows stuff that's going on when we set properties of controls and write code that manipulates them. To understand the limitations of VB and what we may be able to do to address them without changing programming environments, we'll also have to understand what's going on with Windows when VB is told to do things. I'll only introduce the topic in this section, to demonstrate the difference between how images and picture boxes can be used for display. Keep in mind, though, that the real meat of this discussion continues in the next chapter when we talk more about Windows under the hood.

So, first things first: image versus picture box. What's the difference between the image and picture box controls? They are very different in their internal makeup, with the obvious difference shown here:

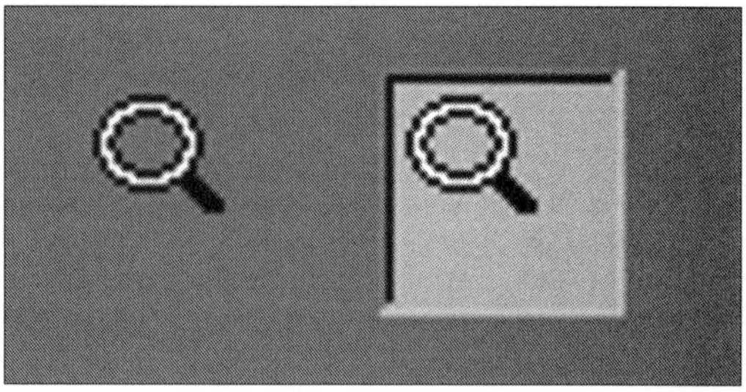

Image Control *Picture Box Control*

Both the image and picture box contain the same cursor file, the magnifying glass, as their picture. The form's background color shows through the transparent areas of the cursor inside the image control, where the picture box's background shows through those same transparent areas. Both cursors display on their parent window's background. Both the image and picture box controls have the form as their VB *container*, but when an image is loaded into the picture box, the picture box is the *window* in which the image is displayed. The image control, on the other hand, is not a window (I'll explain), so the form is the window in which its image is displayed. What the form and picture box have in common is that they are both considered *windows* in the Windows environment. A **window** is a rectangular object that the Windows operating system provides for applications to send information to the display and react to messages sent in the system, usually resulting from user activity. Both VB objects have window handles (the hWnd property) and device context handles (the hDC property) that Windows uses to access them when commands are executed to paint graphics or text, and more. The image control has neither of these properties, because drawing a graphic inside it uses the form's drawing area. This is all transparent to us with VB. We just know that an image control supports transparent images (if the image is transparent); the picture box doesn't because it has a background area, colored by its BackColor property.

Let me explain a little more. To do this, I'll take a step away from VB and discuss things in general terms of what a C programmer would have to do (purely as an example of what VB is doing for us by providing these controls and properties). If we're creating a C-based Windows program, we must write code to create the main window (our form) for the application's display. The functions that do this are called for us by VB, and the window that we create is described by the form properties we set at design time. Whether VB creates the window for us, or we write the code from scratch in C, Windows returns a pointer (window handle) that assigns the new window a number to be used every time something is done to it. The window handle refers to the entire window object, which is the form, including its border and caption bar. Windows also returns a pointer (device context handle) to the drawing area of that window. This is the area that displays the interface components. The hWnd and hDC properties are these pointers. The image control doesn't have them, because this control is little more than a description of a rectangle on the form's drawing area.

How Graphics Display

This topic will become clearer when you get to the next chapter and we discuss more about the GDI (graphics device interface) which is the driving force of all Windows display functionality. Now that you have an idea about the differences between the image and picture box controls, let's take a look at the difference in how they act on screen. If you run **\Code\Chapter1\Imgpic\Imgpic.vbp**, you'll see that it compares the use of the picture box and image controls for creating an animation of a deck of cards being spread open, with the six of hearts as the top card. This is done by creating duplicate copies of the same card, moving it by a small amount each time. The menu selections under the Test menu let you choose one of three options: PictureBox, Image or PaintPicture. PaintPicture is a new capability of forms and picture box controls, so I'll cover that example last. First, let's see how the two controls compare.

The first thing you'll notice is that using controls to create an animation like this is really slow. Actually, this animation would probably never be performed using controls, but this part of the example has a demonstrative purpose. A new control is created for each new card position in the first two menu options. The picture box and image control both act very differently as they perform this animation. This goes back to our previous discussion about picture boxes being windows, and image control representing an area of the form's window (or its container's window, in this case, the form).

Something that happens in the Windows environment, something that VB takes care of for us, is the interception of Windows messages. When part of a window is covered by another, Windows sends a message to the first window when it's no longer covered, so that it can be repainted. When a new picture box is drawn on the form, as each new card in the animation is created and moved downward, the form isn't told to repaint beneath the picture box, because the picture box is a window and is still covering the form's window as long as it's visible. The image control, on the other hand, isn't a window. This would explain why the area beneath the new image control created for the animation is repainted every time there's a new card. Since that area of the form is repainted, within that area, a portion of each image control is redrawn until the top image control is drawn. Run the code to see what I mean.

The point here is that the flicker of the image control makes the animation that it produces appear slower than that produced by the picture box control. This is because of the amount of layer repainting going on, resulting from the new card being copied to the display.

This flicker presented by the use of the image control for an animation is similar to that caused by other non-window controls like labels and shapes. The last attempt at the card animation is using the new **PaintPicture** method of VB4. This is obviously the only way that this animation should be implemented, so this program sample isn't really a comparison of competitive methods, as much as it is a demonstration of how VB handles its graphics display.

PaintPicture

Without creating additional controls, the **PaintPicture** method was able to implement the best alternative to the card animation from **Imgpic.vbp**, using a single picture box with **6hearts.bmp** as its picture. The **PaintPicture** method is only supported by the picture box and form. The purpose of this method is to copy the image from a Picture property (form or picture box) to another device context (form, picture box or printer). At its most basic level, which is all that will be discussed in this chapter, the **PaintPicture** method makes a copy of a picture on the background of a form or picture box display at the coordinates suggested. Just like the image and picture box examples use an incrementing **nTop** variable for the next control's display, the **PaintPicture** command uses the stationary **nLeft** and changes **nTop** to make the next copy on the form's background, from **Picture2**'s picture:

```
Me.PaintPicture Picture2.Picture, nLeft, nTop
```

There's no loading of another copy of the same graphic involved here, so the only overhead is copying from the image that's already loaded to the form's background in a new location. That's why it's so fast. It's easy to see how much less overhead would be involved here.

PaintPicture can also be used in more complex situations where you also want to size the image. Remember that the picture box can't stretch an image, so, until **PaintPicture** was introduced, the image control was the only way to stretch a graphic on the display. In the **Movesize.vbp** example, from the Size menu option, you can choose Image or PaintPicture. They look the same as the dragon grows while flying in place. This time, **PaintPicture** looks to a different frame (picture box) of the animation to paint to the form, and the image control loads from the picture box Picture property into its own. This time, the **PaintPicture** command copies from the **picDragon** picture box to a specific rectangle on the form, which depicts the size of what was inside the picture box:

```
Me.PaintPicture picDragon(m_nFrame).Picture, nCX - nWidth / 2, nCY - nHeight / 2,
nWidth, nHeight
```

To compare the two methods, the image control is sized to the new size of graphic we want to see, then the Stretch property tells whatever picture is loaded into the Picture property to take on that size. The **PaintPicture** method happens in one step, which is to paint to this rectangle specified, and that's what you see.

One important thing to note about using **PaintPicture** is that you need to repaint the form if the window is covered, or you need to keep the form's AutoRedraw property set to true, so that whatever the **PaintPicture** command copies to the form will be retained in memory. VB keeps track of all our controls for us, but not what we paint ourselves.

Coded Animation

Now it's time to look at some of the different ways of putting together animation in code. The heart of this section concerns techniques for coded animation, but, where applicable, I'll also cover some other aspects of the code. The purpose here is to cover some background information about animation that will come up again elsewhere in the book. Though bitmap graphics will be the main type of animation used in chapters to follow, the animations in **Vbanim.vbp** use various controls (as you're already aware) to demonstrate issues with VB. In this discussion, the actual graphics used for the animation are irrelevant. The important thing is how the animation was put across.

The beauty of coded animations as opposed to video, is that, as a programmer, you have complete control over what's about to happen. You plan from beginning to end how the animation takes place. Better yet, you don't have to pre-determine everything. Though it can be played out of frame order, digital video has a predisposed set of frames that can be played. When you create it, you have to decide what will happen from beginning to end. In the case of coded animations, the objects that are animated can be separate from the background behind them. I broke down the types of animations that you can create into the following categories:

- Idle animations
- Scripted animations

- Random animations
- Animation loops

As you read through this section, keep in mind that all of these animation techniques can be used in any combination, to form a single animation sequence.

Idle Animation

Idle time is time when the application is not performing a task resulting from a request by the user. In most applications, this means that the user is either staring at nothing or staring down a group of interface controls in an application window, deciding what to do. An idle animation is one that takes place during times just like these, taking the user by surprise. This can be an interesting way to entertain the user while they decide what to do next.

For example, idle animations can be implemented as sudden interface animations that take place in a specific part of the display, like animating a portion of the background when the user least expects it. It can also be an ongoing interface animation, like a button that flashes until the user presses it or launches another task. In the sample **`Vbanim.vbp`**, the eyes have it! Or maybe you didn't notice the strange pair of eyes following your cursor around the window as you moved it. Well, apart from the fact that I may have an odd sense of humor, you probably noticed that the animation continued as long as you didn't make any other selections, the entire time the application was running.

Actually, this idle animation has two possible states. The eyes can either follow the mouse or the red ball. One of these idle animations is driven by the **`MouseMove`** event, the other by a timed interval that moves a ball to a new, random location on the form. These idle animations are ongoing, so bring to the table some other requirements. While the animation takes place, other Windows messages must be allowed to process so that the user can still make that interface selection they've been distracted from doing. Furthermore, there must be a way to start and stop the animation at the appropriate moments.

Games often use idle animations to add a little bit more fun to the proceedings. For example, if your character, Jim the Monkey doesn't move for a few seconds, he might look towards the screen and start tapping his foot, or perhaps he will whistle or read a book while he waits for you to make your mind up.

The code for the idle eye animation is located inside **`frmEyes`** from the **`Vbanim.vbp`** project. Let's now go through the design and coding behind it.

Starting the Idle Animation

In both scenarios of the idle animation, **`Animate_Eyes`** is the central procedure that moves the pupils. This procedure expects an *x, y* coordinate, showing where the eyes should look, that can be passed by either state of the animation. You toggle between the two states by selecting one of the Method radio buttons, Mouse or Timer. Each is represented by its index through the constants **`ANI_MOUSE`** and **`ANI_TIMER`**. The currently valid constant is held inside the **`m_nAnimMethod`** variable. Each time a different radio button is selected (Mouse is the starting choice), **`m_nAnimMethod`** is updated.

Since the animation is ongoing, unless a specific task is called, the only other thing to do when the state of the animation is selected is to set up the props. **`ANI_MOUSE`** requires just the

MouseMove event to continually call **Animate_Eyes** with the current coordinates. The only check here is that **m_nAnimMethod** is **ANI_MOUSE**, then that the **X**, **Y** parameters are passed along:

```
If m_nAnimMethod = ANI_MOUSE Then
    Animate_Eyes CInt(X), CInt(Y)
End If
```

When **ANI_TIMER** is selected, the **MouseMove** event can't trigger the pupils to follow the mouse because it would interfere with them following the red ball. In this state, a red ball (**shpBall**) is displayed and moved to random positions on the form at each **Timer** interval. Once the ball is moved to a random coordinate, **Animate_Eyes** is called again, this time with the random coordinate of the ball:

```
' get random coordinate for ball
nRandX = Int((Me.ScaleWidth * Rnd))
nRandY = Int((Me.ScaleHeight * Rnd))

' move ball for eyes to follow
shpBall.Move nRandX, nRandY

' change pupil position
Animate_Eyes nRandX, nRandY
```

Since **m_nAnimMethod** is no longer set to **ANI_MOUSE**, there's no danger of the pupils following the ball and the mouse at the same time. That would be truly scary! Preparing for a new state, the only code required is to hide the ball and turn off the timer (if **ANI_MOUSE** is selected) or show the ball and turn the timer back on (if **ANI_TIMER** is selected). This is done via the radio buttons, based on the **Index** clicked:

```
m_nAnimMethod = Index
If m_nAnimMethod <> ANI_TIMER Then
  shpBall.Visible = False
  tmrEyes.Enabled = False
Else
  Randomize
  shpBall.Visible = True
  tmrEyes.Enabled = True
End If
```

Idle Pupil Movement

If you look at the following code, you'll notice that movement is accomplished by setting the Top and Left properties of the pupil shape (**shpPup**) controls. The **Move** method could also be used to set these properties. Nothing new here, because this is beginner VB code. The location of each pupil's move is hard-coded to 15 possibilities around the circumference of the white circle of each eye. Sorry, but calculations for things like a coordinate at the circumference of a circle are saved for later chapters. Besides, this is a true master hack for the quickest possible solution and is exactly how anyone would do it if we were sure of a fixed location. At design time, the shape was moved to each of the 15 locations, then a range of mouse coordinates was planned out for each of those 15 positions.

> *Master hacks* are code snippets written with a clear head, but not optimized to an efficient number of code lines. *Desperate hacks* are quickly interjected lines of code, like optional parameters and statements, like **`if flag = 153 then...,`** that are last minute feeble attempts to fix a bug in a program that you wish never existed.

```
Private Sub Animate_Eyes(ByVal nLookX As Integer, ByVal nLookY As Integer)
'—Description
' the following are 15 hard-coded positions based on the
' possible range of nLookX, nLookY coordinate on the form
' to set the left, top properties of the pupil shapes to
'—

    '1
    If nLookX < picEye(0).Left And nLookY >= picEye(0).Top And nLookY <
picEye(0).Top + picEye(0).Height Then
        shpPup(0).Left = 0
        shpPup(0).Top = picEye(0).Height / 2 - shpPup(0).Height
        shpPup(1).Left = 0
        shpPup(1).Top = picEye(1).Height / 2 - shpPup(1).Height
    '2
    ElseIf nLookX < picEye(0).Left And nLookY < picEye(0).Top Then
        shpPup(0).Left = 0
        shpPup(0).Top = 0
        shpPup(1).Left = 0
        shpPup(1).Top = 0
    '3
    ElseIf nLookX >= picEye(0).Left And nLookX < picEye(0).Left + picEye(0).Width
And nLookY < picEye(0).Top Then
        shpPup(0).Left = picEye(0).Width / 2 - shpPup(0).Width
        shpPup(0).Top = 0
        shpPup(1).Left = 0
        shpPup(1).Top = 0
    '4
    ElseIf nLookX >= picEye(0).Left + picEye(0).Width And nLookX < picEye(1).Left
And nLookY < picEye(0).Top Then
        shpPup(0).Left = picEye(0).Width - shpPup(0).Width
        shpPup(0).Top = 0
        shpPup(1).Left = 0
        shpPup(1).Top = 0
    '5
    ElseIf nLookX >= picEye(1).Left And nLookX < picEye(1).Left + picEye(1).Width
And nLookY < picEye(0).Top Then
        shpPup(0).Left = picEye(0).Width - shpPup(0).Width
        shpPup(0).Top = 0
        shpPup(1).Left = picEye(1).Width / 2 - shpPup(1).Width
        shpPup(1).Top = 0
    '6
    ElseIf nLookX >= picEye(1).Left + picEye(1).Width And nLookY < picEye(0).Top
Then
        shpPup(0).Left = picEye(0).Width - shpPup(0).Width
        shpPup(0).Top = 0
        shpPup(1).Left = picEye(1).Width - shpPup(1).Width
        shpPup(1).Top = 0
    '7
    ElseIf nLookX >= picEye(1).Left + picEye(1).Width And nLookY >= picEye(0).Top
```

```
And nLookY < picEye(0).Top + picEye(0).Height Then
        shpPup(0).Left = picEye(0).Width - shpPup(0).Width
        shpPup(0).Top = picEye(0).Height / 2 - shpPup(0).Height
        shpPup(1).Left = picEye(1).Width - shpPup(1).Width
        shpPup(1).Top = picEye(1).Height / 2 - shpPup(1).Height
    '8
    ElseIf nLookX >= picEye(1).Left + picEye(1).Width And nLookY >= picEye(0).Top
+ picEye(0).Height Then
        shpPup(0).Left = picEye(0).Width - shpPup(0).Width
        shpPup(0).Top = picEye(0).Height - shpPup(0).Height
        shpPup(1).Left = picEye(1).Width - shpPup(1).Width
        shpPup(1).Top = picEye(1).Height - shpPup(1).Height
    '9
    ElseIf nLookX >= picEye(1).Left And nLookX < picEye(1).Left + picEye(1).Width
And nLookY >= picEye(0).Top + picEye(0).Height Then
        shpPup(0).Left = picEye(0).Width - shpPup(0).Width
        shpPup(0).Top = picEye(0).Height - shpPup(0).Height
        shpPup(1).Left = picEye(1).Width / 2 - shpPup(1).Width
        shpPup(1).Top = picEye(1).Height - shpPup(1).Height
    '10
    ElseIf nLookX >= picEye(0).Left + picEye(0).Width And nLookX < picEye(1).Left
+ picEye(1).Width And nLookY >= picEye(0).Top + picEye(0).Height Then
        shpPup(0).Left = picEye(0).Width - shpPup(0).Width
        shpPup(0).Top = picEye(0).Height - shpPup(0).Height
        shpPup(1).Left = 0
        shpPup(1).Top = picEye(1).Height - shpPup(1).Height
    '11
    ElseIf nLookX >= picEye(0).Left And nLookX < picEye(0).Left + picEye(0).Width
And nLookY >= picEye(0).Top + picEye(0).Height Then
        shpPup(0).Left = picEye(0).Width / 2 - shpPup(0).Width
        shpPup(0).Top = picEye(0).Height - shpPup(0).Height
        shpPup(1).Left = 0
        shpPup(1).Top = picEye(1).Height - shpPup(1).Height
    '12
    ElseIf nLookX < picEye(0).Left And nLookY >= picEye(0).Top + picEye(0).Height
Then
        shpPup(0).Left = 0
        shpPup(0).Top = picEye(0).Height - shpPup(0).Height
        shpPup(1).Left = 0
        shpPup(1).Top = picEye(1).Height - shpPup(1).Height
    '13
    ElseIf nLookX >= picEye(0).Left And nLookX < picEye(0).Left + picEye(0).Width
And nLookY >= picEye(0).Top And nLookY < picEye(0).Top + picEye(0).Height Then
        shpPup(0).Left = picEye(0).Width / 2 - shpPup(0).Width
        shpPup(0).Top = picEye(0).Height / 2 - shpPup(0).Height
        shpPup(1).Left = 0
        shpPup(1).Top = picEye(1).Height / 2 - shpPup(1).Height
    '14
    ElseIf nLookX >= picEye(0).Left + picEye(0).Width And nLookX < picEye(1).Left
And nLookY >= picEye(0).Top And nLookY < picEye(0).Top + picEye(0).Height Then
        shpPup(0).Left = picEye(0).Width - shpPup(0).Width
        shpPup(0).Top = picEye(0).Height / 2 - shpPup(0).Height
        shpPup(1).Left = 0
        shpPup(1).Top = picEye(1).Height / 2 - shpPup(1).Height
    '15
    ElseIf nLookX >= picEye(1).Left And nLookX < picEye(1).Left + picEye(1).Width
And nLookY >= picEye(1).Top And nLookY < picEye(1).Top + picEye(1).Height Then
        shpPup(0).Left = picEye(0).Width - shpPup(0).Width
```

```
            shpPup(0).Top = picEye(0).Height / 2 - shpPup(0).Height
            shpPup(1).Left = picEye(1).Width / 2 - shpPup(1).Width
            shpPup(1).Top = picEye(1).Height / 2 - shpPup(1).Height
        End If

    End Sub
```

Stopping the Idle Animation

Animate_Eyes is constantly called until the idle animation is stopped. This is done by selecting another animation from one of the three choices, or exiting. In this case, another form is displayed and another animation interface presented. To make this possible while the idle animation is running, other Windows messages, like button clicks and menu selections, must be allowed to process. One of the reasons for the need for other messages to process is for the termination of the idle animation. If the user exits, starts a process, or goes to another form, the animation must be stopped.

If **Timer** is enabled, it must be disabled so that it doesn't take up unnecessary processor resources. If the form was visible when the animation stops, the **m_nAnimMethod** flag would have to be changed to a value that is not **ANI_MOUSE** or **ANI_TIMER** so that the **MouseMove** events would no longer execute.

Clicking on another animation selection by selecting one of the graphical buttons at the bottom of the form will immediately turn off the timer, before calling the selected animation. Each animation is located within its own form, so they are called with a **Show 1** command. When they return, the timer can be turned back on if applicable. This ensures that the idle animation will continue where it left off.

Notice also that the form that was called is not only unloaded after the code returns, but is also set to **Nothing**. Here's the case for calling the letter animation on **frmLetters**:

```
    frmLetters.Show 1
    Unload frmLetters
    Set frmLetters = Nothing
```

When **Show 1** is called, the other form goes about its animating business. When the user exits, the instruction only hides the form to let code continue processing after the **Show** command. If the form is only unloaded, not set to **Nothing**, the variables on the form continue to retain their most recent values, the objects on the form are not returned to their design-time positions and unexpected results are visible.

Scripted Animation

I can generalize an example of a scripted animation here, but, really, anything goes, as you'll see when we get to the sample code in Chapter 4. Put simply, **scripted animations** are those that follow a screenplay or a pre-planned list of instructions. A demonstration program, or tutorial is a good example of a final application that requires some specific scripting. They are created to step the user through some specific content, whether it be for entertainment, marketing or for teaching purposes. Usually, the scripted part of any animation is not interactive, so calculations and events are not triggered based on some sort of action from the user.

In the animation on **frmLetters**, there are three parts to the script:

- The letters are moved to the center of the screen.
- The letter colors are animated.
- The ball bounces and hits each letter, hiding it.

This is an example of a scripted animation purely for fun, but if the letters read the name of a program or some other important name rather than just the word ANIMATION, this script could be used as a splash screen. Such finishing touches added to a program are best used when the rest of the application is not oriented towards entertainment.

Script Initialization

In the example, all letter positions are predefined at design time. You'll notice that the form starts out with the final position, where each letter should 'land' before the ball starts to bounce. This is what made it easier to define the path of the ball as it bounced on top of each letter. This animation sequence is scripted and doesn't include any code that can really be reused in other animations. For this reason, the entire script for the animation is placed in a single procedure. If the script were much longer, or code somehow needed to be called by another procedure (take a peek at the demo script in Chapter 4), we'd need to break it apart.

The central procedure, **Animate_Letters**, begins by initializing the sequence. The letters' current **Top** positions are stored in an array and the red ball is positioned off-screen to the left:

```
' save original top positions for each letter
For nIndex = 0 To 8
  nLetterTop(nIndex) = labLetters(nIndex).Top
Next nIndex

' move ball offscreen top-left
shpBall.Left = -shpBall.Width
shpBall.Top = -shpBall.Height
```

Next, still initializing, the code loops through the letters, positioning them off-screen to the top, making them visible, then assigning them a random **QBColor** (excluding black, so that they can be seen):

```
' prepare to start animation
For nIndex = 0 To 8
  ' move letters offscreen-top
  labLetters(nIndex).Top = -labLetters(nIndex).Height
  labLetters(nIndex).Visible = True
  ' select a random color from 1 to 15 (exclude black, 0)
  nColor = Int((15 * Rnd) + 1)
  labLetters(nIndex).ForeColor = QBColor(nColor)
Next nIndex
```

The Scripted Scenes

Now for Scene 1 of the script. This is where the letters are moved into their design-time position, directly below their current vertical off-screen position. One letter is moved at a time until it has reached its landing point, but each loop must include a **DoEvents** so that messages can be processed. This way, if the user clicks the exit option (the eyes at the bottom right of the form), the flag, **m_flgExiting**, is set to **True**. This must be checked every time so that the code can exit the entire script. You'll notice this check inside every loop of the script, so that the form exits as soon as the user chooses to do so and isn't kept waiting until the whole script has been completed.

From the first scene's script below, you can see that the animation is scripted. There's no dynamic array of letters. There are 9 index values, from 0 to 8. Movement is not random; it's exactly 25 twips downward each time, until the final destination of the letter is reached or passed:

```
'-SCENE 1:
  ' move letter to center position
  For nIndex = 0 To 8
    For nPos = labLetters(nIndex).Top To nLetterTop(nIndex) Step 25
      If nPos > nLetterTop(nIndex) Then Exit For
      labLetters(nIndex).Top = nPos
      DoEvents
      If m_flgExiting Then GoTo endscript
    Next nPos
  Next nIndex
```

Scene 2 is the color animation portion of the script. Here, an iteration of 500 times will cycle through each of the letters, selecting and assigning a new random **QBColor** for the ForeColor property of each label. Once again, the termination flag **m_flgExiting** is checked on every loop.

```
' SCENE 2:
  ' animate letter colors
  nLetter = 0
  For nIndex = 0 To 500
    ' select random color again
    nColor = Int((15 * Rnd) + 1)
    labLetters(nLetter).ForeColor = QBColor(nColor)
    ' move to next letter
    If nLetter = 8 Then
      nLetter = 0
    Else
      nLetter = nLetter + 1
    End If
    DoEvents
    If m_flgExiting Then GoTo endscript
  Next nIndex
```

In Scene 3 of the script, the ball bounces on top of each letter and hides them one by one. The movement of each ball is also scripted, since each bounce has a preplanned place that it needs to fall on.

This isn't a bad example of what you might do to program movement from point to point without getting into any difficult algebra calculations. Don't worry, you'll see some slick looking path calculations in later chapters, nicely encapsulated in VB classes. Let's go through the logic behind planning each step in the ball bouncing movement.

First, the ball is made visible in its off-screen position, as the initialization of the script suggests. The value for **nSpeed** is set (I'll explain how this is used) and a loop is started that will iterate through each letter from 0 to 8, bouncing the ball on top of each. These steps are shown on the next page.

```
' Scene 3:
  ' show ball
  shpBall.Visible = True
  nSpeed = 30

  For nIndex = 0 To 8
    ' setup ball bounce for this letter
    ' make ball rise
    ' make ball fall
    ' hide letter
  Next nIndex
```

The **For...Next** loop above is, for now, filled in with comments that discuss each part of the ball bouncing for each letter. The first step is to set up the bouncing coordinates for the current letter. The ball starts off-screen, then falls onto the first letter (hiding it), then rises to a position just off-screen at the top of the form, positioned between the current and next letter. Now the ball is ready to fall again onto the next letter. The sequence is repeated until the last letter is hidden and the ball is jetted off-screen to the right.

The ball bounce requires three positions: a start position to fall from, a hit position where it lands on the current letter and an end position off-screen where the ball is now ready to fall again on the next letter. The coordinates for a bounce are calculated for each letter and stored inside the **nBounceX()** and **nBounceY()** arrays. There are three elements in each array, one for each of the three bounce positions. The first and last letters are special cases for calculating the positions, since the ball won't rise to a position off-screen between two letters, the first and last letters respectively. Here's the code that prepares the three points, depending on the current letter:

```
' setup bounce points for this letter
If nIndex = 0 Then  ' first letter bounce points
  nBounceX(IDSTART) = shpBall.Left
  nBounceY(IDSTART) = shpBall.Top
  nBounceX(IDHIT) = labLetters(nIndex).Left + (labLetters(nIndex).Width -
shpBall.Width) / 2
  nBounceY(IDHIT) = labLetters(nIndex).Top - shpBall.Height
  nBounceX(IDEND) = (labLetters(nIndex).Left + labLetters(nIndex).Width +
labLetters(nIndex + 1).Left) / 2
  nBounceY(IDEND) = -shpBall.Height
ElseIf nIndex = 8 Then 'last letter bounce points
  nBounceX(IDSTART) = nBounceX(IDEND)
  nBounceY(IDSTART) = nBounceY(IDEND)
  nBounceX(IDHIT) = labLetters(nIndex).Left + (labLetters(nIndex).Width -
shpBall.Width) / 2
  nBounceY(IDHIT) = labLetters(nIndex).Top - shpBall.Height
  nBounceX(IDEND) = Me.Width + shpBall.Width
  nBounceY(IDEND) = -shpBall.Height
Else 'all other letters points
  nBounceX(IDSTART) = nBounceX(IDEND)
  nBounceY(IDSTART) = nBounceY(IDEND)
  nBounceX(IDHIT) = labLetters(nIndex).Left + (labLetters(nIndex).Width -
shpBall.Width) / 2
  nBounceY(IDHIT) = labLetters(nIndex).Top - shpBall.Height
  nBounceX(IDEND) = (labLetters(nIndex).Left + labLetters(nIndex).Width +
labLetters(nIndex + 1).Left) / 2
  nBounceY(IDEND) = -shpBall.Height
End If
```

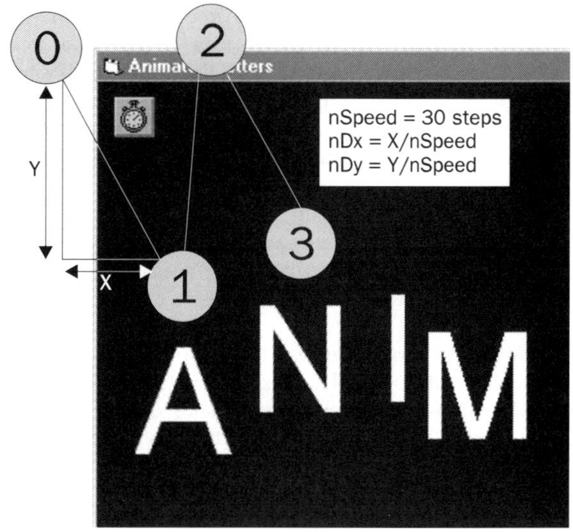

The **nSpeed** variable is used to calculate the ball's movement. This value for **nSpeed** represents the number of points along the X and Y axis that the ball will stop at on its way to its next point destination. A value of 30 is assigned, which means the total X distance moved is divided by 30 to get a delta X movement (**nDX**). The same is done for the Y movement (**nDY**). Of course, this won't be the most accurate, since the division could produce rounding errors and, by the time it reaches the 30th **Move** command, the movement can end up going astray. This is summarized in Figure 1-15, for the first movement from the top left to the first letter:

The ball falls to the current letter with the code below. The **nDX** and **nDY** calculation are based on movement from the bounce position **0** (**IDSTART**) to bounce position **1** (**IDHIT**). Since **nSpeed** is used to calculate the delta movement for both X and Y, the **For...Next** loop iterates from **0** to **nSpeed**, moving the ball by the calculated amount:

```
' calculate movement direction X and Y for fall
nDX = (nBounceX(IDHIT) - nBounceX(IDSTART)) / nSpeed
nDY = (nBounceY(IDHIT) - nBounceY(IDSTART)) / nSpeed
' move ball
For nPos = 0 To nSpeed
  shpBall.Left = nBounceX(IDSTART) + nDX * nPos
  shpBall.Top = nBounceY(IDSTART) + nDY * nPos
  DoEvents
  If m_flgExiting Then GoTo endscript
Next nPos
```

The letter is hidden before the call is made to move the ball to the ending position of the bounce. This time, the calculation is made to move the ball from position **1** (**IDHIT**) to position **2** (**IDEND**) in the **Bounce** array. The movement value for **nDY** will end up negative, which will insure that the loop equation moves the ball upward:

```
' Hide Letter
labLetters(nIndex).Visible = False

' Ball RISE
' calculate movement direction X and Y for rise
nDX = (nBounceX(IDEND) - nBounceX(IDHIT)) / nSpeed
nDY = (nBounceY(IDEND) - nBounceY(IDHIT)) / nSpeed
' move ball
For nPos = 0 To nSpeed
  shpBall.Left = nBounceX(IDHIT) + nDX * nPos
  shpBall.Top = nBounceY(IDHIT) + nDY * nPos
  DoEvents
  If m_flgExiting Then GoTo endscript
Next nPos
```

The scripted animation code speaks for itself. Each scene has a place in the entire animation, one after another. Within each scene was a separately iterated event that had to take place before the next part could begin. That's the thing with scripting, you have to keep it in the order the script expects or you're in trouble! If the ball were to bounce before the letters had arrived to their position, the entire animation would be wrong. My previous comment about unloading the form and setting it to **Nothing** is also relevant here.

If the animation is left part way through, the **Animate_Letters** procedure starts off by saving the Top properties of each label. This expects that the labels are located at their design-time position. Basically, scripting an animation has the added responsibility of ensuring the code that will *always* turn out the way you expect. In other words, be careful.

Now, this script *can* be made more reusable by writing code that moves each control off-screen to begin with and calculates the path to a landing point dynamically. I've saved that for Chapter 4, when VB animation classes make that our central programming focus. What you've just seen is standard VB coding practice to implement the script. It's also a perfect example of a situation where hard-coding is the only way to get it to work exactly as you planned, without spending two weeks on math calculations.

Random Animation

Contrary to the ideals of the scripted animation, a **random animation** requires that the code not need to know where it last left off, or in what order things are to be executed. There are aspects of random animation in several of the animations of **Vbanim.vbp**. The **Timer**-based idle eye animation, the color animation of the letters and the ball animation of **DrawMode** and **FillStyle** are all examples of random animations, but these are just the tip of the iceberg. Here, I'll discuss each of the random animations and describe some of the ways they could be made more random. Each case will bring a different addition to light that will be covered later in the more meaty application examples.

The **Timer** version of the idle animation moves the red ball to a random coordinate on the form each interval. These two lines select random coordinates:

```
nRandX = Int((Me.ScaleWidth * Rnd))
nRandY = Int((Me.ScaleHeight * Rnd))
```

This is fairly uncomplicated—**Rnd** generates a value between 0 and 1 each time. When you multiply the maximum value of each range (**ScaleWidth** and **ScaleHeight** here) by **Rnd** you get a coordinate within that range. Here we do this for both X and Y.

We could make two obvious improvements to this animation to make it more random. First of all, the **Timer** interval is always the same, so if each interval selected a new, random interval before the next ball move is triggered, the animation would be more unpredictable. Random movement, direction and timing are covered in later chapters, and the code is contained nicely inside classes that you can reuse—so keep reading!

The letter animation uses the **Rnd** function to generate a random **QBColor** from 1 to 15. There's no random movement of the letters; they move the same direction into the same position every time. A variation on this script could be to have Scene 1 of the script move the letters into position in random order. Maybe they could even enter on screen from different directions, sometimes landing out of order in the display of the word ANIMATION. This requires a lot of careful coding. Although this example isn't scripted as such in this book, there are other examples of characters appearing and moving randomly that you could apply to this theory.

The appearance of the ball bouncing against the walls of the room is chosen randomly. The ball is normally a solid shape, but since the **FillStyle** and **DrawMode** properties affect how an object appears on another graphic, the results are fairly unexpected. Another way to make this animation more random in nature, would be to move the ball at random distances each move iteration. This could make the ball look as if it had a mind of its own, just for kicks.

The bottom line here is that a random animation gives the user a taste of change and surprise so that they're not able to predict the application every time they see it. To do this, the code needs to be planned that way from the start, so that the graphics, the user interface and any other related issues are in sync with one another.

Loop Animations

Repeated activity is at the heart of animation. As you've probably gathered from this chapter, *animation* is a very generic term that covers a wide spectrum of programming possibilities. Whatever the animation, it's likely that it contains some form of repetition. What that repetition or loop consists of decides what starts and terminates the loop, as well as its contents. I'm going to discuss the code constructs that VB provides for looping, while discussing reasons for using each and reasons for looping an animation. Then I'll compare code constructs to the **Timer** and explain why you might choose one over the other.

Constructing a Loop

Here are some of the central methods that VB provides to construct a repeating code sequence, most of which should look rather familiar:

- **Do While...Loop**
- **Do Until...Loop**
- **Do...Loop While**
- **Do...Loop Until**
- **While...Wend**
- **For...Next**
- **Timer**

The first six are code constructs that repeat based on conditions specified within the code. The last is the **Timer** event for the timer control which is triggered based on a time lapse. Regardless of the format of the animation construct, there's typically a condition which starts the animation and one that ends it. Usually, any animation loop can be written in another way, so it ends up being at the programmer's discretion. Let's see some of the constructs inside **Vbanim.vbp**.

On the first form, **frmEyes**, there's an idle animation as described earlier, with the eyes following either the mouse or the ball as they move to new positions on the form. This is a loop because the eyes continue moving until another animation is called, making it a repeating activity. In this case, the loop itself is driven by events only, **MouseMove** or **Timer**. Since there's no looping construct to break free of when another animation is selected, the **Timer** must be disabled and/or the Form hidden (to stop the **MouseMove** event being triggered) for the animation to terminate. This animation is ongoing until the user chooses to do something else. In this loop, there's no complex content, just the movement of two objects, the eye pupils.

The row of buttons at the bottom of the form are more samples of animation. Let's take the eyes on **frmLetters** in the bottom right corner of the screen, for example. Until the condition is met that the mouse button is pressed over the eyes, there is no animation on the button. This is the start of the animation loop that continues until the mouse button is released, a state which is reflected by the flag, **m_flgButtonDown**. The flag is set to true just before the animation construct is called and to false when the **MouseUp** event is triggered. This time, a **Do While...Loop** code construct is used and the condition is this flagged:

```
Do While m_flgButtonDown
  DoEvents
  nIndex = IIf(nIndex = UBound(g_sEyes), 0, nIndex + 1)
  imgAnims.Picture = LoadPicture(g_sEyes(nIndex))
Loop
```

Once again, this animation can only be terminated by the user doing something—letting go of the mouse button—which means that the number of loops completed is unknown every time the loop is called. In this second looping example, rather than moving something, the button image is being cycled through a number of images that make up the animation. This is an example of a stationary frame animation, where no movement occurs. As you can see from the code, each loop must cycle through the number of frames in the picture filename array (**g_sEyes** in this case), starting from the beginning each time it reaches the end of a cycle.

In **frmLetters**, the animation has several parts. The first part has the code that moves each letter to its pre-planned position on the form and performs a loop within another loop. The outer loop is for each letter, the inner loop moves that letter until it reaches the correct position, then the next letter is up. In both cases, the **For...Next** construct is used. The outer loop through each letter is fixed every time, based on the number of letters, which is always constant. The inner loop is a little more dynamic in that it takes the current letter's position and moves it to another position. These coordinates can vary without breaking the loop. The condition that the current letter reaches its planned destination is met first, and the condition that each letter gets the same treatment is met second. There is no user interaction with this example:

```
For nIndex = 0 To 8
  For nPos = labLetters(nIndex).Top To nLetterTop(nIndex) Step 25
    If nPos > nLetterTop(nIndex) Then Exit For
    labLetters(nIndex).Top = nPos
    DoEvents
    If m_flgExiting Then GoTo endscript
  Next nPos
Next nIndex
```

The second part of the letter animation performs a color cycling animation for a specified interval. Again, there's a loop within that changes the current letter being worked on, but the outer loop is specific in its number of repetitions. There are 500 cycles. Inside each of these cycles, a random letter and a new color for that letter is chosen. Once again, the user plays no part in this loop. It is hard-coded to the 500 iterations:

```
nLetter = 0
For nIndex = 0 To 500
  ' select random color again
  nColor = Int((15 * Rnd) + 1)
  labLetters(nLetter).ForeColor = QBColor(nColor)
  ' move to next letter
  If nLetter = 8 Then
```

```
      nLetter = 0
    Else
      nLetter = nLetter + 1
    End If
    DoEvents
    If m_flgExiting Then GoTo endscript
  Next nIndex
```

These examples don't cover all types of loops that can be useful in an animation. For instance, you could take the example of the frame cycling of the animated buttons and make it so that there's only one cycle through those frames. That would mean that the loop was terminated by completing the cycle, rather than waiting for the user to let go of the button.

There are far too many creative ways of using and triggering loops for us to discuss here, but I hope this has whetted your appetite for further study and development.

Loops and Timing

One very important point to note on timing your animations is the idea of keeping the timing code independent of the actual animation. For instance, the ball animation takes place in the procedure **Animate_Ball**. The user can select the timing on the ball animation as **DoEvents** or **Timer**. This means that we must write the code so that it can be called from two separate loops. Here's how the two loops look:

```
Private Sub tmrBall_Timer()
  Animate_Ball
End Sub
```

```
Do While m_flgDoEvents
  DoEvents
  Animate_Ball
Loop
```

Keeping the meat of the loop inside another procedure adds the flexibility that you might need when it comes to changing the way the code is called.

There's a reason why the **Timer** and **DoEvents** are part of this last comparison for separating the code. The **Timer** event has some limitations with respect to speed. It can never iterate faster than eighteen times a second. This is not a VB thing, but a Windows timer thing, so it happens to C programmers too. This timing is used by all timer facilities, whether the VB control, or a timer message sent using external methods (a Windows programming thing). These timer messages take on low priority to all other events, so your timing may not be on target for every animation loop if other things are going on in the system.

In the ball animation, the **Timer** interval is set to a higher value to slow it down so that you can see how the ball changes as it moves around the room, but the **DoEvents** loop is executed as fast as the CPU can get there to execute it. The reason I called it a **DoEvents** loop is because any time a loop is iterated without the use of an event, like the **Timer** or **MouseMove**, the CPU will not free up to receive other mouse messages and so the loop will never terminate. **DoEvents** checks for other Windows activity so that other messages, like mouse clicks, can be processed.

When you want an animation to go as fast as possible, a **DoEvents** loop is the only way to go. There are some other, advanced timing methods that come from the Windows API and MCI (Media Control Interface). That latter is the only clock that ticks at more than eighteen times per second. Even the **Timer** control, whose interval is set to 10 ticks (which should amount to one hundred times per second) is only performing at eighteen times per second. This is not necessarily an issue, until you get to game programming when you want things to go as fast as possible (i.e. scream!) across the screen. Actually, you'll find that methods sometimes need to be implemented to slow things down on faster machines!

Summary

This chapter's code implements most of the previous animations, using color, character frames and so on, all under the limitations of the VB controls and code. Consider this a therapeutic session to help you overcome the VB separation anxiety that you're going to get in the next chapter. This is that funny feeling you get in your stomach when you start to learn something new that opens up into a really big, unknown area. Let me give you some idea by summarizing how I would use some better techniques to improve on each animation that we've seen in this chapter.

The eye animation had two problems: the shape flicker that comes with the pupils and the red ball. In a nutshell, VB repainting methods suck. To prevent repainting flicker, you'll always need to use something called **double-buffering**. This concept is covered in the next chapter. For similar reasons, we saw other flicker problems in the letter animation when the labels were moved and in the bouncing ball animation when the ball was moved and its **DrawMode** and/or **FillStyle** altered. All of these things, moving controls and changing their appearance, cause the control's container to want to repaint it, generating a non-double-buffered repaint.

We saw another flicker problem with the dragon animations. Though the new frames of the dragon in both the night and day scene are drawn with **PaintPicture** rather than with controls, there's still a moment where the previous frame drawn is erased, before the new frame is drawn. This still causes flicker, once again resolved by double-buffering.

Palettes are another issue. Though we won't discuss palettes in detail until Chapter 3, all samples from this moment forward will work on both palletized systems (256 color) and better. You'll be seeing a lot of palette work, since any application that uses graphics requires special attention in this area over and over and over again.

We'll also take a look at how to have the dragon fly over an image like the castle without hard-coding the bitmap frames. You can make bitmaps transparent if you use some API functions, as we'll see in the next chapter.

Lastly, we can improve animations by better encapsulating movement and positioning, which you'll start seeing from here on in. This chapter has served two purposes. It has shown some different animation concepts and made you aware of what VB can and can't do. Now the fun will begin!

```
rivate Declare Function GlobalFree Lib "kernel32" (ByVal h
rivate Declare Function GlobalLock Lib "kernel32" (ByVal h
rivate Declare Function GlobalUnlock Lib "kernel32" (ByVa
--copying bitmap bits
 copies a global block of data into global memory
rivate Declare Sub CopyMemory Lib "kernel32" Alias "RtlM

--copies global block of data in      B
rivate Declare Function SetDIB      "gdi32" (ByVal m_hd
 ByVal hBitmap As Long, ByVal nStartS      As Long, ByV
 ByVal lpBits As Any, lpBI As BITMAPI      ByVal wUsa

--blits DC to DC
rivate Declare Function BitBlt Lib "gdi32" (ByVal hDestDC
rivate Declare Function StretchBlt Lib "gdi32" (ByVal hDes

--palette methods
rivate Declare Function CreatePalett      "gdi32" (lpLogPal
rivate Declare Function SelectPalette      "gdi32" (ByVal m
rivate Declare Function RealizePalette Lib "gdi32" (ByVal r
rivate Declare Sub AnimatePalette Lib "gdi32" (ByVal hPal

--device context methods
rivate Declare Function SelectObject Lib "gdi32" (ByVal m_

rivate Declare Function CreateCompatibleBitmap Lib "gdi32
rivate Declare Function DeleteObject Lib "gdi32" (ByVal hC

rivate Declare Function CreateCompatibleDC Lib "gdi32" (B
```

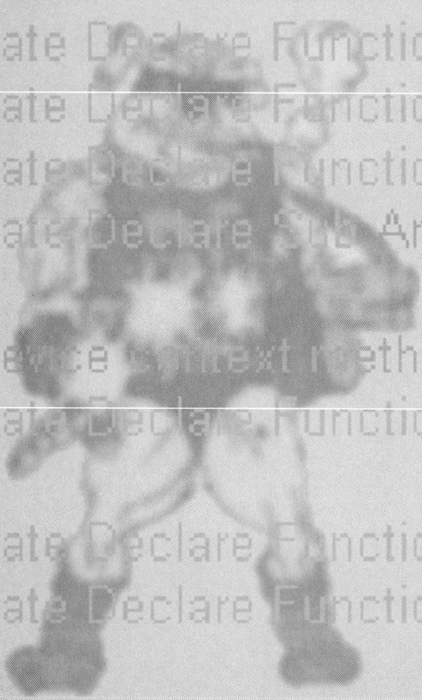

Chapter

2

VB Graphics Primer

Put a C programmer and a VB programmer in the same room for an hour or so and the chances are the VB-er will run out holding his hands over his ears, screaming "Noooo, make it stop!!!" Okay, a slight exaggeration perhaps, but the language that these two Windows programmers speak is frequently quite different. What's worse, the C programmer is often left dumbfounded as to why the other doesn't understand terminology that in his mind is 'trivial'. VB-ers are rather sheltered from the intricate terminology that bombards C programmers right from day one. If they knew it all, they may not have started using VB in the first place!

Now that we've seen some of the animation techniques available when we use straight VB capabilities, it's time to learn some Windows techniques in preparation for a book bulging with animation. Customarily, the C programmer is *forced* to deal with the underlying nitty-gritty of Windows programming, while VB programmers happily design their form displays and get right down to content coding. Getting to the content code quicker is great, but we'll be needing some of this knowledge too, to help us make our animations smoother and give us some new tools for added programming capability. Throughout the book, we'll use the new methods and theories (which we explore in the next two chapters) as we build more elaborate applications that demonstrate various animation techniques.

In this chapter, we'll begin by taking a look at some useful Windows programming concepts which we often overlook, sheltered as we are by the sometimes overprotective mother wing of VB. Let's unleash some indispensable Windows programming methods, along with their full implications so that we can begin to *really* exploit VB for what it's worth!

Windows Programming

Windows programmers do plenty of complex and sometimes horrifying things behind the scenes that you haven't had to worry about (ha! ha!—until now!). You see, this VB shelter has made our lives both easier *and* more difficult—easier because we don't get gray hair when we write our first program; more difficult because when we decide to expand our horizons on the Windows frontier, we need to start understanding all of those things that we didn't *have* to understand in the first place, leaving us... ahem!... a little behind.

All is not lost. Thank your lucky stars that you don't have to open the whole can of worms. You just need to gain an adequate knowledge surrounding a given topic so that you can intelligently use its methods—in short, know enough so that you don't mess everything up. Throughout the book I'll unravel useful Windows concepts bit by bit, uncovering just enough to give you a triumphant programming experience. Right now, you're going to embark on a journey through the GDI (Graphics Device Interface), the heart and soul of Windows graphics programming. If you already know this stuff, bear with me for the moment, because we need to prepare some common ground rules before we set off.

The Windows API and GDI

Once you've used Windows for some time, you'll probably notice that all the programs share many common traits. For example, the interface is in a 'window', usually one of many running at a single time. Even the contents of those windows (i.e. buttons, list boxes, menus) tend to look alike. One of the reasons for this similarity is the fact that Windows programs are *supposed* to follow a standardized interface so that users can quickly grasp new applications they haven't seen before. The other reason is that they use the same underlying Windows programming language, which is the heart of the Windows operating system: the **Windows API**.

Reusable Windows Functionality

As everyone knows, API stands for **Application Programming Interface**. The Windows API (or WinAPI) is a collection of several DLLs that expose functions for use with Windows programs. These DLLs go by the names **`KERNEL32.DLL`**, **`USER32.DLL`** and **`GDI32.DLL`**. Windows uses these three DLLs to provide the interface where other programs are loaded, displayed and used, which means that the functions used by the operating system are also available to us in our own programs. VB automatically calls these functions *for* us, to create the display and perform other Windows functionality, but we can use them directly when we're good and sick of the limitations of VB.

> **Appendix A, *Using DLLs*, provides additional information on what DLLs are, how to use DLLs from VB, and more information about the Windows API.**

The GDI comprises a large library of commands that create, manipulate and display all components of any Windows interface, that covers the window itself, the graphics, the buttons and any other controls displayed in it—the GDI provides access to it all. Virtually anything to do with sending information to the display belongs in the GDI library. The reason for the GDI doing all the work is to standardize the things that Windows programs do, so that it doesn't matter what machine you're on or what the hardware makeup is. The connection between GDI and the hardware components is covered more in Chapter 3, but just be aware that there's an important liaison here that saves programmers a ton of extra work: they can forget the hardware and just concentrate on the code, which is a software programmer's nightmare as it is.

When we're using VB, we take many things for granted. Creating a form (or window), printing text and displaying graphics are all done with many additional calls to the GDI. VB takes care of all that for us. Even controls that VB lets us draw freely and set properties for are created using calls to GDI. When I get to discussions about these GDI functions and how they are presented to us in the VB environment, you'll really see the connection and then be able to extend your functionality. From the 'fix it' list at the end of Chapter 1, you'll learn what you can do to fix each and every one of those animations, as we go through this chapter.

The connection between the device dependence, driver and GDI is that, when a device context is created using a GDI call, it looks to the current device driver to create a compatible device context with the display (or printer if that's the device in question). The reason is that the devices should be interpreting the data in the same way, otherwise you would end up with gobbledygook when the data is displayed in the new device. The DC structure (a GDI structure) holds information about how the device with which it is compatible expects to receive its information.

Windows and Device Contexts

The theory of device independence that drives Windows is supported through the GDI and whatever device driver is being used for output, whether it be for printing or for screen display. Device contexts are a type of Windows object and are a central component of the GDI's device independence. Windows supports four types of device contexts: display, memory, printer and information. For the moment, though, we'll concern ourselves with just the first two.

A window is another Windows object used by the GDI. Windows are a physical part of the display and come in a variety of shapes and styles. Without getting too deep, C programmers can use the GDI to create the equivalent of VB's forms and controls. As far as Windows is concerned, all of these things (well, almost all) are windows, but they just have different descriptions that state how they work, what kinds of user actions they respond to, and so forth. Sound familiar? Each of our controls have different appearances and they each have different events that can be triggered by user and program interaction.

Only certain types of windows have associated device contexts. Windows that have a client area where drawing takes place or where bitmaps are displayed use a device context to support this graphical output. A display device context always comes with a window for their display. VB provides us with two types of display DCs: the form and the picture box. The form's window is the entire object, including the caption bar and border, whereas the picture box's window only has a border. Within each is a drawing area—the DC—calculated by the **ScaleWidth** and **ScaleHeight** properties. Only the form and picture box are capable of supporting graphics display output in VB (like Print, Line and Circle methods), which makes sense since they are the only ones with an associated device context to draw to.

When a window is created with an associated device context, both of these objects need to be tracked by the operating system. The whole concept of Windows is based on the ability to have more than one application open at a time, so when a command is sent to the GDI to draw to a device context, or to alter the appearance of a window, the GDI needs to know what's what. Windows assigns handles (which are really pointers to memory addresses) to every object it creates. Windows have window handles (**hWnd** property in VB) and device contexts have DC handles (**hDC** property in VB). Notice that the form and picture box are the only ones with both, but that almost all controls have **hWnd** properties because, as I said before, they are types of windows.

Windows and device contexts are types of Windows objects that can be manipulated using the GDI. Device contexts also have objects associated with them, which are graphic objects and should sound similar to some of the properties that VB keeps for the form and picture box DCs. Since this is not an 'everything you wanted to know about windows but were afraid to ask' book, I won't get into each and every object listed, but I'll be covering the bitmap, brush, palette and font objects throughout the book. Each of these graphic objects are assigned handles when they are created, but VB encrypts that for us, since we use the property window to set them. This table sets out descriptions for all the graphic objects that we'll be using, including in brackets the related property where applicable.

Graphic Object	Description
Bitmap	Bitmap graphic image (Picture)
Brush	Fill pattern for drawing (FillColor)
Palette	Palette colors for mapping any drawing to the DC including bitmap blitting and selection
Font	Font information for printing text to the DC (Font)
Path	Figures defined by drawing methods (Line, Circle Method)
Pen	Forecolor for drawing (ForeColor)
Region	Defined areas within the DC's client area

When we assign an image to the picture property of a picture box, we're actually 'selecting' a bitmap for the DC of the picture box. When we change the properties of the picture box's font, we're 'selecting' a new logical font for the DC to use when next we use the Print method that outputs text. What a revelation! Some of that Windows terminology is already starting to make sense!

PictureBoxes and Memory DCs

You can use forms and picture boxes to load image data from disk simply by calling the **`LoadPicture`** method. The image data can be loaded into the associated display device context, even when the form or control isn't visible and is stored in memory somewhere until it's displayed. Windows programmers don't have this same convenience for loading images from a file into memory for display. Not only are they forced to write code to *read in* the binary image data (along with its associated palette information, if applicable), they must also allocate a place in memory with all the associated structure information necessary to organize the data. This is a far cry from what *we're* accustomed to, but if your intention is to display all images in a single display device, using **`PaintPicture`** to get them to the screen without flicker or speed delay, storing them in a picture box is an inefficient use of resources, since the picture box uses both a handle to the window and a handle to its device context. This extra overhead can add up if you're thinking about loading all the animation frames you're going to use and any other additional bitmaps that are part of the scene. Sacrificing these extra Windows resources just for the sake of speed and easy coding is something that has to stop.

Enter the memory device context. Display device contexts support display output, printer device contexts support printed output, but you can use memory device contexts to store bitmap information that can be sent to either output type—without the physical device (window or printer) as overhead. Since we're only covering DC's for display, we shall assume that all the DC's we discuss from here onwards are compatible with the display.

I'm not going to get into the code here, but let's talk a little about the theory of this subject. A picture box is a window, with a display DC associated that we can see as long as the control is visible on the form. When the **`Picture`** property is set, the bitmap object of the DC contains the image data. Before this happens, there is a default stock bitmap object associated with the DC as a placeholder. When the DC is created, this bitmap object is initialized to the same color format as the one supported by the current display driver. This ensures that information prepared in this bitmap area fits in with what the output device is expecting.

When a memory device context is created, it associates with this same default bitmap until it receives instructions to 'select' a new bitmap into the DC. This bitmap object is only 1 pixel by 1 pixel. Gee, now *that's* a large area to draw to—NOT! Until a new bitmap is selected into this DC, the drawing area for the DC (to print text or alter pixels) is constrained to that 1x1 area. In short, you can't do a thing until a bitmap is selected into the DC area. I'll be discussing how DC objects are replaced in a later section. This can be done for any of the graphic objects listed in the previous table.

API Animation Sampler

This chapter's main code sample, **`\Code\Chapter2\Apianim\Apianim.vbp`**, demonstrates several examples of using the Windows API, including some advanced animation techniques. Since there's so much going on and the interface, although interesting, may not be totally intuitive, I'll explain what each sample is trying to accomplish before we get to the guts of the code.

The Interface

Take a look at the following figure, showing a screenshot of the interface for this chapter's animation sampler. The film strip at the bottom shows five frames. The first three each begin a different animation sample, the fourth stops the animation and the last (you guessed it!) ends the program. Here's a list of the different animations taking place in the code:

- An animated trash can
- A flying pilot
- A walking kid
- A closing curtain

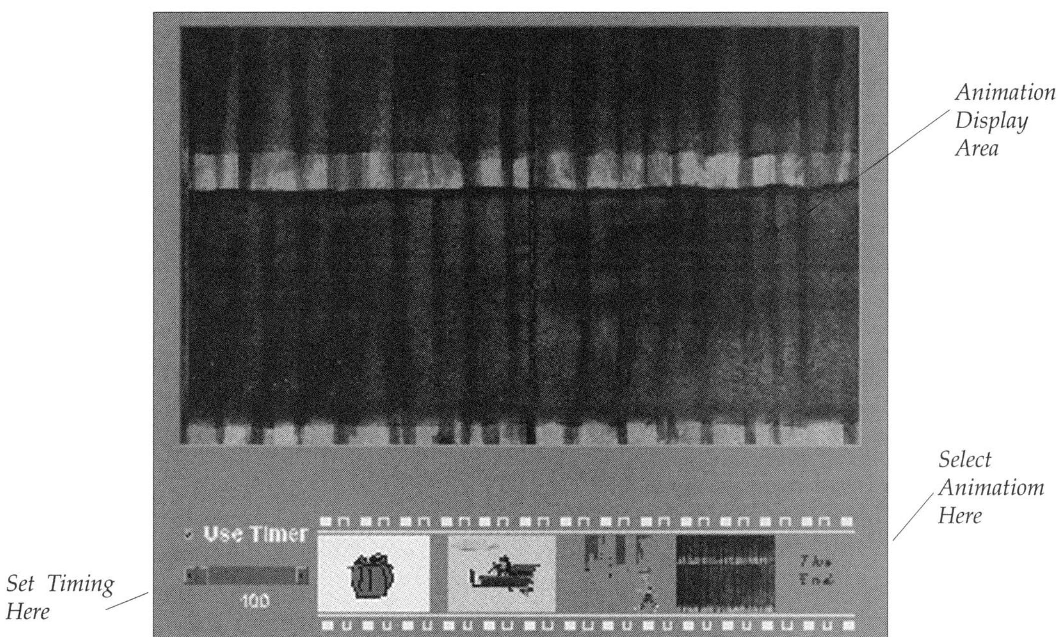

This film strip bitmap acts as the selector for each animation. Hit testing is implemented with empty image controls bounding each frame area on the filmstrip bitmap. The Use Timer check box lets you turn the timer off for each animation, though what it actually does is to set the **`Interval`** property for the timers (**`tmrAnim`**, **`tmrText`** and **`tmrCurtain`**) to a value of 1 rather than 0, so the **`Timer`** event will still execute. When Use Timer is checked, you use the scroll bar to specify a timer interval from 100 to 1000, varying the frequency of each animation loop.

Before you go on, I recommend you run the code sample to get a better idea of the steps and code navigation that I'll be describing for each sample. In this chapter, we'll concentrate on the cool, new code samples, so I'll leave you to investigate the rudimentary code on your own.

What's Happening?

Once you've chosen the animation that you want, the curtain rises and things get going. While each animation plays, if you click on the curtain image in the film strip, the animation will cease and the curtain will fall. The curtain animation marks the beginning of a transition class that we'll be improving and adding to in later chapters.

The animated trash can sample generates random animation by using a controlling timer (**`tmrAnimCtrl`**) to select one of four trash can animations, setting a new interval for its duration. Each trash can animation is introduced by a text animation that uses Windows API calls encapsulated in a VB class for easy reuse.

The flying pilot and walking kid animations both demonstrate transparent sprite animation, using bitmasking techniques. There is more than one layer to the kid animation, as the city scene moves behind the walking kid, demonstrating a simple panning technique that we can compare with more sophisticated animation methods in later chapters.

The pace of each animation sample is driven by the **`Interval`** property of **`tmrAnim`**. This interval is set from the scroll bar next to the animation selector.

Encapsulating Functionality

There are small extensions, donated by the Windows API and a little programming theory, that can sometimes enhance your program's capabilities. You can see these enhancements at work in the sample program, **`Apianims.vbp`**, in the three class modules:

- **`clsLocate`**
- **`clsFont`**
- **`clsBitMask`**

The first, **`clsLocate`**, is used to quickly test a particular point (x, y coordinate) is within a specified rectangle. This is more practical than the lengthy **`If...Else`** statement. The second, **`clsFont`**, is a class that prints text of a specified font inside a device context. At present, we use the Print method for this, but it doesn't allow us to rotate text. This is where **`clsFont`** comes into play. Lastly, **`clsBitMask`**, uses some of the theory in Appendix B to implement bitmasking with numbers, in order to track individual bits of a state variable.

Class Description: clsLocate

This class encapsulates some of the handy Windows API functions that let you quickly compare and receive result sets working with rectangles and points. We'll develop it further in Chapter 5, but here, in this chapter, we'll start it off with a single function from the API, **`PtInRect()`**, which enables you to quickly test whether a single point is within a rectangle.

Using PtInRect()

Consider the following API structures and variables, declared in the general declarations of **`clsLocate`**:

```
Private Type RECT
  Left As Long
  Top As Long
  Right As Long
  Bottom As Long
End Type
Private m_r As RECT

Private Type POINTAPI
  x As Long
  y As Long
End Type
Private m_p As POINTAPI
```

Assume now that **`m_r`** is filled with a valid rectangle of 0,0,100,100 and that **`m_p`** is set to a valid point 10,10. To check whether **`m_p`** is within **`m_r`**, standard VB code, you would need something like this:

```
If m_p.x > m_r.Left And m_p.x < m_r.Right Then
   If m_p.y > m_r.Top And m_p.y < m_r.Bottom Then
      ' successful
      End If
End If
```

The following call to the **`PtInRect`** function performs exactly the same test in fewer lines:

```
If PtInRect(m_r, m_p.x, m_p.y) <> 0 Then
   ' successful
End If
```

Now, no-one is saying that the original was poorly coded, but this is just one of many Windows API functions that are invaluable when you're working with rectangles and points. If you put them all in a room together, the comparative VB-only code is a complete pain.

The **`RECT`** structure parameter is expected as an address to that rectangle information, which means passing the structure *by reference*. The **`POINT`** structure, on the other hand, is expected to be passed as two **`Longs`** (not an address to the structure), which means it should be passed *by value*. The problem is, you can't pass a structure from VB by value, so the declaration from the API Text Viewer doesn't work as it appears. The declaration for the function from there is shown on the following page.

```
Declare Function PtInRect Lib "user32" Alias "PtInRect" (lpRect As RECT, pt As
POINTAPI) As Long
```

You'll notice that I passed it two **Long**s instead of the **POINTAPI** structure! For the **POINTAPI** structure to be passed by value, the two **Long**s within the structure must be passed individually by value, so the declaration ends up looking like this:

```
Private Declare Function PtInRect Lib "user32" (lpRect As RECT, ByVal ptX As Long,
ByVal ptY As Long) As Long
```

When this function is called in the previously listed lines of code, a **RECT** structure is passed by reference and two long values are passed individually (each by value), as the **POINTAPI** coordinate—matching up with the later translation of the declaration. On the VB side, we're actually adding a parameter to the declaration that isn't there—and it works!

Beware though—the API functions that have declarations using the **POINTAPI** structure work with that structure. For instance, the **GetCursorPos()** function, which returns a point into the **POINTAPI** structure, can be passed an empty variable in that form. The declaration and the function call to get the cursor position follow:

```
Declare Function GetCursorPos Lib "user32" Alias "GetCursorPos" (lpPoint As
POINTAPI) As Long
```

```
nRet = GetCursorPos(m_p)
```

That's because when the **POINTAPI** structure is passed to this function, it's expected as an address to the structure, which, like the **RECT** structure, works fine.

> **There are books available that cover the inner workings of DLLs, parameter passing, what the C side is expecting and what VB does in the parameter translation. I've summarized these workings in Appendix A because there just wasn't time to write two books at once!**

How clsLocate Works

The following figure shows the visible functionality of **clsLocate**. There are only three methods in this startup version of the class. You'll notice that I alter the class in later chapters for several reasons. For now, **clsLocate**'s **SetRect** and **SetPoint** methods are used to pass the individual coordinates to the class, to be placed into the class's internal **RECT** and **POINTAPI** structures. This is because the structure definitions can't be public when declared inside a class module, so the rest of the code modules don't understand them. I could have declared another copy of the **RECT** and **POINTAPI** structures in a public module, but then the encapsulation of the class would be gone. (Later I'll be using another method to pass these values, but for now, our focus is on other things.)

Here are the two methods:

```
Public Sub SetRect(x1 As Long, y1 As Long, x2 As Long, y2 As Long)
  With m_r
    .Left = x1
    .Top = y1
    .Right = x2
    .Bottom = y2
  End With
End Sub
```

```
Public Sub SetPoint(x As Long, y As Long)
  With m_p
    .x = x
    .y = y
  End With
End Sub
```

Once this is done, a single call to the **PointInRect()** method calls the API **PtInRect()** function, using **m_r** and **m_p**, returning the functions return in the class methods return value:

```
Public Function PointInRect() As Long
  PointInRect = PtInRect(m_r, m_p.x, m_p.y)
End Function
```

You'll see this used in the **Animate_Kid** sample later in this chapter.

Class Description: clsFont

There are some neat things we can do with text output that VB alone doesn't give us a method for. Oh sure, we can specify our font, its size and other aspects of its appearance through the **FontBold**, **FontItalic** and **FontUnderline** properties, but what about the angle? That's right, if we want to spin some text around on the screen, we can't. We might, for instance, want to label the vertical axes of graphs with vertical running text. How ridiculous is that?

Using the Font Object

Our sample program displays all its graphics output in **picDisplay**. Since a picture control has an associated display device context supporting all graphics output, it goes without saying that it also has an associated font object, like any other DC. The picture box has a **Font** property that shows a dialog allowing you to set the properties of the font for the Print method. Behind the scenes, VB already has what is called a **LOGFONT** object selected into the DC. When you set properties for the font, VB is calling the Windows API functions that change the **LOGFONT** associated with the device context. There is a Windows structure that holds this information.

To gain access to all of the properties of this font object, we must create our own version of the structure and make our own call to select the font into the device context. Not a problem! The **LOGFONT** Windows API structure is shown at the top of the following listing. Some of the elements in **LOGFONT** go into more detail than we require at the moment, but you can see that the height and width can be specified, which constitutes the point size in the font dialog box. The weight sets the level of boldness the text has and the font name element is clear. What's new and exciting is the escapement element, which represents the angle of the text's output to the DC. Simply altering this value makes the text in our trash can animations rotate!

```
Option Explicit

'---API structures---'
Private Type LOGFONT
   lfHeight As Long 'font height
       lfWidth As Long 'font width
       lfEscapement As Long 'angle of line of text
       lfOrientation As Long
       lfWeight As Long 'level from normal to bold (0 - 1000)
       lfItalic As String * 1
       lfUnderline As String * 1
       lfStrikeOut As String * 1
       lfCharSet As String * 1 'ansi, symbol etc.
       lfOutPrecision As String * 1
       lfClipPrecision As String * 1
       lfQuality As String * 1
       lfPitchAndFamily As String * 1
       lfFaceName As String * 24 'font name
End Type
Private m_Font As LOGFONT

'---API functions---'
' DC
Private Declare Function DeleteObject Lib "gdi32" (ByVal hObject As Long) As Long
Private Declare Function SelectObject Lib "gdi32" (ByVal hdc As Integer, ByVal
hObject As Long) As Long
' font
Private Declare Function CreateFontIndirect Lib "gdi32" Alias
"CreateFontIndirectA" (lpLogFont As LOGFONT) As Long
Private Declare Function TextOut Lib "gdi32" Alias "TextOutA" (ByVal hdc As Long,
ByVal x As Long, ByVal y As Long, ByVal textstr$, ByVal textlen As Long) As Long
```

The class module **clsFont** declares the variable **m_Font** from the **LOGFONT** structure, along with several other private variables that are used within the class. There are also a few required Windows API functions that we must use, to make this class functional. There is a default font object that exists when a DC is created. This font object is the stock object that should be replaced to customize printed text on the DC. This is done by using the **SelectObject** API function, which returns the handle to the currently selected font object and associates a new logical font with the device.

TextOut vs. VB's Print Method

The **PrintText** method of **clsFont** is the place where the picture box DC is assigned its new logical font. These are the steps that VB goes through for us to change the font, based on our selections in the font dialog box. Once the structure has been filled in with the appropriate values, we can create the new font object .

CreateFontIndirect takes our logical font structure and returns us a handle to a font object. We need this handle to make the call to **SelectObject**, which selects the new font into the DC. As with the selection of any windows object into a DC (font, bitmap, palette) the function returns the handle to the previously selected or stock object of the same type. We save this so that we can select it back in when we're done:

```
hFont = CreateFontIndirect(m_Font)
hOldFont = SelectObject(hdc, hFont)
```

Once the desired font object has been selected into the DC, any text printing done on that DC will reflect the currently selected font. Just because we're using API calls, it doesn't mean that VB doesn't know what we've done by selecting the new font object into the DC. VB may have created the picture box for us and may have given us the handle to the device context, but from there, whether we edit the font by using the dialog box or by using API calls as we've just done, the DC is what keeps track of the current font object.

What I'm getting at is that, though the **`TextOut`** API call is what C programmers would have to use to exercise a print instruction to a DC, our VB Print method will still work if we set the **`CurrentX`** and **`CurrentY`** properties of the picture box DC. **`TextOut`** performs the same function as the Print method, using the selected font at the specified coordinates:

```
nRet = TextOut(hdc, m_nPosX, m_nPosY, m_sText, Len(m_sText))
```

Once the text has been printed and we've had our way with the font object, the original (not necessarily the stock object, but whatever font handle was returned to us when we selected ours) must be restored to reflect the DC's previous state. There are several reasons for this. First, VB had set up a font object before we went and changed it and it's polite to restore that when we're done. Second, we point to font objects with handles, which uses Windows resources. These resources can't be freed while selected into a DC, so we must select the font object out of the DC, then delete it:

```
hFont = SelectObject(hdc, hOldFont)
nRet = DeleteObject(hFont)
```

When you're using API calls that alter VB forms and controls, you should remember to always return things the way you found them. Unexpected occurrences have been known to drive more than one good programmer over the edge!

Font Animation

Here are the steps for creating the pivoting font animation, made possible by using Windows API calls. The next figure also describes the contents of **`clsFont`**, so you should refer back to it as we work through how to use the font class:

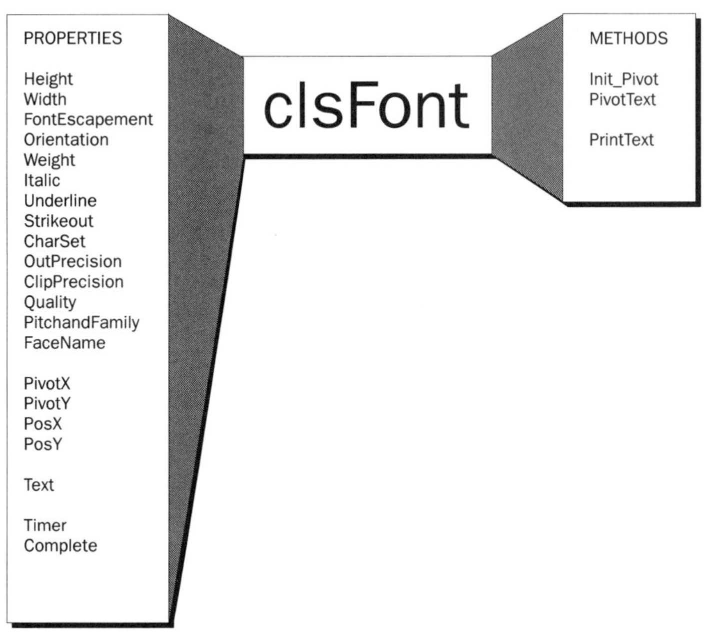

1 Create a font object from **clsFont**. To instantiate the font class, you must declare a variable. You do this in the general declarations of **frmAPIAnims**:

```
Dim m_objFont As New clsFont
```

2 Initialize the **LOGFONT** structure. We don't want to have to set every property of the font structure each time we want to create the class. In the class initialization event, the font's default values are prepared. Notice that from **lfItalic** onwards these are single character strings (bytes) and so must be set to the character representation of each number value. Try replacing the **Chr$(0)** with just **0** and watch what happens to the text!

```
With m_Font
     .lfHeight = 30
     .lfWidth = 10
     .lfEscapement = 0
     .lfOrientation = 0
     .lfWeight = 400
     .lfItalic = Chr$(0)
     .lfUnderline = Chr$(0)
     .lfStrikeout = Chr$(0)
     .lfOutPrecision = Chr$(0)
     .lfClipPrecision = Chr$(0)
     .lfQuality = Chr$(0)
     .lfPitchAndFamily = Chr$(0)
     .lfCharSet = Chr$(0)
     .lfFaceName = "Times New Roman" & Chr$(0)
End With
```

3 Prepare font object for use. Some other class properties must be initialized that are based on the code that is driving the font spinning animation. These are the Timer, which will be started when the animation is told to begin, and the coordinate on which the text pivot is based. Also, since the device context being used is the VB picture box **picDisplay**, it can be used to set the **ForeColor** of the text, since this isn't part of the Windows font object's structure. (Actually, the **ForeColor** is a brush object, but that's another story altogether—as we'll see in Chapter 4.)

```
picDisplay.ForeColor = RGB(255, 0, 0)

With m_objFont
   .Timer = tmrText
   .PivotX = picDisplay.Width / 2
   .PivotY = picDisplay.Height / 2
End With
```

4 Initialize the text pivot. To start the text pivoting animation, the class procedure's **Init_Pivot** method is called. This is done at the end of the **tmrAnimCtrl_Timer** event *after* it has selected the current animation for the trash can and set up the next animation's random interval. **Init_Pivot** does the following:

```
' setup values
m_nComplete = False
m_Font.lfEscapement = 0

' start text animation timer
m_tmrAnim.Enabled = True
```

Notice that this function starts the timer for the text animation after it initializes the complete flag to **False**, and the text angle to **0**. This is a convenient way to ensure the timer event that calls the **PivotText** procedure isn't started before the global class variables have been prepared.

5 Animate the text. The **tmrText_Timer** event calls the **PivotText** procedure until the **Complete** property for the class is set to **True** (which is when the pivot has gone full circle). When **Complete** is found **True**, the timer is disabled and the final call is made to the **PrintText** method of the class (the same as Print method for the picture box in VB) after changing the color and weight of the font (400 is normal, 700 is bold):

```
If m_objFont.Complete Then
    tmrText.Enabled = False
    ' print black text at current pivot position
    picDisplay.ForeColor = RGB(0, 0, 0)
    m_objFont.Weight = 700
    m_objFont.PrintText (picDisplay.hdc)
    picDisplay.ForeColor = RGB(255, 0, 0)
    m_objFont.Weight = 400

    ' start the animation control timer again
    ' now that text animation is complete
    tmrAnimCtrl.Enabled = True
    tmrAnim.Enabled = True

Else
    ' not complete, continue pivot
    m_objFont.PivotText picDisplay
End If
```

PivotText is passed the picture control whose DC will be assigned the new logical font. Since the angle of the text is being changed in this function, new coordinates for text output are calculated based on the current quadrant of the angle. The escapement angle is incremented from 0 to 3600 by 180 each time. When it reaches 3600, the pivot is finished and **complete** is set to **True**.

```
nDX = pic.TextWidth(m_sText) / 2
nDY = pic.TextHeight(m_sText) / 2

'figure out next xy coordinate based on text angle
nEsc = m_Font.lfEscapement
If nEsc = 0 Then
  m_nPosX = m_nPivotX - nDX
  m_nPosY = m_nPivotY
ElseIf nEsc > 0 And nEsc < 900 Then
  m_nPosX = m_nPivotX - nDX
  m_nPosY = m_nPivotY + nDY
```

...

```
ElseIf nEsc = 3600 Then
  m_nPosX = m_nPivotX - nDX
  m_nPosY = m_nPivotY
  m_nComplete = True
End If

' print text output
PrintText pic.hdc
' increment font angle for next time
m_Font.lfEscapement = m_Font.lfEscapement + 180
```

Class Description: clsBitMask

Now, let's make some sense out of that stimulating discussion about numeric bits in Appendix B. There are some slick coding methods that can be implemented using bitmasking theory. Look out, this stuff is catchy! This chapter's code sample uses bitmasking both directly and indirectly: directly to store several flags in a single number value and indirectly through the raster operations described in the next section.

Bit Functionality

If you've read the appendix or are familiar with computer mathematics, you'll already know that you can use a single number to track several flag values by setting individual bits of the number on or off (1 or 0). I included a class module, **clsBitMask**, that provides functionality for a single number value. In the global declarations section of the class, there's an array of long values, called **m_nBit()** internally:

```
Private m_nBit() As Long

     'In the class Initialization event, m_nBit() is filled in as follows:
     ' start value at 0
       m_nValue = 0

       ' initialize array of hex values each representing
       ' a single m_nBit turned on
       ReDim m_nBit(-1 To 15)
       m_nBit(-1) = 0      'used to turns all m_nBits off

       m_nBit(0) = &H1
       m_nBit(1) = &H2
       m_nBit(2) = &H4
       m_nBit(3) = &H8
       m_nBit(4) = &H10
```

```
        m_nBit(5) = &H20
        m_nBit(6) = &H40
        m_nBit(7) = &H80
        m_nBit(8) = &H100
        m_nBit(9) = &H200
        m_nBit(10) = &H400
        m_nBit(11) = &H800
        m_nBit(12) = &H1000
        m_nBit(13) = &H2000
        m_nBit(14) = &H4000
        m_nBit(15) = &H8000
```

Each array item is set to a hex value that corresponds to the value of a number if that particular bit is on. This is consistent with the examples in Appendix B, which compare two numbers using bit operators. In each bit operation, there is a number to change and a number that is used to make the necessary change, both represented in binary.

The class module's functionality is shown here. The purpose of the class is to work with a single number, manipulating its individual bits on and off to hold flag information. The class has two properties: **`Value`** and **`Bit`**. Value always starts at 0 (which means no bits are turned on). This is the module variable (**`m_nValue`**) that is manipulated with the three methods provided to turn bits on and off and to ask whether bits are on. **`Bit`** takes one parameter (the bit position you want to ask the hex value for) and returns to the property's value that item in the **`m_nBit()`** array.

```
Public Function BitsOn(nBits As Long) As Boolean
'---Description
' returns true if the bits set in nBits are all on
' in m_nValue, false if they are not
'---
    BitsOn = (nBits <> 0 And nBits = (nBits And m_nValue))
End Function

Public Sub TurnBitsOff(nBits As Long)
'---Description
' turns bit values set in nBits off in m_nValue
' other bits in nVal retain their current values
'---
    m_nValue = m_nValue And (Not nBits)
End Sub

Public Sub TurnBitsOn(nBits As Long)
'---Description
' turns bit values set in nBits on in m_nValue
' other bits in m_nValue retain their current values
'---
    m_nValue = m_nValue Or nBits
End Sub
```

Working with Bits

The **Animate_Kid** procedure of **frmAPIAnim** uses this class module's functionality. I won't walk through the code that actually performs the animation at this point, but I'll explain what the animation does and how the **clsBitMask** object was used to track the various states of the animation.

First of all, in the global declarations of the form, the following lines of code set up the bitmask object and the constants that will point to each bit, starting at 0, that will represent a state of the animation:

```
Dim m_nStateKid As New clsBitMask
Const BIT_CITYMOVING = 0
Const BIT_KIDSTOPPED = 1
Const BIT_STOPKID = 2
Const BIT_KIDOVERLAPS = 3
```

The nice thing about using the bitmask class is that if we need a new state for the animation, we can simply add it to the constants, moving to the next bit. We can go up to the fifteenth bit using the current version of **clsBitMask**, but since **m_nValue** is a **Long**, it could, in theory, go up to 32 flags. We need to fill in the **m_nBit()** array for this to be possible.

The **Load_Kid** subroutine is called before the animation sequence is run. This takes care of loading all the images used for the animation into their respective picture box controls, initializing size position and movement variables and starting the timer (**tmrAnim**) so that the animation will begin. The **Animate_Kid** subroutine is called at every timer interval, where the animation is done and the current state is updated at each interval. Since the animation can be restarted in the same session, the following line of code in **Load_Kid** resets the bitmask object value to 0, which means that all bits are off:

```
m_nStateKid.Value = 0
```

As there is more than one thing happening at the same time, the **Animate_Kid** subroutine performs many tests, so I'll cut it up into bite-size morsels for easy digestion. For now, we'll concentrate on the state tracking being performed, but keep in mind that the routine uses some methods that we'll look at in the next section. I'll point these functions and methods out as they arise.

The four figures on the following page show the states of the animation that need to be tracked. The animation begins with the kid walking on screen from the right and moving towards the center of the screen. When the kid reaches center of the screen, he stops and the city bitmap is moved onscreen from the right, the kid still animating in place. At some point, the city will reach the center of the screen, where the kid is animating, which requires some special screen updating procedures to keep the display smooth. The overlap flag must be turned on at this point. Once the city has passed the center of the screen, the kid begins moving again, the overlap flag can be turned off and the city and kid can continue moving until they are off the screen in their respective directions.

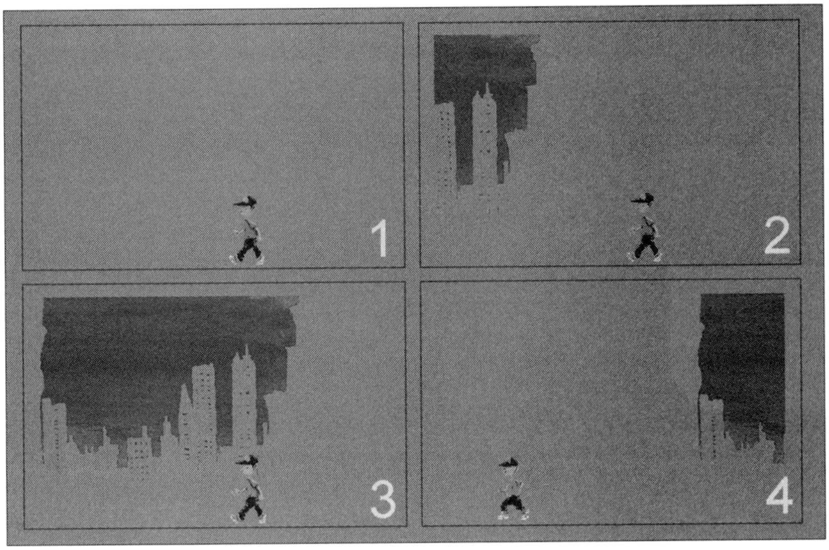

Now let's see how the code handles these steps in the animation. Following are the steps that summarize the animation loop, focusing on state updating and the reasons for doing it. I'll show the code that pertains to each step, but I'll only be describing the state manipulation in detail. We'll look at screen updating routines in the next section.

1 Declare local variables. The variables that are not required to be reset each time the animation loop is called are set up here.

2 Remove the old city and kid. We'll cover how the screen is updated later, so I won't get into the code that performs this function. The idea is that before the kid and city are moved their respective last position should be erased from the display, making room for the next position they are displayed at.

```
' city
If m_nStateKid.BitsOn(m_nStateKid.Bit(BIT_CITYMOVING)) Then
  nRet = PatBlt(m_objMem.hdcWork, m_nCityX, m_nCityY, m_nCityWidth,
                     m_nCityHeight, BLACKNESS)
End If
' kid
nRet = PatBlt(m_objMem.hdcWork, m_nKidX, m_nKidY, m_nKidWidth, m_nKidY,
BLACKNESS)
```

3 Move the city and kid animations. The **BitsOn** method of **clsBitMask** returns true if the bit value(s) passed it is on in the **m_nValue** variable. If the city has begun moving, the bit in position **BIT_CITYMOVE** will have been turned on and the left coordinate for the city bitmap will be incremented:

```
' if city is moving, move city
If m_nStateKid.BitsOn(m_nStateKid.Bit(BIT_CITYMOVING)) Then
  nOldCityX = m_nCityX
  m_nCityX = m_nCityX + nCityDX
End If
```

If the kid has reached center screen, the bit in position **BIT_KIDSTOP** will have been turned on and the section that moves the kid will not be executed:

```
' if kid is moving, move kid
If Not m_nStateKid.BitsOn(m_nStateKid.Bit(BIT_STOPKID)) Then
  nOldKidX = m_nKidX
  m_nKidX = m_nKidX + nKidDX
End If
```

4 Update the current kid frame. This is always performed, even during the kid's stationary period in the center of the screen:

```
m_nCurrFrame = IIf(m_nCurrFrame = (NUM_KIDFRAMES - 1), 0, m_nCurrFrame + 1)
```

5 Copy the new city and kid. Here the city is copied to the screen at its new position, if the **BIT_CITYMOVE** bit is on:

```
' copy city
If m_nStateKid.BitsOn(m_nStateKid.Bit(BIT_CITYMOVING)) Then
    nRet = BitBlt(m_objMem.hdcWork, m_nCityX, m_nCityY, m_nCityWidth,
m_nCityHeight, picCity.hdc, 0, 0, SRCCOPY)
End If
```

The current kid frame is also copied to the new kid position, again using methods that we'll describe later, with two successive API function calls. This technique uses **raster operations**, but is also known as **masking** and we'll describe it in more detail later. Notice there are no state checks for the kid copying, since it's always updated:

```
' copy kid frame
nRet = BitBlt(m_objMem.hdcWork, m_nKidX, m_nKidY, m_nKidWidth,
m_nKidHeight, picKidMsk(m_nCurrFrame).hdc, 0, 0, SRCAND)
nRet = BitBlt(m_objMem.hdcWork, m_nKidX, m_nKidY, m_nKidWidth,
m_nKidHeight, picKid(m_nCurrFrame).hdc, 0, 0, SRCINVERT)
```

6 Determine the amount to copy to the display. This section contains a rather lengthy piece of decision-making code that checks for a few possibilities to determine the area that should be painted to the display area at one time. If the walking kid isn't overlapping the city at all, there's no visual disruption caused by copying the city and kid separately to update their new screen coordinates. However, if the city and kid *do* overlap at any point, we should copy the entire area at once so the update is smooth. We'll look at part of this later in the chapter when we discuss double-buffering, but most of the decision making is done by a series of checks for the overlap of the top left or top right corner of the current kid frame and the city rectangle.

7 Update **m_nStateKid**. Now that all the new coordinates have been settled and the screen has been updated, the state of the animation segment may have changed, as per the descriptions in the previous figures. The following code is where the bitmask object is set according to the current state of the animation:

```
If m_nStateKid.BitsOn(m_nStateKid.Bit(BIT_CITYMOVING)) Then
     If (m_nCityX + m_nCityWidth > picDisplay.Width) Then
       m_nStateKid.TurnBitsOff m_nStateKid.Bit(BIT_STOPKID)
     End If
     If (m_nCityX > picDisplay.Width) Then
       m_nStateKid.TurnBitsOff m_nStateKid.Bit(BIT_CITYMOVING)
     End If
Else
     If (m_nKidX < picDisplay.Width / 2) Then
        ' if kid still moving, initialize city animation
        If Not m_nStateKid.BitsOn(m_nStateKid.Bit(BIT_KIDSTOPPED)) Then
          m_nStateKid.TurnBitsOn m_nStateKid.Bit(BIT_STOPKID) Or _
                      m_nStateKid.Bit(BIT_KIDSTOPPED) Or _
                      m_nStateKid.Bit(BIT_CITYMOVING)
        End If
     End If
End If
```

If the city is moving, a check is done to see if its right side has reached the end of the display area. If it has, the kid can start moving again, so the **BIT_KIDSTOP** bit can be turned off. If the city has disappeared off the screen, the city can stop being moved so the **BIT_CITYMOVE** bit is turned off.

If the city isn't moving, we run a check on some kid-related states. If the kid's left position has reached the middle of the screen, the city can start moving and the flag that notifies us that the kid has been stopped, and **BIT_KIDSTOPPED** can be turned on. Notice that we can do this with one call to the **TurnBitsOn** method of the bitmask class. By OR-ing the bits, the value of the bits sent to the function to be turned on is each of the **BIT_CITYMOVE**, **BIT_KIDSTOPPED** and **BIT_KIDSTOP** bits turned on—bit positions 2, 1 and 0 respectively. This is why rather than passing the function the bit position to turn on, I pass the actual numeric result of the bits I want turned on. This way, they can be OR-ed right from the function call.

Moving Bitmap Data

Chapter 1 used just VB to orchestrate the animation samples described. You've already seen what VB can and can't do with its conspicuous screen updating methods to provide smooth animation. Guess what—you can use Windows API calls to replace VB methods altogether. Stamping out ugly flicker has never been so easy, so let's see what the API can do.

Preparing a Memory DC

We've already discussed the memory DC in this chapter, so you should be clear on how to use it—to store graphical data before it's displayed on the screen without using the picture box, which uses more overhead. Here, I'll discuss how to create the memory DC using Windows API calls and what you end up with at the end of the process.

The class module, **clsMem**, is where the memory DC is created for use in both samples in this chapter. We'll describe this class in full detail in a later section, so for now I'll just show you the relevant lines of code that do the job. As we said earlier, memory DCs are created to emulate a display DC without being visible inside a window. This saves on resources because it means that you only need a handle to a device context, not an additional window handle. By emulating a display DC, a memory DC takes on its color support. Put simply, if you're running 256 color, so will the memory DC; if you're running hi-color, so will the memory DC.

The following call to the **CreateCompatibleDC()** function, found in the **CreateDoubleBuffer()** method of **clsMem**, creates the memory DC:

```
m_hdcWork = CreateCompatibleDC(m_hdcDisp)
```

The variable **m_hdcDisp** holds the **hDC** property of the picture box **picDisplay**. Any other display DC could be passed to the **CreateCompatibleDC()** function and it would still create a memory DC in the same format as the current display device, since they all reflect the same color support. The return from this function is a handle to a memory DC, in this case, a **Long** value named **m_hdcWork**.

Once the memory DC has been created, it's like the empty picture box control, without any graphical data, but with a bitmap object, the stock object of 1x1 pixel, selected into it. Since we're going to be copying more bitmap data into this memory DC, to fill it with a valid bitmap, the 1x1 area needs to be sized to whatever the dimensions of the graphics data that is being copied into it will be. The **CreateCompatibleBitmap()** function creates a new bitmap object, reflecting the dimensions requested. This monochrome bitmap will be used to replace the stock bitmap in the new memory DC, to increase the size of the bitmap's area for copying new graphics. Calling this function returns a handle to this new bitmap object, also created compatible with the current display device:

```
m_hbmpWork = CreateCompatibleBitmap(m_hdcDisp, m_nDispW, m_nDispH)
```

Now, we must use the **SelectObject()** function to select the new bitmap into the new memory DC, increasing its area. In this case, we're replacing the bitmap object, so the handle to the old default bitmap is returned to us from this function, while we use the handle to the new bitmap to assign the DC its new bitmap.

```
m_stbmpWork = SelectObject(m_hdcWork, m_hbmpWork)
```

A bitmap object can only be selected into one DC at a time, a one-to-one relationship. Though a picture box with a loaded image *does* provide an **Image** property (the same as the bitmap handle returned from **CreateCompatibleBitmap()**), this image data has already been selected into the device belonging to the picture box. The most efficient way to create the bitmap of the required dimensions, without using the resources of a picture box, is to call **CreateCompatibleBitmap()**. We don't care what the bitmap looks like, we just need the DC increased to a particular size.

Always save the handle returned from calls to **SelectObject()**. When it's time to free resources, we must delete any object selected into a DC. For this, we first need to select it *out* of the DC with a call to **SelectObject()**, reselecting its original object, which returns the handle to the object we want to delete.

BitBlt() and StretchBlt()

Now we have a DC in memory, just waiting to have information blasted into it. Since we're not using a picture box control provided by VB to access a device context, we need to learn some Windows API functions that are available to us for getting data into the DC. There are several functions that move pixels from one DC to another, which means we can move pixels from the picture box **hDC** to any memory DC we create. Until we do this, the memory DC will just have a monochrome bitmap of whatever dimensions we initialized it to before selecting it into the DC.

The two Windows API functions that we need are **BitBlt()** and **StretchBlt()**. These are quite similar, so I'll just stick to **BitBlt()** first, then explain what **StretchBlt()** does by comparison. We can use **BitBlt()** to copy the image data from a picture box control into a memory device context, to keep a copy of the original in memory without using a second picture box. The following call to **BitBlt()** (the declaration is at the end of the chapter) copies the contents of a picture box control into a memory DC:

```
nRet = BitBlt(hdcMemory, nDestX, nDestY, nWidth, nHeight, Picture1.hDC, nSrcX,
nSrcY, nROP)
```

The parameters passed to **BitBlt()** are as follows:

- **hdcMemory**: the destination DC
- **nDestX, nDestY, nWidth, nHeight**: the destination rectangle to copy the data to
- **Picture1.hDC**: the source DC
- **nSrcX, nSrcY**: the coordinate to begin copying from the source DC
- **nROP**: the raster operation code for combining source and destination pixels

This function takes the information from the source, starting at the **nSrcX**, **nSrcY** coordinate, for a width and height of **nWidth** and **nHeight**, and copies it to the destination, starting at **nDestX**, **nDestY**. The last parameter is called a raster operation code, which tells Windows how the source and destination should be combined in this copying procedure. There are many settings for this, which we'll discuss shortly. One of the most commonly used settings is represented by the Windows constant **SRCCOPY** defined below:

```
Private Const SRCCOPY = &HCC0020
```

Sending this value, **SRCCOPY**, in the **nROP** parameter tells the function to copy the bits, pixel for pixel from the source DC, as shown on the following page.

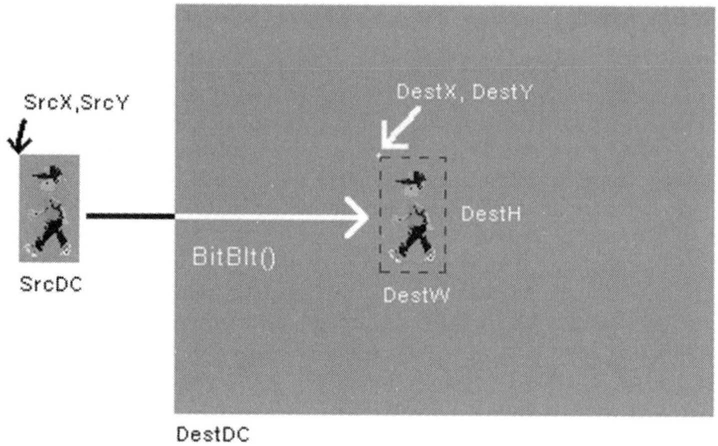

This works to and from any DC, whether it's from picture box DC to picture box DC, memory DC to memory DC, or some combination of the two. Since memory DCs aren't visible on the display anyway, they always work as is when it comes to copying data. Picture boxes, on the other hand, need a few properties to be set a certain way, which we'll discuss when we compare the **PaintPicture** and other blitting methods next.

Now for **StretchBlt()**. What does it do? It works exactly like **BitBlt()** with a few additional parameters and some added functionality. The following call to **StretchBlt()** adds two parameters: **nSrcWidth** and **nSrcHeight**:

```
nRet = StretchBlt(hdcMemory, nDestX, nDestY, nWidth, nHeight, Picture1.hDC, nSrcX,
nSrcY, nSrcWidth, nSrcHeight, nROP)
```

These make it possible to take the contents of a specified rectangle from one DC, copying it to a rectangular area on another DC of a different size. The next figure demonstrates two possibilities: stretching the pixels to a larger area or squeezing them to fit a smaller area on the destination DC:

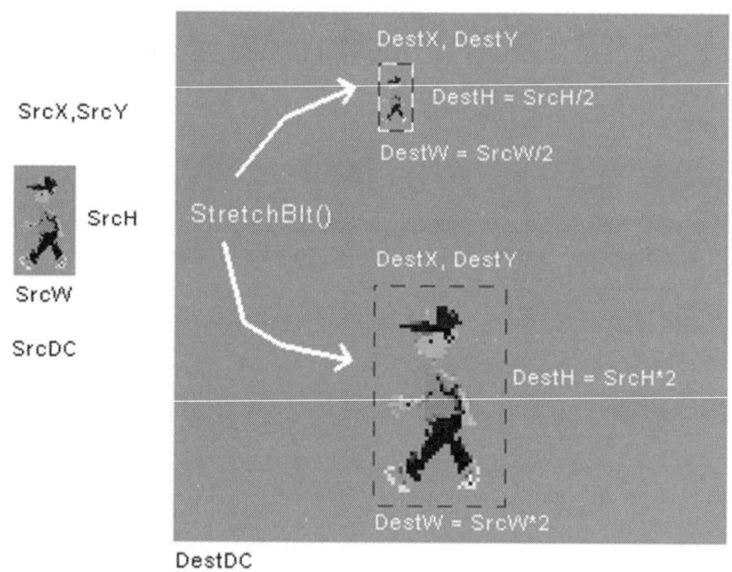

Before we look at when this becomes really useful, we'll compare the use of these blitting functions to **PaintPicture**, so you'll understand what happens with VB in a little more detail, compared to the Windows API ways of doing things.

PaintPicture vs. Blitting

We discussed the basics about the **PaintPicture** method in Chapter 1. Now, you can probably see the similarities between this method and the **BitBlt()** and **StretchBlt()** Windows API functions. The parameters and actual instruction may be laid out differently, but the results are the same. Actually, **PaintPicture** is more like **StretchBlt()**, since it accepts the source and destination dimension information, allowing the rectangles from source to destination to be different, thereby altering the resulting appearance of the source.

No matter where the graphics are that you're using for display data, somehow, some way, the data must be displayed. If there's just one image, you can do this by loading the image in a picture box control and displaying it, but if you're using several graphics, as with animation, you can't load all of them into the display picture box. In VB3, you would have to use more picture boxes or image controls to display other graphics over the background graphic. In VB4, you can use **PaintPicture**. Regardless, these other graphics need to be loaded into their own DC for animation to be possible.

Any animation that uses a picture box as the display DC and other picture boxes to load graphics, need only make the display DC visible to the user. It's your code that enforces when other graphics are copied to the display. This chapters second example, **\Code\Chapter2\Testblit\Testblit.vbp,** uses a simple background graphic of a sky and another small graphic which is a bull's-eye ball on a black background. These two are loaded into picture boxes and the Test Run menu copies the sky to the display DC in the method selected (**PaintPicture** or **Blit**). The Copy Ball button copies the ball onto the display, on top of the sky background. The Move Ball button copies the ball in a new position each time you click it.

There are several properties that the menus allow you to change for each of the picture controls. The Display Properties menu alters the display DC properties and the Graphics Properties menu alters the properties of both graphic picture boxes. You can play with this sample later, but I'll sum up the key points of what happens to the copying of data, with each of these properties settings. The interface for this sample is shown here:

Menu Selections

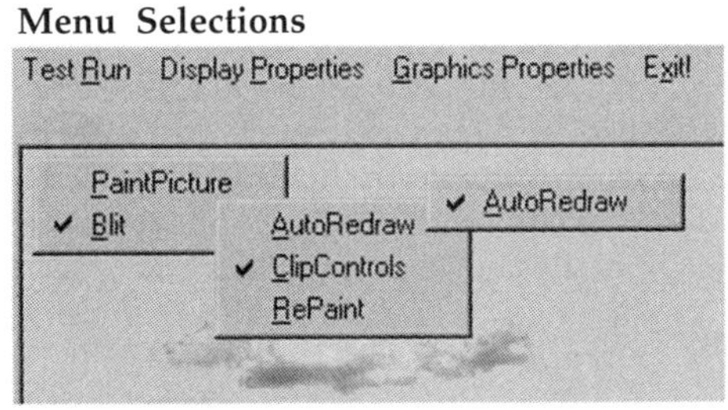

Button Functionality

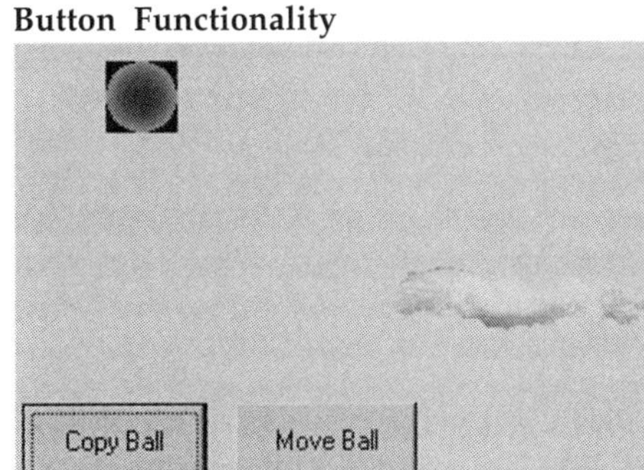

Graphics Properties: *AutoRedraw*

This menu affects the picture boxes that hold the graphics data we want to **PaintPicture** or **Blit** to the display DC. If **AutoRedraw** is true, the contents of these picture boxes are retained in memory. Even if they're hidden, you can copy the data from them to the display using either method. Turning **AutoRedraw** off causes the DC used for **PaintPicture** or **Blit** methods to pick up junk to copy to the display.

Display Properties: *AutoRedraw*

This works differently, depending upon how information is copied to the display. If **AutoRedraw** is set to false, both the **PaintPicture** command and the **BitBlt()** command can copy data to the display DC. The catch is that if the window is covered by another window, there's no repainting done unless you write code to do so in the **Paint** event of the displayed picture box, which we have done.

With **AutoRedraw** set to true, the picture placed on the picture box with the **PaintPicture** method will not be erased, since Visual Basic will take care to repaint the window for you (with the **Paint** event.) It will know what you have drawn to the picture box with the **PaintPicture** commands and it will retain that information in memory, copying it back to the display each time it repaints. **BitBlt()**, however, won't work this way because Visual Basic doesn't know that the contents of the picture box have changed from those that it keeps in memory for the picture box since we have side stepped VB with the **BitBlt()** API call. The picture box is actually keeping a copy of the contents of the display in memory, it's keeping a copy of things VB knows was sent there only through its own methods, i.e. the **PaintPicture** method and other VB drawing methods, but not Windows API calls. In this scenario, the **BitBlt()** command will never successfully copy data to the persistent display of the DC, since it will be perpetually erased by the picture box's blank copy of the DC in memory.

Display Properties: *ClipControls*

ClipControls determines whether or not the rectangles where the buttons lie on the display picture box are included in the **PaintPicture** or **Blit** command. If this property is set to false for the display picture box, both **PaintPicture** and **BitBlt()** will cover the buttons with their data copying command if the data covers that area of the display. The buttons are still there, but VB won't repaint them until it receives a paint message for the display area (**AutoRedraw** has to be false for this to happen). When the user clicks that area of the display, you'll find the buttons will re-appear—you just have to remember where they are! If **AutoRedraw** is set to true and **ClipControls** is false, **BitBlt()** won't work (because of **AutoRedraw**) but **PaintPicture** will show the button with a flicker, because for a split second they'll be covered by the **PaintPicture** command. Then the paint message will cause VB to repaint the controls again.

One thing to note here is that if **ClipControls** is changed, you can't alter the property at run time; you must use a different picture box control for the display. There are two picture boxes used for the display DC. The container property of the buttons is changed when **ClipControls** is changed so that it seems to be the same display DC used. The difference, of course, is that the **ClipControls** property differs for each control.

Display Properties: *RePaint*

This menu selection is used as a flag for the **Paint** event in both display DCs (based on the **ClipControls** setting). This is required when **AutoRedraw** is false, so that if the window is covered, the display can be sent data again, be it by **PaintPicture** or **BitBlt()**. Notice that the update is without a ball, since the update is coming from **picSky**. This is why we needed to use thereason behind the discussion of double-buffering technique, where a copy of the actual display data is kept in a memory DC, similar to the way that VB keeps a copy of it when **AutoRedraw** is true. If **BitBlt()** is used, the only way to do this is to keep a memory DC constantly updated with the same information that the display gets. We'll see how that works next.

The Test Run menu lets you choose between **PaintPicture** and **Blit** to perform the copying of the background graphic to the display DC. The Properties menu shows the settings that you're choosing for the display DC's **AutoRedraw** and **ClipControls** properties. Altering these two properties affects the outcome of both data copying methods, as we'll explain. The setting for **ClipControls** switches the current picture box for display, since you can't alter this property at run time. Once the background is copied to the display DC, the Copy Ball button should be clicked to copy the ball to the display. The Move Ball button will move the ball to a new position on the display. In all cases, whichever drawing mode selection was made from the Test Run menu is used for all copying instructions, for background and ball.

> **PaintPicture may seem more convenient at first, since you can send fewer parameters if you like, but this can also cause some ghost-chasing adventures too. Try altering the cmdMove code, removing the trailing m_nWidth and m_nHeight parameters from the following line:**
>
> ```
> m_picDisplay.PaintPicture picSky.Picture, m_nLeft, m_nTop,
> m_nWidth, m_nHeight, m_nLeft, m_nTop, m_nWidth, m_nHeight
> ```
>
> **Then ask yourself how long it would have taken you to figure out that the remaining area of picSky from m_nLeft, m_nTop was being stretched to fit m_nWidth and m_nHeight on m_picDisplay.**

Bitmasking for Transparency

When you use GDI functions to move image data, you can add some additional operations to the method in which the data is copied. Since data is copied pixel for pixel to another DC area's pixels, equivalent source and destination pixels can be compared before the resulting pixel color is determined. Confused yet? Don't be.

There's a trailing parameter to both **PaintPicture** and the blitting functions that specifies what's known as **raster operation code**. We mentioned this briefly when we discussed **BitBlt()** and **StretchBlt()**. This parameter can be set to several predefined values that are used by the function in question to decide how the source and destination data should be compared.

This operation code can perform bit-wise operations on the transferred pixel bits (see Appendix B for a quick revision of bit-wise operations), not unlike the bit-wise operations performed on numbers in the class module **clsBitMask**. Color information, after all, is stored as numeric values that Windows knows how to read and understand.

The raster operation value is particularly useful for things like creating transparency for a rectangular bitmap graphic. The pilot and kid animations both make use of this process, since the animations aren't moving over a solid color background for the duration of the animation. I'm going to demonstrate the use of three different raster operation codes. Here are their definitions as Windows constants:

```
Public Const SRCCOPY = &HCC0020
Public Const SRCINVERT = &H660046
Public Const SRCAND = &H8800C6
```

To create the pilot animation, there's a sky bitmap (for the background) and three pilot frames (for the animation over the background). The background bitmap can be copied from the picture DC that holds it to the display, pixel for pixel. This means that the raster operation code of **SRCCOPY** is used for this transaction. First, the sky bitmap is loaded into **picBg**, in the **Load_Pilot** animation, then it's copied to another DC pixel for pixel, using this code:

```
picBg.Picture = LoadPicture(g_sPath & "sky.bmp")

nRet = BitBlt(m_objMem.hdcWork, 0, 0, m_objMem.Width, m_objMem.Height, picBg.hdc,
0, 0, SRCCOPY)
```

The destination DC in this case is a memory DC pointed to by the **clsMem** object, **m_objMem**, which we'll cover a little later. The source is **picBg**, and whatever is being held there, will be displayed pixel by pixel by **hdcWork**.

What you don't see is that there are three additional bitmaps required for the pilot animation. To create the illusion of just the pilot flying across the screen, we need a second bitmap for every frame of the animation. Without it, you would see a pilot in a black box flying across the sky, just like the ball in **Testblit.vbp**, which shows the rectangle background.

We can use the raster operations to create this illusion, using two special copies of each pilot animation. Using the first pilot frame as an example, the figure below shows both a bitmap containing a copy of the pilot on a black background (**Pilot1.bmp**), and a 'mask' bitmap (**Pilot1m.bmp**) containing another version of that same graphic:

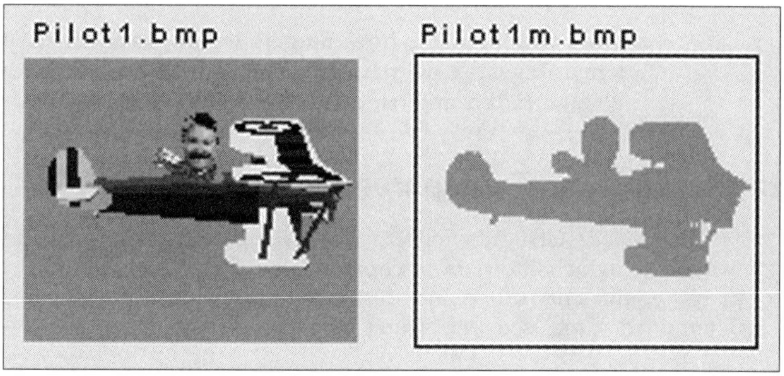

For each frame in the animation, we need two picture box controls to load the animation bitmaps. We do this in the **Load_Pilot** routine:

```
picPilot(0).Picture = LoadPicture(g_sPath & "pilot1.bmp")
picPilot(1).Picture = LoadPicture(g_sPath & "pilot2.bmp")
picPilot(2).Picture = LoadPicture(g_sPath & "pilot3.bmp")
picPilotMsk(0).Picture = LoadPicture(g_sPath & "pilot1m.bmp")
picPilotMsk(1).Picture = LoadPicture(g_sPath & "pilot2m.bmp")
picPilotMsk(2).Picture = LoadPicture(g_sPath & "pilot3m.bmp")
```

How does this work? Just as numbers can be interpreted in binary form, so can images. Each pixel is represented by a number value that describes the color for that pixel. When they're copying bits, raster operations compare the numbers for each pixel, based on the specified operation. In this case, we use the other two constants described earlier: **SRCINVERT** and **SRCAND**. Each time a pilot frame is 'blitted' to the same memory DC, the following two calls to **BitBlt()** are made:

```
nRet = BitBlt(m_objMem.hdcWork, m_nPilotX, m_nPilotY, m_nPilotWidth,
m_nPilotHeight, picPilotMsk(m_nCurrFrame).hdc, 0, 0, SRCAND)

nRet = BitBlt(m_objMem.hdcWork, m_nPilotX, m_nPilotY, m_nPilotWidth,
m_nPilotHeight, picPilot(m_nCurrFrame).hdc, 0, 0, SRCINVERT)
```

Both calls use the same x, y coordinates and width and height for the bitmap area—all six pilot bitmaps have the same dimensions. Assuming the value of **m_nCurrFrame** is 0, the first set of pilot bitmaps will be called for. The first call copies the entire rectangle of the **Pilot1m.bmp** contained in **picPilotMsk(0)** from this source DC to the memory DC at the current set of coordinates. This time, the raster operation, **SRCAND**, is used, which produces the first effect shown below. The black part of the bitmap, which is shaped like the actual pilot, is copied to the DC as black. If you look at our bit-wise operations in Appendix B, you'll see that AND-ing 0 with any bit value yields 0. In color terms, the value of black is 0, so black is what we see. Every white pixel of the mask bitmap is represented by all bits carrying a value of 1. AND-ing 1 with another pixel's value leaves the original pixel in tact. This is why the sky shows through and only the black pilot is drawn to the memory DC.

The next step is the **BitBlt()** call using **SRCINVERT**, which performs the same operation as the Boolean **XOR** operator (explained in Appendix B). The contents of the pilot area are now mixed with colors, which means that the pixel values include some varied combination of 0 and 1 bit values. These values are being **XOR**-ed with 0, since the same area on the memory DC is the black-filled pilot, which copies the pixels as they appear in the source bitmap. Conversely, **XOR**-ing the black area of the source bitmap with the destination leaves the destination pixels in tact. If this logic doesn't seem to make sense, you can review the Appendix discussion of bitmasking operations and walk through the logic. It should be pretty straightforward.

The white and black colors of the mask bitmap must be *pure* white (255, 255, 255) and *pure* black (0, 0, 0). The background black of the actual bitmap must also be pure. Be careful with the content colors of the sprite, though. For instance, if the pilot image contained any pure black pixels, they wouldn't be copied and we would see the sky right through. You can fix this by altering any pure black pixels to off-black by a slight change to one of the red, green or blue values.

So, there are two steps to creating transparency, which are taken each time a pilot frame or a kid frame is copied throughout those animations. For the record, `PaintPicture` can also be passed these raster operation codes in its final parameter, giving the same results. There are other reasons why `BitBlt()` is used instead, which we'll cover in the next section on double buffering.

Smooth Display Updates

Now it's time to wrap up the theory of the code samples and see why we had to use memory DCs. We'll also discuss the use of `clsMem` and `clsWipe` to put this sampler together.

Double Buffering

First up is double buffering, that long awaited discussion that should clear up any doubts you had about using memory DCs versus the picture box control for building animations. Let's go!

How It Works

Sprite animation is a good illustration of double buffering techniques. First, let's see an example of what happens when you move a sprite across the display area, using the flying pilot as our sample. Here's the transition from frame to frame:

1 The pilot flies. The sky background is copied to the display first, then the pilot sprite is copied over the top in its current animation position:

2 The pilot doesn't fly. Before the next frame of the pilot can be displayed, the previous frame must be replaced with sky again, or else we'll see two copies of the pilot on the screen, overlapping each other by the amount of animation movement. The red box outlines the area of sky that had to be copied back to the screen:

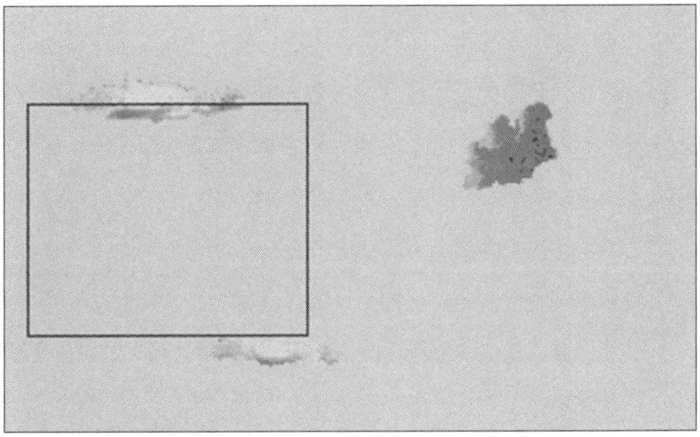

3 The pilot flies. The next frame is copied a small amount to the right of the previous frame:

Steps 2 and 3 describe the transition from the previously displayed pilot frame. These steps are repeated every time the animation moves. There's just one problem: if we're drawing to the display DC, each transition has a moment where just the sky is displayed, when the previous frame is overwritten with sky. Aha! That's what causes flicker! This is exactly what you were seeing during the dragon animations from Chapter 1, because no techniques were used to do an update to the display of the entire change area.

Enter the memory DC. We need a place, offscreen in memory, where we can do steps 2 and 3, and then perform a single fourth step to copy the entire area that changed to the screen. This means that we get only *one* screen update every time and no flicker because we never get to *see* the erased pilot. We just get to see him once he's moved—that's it!

The source components that provide this double buffering capability are:

- Original pilot frames
- Original background
- Memory buffer
- Display area

Let's take a look at them.

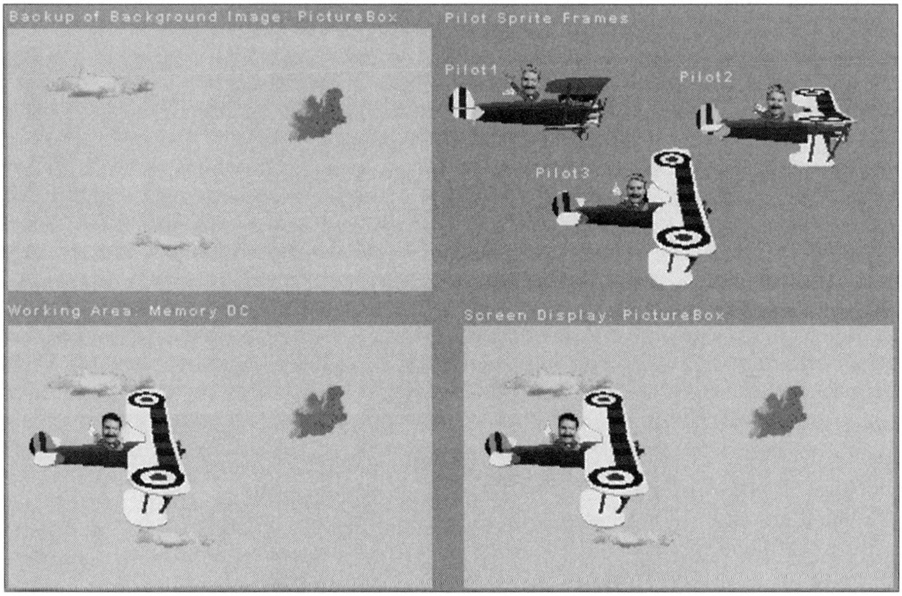

As you know, each pilot frame is loaded into a picture box control when the animation is set up in the **Load_Pilot** procedure. The sky background is also loaded into the **picBg** picture box, which stores the current background for each animation. The only method that VB provides for us to load images into memory at run time is the **LoadPicture** method of a picture box control, so this is the method we employ for now. The **picBg** control holds the untainted copy of the sky background, which is used to overwrite the area where the last pilot frame is, as in Step 2 in the previous section. The **picDisplay** control is the visible picture box on the form which gives us a display DC to copy data to. The last and most important component is the memory DC we use as the 'working' area. Now we'll take you through the reasons for using a memory DC instead of a picture box's DC to build the next display.

Firstly, resources. The picture box takes up Windows resources by using a window as well as a device context. This is needless overhead when the picture box isn't being used to load graphics into memory *or* display data on the screen.

Secondly, it doesn't work properly anyway! If you're not convinced by the resource issue, it should be enough to say that there are flaws in the procedure when a picture box is used. You can copy information (with **PaintPicture** or an equivalent API call) into a picture box that is displayed. If the picture box isn't displayed, **PaintPicture** can successfully copy buffer where **BitBlt()** can't. You could successfully move your pilot across the screen on a hidden picture box control as a working buffer, using **PaintPicture** only.

The problem is that when you try to copy that data in the working buffer of the hidden **PictureBox** control to the displayed **PictureBox** control, the error message Invalid Picture comes up. This is because there was no picture loaded into the **PictureBox** control using **LoadPicture**, which is just like the display DC, where no picture is loaded, just data copied to it via **PaintPicture** commands. You can see the data in the working buffer if you display it, but there's no drawing area selected into the DC, since no image has been loaded, so VB doesn't know that there's information in the DC area. VB uses **`PaintPicture`** to move data, but it depends on the picture property being set to a valid image before it will believe the data is there.

OK, so why not load a fake picture into the background of the hidden working buffer, then do all the **`PaintPicture`** you want, then copy the data to the display. Fine, this would work, but it seems a lot of trouble when there are API calls ready and waiting that use fewer Windows resources and do the job just fine!

Thirdly, it's just silly. With efficient and easy-to-use API calls at our fingertips, why bother?

Dirty Rectangle Updates

With double buffering, the only complex part of the process is figuring out which area should be copied to the screen. After he's moved the pilot, the lazy programmer will update the entire display area. That's a huge no-no, though, because if you constantly update the entire display when only a small portion of it has changed, you're slowing down the display update process unnecessarily by moving a lot of data which remains the same.

How the changed area, or **dirty rectangle**, is calculated is pretty easy when you're talking about just moving one object in one direction by a constant value, since the rectangle width and height becomes the width and height of the object in question, adding the amount of movement in either direction. When there's more than one object moving, as in the **`Animate_Kid`**, you need to make some more complex decisions to determine the area that needs to be copied to the working buffer and display at a given moment. These decisions for the kid animation are the most difficult of the lot, so we'll go over them now.

The working buffer is used to compile a change in the display, without flicker. This doesn't mean that all objects that are being moved need to be updated to the screen in one fell swoop. How would it be if the city and kid were both moving but not yet overlapping each other and the dirty rectangle became the union of both objects on the screen? This is inefficient screen updating that can spoil things for the user. That's why there's a lengthy process during that animation, each time the loop is encountered, to decide how much of the screen should be not only updated to the working buffer, but also to the display.

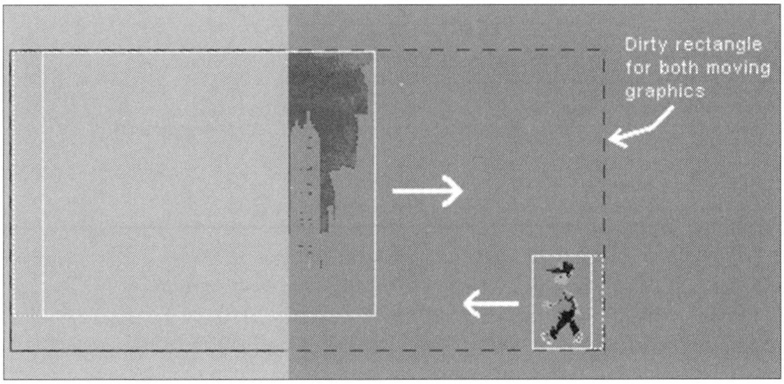

If the city and kid never overlapped, they could always be updated to the screen. In this case, both objects have their own direction and their own movement quantity (both only moving along the X-axis) that helps to calculate the dirty rectangle in its simplest form. Once both graphics have been moved, their individual dirty rectangles can be copied to the screen separately.

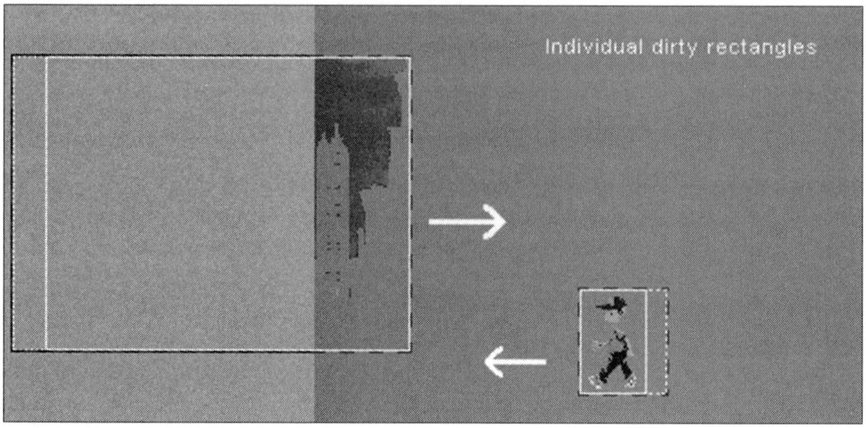

When these two graphics overlap, if they were to be updated to the display separately, there would be a moment where part of the kid disappears from the city scene, which would look silly. For this reason, some rectangle overlap checking must be done to ensure that the appropriate screen update is performed. By the time the dirty rectangle calculation is performed, both graphics have been erased, moved and copied to their new location in the working buffer.

The dirty rectangle calculation is only performed if the city is moving (**BIT_CITYMOVING** is turned on in **m_nStateKid**). Here's where the **clsLocate** object is used to determine whether there is overlap between the city and the kid rectangles:

```
' determine dirty rectangle for city checking kid overlap area
If m_nStateKid.BitsOn(m_nStateKid.Bit(BIT_CITYMOVING)) Then
  ' check for overlap
  locOverlap.SetRect nOldCityX, m_nCityY, nOldCityX + nCityDX +
                     m_nCityWidth, m_nCityY + m_nCityHeight
  locOverlap.SetPoint nOldKidX, m_nKidY
  If (locOverlap.PointInRect <> 0) Then
    ' kid top-left overlaps city
    m_nStateKid.TurnBitsOn m_nStateKid.Bit(BIT_KIDOVERLAPS)

    ' start blit at old city coordinates
    nBlitX = nOldCityX
    nBlitY = m_nCityY

    ' kid top < city bottom, subtract overlap difference
    nOverlap = (m_nCityY + m_nCityHeight) - m_nKidY
    nBlitHeight = m_nCityHeight + m_nKidHeight - nOverlap
```

```
        ' kid left < city right, subtract overlap amount
        nOverlap = (m_nKidX + m_nKidWidth) - (m_nCityX + m_nCityWidth)
        If nOverlap < 0 Then nOverlap = 0
        nBlitWidth = m_nCityWidth + m_nKidWidth - nOverlap
      Else
        locOverlap.SetPoint nOldKidX + m_nKidWidth, m_nKidY + m_nKidHeight
        If (locOverlap.PointInRect <> 0) Then
          ' kid top-right overlaps city
          m_nStateKid.TurnBitsOn m_nStateKid.Bit(BIT_KIDOVERLAPS)
          nBlitX = m_nKidX
          nBlitY = m_nKidY

          ' kid top < city bottom, subtract overlap
          nOverlap = (m_nCityY + m_nCityHeight) - m_nKidY
          nBlitHeight = m_nCityHeight + m_nKidHeight - nOverlap

          ' kid left < city right, add overlap difference
          nOverlap = nOldCityX - m_nKidX
          nBlitWidth = m_nCityWidth + nOverlap
        Else
          ' kid and city do not overlap
          m_nStateKid.TurnBitsOff m_nStateKid.Bit(BIT_KIDOVERLAPS)
          nBlitX = nOldCityX
          nBlitY = m_nCityY
          nBlitWidth = m_nCityWidth
          nBlitHeight = m_nCityHeight
        End If
      End If

      ' copy city
      nRet = BitBlt(picDisplay.hdc, nBlitX, nBlitY, nBlitWidth + Abs(nCityDX),
         nBlitHeight, m_objMem.hdcWork, nBlitX, nBlitY, SRCCOPY)
    End If

    ' copy kid if not already copied with city overlap
    If Not m_nStateKid.BitsOn(m_nStateKid.Bit(BIT_KIDOVERLAPS)) Then
      nRet = BitBlt(picDisplay.hdc, nOldKidX, m_nKidY, m_nKidWidth +
         Abs(nKidDX), m_nKidHeight, m_objMem.hdcWork, nOldKidX, m_nKidY, SRCCOPY)
    End If
```

The overlap can't just check for the current position of each graphic. It has to check if there is overlap for the entire dirty rectangle for each as an individual, since that's what would be updated separately to the screen if there is no overlap.

The overlap of the city and kid can be in one of two positions. The kid can be overlapping with the left coordinate of its dirty rectangle, or the right coordinate of its dirty rectangle. As the following diagrams demonstrate, this is what determines the coordinates for the entire dirty rectangle of the movement for both.

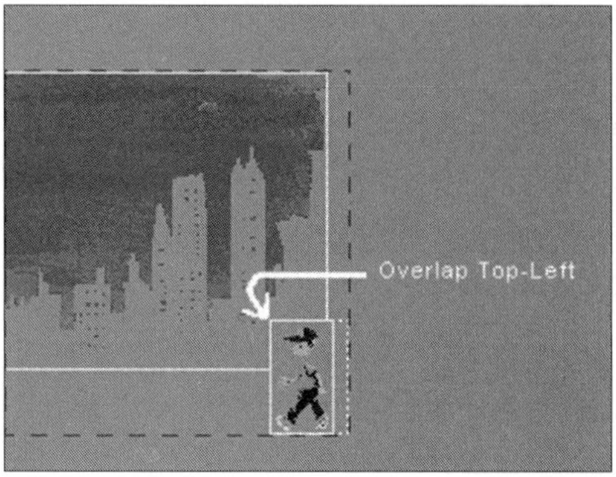

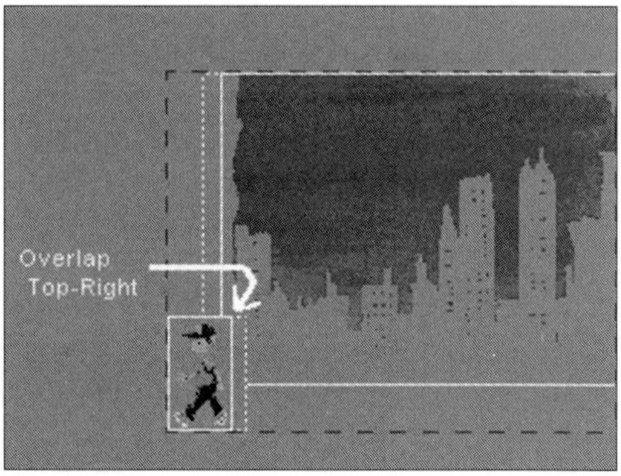

The values for **nBlitX**, **nBlitY**, **nBlitWidth**, and **nBlitHeight** are filled in, based on the results of each of the overlap tests using the **clsLocate** object, **locOverlap**. If the city and kid don't overlap, the values for these variables become the dirty rectangle of the city alone and the kid will be copied separately using its dirty rectangle directly afterwards (if the **BIT_KIDOVERLAPS** bit is turned on, it means that there was no overlap and the kid should be blitted separately).

Class Description: clsMem

There's nothing worse than having to look up the Windows API functions you need every time you start a new project. The double buffering technique that we've just discussed is something that virtually all animations need to use to keep screen updating smooth. The class module, **clsMem**, is a reusable class that enabled me to plug in my double buffering methods without looking up any API functions, constants or processes. We'll build on this class throughout the book, but, in this chapter, we'll use it in a preliminary state in the animation samples.

The following figure shows the class object's exposed properties and methods in its current state. The purpose of **clsMem**, is to create and work with the working area of the double-buffer—a memory device context created to build the next display, which ultimately gets copied to the display. This class acts as a crucial part of double-buffering activity, supplying methods and properties needed to access this working area throughout the project. There need only be one **clsMem** object per project.

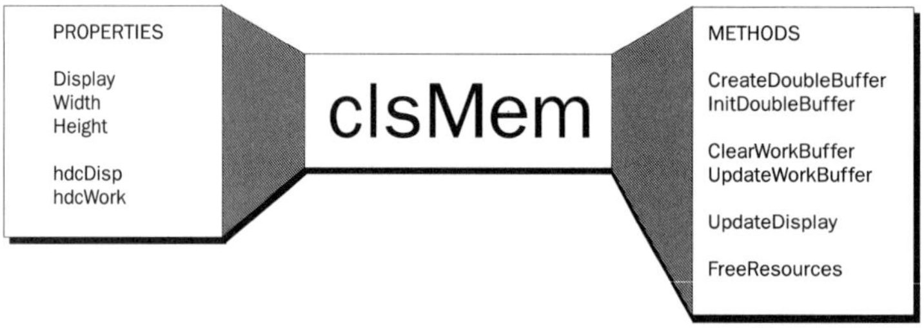

As you can see in the double-buffering diagram above, **hdcWork** is the only DC that is a memory DC. The copy of the background graphic remains in the picture box control that loaded it. The display DC, of course, must be in a window, along with a picture box control.

I'll use **Testblit.vbp** as the example for using **clsMem**, since it's a simpler example. To use this class, you should create a class object at the start of the application sample, which, in this case, is created as a module level variable of the main form:

```
Dim m_objMem As New clsMem
```

Since the class doesn't know where the data is going to be displayed, there's a class property, **Display**, which is set to either a form or picture box, in order for the class to prepare its dimensions for display, and the DC handle to copy display data to. Then the **CreateDoubleBuffer()** method for the class is called, which uses the Windows API (encapsulated into the class with private function declarations) to create a memory buffer and select a bitmap object the same size as the display DC being used for the application:

```
With m_objMem
  Set .Display = m_picDisplay
  .CreateDoubleBuffer
  .InitDoubleBuffer picBg
End With 'objMem
```

Now the working area pointed to through **clsMem**'s **hdcWork** property (the handle to the work area's device context) is created and filled with the sky background that was loaded into **picBg**. When the Copy Ball button is clicked, the ball is copied to its current position in the display. Since no movement is taking place, there's no need to erase the previous position of the ball from the display. The following lines of code just copy the ball graphic from its DC to the working area and then the working area is updated to the display:

```
With m_objMem
  .UpdateWorkBuffer picBall.hdc, m_nLeft, m_nTop, m_nWidth, m_nHeight, 0, 0
  .UpdateDisplay m_nLeft, m_nTop, m_nWidth, m_nHeight
End With
```

Since the ball is being copied to the display without transparency (as in the bitmasking discussion earlier) the assumption of the class is that the raster operation is to copy data as is to the display, using **SRCCOPY**. This is encapsulated into the class, so it saves a few parameters to pass to the methods that both update the working buffer and the display DC. In this case, it wasn't really necessary to use the double buffering capability of the class, since the same information copied to the working buffer is also copied to the display. This is really useful when the ball is moved that this becomes useful.

When the user clicks on Move Ball, the following lines of code erase the previous position of the ball, copy it to the new position, then copy the entire update to the work buffer to the display DC:

```
With m_objMem
  .ClearWorkBuffer picBg.hdc, m_nLeft, m_nTop, m_nWidth, m_nHeight
  .UpdateWorkBuffer picBall.hdc, m_nLeft + nMoveAmt, m_nTop, m_nWidth,
              m_nHeight, 0, 0
  .UpdateDisplay m_nLeft, m_nTop, m_nWidth + nMoveAmt, m_nHeight
End With
```

As I said, calculating the changed area that the screen should have updated can be tricky, but in this simple example, the ball is moving from left to right only and the movement amount is fixed, so the entire update rectangle is obvious. Wait till you get to Chapter 5!

For reasons that will become obvious as **clsMem** is buffed out and other related classes like **clsBitmap** are created, you'll see why I didn't add additional parameters to the methods of **clsMem** with respect to raster operation codes. For this reason, the pilot and kid animations use **clsMem** in a different way for double buffering. In these examples, **clsMem** is used to access the handles to the work area device context and the creation and initialization of that device context, but not to erase previous positions of animations using the methods provided. That is because, clearly, the bitmaps themselves should hang on to that kind of information so that the class doesn't need to be passed a parameter, but an actual bitmap structure (or class) that tells it where the bitmap is, what its location is and so on. Coming soon to a chapter near you!

Class Description: clsWipe

One very important topic of any animation application is that of **transitions**. For instance, how horrible would it be if the curtain disappeared before one of the animation selections where shown. What kind of presentation is that for each animation? So, rather than keep this animation simple-stupid, and just offering you a curtain that had no intention of rising and falling as a curtain should, I give you a curtain that does exactly what you would expect. In doing so I introduce a new Windows API function, **PatBlt()**, and put together a simple wipe class to get us ready for Chapter 4 where the really sophisticated transitions take place.

PatBlt()

I needed a simple outlet for the **PatBlt()** function, another Windows API function which is part of the family of blitting functions. The curtain example fits perfectly in this plan. If you run the **Apianims.vbp** application, you'll probably notice that the curtain always wipes from or to a solid color background. The choices for this solid color are white and black. This isn't coming from a DC, however. The area is being painted a solid color by using the **PatBlt()** function.

This function copies information, not from another device context, but from the same destination device context that is receiving the final results. The rectangle specified by the parameters passed to **nDestX**, **nDestY**, **nWidth** and **nHeight** is the rectangle that is painted on the DC specified by **hdcDest**. The source information comes from the same DC, but rather than from the contents of the DC's bitmap, it comes from the contents of the DC's brush object.

```
nRet = PatBlt(hdcDest, nDestX, nDestY, nWidth, nHeight, nROP)
```

I won't go into too much detail on brushes here, since we'll see more in Chapter 4. What I can say now is that if the brush is a solid color and **nROP = PATCOPY**, the rectangle will be filled with that solid color. You can also pass two other constants that are used in **clsWipe** to copy a color that ignores the brush color altogether. They are declared as follows:

```
Private Const BLACKNESS = &H42
Private Const WHITENESS = &HFF0062
```

> **The constants BLACKNESS and WHITENESS look to the system palette for the first and second index in the palette if this is used in a palettized environment. Though these two colors are, by default, always part of the system palette in these positions, they can be changed by another program, which would account for any unexpected results.**

PatBlt() is a very speedy way to fill in the destination DC with a solid color. It's faster than using another DC filled with black and using **BitBlt()** to perform the same function.

Wipe Functionality

With the curtain animation in mind, I started a wipe class as a prelude to Chapter 4 in which I wanted to use a much more sophisticated transition. This class has two transitions so far: one to wipe a DC's contents upwards and offscreen, exposing a solid color, the other, to wipe a DC's contents downwards and onscreen, from a solid color. The class's functionality is described here:

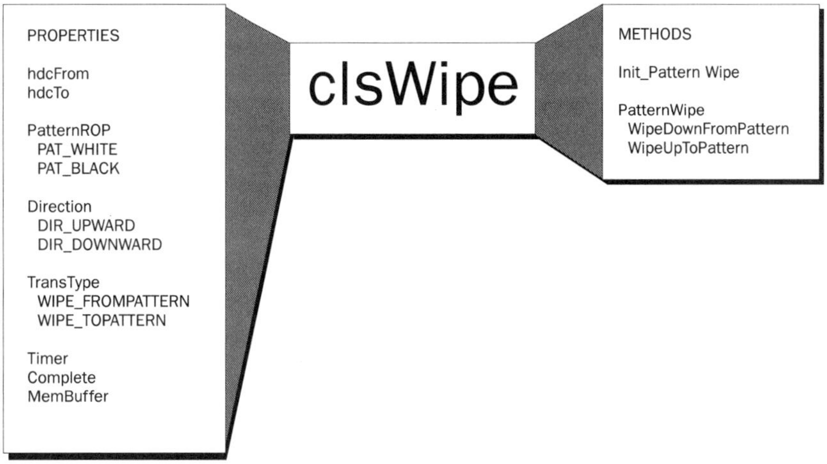

Since the curtain starts out as the display on the screen when **Apianims.vbp** is first run, it makes sense that the first animation with the curtain is to move the curtain upward within the display. This curtain animation is called by selecting an animation from the film strip selections. If the trash can or pilot is selected, the curtain wipes to a white screen before the animation begins. If the kid animation is selected, the curtain wipes to black. In preparation for the wipe animation, the **clsWipe** object, **m_objWipe**, must have certain properties initialized:

```
With m_objWipe
   .PatternROP = .PAT_WHITE
   .Direction = .DIR_UPWARD
   .hdcFrom = picBg.hdc
   .Init_PatternWipe
End With
```

You can see in the above code sample that **PatternROP** is set to white, which is the color that we want the wipe to use. This property is used in the **nROP** parameter of the **PatBlt()** function. The **Direction** property is used to tell the wipe method which direction the curtain is going. If the curtain is being wiped upward, the **hdcFrom** parameter is set so that the Wipe method will know which DC to use for the transition. Since wiping upward means that the pattern wipe is moving from the curtain to a color, there's no need to set up the **hdcTo** property in this instance.

Init_PatternWipe, makes a call to the method provided by the class that sets up the wipe variables to start fresh. Here's the method:

```
' set position based on direction
If m_nDirection = m_DIRUPWARD Then
    m_nPosX = 0
    m_nPosY = m_nHeight
ElseIf m_nDirection = m_DIRDOWNWARD Then
    m_nPosX = 0
    m_nPosY = 0
End If

m_nBlockCount = 0
m_bComplete = False

' start wipe timer
m_objTmr.Enabled = True
```

To set up each wipe, the starting positions for each wipe (**m_nPosX** and **m_nPosY**) must be initialized, along with a counter that keeps track of the number of blocks that have been copied for the wipe (**m_nBlockCount**, which is incremented each time the timer calls the wipe procedure) and **m_nComplete** (which always starts as **False**). Before the setup is complete for the wipe, the timer that **clsWipe** has been assigned is enabled. The timer's **Timer** event will call the **PatternWipe** method each interval.

Now, the **PatternWipe** method will be called each timer interval, which will decide, based on the **Direction** property, which pattern wipe to use. **WipeDownFromPattern** and **WipeUpToPattern** are the only two pattern wipes belonging to the class, though we could easily alter these to reflect different wipe directions and specifications. The **PatternWipe** method has these lines of code:

```
If m_nDirection = m_DIRUPWARD Then
    WipeUpToPattern
ElseIf m_nDirection = m_DIRDOWNWARD Then
    WipeDownFromPattern
End If
```

This figure demonstrates the variable use and steps to the upward wipe from curtain to a solid color of black:

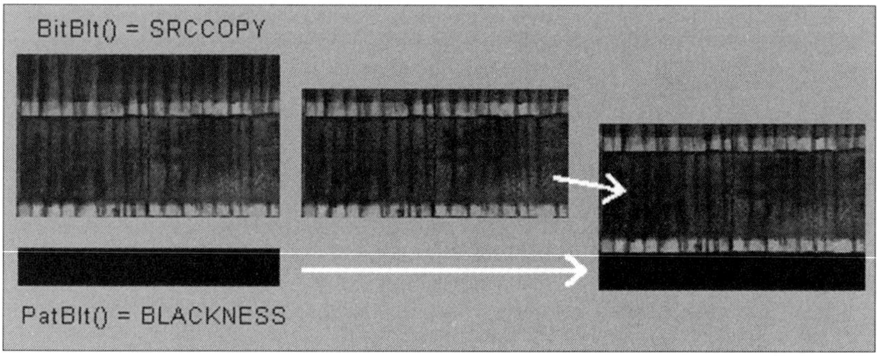

At each timer interval, a smaller portion of the curtain DC is copied into the work buffer and a larger portion of the work buffer is **PatBlt()** with a solid color. The color is based on the setting for the **PatternROP** property; **PAT_BLACK** in this case. Calculating the portion of the curtain and solid color to copy to the working buffer is easy, using the **m_nBlockCount** variable which, multiplied by the size of each wipe block, gives the height of the **PatBlt()** rectangle. That is the Y position that the curtain DC should be copied from. The height of that DC minus the Y position should be the height of the curtain rectangle to copy. Let's look at the code:

```
With m_objMem
  ' copy hdcFrom data to working buffer
  nRet = BitBlt(.hdcWork, m_nLeft, m_nTop, m_nWidth, m_nHeight -
          m_nBlockCount * m_nBlockHeight, m_hdcFrom, 0, m_nBlockCount *
          m_nBlockHeight, SRCCOPY)
  ' copy pattern fill
  nRet = PatBlt(.hdcWork, m_nLeft, m_nHeight - m_nBlockCount *
          m_nBlockHeight, m_nWidth, m_nBlockCount * m_nBlockHeight,
                              m_nPatternROP)
  ' update display with working area
  .UpdateDisplay m_nLeft, m_nTop, m_nWidth, m_nHeight
End With
```

Since the display is changed in each wipe, this animation requires a complete screen update when all is done. Once the entire area has been **PatBlt()** with the selected color, the operation is flagged as complete by setting the **m_nComplete** variable to **True**. The **Timer** event checks this value each interval before continuing, so this should trigger the end of the animation:

```
If m_nBlockCount * m_nBlockHeight >= m_nHeight Then
    m_bComplete = True
Else
    m_nBlockCount = m_nBlockCount + 1
End If
```

The **WipeDownFromPattern** method begins with the memory DC being filled with the previously selected color (by way of a call to **PatBlt()**). When the user chooses to stop the animation, they do so by either selecting the curtain or another animation frame, from the programs interface. **PatBlt()** then fills the display DC with the color stored in the memory DC before the curtain wipe fills the screen with a curtain. Though it may be more effective if the curtain were to drop down over the display's current state rather than a solid color fill of black or white, this requires some additional steps which we'll use in Chapter 4.

Summary

Understanding how Windows programming works and how it relates to VB's environment will help you to better determine when and how to add functionality to your VB apps. There's almost *always* a way to get what you want out of VB, in one way or another. You won't believe the control you'll gain over your VB code when you get under the Windows hood.

In your 'not-so-spare' time, you may want to play a little more with some of the techniques described in this chapter. Don't worry, we'll be using them over and over again masked only by new variable names and program interfaces. If you feel the sudden urge to frolic about with a few of your favorite Windows techniques, here are a few suggestions:

- Add some variety to the font animation by altering the escapement in different ways, along with size and color.
- Add a closing bounce to the start of the curtain rise and the end of the curtain fall transitions, rather than simply using the constant timer interval.

So many tricks to try, so little time. Well, stay tuned! We still have a little more Windows theory to get under our belts as we jump headlong into animation, multimedia and more! Next up, palettes and scary bitmap details, so don't go away!

```
rivate Declare Function GlobalFree Lib "kernel32" (ByVal h
rivate Declare Function GlobalLock Lib "kernel32" (ByVal h
rivate Declare Function GlobalUnlock Lib "kernel32" (ByVa
'--copying bitmap bits
' copies a global block of data into global memory
rivate Declare Sub CopyMemory Lib "kernel32" Alias "RtlM

'--copies global block of data in   B
rivate Declare Function SetDIB     "gdi32" (ByVal m_hd
  ByVal hBitmap As Long, ByVal nStartS   As Long, By
  ByVal lpBits As Any, lpBI As BITMAPI    ByVal wUsa

'--blits DC to DC
rivate Declare Function BitBlt Lib "gdi32" (ByVal hDestDC
rivate Declare Function StretchBlt Lib "gdi32" (ByVal hDes

'--palette methods
rivate Declare Function CreatePalett    "gdi32" (lpLogPa
rivate Declare Function SelectPalette     "gdi32" (ByVal m
rivate Declare Function RealizePalette Lib "gdi32" (ByVal n
rivate Declare Sub AnimatePalette Lib "gdi32" (ByVal hPal

'--device context methods
rivate Declare Function SelectObject Lib "gdi32" (ByVal m_

rivate Declare Function CreateCompatibleBitmap Lib "gdi32
rivate Declare Function DeleteObject Lib "gdi32" (ByVal hO

rivate Declare Function CreateCompatibleDC Lib "gdi32" (B
```

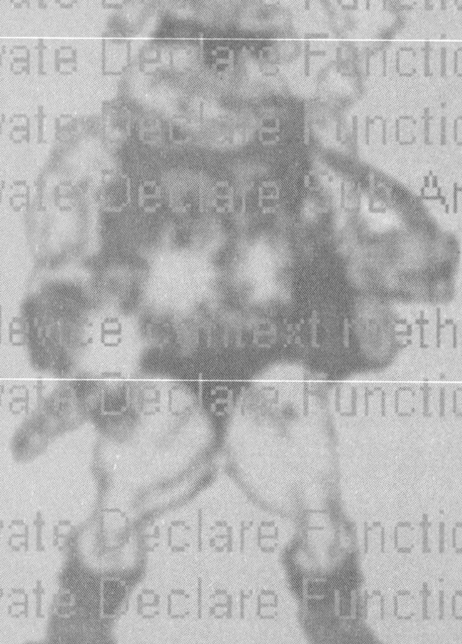

Chapter

3

Windows Graphics Primer

Oh boy! Now for the scary stuff! Up until now, you've had but a teaser on graphics techniques. Without getting into the meat of the subject, I explained how to copy graphics into memory, as well as how to copy them to the display area using techniques such as bitmasking, double buffering, movement and transition. This provided an introduction to using the Windows API to shove graphics data around. Just as a precautionary measure, gather your smelling salts because there's a lot more to working with bitmap data than *that* humble introduction! To play with the big boys and write killer applications that use killer graphics, you'll need a solid grip on graphical reality. By casually locking horns with VB and slinking behind the driver's seat at run time, you can do just that!

This chapter will give you the low-down on the mechanics of graphics display, how bitmap graphics are stored and laid out, how they can be accessed and the methods that provide this, and the ability to manipulate and display the final results. As a special treat, we'll dig into the issues that palettes bring to the table. Not only will you learn the basics about how palettes work, but you'll also get a chance to manipulate them for idle fun and frolic! Don't get your hopes up, though. No matter how much you know about palettes, it seems that every new application introduces yet another fearful twist, which is why I'll also be covering additional information on that topic in later chapters.

The Mechanics of Display

Using Visual Basic makes it easy to overlook the particulars about how display data is delivered to the screen. If you're planning to dive into game programming, you'll definitely need an in-depth knowledge in this area, considering the speed with which the graphics should be hammered to the screen. This can make or break your game's *je ne sais quoi*. Though this book is but a primer to multimedia entertainment and games—that place where hardware knowledge is inescapable—it's still useful to understand the fuss of graphics delivery while creating killer animations. I figure what the heck, I'll toss you smack into the middle of some gory graphic details just to put a little spice into an otherwise dull day. Yes, this *will* require a glimpse at some hardware-related issues—that unpopular tea-time subject—but I'll keep it simple and clear, feeding you one small and digestible bite at a time. If you're already a graphics guru, go ahead and speed read through the next couple of sections.

An Overview: from File to Display

With Visual Basic, displaying data can be as simple as creating forms, adding and organizing their contents, and then manipulating them to display what you wish. Almost magically (not really though) those VB instructions update the screen. Without further delay, allow me to formally introduce the contributing factors to the display of information:

- The monitor
- The video card
- The video driver
- Many program instructions

Oh, so you've already met? Well, just in case you haven't, I'll go ahead and summarize their part in data display, *before* we get knee-deep in bitmap data.

I guess you could say that there are more than a few things going on to get you your screen display. When we're talking about image data, you know that the image files, when stored on disk, must somehow be read into memory to be displayed. Consider this figure as a summary of the places that an image file's data visits on the way to the screen:

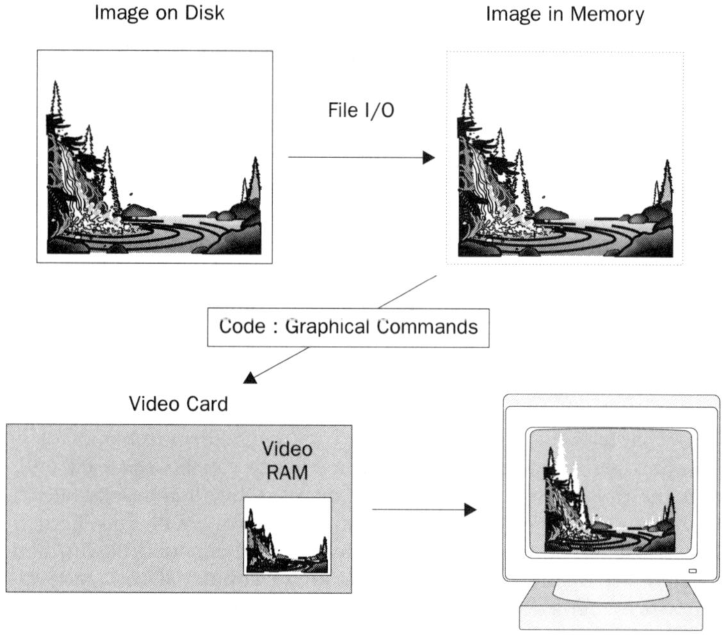

To explain this, let's escort the image data shown in the diagram from disk to display.

Reading data into memory

Reading a graphics file into memory requires instructions, be it the **`LoadPicture`** method of the picture box control (which, incidentally, does much more than just load the image data into memory, since it obviously updates the display as well), or some other low-level functions that read data from disk. I'll be walking you through a VB class that uses VB combined with the Windows API functions necessary to get raw bitmap data from a file into memory. The point of this exercise is to make the image data accessible to the code that takes it to the display, without having to see it right away.

Data organization and manipulation

Once image data has been read into memory, it needs to be organized in some format that other program code can comprehend when using manipulation and display instructions on the data. (This will make more sense when I go through an example of how image data is laid out.) How this data is organized in memory has an effect on what code can subsequently act on the data and what commands can be used to send the information to the display. There are several ways this type of binary information can be stored in memory, along with several methods that can be used to perform actions on that data. I'll be outlining the available graphics coding methods in this chapter, then we'll use one of those methods in a bitmap class to work with bitmap data. Generally, the decision on how the data is stored, along with the functions that will manipulate it, is based on efficiency and ease of implementation. This usually involves some sort of trade-off.

From memory to display

Once the data has been safely stored in memory, and altered to your satisfaction, a suitable method (based on how the information was stored and manipulated in memory) is used to send it to the display. As you can see from the previous figure, the data isn't actually sent directly to the screen *per se*. The video card gets a hold of the data first and puts it into *its* memory area. This is where the screen display is actually stored and is the place from where the monitor sucks its display information. The video card is constantly sending data to the display device, so it updates to the video card almost as soon as it's sent to the display. Obviously I'm smoothing over a much more complicated discussion which we'll be attacking presently. Plenty more is happening in this last step that requires a small interlude to describe each component's part in the process.

The Display Device

Unless you're a hardware guru, you probably don't need to know how a display device works any more than you need to know how a stove element gets its heat. (It heats up, it gets hot, you shouldn't touch it!) Just so that you can follow conversations that we'll have later, I'll summarize the workings of a display output device. If you're already familiar with them, bear with me and treat it as a good time for a little revision. The display you see is created with many dots of light, generated by the inner workings of the hardware. Each dot retains a color significant to the display, and this is sent via an analog signal from the video card. We'll look at the video card later, but right now we're interested in how the data is presented to the naked eye. The actual display device retains characteristics that influence the resulting output. Here are some elements that affect the inner workings and capabilities of a display device:

- The hardware makeup
- The dimensions
- The refresh rate

Hardware makeup ... Hmmm, I wonder if I could be a little more vague? Well, I'm referring once again to the mechanics of how the display information gets to the display device. The dots of light are organized in a matrix format. Each dot in the matrix is represented by a color specific to the display. The specifics of the color and matrix location are sent by the video card through its output port. This is the analog signal that the display device can understand and send to the display. Any more information on display technology would undoubtedly turn you into a hard-core hardware geek, so I'll stop right here.

The **dimensions** of the display area affect the appearance of what's been sent to the screen. As you already know, what you see on the monitor is built from many individual dots of light (better known as **pixels** or **picture elements**), each having a color value appropriate to the current display.

The size of each pixel that builds the display is not fixed, so the rays of light can be different sizes. Their size is the product of the available display real-estate (or monitor dimensions) and the current resolution (rows and columns of pixels to display). The display hardware is responsible for the dimensions available, the device driver for the resolution (more on this later). Here's a visual for you. If the resolution is changed from 640x480 to 800x600, thus increasing the number of rows and columns of pixels displayed, facilitating this change requires the pixel size to shrink. The figure on the next page shows what happens to a 640x480 window's appearance in both display resolutions:

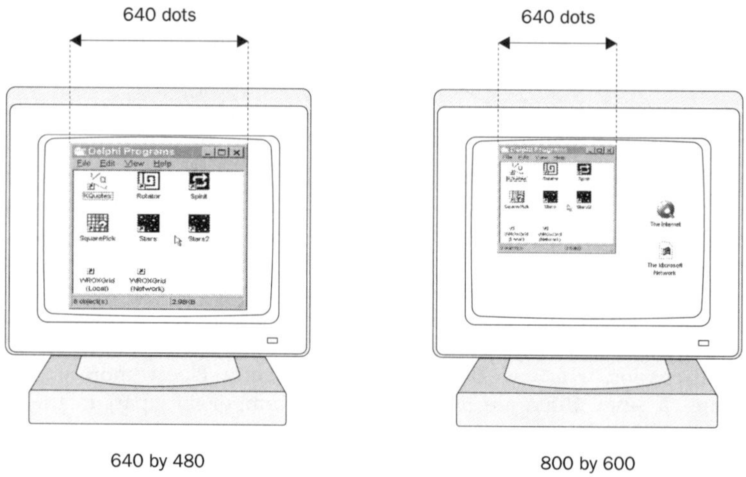

Pixels get smaller in larger display resolutions

The **refresh rate** refers to the number of times per second the entire display area is sent its current pixel information. Individual light beams that burn each pixel color into the monitor are not persistent. However, before the light beam fades, that same pixel is beamed again to refresh the display. Pixel updates are usually completely inconspicuous because of the rapidity of the refresh rate. 72Hz is an acceptable and common rate among standard video cards and monitors. This means that the entire screen display is sent to the screen 72 times each second. The monitor *does* have a refresh limit that will restrict the speed with which the video card is allowed to send its data and that will be the ceiling speed for this transaction. So, as important as it is to have a good video card, the monitor too must be worth its salt!

The intricacies of how the display device puts forth its pixels is not of great concern from a programmer's standpoint, but display real-estate and monitor refresh *are* meaningful. These characteristics become more important when they're combined with the video card and driver. It's the display device's capabilities that depicts what the other two can request support for. Clearly, this leads us to the following topics: the roles of the video card and device driver.

The Video Card

The video card takes charge of sending the pixel coordinates and color information to the monitor for display. As we've mentioned, analog signals are sent through the video card's output port, where a monitor connected to it will be awakened to respond to the signal. The video card has a special place in its heart where it keeps the display—the video card's RAM (this can be VRAM or DRAM)—which, as it sounds, is the video card's active memory. Video hardware directs information from its RAM and pixel-by-pixel sends the data, converted from digital information to an analog signal, through the monitor connection. We won't talk about how that information gets to the RAM just yet. Let's consider the characteristics of the information display that the video card specifically contributes to.

> **Memory device contexts created as per the previous chapter's discussions supply an area in memory where the display can be built before it's seen. Video card RAM supplies a similar area belonging to the video card instead of to the PC. The difference is that the display comes from there, and thus display DCs are associated with this area.**

Display output capabilities—color, resolution and speed—rest on the shoulders of the video card. Aspects which affect display performance include:

- Bandwidth
- Refresh rate
- VRAM
- Driver software
- Graphics accelerators

The **bandwidth** is calculated by multiplying the video card's (not the monitor's) refresh rate by the number of pixels being displayed. The more pixels being displayed, the more time it will take to complete a full screen update (remember this is performed pixel-by-pixel). Obviously, the wider the bandwidth, the more throughput on a single pass and the more flicker on the screen as it gets updated.

> **Flicker is not only caused by poorly managed screen updates. Hardware flicker is caused when individual pixel updates are noticeable to the eye. This happens when burned monitor pixels have had a chance to begin fading before the next refresh has reached those pixels in the display.**

Refresh rate capabilities of the video card are limited by the capabilities of the monitor receiving the data. The lowest common denominator wins, but typically 70–72Hz is considered the minimum acceptable resultant refresh rate. Different video cards have widely differing refresh capabilities. For example, high- performance cards with a high refresh rate are the most popular amongst game freaks.

VRAM/DRAM are types of memory that can be present on the video card, determining the available storage space for display data. Consider a display resolution of 640x480, with 256 color depth (or 8 bits per pixel, which comes to 1 byte). This would require 307,200 bytes (640 rows x 480 columns x 1 byte) of memory on the card to hold one screen full of data. If the color depth was 24-bit, you can multiply that by three and you need at least 1MB. Then what if the resolution increased to 800x600? What about 1024x760? Can you see why some video cards don't support higher resolutions for display output? It all depends on the video card's memory availability. Resolution and color are in a perpetual fight over available video memory (more color for less resolution and vice versa). The good thing is, you don't have to address this issue directly, since the only drivers available for a given video card will be those its memory can support.

Graphics accelerators are processors (or CPUs) residing on the video card. Rather like a sound card which allows asynchronous processing, a graphics accelerator takes the command set and carries it out while the PC's CPU is set free to continue processing the next instruction. This multiprocessing is what speeds up everything, especially when the application is graphics-intensive.

The Video Driver

Before Windows came along, DOS programmers had to write code for specific individual video cards existing in the market. With the advent of Windows and the GDI, video drivers began shipping their hardware with support for the mandatory command set that GDI required, enabling it to gather the graphics data sent to it by GDI commands. This is, of course, because the GDI contained the central graphics instructions that all Windows programs call to get data to the screen. At this point, programmers were free to concentrate on those generic graphics functions that would work with any installed driver. Since video hardware is unique, the drivers shipped with it now knew how to communicate with the hardware and software using the default GDI command set.

The video driver has several functions that assist in this new procedure for data display, including what the video card's display area supports, as far as resolution and color are concerned. Drivers are responsible for:

- Resolution and color
- Translating GDI commands
- Increasing software performance

Resolution and color for the display device are representative of the display driver that Windows considers current. As we've mentioned, the amount of memory on the video card will directly affect the possible resolution and color combinations that can be supported by the drivers shipped with the card. Several drivers will be supplied for a given card, each supplying a unique resolution and color combination falling within these boundaries: 640x480 (16-bit color), 800x600 (256 or 8-bit color).

Remember when we created memory DCs in Chapter 2? The currently installed video driver is used by the GDI when all device contexts (display or memory) are created. The color information (we'll be diving into those details further on) of the DC must reflect that of the current driver, since that is what is being currently supported. For instance, if the driver uses 256 colors then the DC must also be capable of supporting 256 colors, so that the DC information sent to the display is already in the format that the video card is supporting through the driver. Display DC's are, of course, stored in video memory, since their contents are seen on the current display.

Translating GDI commands is another central function of the video driver. I mentioned that there is a basic GDI command set that must be supported by every Windows video driver, but the driver must know how to translate and gather display information by referring back to the GDI when more sophisticated commands called do not reside within the driver's command set. This isn't a problem, as the basic command set enables the driver to at least compile and send display data from pixel by pixel data that the driver can understand and send to the video card.

The driver can increase software performance when it supports *more* than the basic command set from GDI. What should be apparent from the previous paragraph is that drivers supporting a more sophisticated GDI command set will send data to the video card faster, thus improving performance. Beyond the basics, drivers can also support functionality like line drawing or transparent blitting, which the driver will then use to send the data to the video card, instead of returning the command to the GDI for more detailed information. This increases performance significantly, since the GDI must send the data over the CPU bus to video memory, which is done much more slowly on a pixel by pixel level. How does the driver actually request the more detailed data? We don't care unless we have to write the driver ourselves... (Which we don't thank goodness.)

*Did you know that a **driver conflict** with your system is a polished term that really means there's a 'bug' in the driver software? A collection of drivers will most likely not have the same 'conflict', so if you choose one in the group for a different resolution/color combination, it will probably work. Drivers are often updated frequently by their manufacturer for this reason, so it's well worth your while to call them or check the Internet and/or Compuserve for recent updates.*

All the information that we've just covered regarding the monitor, video card and its drivers is going to prove very useful to you. Just understanding the basic process of information display from every angle of functionality will enable you to make intelligent decisions about how you wish to format, display and use graphical data. Remember that graphical data does not just include images, but also covers text, lines, points, and so on. Essentially, anything that you can do to manipulate your display with the GDI is a form of graphical data that will eventually be seen by the display. Since the image data is an important part of animation, I'll move on to discuss bitmap graphics in more detail.

Bitmap Graphics

If you don't know already, I'll bet that at least once when you were loading a bitmap into an imaging program or picture box control, you wondered how that image data was stored and arranged on disk. I don't mean the really low-level 1s and 0s that are contained in the file, seen when you type **`debug <filename>`** at the DOS prompt. (If you've never done that before, try it for kicks. It's a trip!) What I *am* referring to is the logical layout of the image data. In order to play with the big boys, you have to get a grip on what graphics are all about. Now, if you already know this stuff, let me state that the person I'm writing to now is the one who's reading this section and saying "Oh! *Now* I get it!". The rest of you folks can come along for the ride till we get to the really meaty section of the chapter.

Data Organization

There are two main categories of data organization for bitmap graphics. The first is the file format, which is how the information for the image is laid out on disk. The second is the format of DDB or DIB, which concentrates on what information is stored about the image (is color information there or not?). Understanding these two concepts is the next step in being able to work with bitmap graphics in code.

File Formats

If you ask me, the term *bitmap* is used pretty loosely. Bitmap graphics in general are referred to as *bitmaps*, but amongst this primordial soup is also an authentic bitmap format. Bitmap graphics are **non-vector** (or **raster**) image data, organized as an array of image data that is written to disk. (Vector graphics differ in that they are instructions on how to build the image rather than the actual image bit by bit). Each array item describes the color information for a single pixel in the image.

Before I get into the details of the 'authentic' bitmap format, let me touch on the concept of file formats for bitmap graphics. Using VB doesn't give us much reason to consider the details of the file formats we're loading, how their data is laid out, or how they're stored and used at run time. We know that forms, picture boxes and image controls support the display of icons, Windows metafiles (which, incidentally, are a form of vector graphics), and 'true' bitmaps, but a graphic image can be saved in more formats than you can shake a stick at.

Consider the following short list of file formats that can be used to organize a bitmap's contents:

*.BMP, *.GIF, *.TIF, *.TGA, *.CMP

This is but a sample of the possible formats that most image applications would support. Compared to the picture box control's lame selection, an imaging program will offer numerous formats, all standardized (or should be) across the board so that different programs can read data saved from another, as long as the format is consistent—shame on them if it's not. So how does a program recognize the image data's format?

Although the file extension usually corresponds to the format used to save the image data, this is not a guarantee. Filenames can be altered. Most file formats are identified by a unique ID that gets saved as part of the actual file's contents which the user can't change (at least, not easily). When it's loading a bitmap from disk (which we'll be doing in a minute) the first thing that the read-code should do is check for the file format identifier to see how the data is stored. To make things awkward for the programmer, the inventors of *some* file formats placed their file identifiers in different parts of the file, or didn't use one at all! We won't be looking at all of these formats, but you'll get the gist of reading and using bitmap data when we look at the bitmap class.

Aside from a unique ID, file formats also use proprietary methods for organizing image data. This is not a problem once you've discovered the file format by its identifier, but you can see why standardization of these formats is imperative. The application reading in the data relies completely on this standardization to display the data with integrity. Regardless of format, all bitmap graphics saved to disk are device-independent bitmaps (or DIBs), another loosely used term that I'll resolve in the next section.

DDBs and DIBs

Now *there's* a couple of acronyms for ya! DDB this, DIB that...you must come across it at least once a day somewhere in your travels through VB land. DDBs are device-dependent bitmaps and DIBs are device-independent bitmaps. Well *that's* great, but what the heck does it all mean? I'll start with a little history that will lead us to the birth of the 'true' bitmap.

Long ago in a land far far away, there was only one file format—the device-dependent bitmap. When an image was created using a graphics program, it was saved to disk based on the current video device. When that same file was loaded on any machine with a different device setting, its display integrity wasn't preserved. No color information was stored with it that could be interpreted programmatically and set up for correct display. This was the epitome of device dependence, and thankfully is no longer.

Color By Numbers

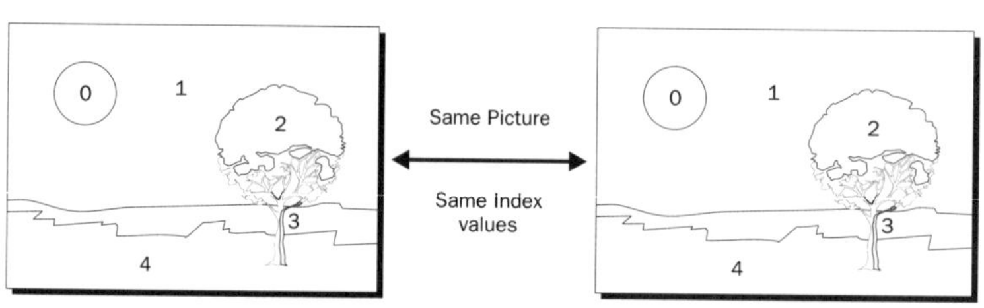

Palette Device #1

Orange	Light Blue	Green	Dark Brown	Light Brown
0	1	2	3	4

Palette Device #2

Light Blue	Pink	Purple	Orange	Green
0	1	2	3	4

A standard format was soon developed for device-independent graphics, known as the **device-independent bitmap** (the **DIB**). This format included color information to preserve the integrity of bitmaps saved to disk, later viewed in a different display environment. This completely obliterated the DDB, at least, insofar as images saved on disk. With respect to the above figure, the pixel array could still point to the same indices, but now the palette too was stored on disk so the next time it was displayed, that palette would hopefully be used by the displaying applications. Alternatively, the RGB values could now be stored in the pixel array instead of a reference to a palette index.

All bitmap file formats (as discussed in the previous section) store their image data as DIBs. However, this is this original DIB, the Microsoft DIB Format, that retains the title of the 'authentic bitmap'. Files with the extension `.bmp` or `.dib`, are both true bitmaps, identified by the signature `BM` in the first two characters of the file. It became a standard for bitmaps to be saved as DIBs so that different display environments would know how to display the data. This doesn't always go as planned, since the current display device can only offer those colors available in the system at one time. At worst, a color close to the one requested will be sought out, a far cry from just pointing to the same index position and hoping for the best. We're going to r-r-r-rip the entire process apart as we read in the bitmap, gather and organize its information and see what we can do with the colors to get the best possible results.

But wait, there's still more to know. The concept of the DDB didn't die completely. When an image is read from disk, it's up to the programmer how the information is organized in memory. Windows provides structures for organizing related bitmap information that mirrors standard DIB bitmap information, but the actual image data (the pixel array and palette), once in memory, can be used as device-dependent (DDBs) or device-independent (DIBs). In the next section, we'll explain the different programming methods available now to store the image data and then transfer it to the display device.

Programming Methods

All image data on disk must be loaded into memory using some method of file input. Your choice of file I/O will follow suit with the tools available to you in your current development environment. As you'll see when we get to the code, we can use VB's file I/O methods just fine to read in image data manually, at which point the issue then becomes, what do we want to do with it?

In order of appearance in the evolution of speedy Windows graphics handling, we have the GDI, WinG, DIBSection, and Direct X's DirectDraw methods. No one method necessarily out-does another, simply for the reason that they're all useful in different ways. We won't use all of these graphics handling methods in this book, so I'm not going into too much detail here. Let's take a look at the decision-making process for a method of programming graphics, then we'll see what each has to offer.

Choosing a Method

I'm going to address some pertinent questions before describing for you the methods you can choose from to handle graphics. For instance, why are there choices for handling graphics? What is it that should make me choose one over another? It seems there are four main issues that should drive your decision. They are:

- Data manipulation requirements
- Performance needs

- Platform support
- Development capabilities

Data manipulation requirements refers to what you'll be doing to the bitmap once it's loaded into memory. What you do to the data affects the choice to use DIBs or DDBs. For example, if you're loading in a predrawn image for use as a background or animation and don't intend to alter it in any way before it is displayed, you'll want to use the data as a DDB to maximize performance. All bitmaps become device-dependent when they reach the display, since the display is ruled by the current device driver. It makes sense that it's faster to copy data from a DDB, since it's already in the format that the screen expects. Conversely, if your intention is to blend or alter pixels directly, possibly to weave that image into a complex background image, you're better off accessing the pixel matrix directly, so a DIB would be best.

Performance needs relate to the application itself. Whereas a game requires animations to be as lickety split as they can get, animation used in conjunction with a demonstration program or as an interface enhancement may not require the same performance figures. Not only does this affect the choice of image delivery, but it may affect what you decide to do with the data, so that you *can* use the fastest delivery method.

Platform support has now become an issue since software can run on Windows 3.x, Win32S, Windows NT, or Windows 95 environments. Some of these support *all* of the graphics methods, some do not. You'll need to be aware of what your target is for the application, then choose the best method for you.

Development capabilities means 'What are you programming in?', 'What are you capable of programming?', and 'How much time do you have?. All of these issues directly affect your decision of programming method as well. You need to weigh this with the others to come up with a final decision.

GDI

The GDI (Graphics Device Interface) is the command-set introduced with Windows that talked to the various device drivers for the programmer through its commands. Programmers were provided with a set of graphics drawing and data-moving functions, some of which you've already seen with **`BitBlt()`** and **`PatBlt()`** operations, implemented through a GDI device context. All GDI functions rely on the bitmap's association with a device context to implement any drawing methods. The benefit here is that the display data is already compatible with the display device, and so is displayed with minimum effort, since it is sent to the screen without conversion. In other words, things happen very, *very* fast.

Of course, data originating from disk must be moved into the bitmap associated with the DC. This is the translation that changes the data from DIB format to DDB format. This step is skipped when the picture box control is used to load the image data, since this process puts the image data into a device context, which means that it's already gone through the conversion from DIB to DDB. If we were to read the data in from disk ourselves using file I/O methods (and we will), you'd see that the data uses the same amount of memory as required on disk. The data is read into a memory buffer, pointed to by a memory address and is accessible via a pointer created when the space was allocated by the file I/O process. To get this pixel data, byte for byte, into the associated bitmap of a device context, you must use **`SetDIBits()`** (covered later in this chapter). This function takes the DIB and converts it to the DDB format the current device supports, from which point GDI can understand the DDB data using its associated device context.

With GDI, accessing a bitmap's pixel data through its association with a DC is available only through GDI methods. There's no longer a pointer to the raw bitmap data once the data belongs to the DC. But GDI functions **GetPixel()** and **SetPixel()** (methods for changing individual pixels) are much slower than using a pointer to access the same data, which is a capability that WinG introduced and DIBSection improved.

WinG

WinG was introduced to provide device-independent and platform-independent ways to get better graphics performance in Windows. DOS game programmers traditionally do lots of pixel level graphics manipulation, a very slow process with GDI methods without that pointer to that graphics data, which provides direct access to the raw bitmap data since you don't have to go through the DC. For a DOS programmer to port to Windows and be happy, they had to have the ability to perform this direct data manipulation, still keeping the DC available for display compatibility and faster screen transfers.

WinG introduced a device context that uses a DIB as the drawing surface, instead of a DDB. The figure below conceptualizes the difference between the standard DC processes that associate a bitmap to a regular device context and the use of a DC that points to a DIB instead. This gave programmers access to the bitmap data through the DC, as well as using a pointer to the bitmap data in memory. WinG came with its own command set (a subset of GDI) that worked specifically with its DCs. This meant that you could use a pointer for those pixel level alterations that worked speedily in this manner and use a GDI-like command to blit information quickly in a device-dependent manner to the display.

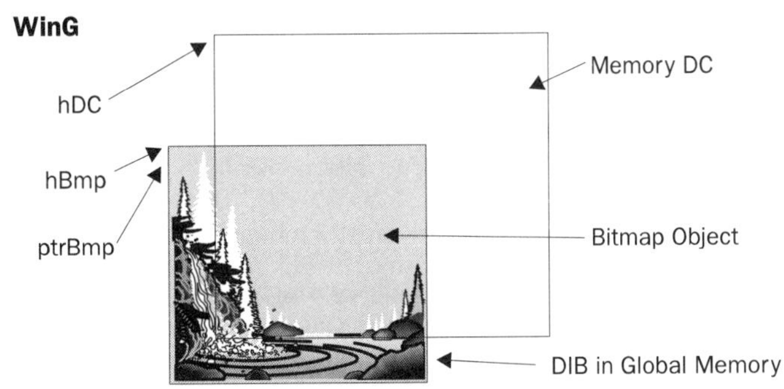

The WinG libraries (the DLLs that provide WinG functionality) were also optimized (or, hacked in) with some special speed improvements in transferring data to the screen based on the current device. An advantage of these WinG libraries is that they also provide platform independence because their command set works on both 16 and 32-bit environments. Actually, under NT or Windows 95 operating systems, WinG commands translate into their native DIBSection commands (discussed next).

This book is directed at 32-bit application development only, so I won't be describing WinG methods through VB. DIBSection, which is available to VB with a little help from a DLL, will be the method we use to manipulate DIBs and you'll see how it can be done in Chapter 7.

DIBSection

In Windows NT and 95, we're no longer restricted to associating DDBs to memory device contexts. A new DIB data construct, affectionately known as **DIBSection**, is available on both operating systems. Thus, DIBSection is the replacement for WinG in both 32-bit Windows environments. Like WinG, DIBSection lets you associate a DIB drawing surface with a device context. The difference is that it's a GDI device context! GDI understands the DIBSection bitmap structure, so you get the DC's bitmap handle *and* the pointer to the raw bitmap data, while continuing to use GDI commands without learning a new and limiting command set as with WinG. So you can have your bitmap and blit it too!

You can use *all* of the GDI drawing functions that you're accustomed to, that weren't provided through the WinG device context. This leaves WinG being useful only for those who want to write code compatible with both 16-bit and 32-bit platforms, while sacrificing some of the functionality and speed they *could* have had using straight 32-bit methods. DIBSection also leaves WinG in the dust by supporting both 8-bit *and* 24-bit DIBs (WinG only handles 8-bit DIBs). To be blunt, DIBSection is WinG without the hacks that came with it.

In Chapter 7, we'll discuss changing the pixel values on an individual basis and how to use those methods, which will show just how useful DIBSection and direct pixel access can be. It will also provide an introduction to image manipulation techniques that could spark new and exciting animation ideas, or just ideas for working with graphics at a lower level.

Ah ... DirectX

Animation-based applications have, in the past, all gravitated to the DOS environment for one reason. They kick! The speed with which your code can send updates to the screen is about as fast as it comes, because you send the data directly to video card memory. Almost immediately , the screen is updated! (Oh...so *that's* why we talked about that boring stuff!). This direct access to the hardware has a rather gruesome caveat in the DOS environment. You had to customize the application for all the devices (the video card being one) that your application would use. Not a pretty sight, but though Windows provided an interface to those devices, it was always too slow for games, so there were no alternatives.

Direct access to the video card combined with coding methods like double-buffering, page flipping and dirty rectangle animation, made screen updates far surpass the capabilities of the Windows equivalent. That is, until **DirectX** (formerly known as the Games SDK) arrived on the scene. The latest step in great Windows animation and game programming makes direct video card access possible under Windows. Hooray!

The only problem is using it from VB. Although Visual Basic is not as quick as languages like C, we can still benefit from some of the great functionality DirectDraw and his cronies will provide us with.

Working with Bitmap Data

After a quick summary of how to work with bitmap data, I guess it's time to talk about what that bitmap data looks like. What I'll go through here is how the Windows DIB appears on disk, what the Windows structures are that organize the information in memory when reading the data (or writing it for that matter) and how this information is encapsulated in the bitmap class, `clsBmp`, to make working with them much easier.

The Windows DIB

Earlier in this chapter, I described briefly how image data was stored on disk. You know how the bitmap pixel data is described as an array of either indices into a color table, or actual RGB color values. Now let's compare 8-bit and 24-bit DIB layout from the perspective of file format information, which means structure.

DIB Layout

The following figure sums up the structural appearance of 8-bit and 24-bit DIB formats on disk. The only difference between the two is the inclusion of a color table in the 8-bit example. So, saved with the Windows DIB is a file header, a bitmap header, an array of color information (if applicable) and an array of pixel information. As you know, pixels are either described by indices into the included color information table, or actual RGB values, in array fashion.

DIB vs DDB structure on disk

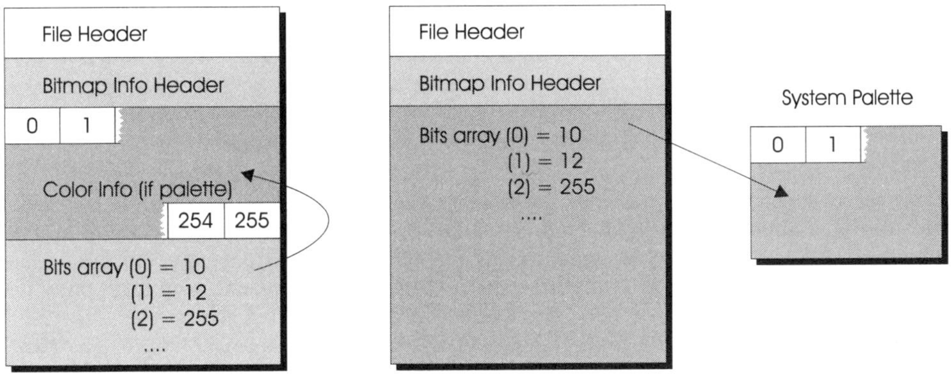

DIB DDB

The reason for using DIBs in the first place was to store image data, but also to include its color information. So what happens to that information on disk when you read the data into memory? Well, we'll get to the actual code in a moment, but the concept is that if the data requires a color table, you'll also need one in memory. If pixels are described by RGB, they'll be read in as part of the image data block in memory. The question is, what happens when the DIB is taken from disk to memory and then converted into a DDB for use with the GDI? Device contexts, whether display or memory DCs, are always compatible with the current display driver, so any DIB read from a file is converted to that format either when it's copied to the display DC, or when it's copied to a compatible DC in memory, since both are device-dependent.

The table on the next page nicely summarizes the steps a DIB makes to a DDB based on its format on disk and the current device driver. Since the 8-bit version includes a color table and is a more complex and common undertaking, I'll be describing how that data is organized when read into memory, using predefined structures and commenting on the differences with 24-bit DIBs where applicable.

Bitmap Colors	Device Support	Process to DDB
8-bit	24-bit	Windows translates each pixel from index into the color table to actual RGB values from that color table. A lookup table is not required by the device context.
24-bit	24-bit	No translation necessary since all RGB values in bitmap are supported by a device context which doesn't require a color table.
8-bit	8-bit	Windows maps the indices for the bitmap's lookup table to that of the device, approximating the closest match when the device palette doesn't support a requested RGB value directly.
24-bit	8-bit	Windows creates indices for each of the bitmap pixel's RGB values by matching that RGB value with the closest RGB value it can find in the palette of the device. At that time, the bitmap is no longer represented by RGB values but indices that point to a (hopefully) close match in the device's color palette.

DIB Structures

First, let me describe the structures that will hold the header information from the DIB. Information is written to disk in the order displayed; first the header information, and then the color and bitmap data. Header information for the bitmap is organized by the pre-defined structures: **BITMAPFILEHEADER**, **BITMAPINFO**, **BITMAPINFOHEADER**, and **RGBQUAD()**.

The **BITMAPFILEHEADER** is the first 14 bytes of the bitmap file format. Notice the **"BM"** signature expected in the **bfType** element of the structure. This is what should tell us that the DIB we're reading is indeed the DIB format we're expecting.

```
Private Type BITMAPFILEHEADER
    bfType As Integer           '"BM"
    bfSize As Long       'file size in bytes
    bfReserved1 As Integer      '0
    bfReserved2 As Integer      '0
    bfOffBits As Long       'where bitmap bits begin
End Type
```

BITMAPINFO information starts at byte position 15. It extends to whatever length holds both the **BITMAPINFOHEADER** structure's length and the array of **RGBQUAD**, the color entries (this is the variable part of the structure size since not all DIBs require a color table). Normally, the definition of this type, **BITMAPINFO**, should not be defined as a fixed array of **bmiColors** from 0 to 255 entries, unless you can be sure that each bitmap being read in will contain that number of palette entries in the file data. I'll explain when this can be changed later, but, for now, I'm assuming the easiest case.

```
Private Type BITMAPINFO
    bmiHeader As BITMAPINFOHEADER   'bitmap information
    bmiColors(0 To 255) As RGBQUAD   'color information
End Type
```

```
Private Type BITMAPINFOHEADER
    biSize As Long          'byte size of structure
    biWidth As Long         'pixel width
    biHeight As Long        'pixel height (+ve/-ve)
    biPlanes As Integer     '1
    biBitCount As Integer   'bits-per-pixel
    biCompression As Long   'compression type
    biSizeImage As Long     'byte size of image
    biXPelsPerMeter As Long    'vertical resolution
    biYPelsPerMeter As Long    'horizontal resolution
    biClrUsed As Long          'number of colors used
    biClrImportant As Long     'number of important colors
End Type

Private Type RGBQUAD
    rgbBlue As Byte         'value of blue
    rgbGreen As Byte        'value of green
    rgbRed As Byte          'value of red
    rgbReserved As Byte     '0
End Type
```

Class Description: clsBmp

Our bitmap class, **clsBmp**, defines these structures used to read and interpret the Windows DIB (or authentic bitmap) file format. The purpose of **clsBmp** is to encapsulate properties and methods that pertain to reading, displaying and working with bitmaps in a single place. Who needs to type in umpteen variables that describe every bitmap that is ever used in an application when you can do it this way and just reuse the class information.

Since I'm taking you away from VB methods in order to learn the low-level aspect of things, as well as to make certain functionality more efficient, there are many API calls that are encapsulated, and some advanced techniques that you sure don't want to have to write from scratch every time you try to use them. This is all part and parcel of the class.

Each aspect of **clsBmp** functionality is described throughout this chapter. Basically, you need to read a bitmap from disk before using it in the display, so **ReadImage** provides that functionality, taking the responsibility away from the **LoadPicture** command. Along with this process is a series of steps to create a place for the bitmap in memory (instead of the picture box control) and to store the color information (described later) for the image being loaded. Throughout the rest of the code, the class provides useful information about the image like size (this list will grow) to make it easier to work with the bitmap and its interaction with the display.

This class is also the beginning of a long line of classes that will interact with each other for each animation sample in this book to come. There will be additional properties and methods that are built on and later altered to fit with the class that you see here in this chapter.

File I/O from VB

Now it's time to get down and dirty with the bitmap bits. This section will only deal with the Windows DIB format for bitmaps data. Showing you how to read in other complex file formats would take a book in itself, because each format requires attention to many details. The purpose here is to show you how to read graphics from disk to memory, for use in your program. The Windows DIB is more than suitable for this purpose.

Reading Binary Data

Now, I'm going to step you through **ReadImage**, mentioned earlier as one of the bitmap classes methods for reading in our bitmap data from a file. This method uses VB methods for file I/O, and the predefined structures discussed in the last section for organizing DIB data and some Windows API calls for allocating the memory to place the bitmap data for later use.

The following steps outline the contents of the **ReadImage** method where we see how to read in bitmap data from VB, with the help of a few useful Windows API function.

1 Open the file for a binary read. The VB **Open** command gives us access to the file, just as well as any API call, so I used it. As the **FreeFile** command is documented, it returns the next free file handle available, so the **fh%** variable is used throughout as our file handle to the **Get** function.

```
nFile = FreeFile
Open m_sBmpFile For Binary As nFile
```

2 Read the first 14 bytes into the **BITMAPFILEHEADER** structure. We know this is always 14 bytes for a standard DIB, so once it is confirmed that this is indeed a standard DIB by checking the value of **bfType**, you can be sure that the rest of **m_bmFileHeader** is filled in with the right values. The read starts at the first byte, specified by the second parameter to the **Get** function, reading the number of bytes in the **BITMAPFILEHEADER**, which is defined by the structure.

```
Get nFile, 1, m_bmFileHeader
```

Checking the value of **bfType** requires a little more effort than just comparing the uppercase value of **bfType** to **BM**. Sure, **bfType** is two characters in length (more accurately two bytes) but it is in binary format, which means that to read each byte as a character, each byte's value must be translated individually to its character value, from their ASCII equivalent.

The value of **bfType**, if it is indeed **BM** in character format, is decimal 19778. Hmmm, that means a lot. Well, in hexadecimal this is 4D42—42 is decimal 66 or character **B**, 4D is decimal 77 or character **M**. OK, that's easy, but reading it and converting in code are two different things. To get the first byte, hex 42, the entire decimal number must be **AND**-ed with a number representing that first byte in the two byte decimal, full of 1s—hex FF. This will return all the bits that were turned on in the first byte (16 bits) to make the hex number 42, decimal 66. Here, I'm using the same technique as discussed in Chapter 2, bitmasking. I return the character value of that byte and put it into **sSignature**:

```
sSignature = Chr$(Val(m_bmFileHeader.bfType) And &HFF)
```

Getting at the second byte is a little less trivial. **AND**-ing the entire decimal value with a number that represents the second byte full of 1s—&HFF00—will return hex 4D00. Close, but no cigar. In decimal terms, this value is 19712. The fact that 4D is in the second byte makes it a higher number, so the next step is to get at just that byte as if it were a single byte number. I want 4D to be the return which is 77 or **M** in character format. This is done by using the modulus (\) of dividing this second byte's value in decimal by the first byte of 1s—hex FF. This too is converted to a character value and added to the **sSignature** string:

```
sSignature = sSignature & Chr$(Val(m_bmFileHeader.bfType And &HFF00&) \ &HFF)
```

Now, I can compare the uppercase string to **"BM"** and get the right answer:

```
If UCase$(sSignature) <> "BM" Then
  ReadImage = False
  Exit Function
End If
```

> **Generally, if one of the elements of this structure gives you unexpected results while you're testing your code, you've either got a `Long` where an `Integer` should be in the `Type` declaration (or vice versa) or the data you're reading is not what you're expecting.**

3 Read in the **BITMAPINFO** structure. Following with the previous step, the next **Get** command will read starting at the byte following the **BITMAPFILEHEADER**. As for the declarations in **clsBmp**, the size of the **BITMAPINFO** structure is 40 bytes for the **BITMAPINFOHEADER** structure and another 4 bytes per palette entry. There are 256 items in the fixed **RGBQUAD** array in the **BITMAPINFO** structure, so 4 * 256 is the number of bytes, additional to the first 40, that will be read if **m_bmInfo** is passed as the variable to fill in by the **Get** function.

```
Get nFile, Len(m_bmFileHeader) + 1, m_bmInfo
```

Now, **m_bmInfo.bmiHeader** should have its 40 bytes of information. Also, regardless of whether this is a palettized bitmap or not, the **m_bmInfo.bmiColors()** array will now have 256 entries filled with data. The problem is, this array may not have valid color information because the data read in after **m_bmInfo.bmiHeader** may have been part of the image data. In fact, the only way this will result in valid image data is if the image file has a palette and if the palette has 256 entries.

If the **BITMAPINFO** structure looked like this:

```
Private Type BITMAPINFO
    bmiHeader As BITMAPINFOHEADER   'bitmap information
    bmiColors As String       'color information
End Type
```

Then before the previous step, if **bmiColors** was set to the correct size to receive only the number of bytes that are taken in the file by color information, you would have seen the following steps:

First, get **bmiHeader** portion of **m_bmInfo** to find out the number of colors in the file:

```
Get nFile, , m_bmInfo.bmiHeader
nColors = m_bmInfo.bmiHeader.biClrUsed
```

Second, pad the **bmiColors** string to four bytes for each color, if any color table exists:

```
If nColors = 0 Then
  If m_bmInfo.bmiHeader.biBitCount = 8 Then
    nColors = 256
```

```
    End If
  End If

  If nColors > 0 Then
    m_bmInfo.bmiColors = Space(nColors * 4)
    Get nFile, , m_bmInfo.bmiColors
  End If
```

Not only would this take the file pointer right up to the byte where the image data begins, but it would make it unnecessary to count the number of palette entries being read from the **bmiColors()** array, as I do in **clsBmp**. Since the **RGBQUAD** array has to be fixed if it belongs to a structure, it makes it so easy to read the color table information, the following steps move the file pointer to the image data and I leave the **bmiColors()** array filled with possibly superfluous data (I'll show you how that is addressed later):

```
  If nColors = 0 Then
    If m_bmInfo.bmiHeader.biBitCount = 8 Then
      nColors = 256
    End If
  End If
  If nColors > 0 Then
    sRgbPal = Space(nColors * 4)
    Get nFile, Len(m_bmFileHeader) + Len(m_bmInfo.bmiHeader) + 1, sRgbPal
  End If
```

4 From the **BITMAPINFOHEADER**, get the image size. This value, filled in by the previous step, tells us the number of bytes the image data alone takes up. This is the number of bytes that should be allocated in memory to read in the rest of the data:

```
  nBmpSize = m_bmInfo.bmiHeader.biSizeImage
```

5 Allocate space in memory for the size of the image data. Here's where yet another can of worms is opened. Now we really have to dig into the C-style code to get our image data into memory. You see, up to now, we've just read in small amounts of binary data, and that data is clearly defined by its structures. Now we're talking raw bitmap bits which are just one byte after another of either indices to a color table, or actual RGB values written one after another to the binary file. This can be a rather large amount of information. The largest string variable we can define in VB still has a limit (even in 32-bit) of 64K.

There are Windows API functions that allow us to rent some space, larger than 64K in size, to place data such as this as we read it in. The idea is to get the entire array of bytes representing the bitmap data into the same contiguous block of memory so that it can be copied to the display with integrity. What this is doing, in an abstract sense, is allowing us to create a really big string variable in memory, since VB can't support a string variable that big.

Using the **GlobalAlloc** function found in the Windows library **KERNEL32**, we can rent this space for the bitmap bits. This function returns a handle to the allocated memory (yet another windows object that requires a handle to access it later), which gets stored in **m_hGlobMem**. The first parameter can accept several flags, describing the type of allocation. **GMEM_MOVEABLE** tells the function to allocate moveable memory, which ensures that if Windows needs to shuffle where things are stored in memory, it can. **GMEM_ZEROINIT** ensures that the contents of the memory object are initialized to zero. This way, we know we're not writing on top of garbage and, if we don't write anything, we could figure it out by checking the contents which, if zero, means that it didn't work:

```
m_hGlobMem = GlobalAlloc(GMEM_MOVEABLE Or GMEM_ZEROINIT, m_nBmpSize)
```

We now have an empty block of memory which is the size of the image data for the file that we're about to finish reading. Note that the new memory block is the size of just the image data, but the structures are part of the file.

There's still another step to take here, since the return from **GlobalAlloc** is not a pointer. I used **GMEM_MOVEABLE** as one of the flag settings and the **GlobalLock** function must be used to lock the memory object and return us a pointer to the first byte of that same block of memory. This pointer is returned into the variable **m_ptrGlobMem** and is necessary for other function calls that deal only in pointers to memory addresses, rather than handles to memory objects.

```
m_ptrGlobMem = GlobalLock(m_hGlobMem)
```

> **Notice, once again, the use of bitmasking with the first parameter of GlobalAlloc (see Appendix B). This value can be one of, or a combination of many different bits turned on. GMEM_MOVEABLE and GMEM_ZEROINIT represent the value of two different bit positions and by OR-ing these two, those positions will be flagged to the function.**

6 Calculate byte alignment. Just before we jump from preparing the area in memory for the bits to be read into reading in the data with the **Get** function, we need to figure out one other piece of information about the bitmap file. The bitmap bits are organized with the height and width of the bitmap when displayed in mind, which is why part of the header information includes things like width and height, along with the rest of it.

A scan line is the width of the bitmap, as you would see when it's displayed in a window. Otherwise, the actual bits aren't lined up as we see them; they are linearly stored, one after another, until the end of the binary file. There are as many scan lines as the height of the bitmap and there's a rule about scan line width that you must follow when you're reading in the bitmap for display.

Byte Alignment and Scan Lines

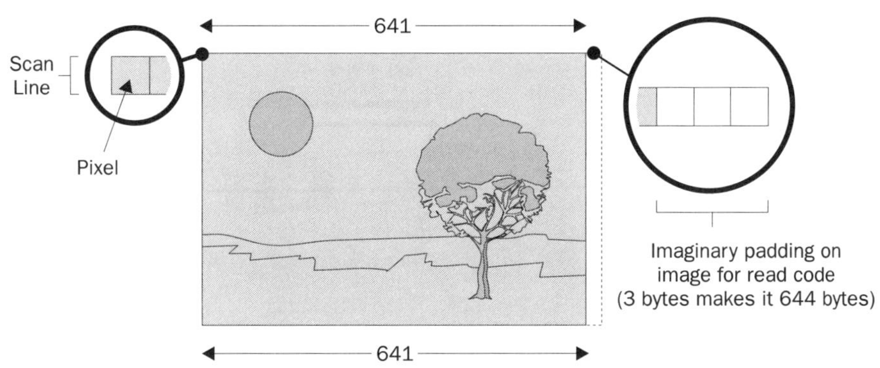

The number of bytes in the bitmap divided by the height of the bitmap (or number of scan lines) returns the width of the bitmap. For the bitmap to be displayed properly, this width must be a multiple of four bytes (or **DWORD** aligned). This is called the **byte alignment**.

In the code, there's a loop that reads in the bitmap data from file. Normally you would want to read in as much data at one time as you can, as each loop grabs a chunk of data using the **Get** function. If the bitmap is aligned on a 4-byte boundary, this is fine, but if it isn't then each scan line must be padded with extra bytes so that it's **DWORD** aligned. In these situations the data should be read in one scan-line at a time, and each read should be padded with the remaining difference between the required byte alignment and scan-line. **nScanPad** holds this difference before the loop is started. In this calculation, **nReadBytes** is set to either the larger chunk (32000 bytes is what I chose for each binary read), or the width of the bitmap.

```
nScanPad = (nBmpSize / m_bmInfo.bmiHeader.biHeight) Mod 4
If nScanPad Then
  'scan line not DWORD aligned, read in scan lines individually and pad
  nReadBytes = m_bmInfo.bmiHeader.biWidth
Else
  'scan line is DWORD aligned, read in larger chunks
  nReadBytes = 32000
End If
```

7 Read in the file. The rest of this code starts the read offset (**ptrGlobOffset**) at 0, which is then incremented after each read, serving as a byte counter for the amount of data we've read from the start of the image data in the open file. The **Get** command reads chunks of the bitmap data, starting where we left off in the last **Get** command, into the read buffer (**sReadBuffer**), which is initialized to the size of the next read chunk. The amount read into the buffer is specified by the byte alignment calculation. Of course, before copying from the read buffer into the allocated memory area, we check to see how much there is to copy, in case we've reached near the end of the bitmap's data (the amount left may vary).

The **CopyMemory()** function is an API function used to move data from one place in memory, to another, using pointers. This is why we needed a pointer to that global area in memory, created with **GlobalAlloc()**. Each time a chunk is read into the variable **sReadBuffer**, it must be copied into the global area in memory. **CopyMemory()** takes the contents of **sReadBuffer** and copies them to the address pointed to by **ptrGlobalMem**. Actually, since we want to keep track of where the memory address with the bitmap starts, **ptrGlobMem** is kept intact and **ptrGlobOffset** is incremented each time. The address where **CopyMemory()** starts to copy the next read of bitmap data must be moved, so that the previous write is not overwritten.

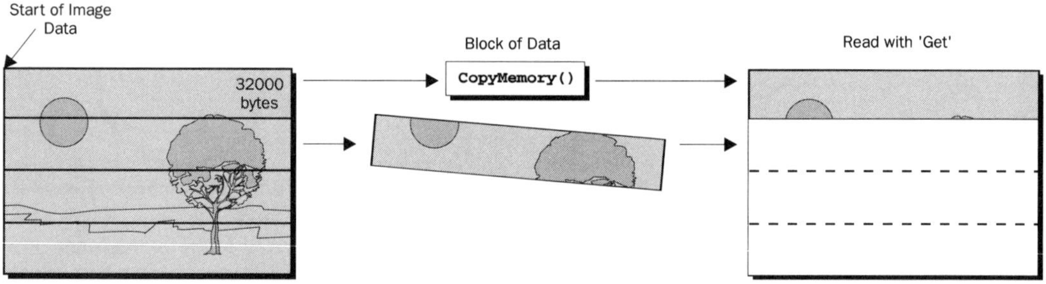


```
' set starting global offset
ptrGlobOffset = 0

' read data into buffer in a loop until all data has been read
Do While nBmpSize > 0
  sReadBuffer = Space(nReadBytes)
```

```
    Get nFile, , sReadBuffer

    If nReadBytes < nBmpSize Then
      nReadSize = nReadBytes
    Else
      nReadSize = nBmpSize
    End If

    ' write data to next position in memory
    CopyMemory m_ptrGlobMem + ptrGlobOffset, sReadBuffer, nReadSize

    ' increment memory offset, including padding if any
    ptrGlobOffset = ptrGlobOffset + nReadSize + nScanPad

    ' decrement size to read in, padding not included here
    nBmpSize = nBmpSize - nReadSize

  Loop

  Close nFile
```

8 Prepare a device context and DDB for the data. This is another method encapsulated in **clsBmp**, which is covered in detail in the next section, along with the process that moves the raw bitmap data into the DDB.

```
  CreateDDB
```

9 Free global memory. Once the data has been safely stored in DDB format from this blob of binary data that's in memory, the globally allocated memory that contains the data as we originally read it must be freed. Both **GlobalUnlock()** and **GlobalFree()** take a parameter of the handle to the global memory object. **GlobalUnlock()** reverses the **GlobalLock()** procedure, freeing the hold Windows had on that memory object. Subsequently, **GlobalFree()** can release that memory, erasing the contents originally placed there:

```
  nRet = GlobalUnlock(m_hGlobMem)
  nRet = GlobalFree(m_hGlobMem)
```

From DIB to DDB

Now, somewhere between reading the bitmap data into memory and erasing that memory, we must have put the image data somewhere where we could access it ... right? The method **CreateDDB** supplied with the **clsBmp** class does just that. It uses some of the concepts for creating memory DCs to hold image data that we've already covered in Chapter 2. However, the catch here is that the data is not being blit from a picture box control to the memory DC. This time, the data has to be moved using another method, which converts it from a DIB to a DDB. When the picture box reads in the bitmap data, it is already converted to a DDB, since it's contained inside a device context. But that would be no fun because then we wouldn't have had the pleasure of feeling cool by reading in the data ourselves! Let's see what happens now.

Creating the DDB

There are a few additional steps here that make this a different process to just creating a memory DC for receiving the image data. Now we're going to be including palettes in our discussion, so I'll put a placeholder where the steps are different and where the discussion will be filled in later on this chapter.

1 Prepare a memory DC and bitmap surface. Using the methods explained in Chapter 2, a memory device context and an empty device-dependent bitmap of the appropriate dimensions are created. The property **hdcDisp** belongs to the bitmap class and stores the display DC that the application is sending data to:

```
' prepare a memory DC
m_hdc = CreateCompatibleDC(m_hdcDisp)
' prepare a bitmap to hold DDB
m_hBmp = CreateCompatibleBitmap(m_hdcDisp, m_bmInfo.bmiHeader.biWidth,
m_bmInfo.bmiHeader.biHeight)
```

The fact that the bitmap object created by **CreateCompatibleBitmap()** is device-dependent was secondary in Chapter 2, but now that you're familiar with the concept of device-dependence, I can get into this in a little more detail. When a memory DC is created, it's created in the same color format as the display device currently supports. The stock bitmap object created with the memory DC is a 1x1 DDB. **CreateCompatibleBitmap()** is a necessary step to filling out the memory DC's dimensions, in order to have a surface area to blit to from another DC. This was how we put the contents of the picture box control's DC into the memory DC, by blitting from one to the other.

In a nutshell, to initialize or change the pixel values of a bitmap area belonging to a DC, there needs to be a surface area containing valid pixels. The fact that the bitmap created is device-dependent is due to the fact that it's selected into a standard GDI device context and those device contexts don't understand data pointed to in memory.

2 Set up the logical palette. In Chapter 2, we didn't do any special palette preparation for our memory DCs because we hadn't broached that subject. Nothing went particularly wrong, but some background things were going on that could offset potential problems with the display of those bitmaps. This opens up a palette discussion which we'll cover in detail in the next section. I'll skip over this part for now, but keep in mind that once the memory DC is ready with the correct dimensions for copying data, the palette would be the next thing that is set up, to ensure that the bitmap's correct colors are reflected in the DC.

3 Copy DIB bits to DDB surface. Normally, when you've created a compatible bitmap, it's selected into the compatible DC in preparation for a call to **BitBlt()** to copy another DC's bits into the new one. This also has to be done so that other drawing functions belonging to the GDI library can be performed on the pixel data of the DC's bitmap object. Notice that we haven't yet selected the bitmap object into the memory DC. That's because we've got a blob of raw image data, stored in a global area of memory right now and these are the bitmap pixels we need to transfer to the memory DC, so that we can do things like blit the data to the display.

The problem is that the data isn't contained in a bitmap object that the memory DC understands and we must use a different method to get the image data into the bitmap object and then selected into the memory DC. We need to copy the DIB to the DDB surface area, which has already been assigned the same size as the image requires (see Step 1), before the **SelectObject()** function can associate the bitmap object with the memory DC. **BitBlt()** won't be able to transfer the data this time, which is why the compatible bitmap isn't yet selected.

The function **SetDIBits()** is used to read data from memory via a pointer to a memory address and copy it into a bitmap area. The function reads the data pointed to by **m_ptrGlobMem** and uses **m_bmInfo** to know when to stop reading from the global area, using the **biSizeImage** element. (Actually, **m_bmInfo** is used for plenty more than that, but we'll talk about the rest in another section, since this function, **SetDIBits()**, is doing a lot more than meets the eye.) The information from memory is copied to the compatible bitmap, **m_hBmp,** one scan line at a time (scan lines are defined by the **biHeight** element). Once the **SetDIBits()** function returns, the DDB pointed to by **m_hBmp** will contain the information that was located in memory from our **ReadImage** method. Now, the DIB turned DDB can be selected into the memory DC, ready for blitting as we did in Chapter 2.

```
nRet = SetDIBits(m_hdc, m_hBmp, 0, m_bmInfo.bmiHeader.biHeight,
m_ptrGlobMem, m_bmInfo, DIB_RGB_COLORS)

m_hStock = SelectObject(m_hdc, m_hBmp)
```

If this were a DIBSection (discussed earlier) instead, the data could be changed and the DC would reflect the changes. In the case of the DDB, no changes to the bitmap data can be made after its selection, but you can draw to the DC surface, on top of the bitmap.

Now we have a memory DC, pointed to by **m_hdc**, associated with the information we read from disk. Essentially, these steps covered what the **LoadPicture** method would do to read an image from disk, only we've saved some overhead by not using the control. But, as with the **LoadPicture** method, we have still performed some inefficiencies in that there was a point in time when two copies of the data were held in memory at once. One was held in a global memory object, the other was copied to the DDB. Of course, this is only temporary until we free some memory, but it's a situation that you won't come across when you're using **DIBSection**. (We'll cover this in Chapter 7.)

Setting and Moving DIB Bits

Now, let's explain what the heck **SetDIBits()** is doing. This is a Windows API function that enables you to copy device-independent bitmap data into a device-dependent bitmap. Since DDBs must be organized in a color format that matches the current display device, there is also a conversion that takes place whereby the function converts the pixel data and its color table if one, into the same format as expected by the DDB. The following line of code is the function call made to **SetDIBits()** from the **CreateDDB** method of **clsBmp**:

```
nRet = SetDIBits(m_hdc, m_hBmp, 0, m_bmInfo.bmiHeader.biHeight, m_ptrGlobMem,
m_bmInfo, DIB_RGB_COLORS)
```

First, let's talk about the DDB and DIB information passed. The **m_hBmp** variable points to the DDB bitmap surface created to store the DIB data, which has not yet been selected into a device context. **SetDIBits()** gets at the DIB image data using a pointer to that block of memory storing the data, **m_ptrGlobMem**, which you'll recall came from the **ReadImage** method.

The function also looks at the **BITMAPINFO** structure, **bmInfo**, to see if there's a color table present, which is where the last parameter comes into play. It can be one of **DIB_RGB_COLORS**, or **DIB_PAL_COLORS**, declared as follows:

```
Private Const DIB_RGB_COLORS = 0
Private Const DIB_PAL_COLORS = 1
```

This parameter doesn't refer to the existence of a color table, but to whether or not a color table that *does* exist holds RGB values (which it will almost always hold) or another set of indices that should point to a logical palette (we'll describe palettes and color later, so hang in there if this doesn't make sense yet). If **bmiColors = 0**, the DIB is assumed to be described by full RGB values for each pixel, rather than an index into a color table, and is read as such.

The third value of **`0`** passed tells the function to start at the first scan line in the bitmap and the fourth (**`m_bmInfo.bmiHeader.biHeight`**) represents the number of lines to scan. Keep in mind that there are two types of Windows DIBs. The array of pixel information can be stored either top down or bottom up. A negative value in the **`biHeight`** element in **`BITMAPINFOHEADER`** indicates that the DIB has been stored bottom-up.

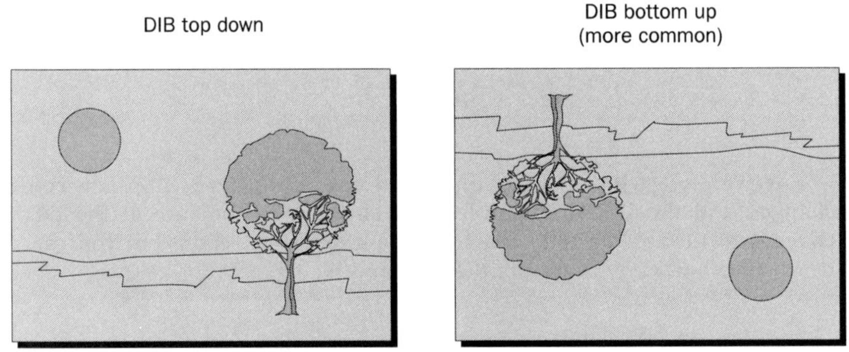

Ah ... now for the first parameter: the device context passed in this example through **`m_hDC`**. If the data is being copied to the DDB which hasn't yet been selected into the DC, what is it needed for? I'll explain part of this now, but the rest should fall nicely in place when we discuss palettes next. Let's assume that the bitmap is an 8-bit DIB with palette information available to the function through the **`BITMAPINFO`** structure. This palette may not be the same palette as the device context is currently using, so the **`SetDIBits()`** function will look to the RGB values it needs for the bitmap and try to map the closest possible indices with the colors available in the DC's palette, because this is the palette the bitmap must use as a DDB.

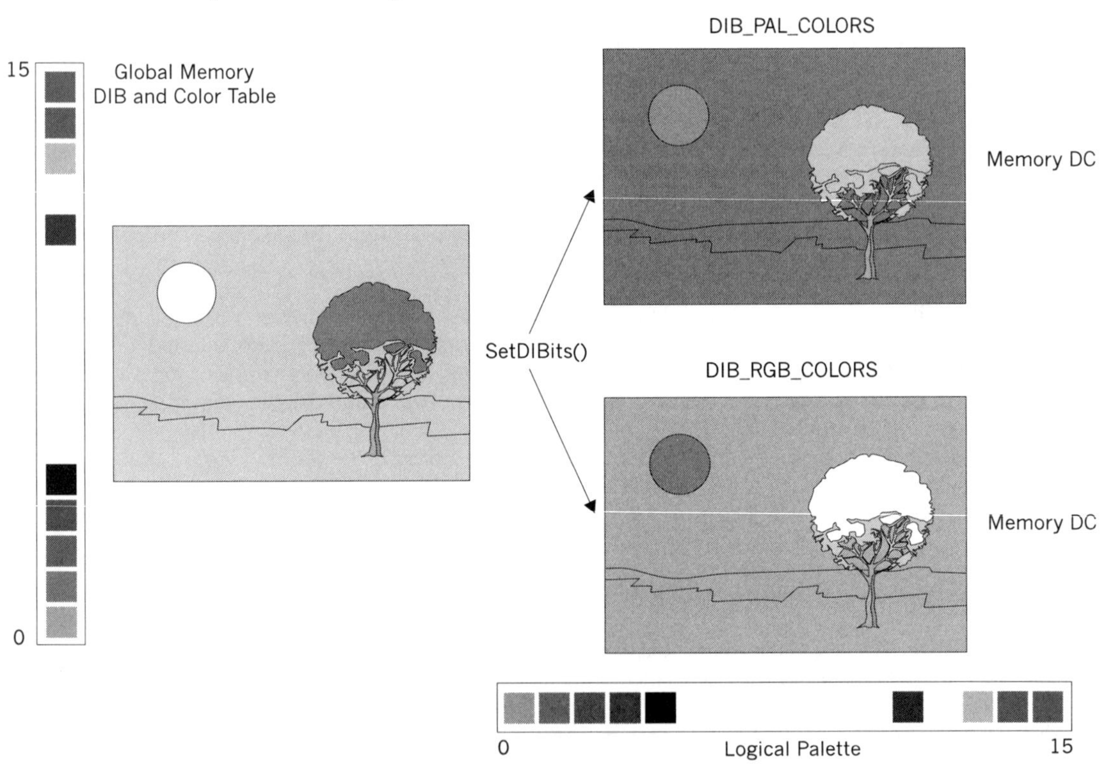

If the last parameter is set to **DIB_RGB_COLORS** then the closest match for each color table entry is found in the DCs color table (or logical palette). Funny things can happen when **DIB_PAL_COLORS** is turned on. Since there is no 'find closest match' going on, the palette entry number in the table is mapped to exactly that color entry in the logical palette of the DC. You want to be pretty sure of that DC palette before using a process like this.

If the palette inside the DC matches the color table of the bitmap (a process you'll see shortly), the mapping from color table to palette is 1:1. If the DIB is 24-bit (no color table), the RGB values have to be mapped to a closely matching color provided by the DC palette, in which case the image can lose significant detail unless the palette is a close fit to the actual shades in the image.

> **We should point out here that now the DIB has been converted to a DDB, there is no conversion necessary when the contents of the memory DC are copied to the display using one of the appropriate blitting functions. These functions require that the data is in the same format (i.e. palettized or not), so this saves time transferring palettes.**

So you think palettes are a pain? Well...um... they are. So is stopping for gas when you're late for a hot date, but-cha gotta do it if ya wanna get there. Naturally, once you've accepted the palette challenge, next time you'll find it's less work. Note that I didn't say *easier* because that's never a guarantee; it's *always* likely to be a pain. To what extent you implement palette handling in your applications really depends on what the application is used for, and also on you, of course. We won't cover all the details in this chapter, but you'll get a glimpse at who the players are in palette-land and then we'll have some fun with them before we get to the serious stuff in later chapters.

Now that you've seen how the Windows DIB is laid out, how it's read into memory using its appropriate structures, and have observed the conversion of the DIB to DDB format, let's backtrack and fill in the missing parts that concern palettes. In the process, I'll give you the dirt on color and how you can have some fun with it!

Palettes and Color References

Windows understands color as combinations of three colors: red, green and blue (RGB). To create one of the many millions of colors in the spectrum, the intensity of each color is specified from 0 to 255, resulting in a different color when all three are combined. If all three colors are given an intensity of 0 (R=0, G=0, B=0) then the absence of color (or black) is generated. Conversely, if all three are at full intensity (all are 255), then the result is white.

Color References

Color values as read by Windows functions are defined in hexadecimal, in a special format known as a **COLORREF**. Color references are used all over the place, even in VB. Take a look at the property window for a form and look at the values for **BackColor** and **ForeColor**. They're written in hex aren't they? If you ever wanted to know how the heck this hex value gets interpreted, and/or created, here's your chance ... read on!

Actually, that hex value can be broken down into structure-like elements. There are four bytes that make up the color value, which makes sense, especially for the RGB values, since a byte can hold a number up to 255 or hex value FF. The color white is defined by the hex value &H00FFFFFF& and black is &H00000000& (or &H0). On the next page, you can see what a colour reference would look like in VB terms if it were a Windows structure :

```
Type COLORREF
        crType as byte
        crBlue as byte
        crGreen as byte
        crRed as byte
End Type
```

The high-order byte, **crType**, describes how the color reference should be interpreted. If **crType** is &H0, the value for **crBlue**, **crGreen** and **crRed** will be interpreted as a value from 0 to 255 for the corresponding color element. If **crType** is &H80, the last three bytes are interpreted as one value, which represent an index into the Windows system colors as set by Control Panel for the desktop. The default **BackColor** (for example) for a new form will show a **COLORREF** of &H80000005& (if the form's **Appearance** property is **Flat**, not **3D**). This tells VB to get the Windows system color at index position &H000005& in the system palette (I'll discuss this one). If you change the value of **BackColor** by selecting the color white from VB's palette for that property, notice the &H8000005& changes to &H00FFFFFF& .

Palette Entries

Color references and palette entries have much in common, yet they're used very differently. The red, green, and blue elements of a **COLORREF** are each **Byte** values, so are **PALETTEENTRY** RGB values. Notice, though, that the RGB values in a **COLORREF** are stored in the opposite order to that of a **PALETTEENTRY**. The **PALETTEENTRY** structure (this really is a structure defined in the Windows API) looks like this:

```
Type PALETTEENTRY
        peRed As Byte
        peGreen As Byte
        peBlue As Byte
        peFlags As Byte
End Type
```

As you'll soon discover, this structure is used with logical palettes, in array format, to store color information in a lookup table of sorts. We'll see that put to use soon enough. However, there's yet *another* way to store color information—using the **RGBQUAD** structure. We discussed this earlier when we talked about saving a bitmap to disk. For comparison purposes, here it is again:

```
Type RGBQUAD
    rgbBlue As Byte
    rgbGreen As Byte
    rgbRed As Byte
    rgbReserved As Byte
End Type
```

This structure was referenced by the **BITMAPINFOHEADER** structure in array format. **SetDIBits()** read this as the color table attached to the DIB and appropriately remapped the color indices to that of the logical palette that was associated with the device context.

Why are there so many ways to store this color information and how are you supposed to know when to use each? Well, the when to know part comes with exposure, because these different color structures are not nearly as confusing as they may seem. When an API function asks for a color reference or a color value, a 4-byte parameter is asked for as a color reference. This means a long value that has either a color value or a requested index. When a bitmap is saved to disk and read from disk, an array **RGBQUAD** structures is used to hold the number of palette entries the bitmap image requires. This is a standard that must be followed, or the image data will not be understood as it should be, just like the way a Windows DIB always has **BM** as the first two characters in the file saved to disk. Lastly, when a palette is created, the **PALETTEENTRY** structure is used to organize the color information and store flags for each color that are used by the palette. We'll be covering this now as we move into a discussion of palettes.

The Hardware/System Palette

First let me introduce you to the system palette, since it plays such a fundamental role in the display. The display device can always generate any combination of RGB values to create any number of colors. The problem comes when we try to display them all at once. When you learned about the display device, you also discovered that not all display modes support all colors. The number of colors that can be displayed is determined by the current video device driver. The programmer must use programming methods in 8-bit display modes to generate the closest possible likeness for a given display. The system palette is the palette that stores the currently available 256 colors that can be displayed if the current mode is indeed palettized.

How the system palette works is fairly straightforward. There are 20 reserved colors that *shouldn't* be changed. These are the colors that the Control Panel settings for the desktop are currently using. In a 256 color palette, these 20 colors reside in the first and last 10 entries, leaving 236 colors free for use by any other window displays currently on the desktop.

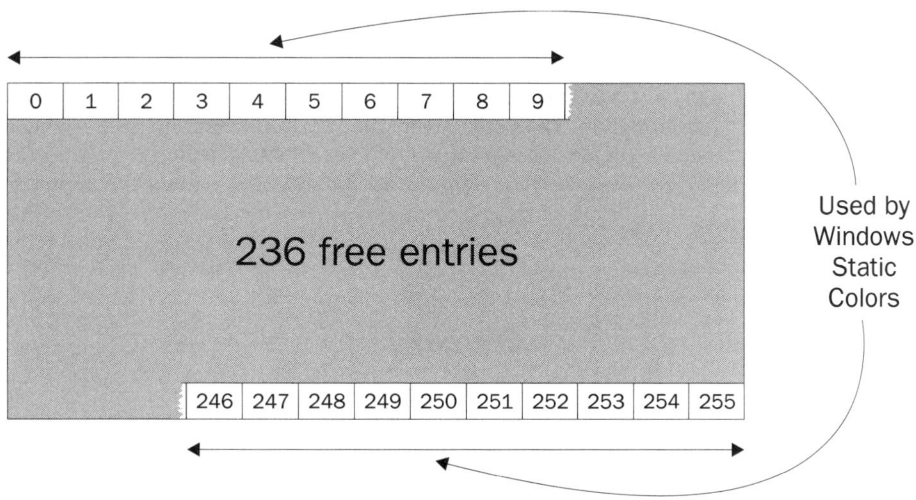

So if many applications are open at once, all displaying different colors, how does the system palette support them all? Well, it doesn't. When a window becomes the topmost window in the desktop, *it* should be the window whose palette is reflected in the system palette, the background windows taking second priority. The Windows Palette Manager takes care of sending the necessary Windows messages to all display device contexts (or, windows) informing them of changes that will or have taken place to the system palette. Since this is the master palette for the entire screen display, any changes to it will affect all windows, even those that don't have the current focus. The important window, however, is the one that has the current focus, i.e. the one the user is using at the moment.

When your application gets the appropriate message from the Palette Manager, you want to respond by telling the system palette what colors *your* window needs to be displayed properly in 256 colors. You can't alter the system palette directly, but you *can* send it a request for new colors, using a logical palette and hope for the best. Let's take a look at logical palettes next.

Creating a Logical Palette

Logical palettes are yet another Windows object that can be selected into a device context. The system or hardware palette is part of the entire physical display, which means that it's used for all windows visible on the screen, not just one. Since each window may require different colors to display their information properly, it seems fitting that they would individually want to keep record of their favorite colors and ask for them whenever they get the focus.

LOGPALETTE

Logical palettes are used to store information about a window or, more accurately, its device context. An array of **PALETTEENTRY** structures is what stores any number of colors the DC needs for display, up to 256 since the system palette doesn't hold more. If the DC were to contain just a single bitmap graphic, this information should reflect how the information on its bitmap surface should be displayed. To describe the use of the logical palette, I'll walk through the code used in the **clsBmp** class module that gathers the DIB's color information, creates a logical palette from it and then selects that logical palette into the DC that will house the bitmap data.

After the image data has been read into memory and the compatible bitmap where it is destined has been created, a logical palette is created from the bitmap's color information in the array of **RGBQUAD** structures. From the **CreateDDB** method of **clsBmp**, a call to **GetDIBPalette()** is made, which returns the handle to a logical palette:

```
m_hPal = GetDIBPalette()
```

Inside **GetDIBPalette()**, a **LOGPALETTE** variable is created and filled in with the RGB values from the bitmap header information. Let's talk about the **LOGPALETTE** structure, which you haven't seen yet. The logical palette structure uses an array of **PALETTEENTRY** structures to define the actual array of RGB data, but also contains some other information. Here's the contents of **LOGPALETTE**:

```
Private Type LOGPALETTE
    palVersion As Integer
    palNumEntries As Integer
    palPalEntry(0 To 255) As PALETTEENTRY
End Type
```

Much like the **BITMAPINFO** structure does with **RGBQUAD**, the **LOGPALETTE** structure defines a fixed array of **PALETTEENTRY** structures from 0 to 255. There may not be 256 entries needed for the palette we are about to create, so this means that there will be superfluous information in any remaining, unfilled array items. This isn't really a problem, but I'll explain how this affects the use of the palette further on.

The **palVersion** element is set to **&H300** because this value works for both Windows 3.x and both Windows NT and 95 (it defines the version compatibility of the palette structure). The number of palette entries used is stored in the **palNumEntries** element, but it originates from the bitmap header information's element, **biClrUsed**. I perform a check in the code that checks the bit-count of the image data (using **biBitCount** from **BITMAPINFOHEADER**) to see if a palette is going to be used. If the bit-count is 8 (for 8-bit), the **palNumEntries** variable is set to 256. The reason for this is that if there are 256 colors used in the image, the **biClrUsed** value will be 0 instead of 256, so this has to be caught in order to ensure that the array is filled with the RGB values needed for the logical palette. Here's the code for this test:

```
Dim logPal As LOGPALETTE

  logPal.palVersion = &H300
  logPal.palNumEntries = m_bmInfo.bmiHeader.biClrUsed

  If Not logPal.palNumEntries Then
    If m_bmInfo.bmiHeader.biBitCount = 8 Then
     logPal.palNumEntries = 256
    Else
     MsgBox "This bitmap is not an 8-bit image and will not use a palette!"
    End If
  End If
```

Here's where the palette entries are set, the RGB values coming directly from the RGB values of the **RGBQUAD** array of the **BITMAPINFO** structure. The order of the elements in each structure may be different, but using the name of each element, this almost seems transparent:

```
For nIndex = 0 To logPal.palNumEntries - 1
  logPal.palPalEntry(nIndex).peRed = m_bmInfo.bmiColors(nIndex).rgbRed
  logPal.palPalEntry(nIndex).peGreen = m_bmInfo.bmiColors(nIndex).rgbGreen
  logPal.palPalEntry(nIndex).peBlue = m_bmInfo.bmiColors(nIndex).rgbBlue
  logPal.palPalEntry(nIndex).peFlags = PC_RESERVED
Next nIndex
```

PALETTEENTRY Flags

The last element of the **PALETTEENTRY** structure is **peFlags**, which can take on several possible values. It can be 0, or one of the following:

```
Public Const PC_RESERVED = &H1
Public Const PC_EXPLICIT = &H2
Public Const PC_NOCOLLAPSE = &H4
```

The goal of creating a logical palette is not just to select it into a device context, but to tell the system palette to use the colors in a DC's palette. If all goes well, every entry should ideally be updated to the system (as you'll see later, this rarely happens) but there are some rules that you should follow as the entries are sent to the system palette. That's where these flags come in. Generally, when you're creating the palette, all entries will take on the same flag setting, but you can set them individually.

If **peFlags** is **0**, when the palette entry is mapped to the system palette, the closest matching color will be sought and that index will be the one used for the specified color. **PC_NOCOLLAPSE** changes this process so that the palette entry will look for an empty system palette entry first. If it doesn't find one, it looks for the closest matching color. In both of these cases, other logical palettes that are mapped to the system palette subsequent to this one will be able to use the colors that this palette updated to the system (which means other logical palettes can map to these new system palette entries), but **PC_RESERVED** changes this, since this setting for **peFlags** makes the palette entry unavailable for other logical palettes to map to. The setting **PC_EXPLICIT** works differently than all other **peFlags** settings in that, in a way, it maps the system palette back to the logical palette. The values for **peRed**, **peGreen** and **peBlue** are now no longer considered as an RGB color because the low-order byte is used to point to a palette entry in the system palette (this flag is used if you want to see the contents of the system palette in the logical palette you create).

You probably noticed that **peFlags** is set to **PC_RESERVED** in the example for this chapter. There's a reason for this. **AnimatePalette()**, the Windows API call that we'll be using to have some palette fun, only works with those palette entries that are reserved, i.e. those can't be mapped to by other palettes that try to do so. I'll get into that when we talk about the code that works with palettes.

After all this preparation, transferring image color values to palette values and setting up the flags, we're ready to actually create the palette. Filling the structure simply increases the palette's values, but the **CreatePalette()** Windows API function is what will return us an object handle (there's that object handle again) to the new logical palette, which is what is used in numerous calls to the Windows API, to use them. In this case, the handle is returned by the **GetDIBPalette()** function to the calling procedure as shown earlier:

```
GetDIBPalette = CreatePalette(logPal)
```

Creating a new logical palette simply allocates a new Windows palette object, and as all other objects are, this one too is accessed via a *handle*. The handle value is returned to **m_hPal**, which we'll use to access the logical palette.

Working with Palettes

Now that you understand what system and logical palettes are, and how the logical palette can be created from the color table for a DIB (though you can probably see it is also possible to create a palette of your own invention too), it's time to get working with those palettes. This may seem pretty straight forward, but it can get pretty scary at this point. It's easy to create a logical palette and make sure that the DC you copy the bitmap into reflects it, but it's not so easy to get the system palette to reflect all of this.

Selecting a Palette

When a device context is created, it starts out with some default objects that can be replaced programmatically. The palette object is one of them. The logical palette we just created doesn't do us any good unless we use it by associating it with a DC (this can be a display or memory DC). The reason this is done before the call to **SetDIBits()** is so that an appropriate logical palette would be used for mapping the colors from the DIB to the DDB. When we discussed the mapping of color information from the DIB to the DDB, I said that the DC was used as a reference for what colors were available and the diagram demonstrated a simple example using just four colors. The number of colors in the DIB information and the DC actually may not be the same, depending on the situation.

The palette object that the DC starts with at its inception is the one that the system generates and definitely not the one that our bitmap needs unless we're really lucky. (If you feel *that* lucky, you ought to be in Vegas rather than reading this book!). You need to choose another more appropriate palette if you want to see the colors in the image data properly. The process of getting the color information and bitmap bits from memory as a DIB into DDB format and associated with a device context is done with the **SetDIBits()** call alone. The only catch is that a palette matching the colors in the DIB should be available for a good match.

As with other GDI objects, palettes are 'selected' into a DC using an API function. Rather than the generic **SelectObject()** function, **SelectPalette()** can be used for palettes. Unlike bitmap objects, a palette object can be selected into more than one DC, so that each one can share the same colors. Any changes made to that logical palette will affect all DCs it's currently selected into, thus updating all images. We need to go through one more step before the call to **SetDIBits()**

will work. When **SetDIBits()** creates a DDB, it doesn't *exactly* use the memory DC's palette to map the DIB's colors. It expects the system palette to also reflect the same colors as the DDB it is created (device-dependent bitmaps reflect the current display mode). For this reason, the logical palette must be 'realized' by the system beforehand. The following two functions take care of both of these steps in preparation for the **SetDIBits()** call:

```
m_hOldPal = SelectPalette(m_hdc, m_hPal, False)
nRet = RealizePalette(m_hdc)
```

The call to **SelectPalette()** takes three parameters. The first is the DC into which to select the palette. The second is the palette handle and the third, a **True/False** value. When it's **False**, as shown in the code sample, the system palette is recognized as a *foreground* palette, not to take second to any windows without the current focus. That means that if another application had the focus and its palette was mapped to the system palette, when your application gets the focus, you want first priority to map to the system palette. Since the system palette is probably full, somehow the system needs to be told that it's full with values that are not valid for the window with the current focus. If this flag is set to **True**, your logical palette will be mapped to the system as a second priority to the current window with the focus.

The next call to **RealizePalette()**performs the mapping to the system palette. The function takes a DC and maps the DC's logical palette to the system, based on the setting for each entry in **peFlags**. As you can probably guess, there won't always be 256 free entries that the system palette can spare for this process. That's why this whole process of using palettes and updating the system palette needs to be intelligently handled so that you address the possibility of not getting all the colors you want when **RealizePalette()** is called. Don't laugh it off quite yet, the next section deals with some of these issues.

Palette Mapping Issues

Now that you know the basic steps of creating and realizing a palette for the first time, it's time to discuss what can go wrong. There are a few other things that you need to consider, depending on the situation. We'll go through a few of these now and explore them some more in later chapters when we create some graphics-heavy applications.

Using multiple bitmaps

In this example, there is only one graphic displayed at a time, so to realize that graphic's palette to the system doesn't conflict internally with other graphics you might want to display. The TV bitmap is generated with the static system colors (red, black, blue, gray) and so doesn't add any further requirements to the palette the bitmap requires. When more bitmaps are used, it's important that they reflect the same palette in the memory DC, so that when they are copied to the display, no fighting takes place over the valuable system palette entries. This would be called a **palette flash** and I'll talk more about handling this with multiple graphics in the next chapter.

Palette message handling

This refers to notifications about changes to the system palette. Primarily, the application needs to know when it becomes the topmost window, so that it can yell to the system palette, "Hey, pick me! Pick my logical palette now!". In this chapter's example, VB's paint event is sufficient for notifying us of such changes. Each time a paint event is triggered, not only do I repaint the bitmap (since it's not persistent in the picture box, I need to do this), but I also re-realize the display's logical palette. This is done in the Blit method of **clsBmp** in this sample:

```
m_hOldPal = SelectPalette(m_hdcDisp, m_hPal, False)
nRet = RealizePalette(m_hdcDisp)
```

```
nRet = StretchBlt(m_hdcDisp, 0, 0, m_nDispWidth, m_nDispHeight, m_hdc, 0, 0,
m_bmInfo.bmiHeader.biWidth, m_bmInfo.bmiHeader.biHeight, SRCCOPY)
```

Juggling available system palette entries

There's aren't always as many free entries as you may think. Already, due to the existence of the 20 static system colors, your palette entry positions have been cut down from 256 to 236. (There are ways to override the system colors, but this would affect default window appearances and should only be used under special circumstances.) Even worse than the 20 entries already lost, other logical palettes may have requested positions in the system palette. Priority is always given to the topmost window's logical palette, but if there are several picture box controls on the same form and all of these are device contexts that use logical palettes for *their* contents, it becomes unlikely that all three logical palettes for this form will be able to share the system palette. While a closest match is sought for the later calls to **RealizePalette()** for one of these picture box controls, the palette flash is inevitable. Once they settle into their mapped system entries, after the flash, there's a calm display. However, all of the images will likely not appear as they were intended.

Palette mapping speed

This refers to the need for translation (or not) from logical palette indices to system palette indices. Since the system palette reserves the first and last ten entries for the Windows static colors, the logical palette entries may not end up in the same index position as they were in *its* structure. An identity palette, which we'll create in Chapter 6, aligns the system colors to the logical palette to be used. This means that if your palette was supposed to be 256 colors, it will be truncated to 236 from the last entries, so that the 236 that would have made it to the system anyway are actually the 236 now inside the logical palette. This process happens regardless of the mapping procedure (except in very special cases), and actually helps improve the blitting speed if it's done in the memory DC already, so that it's an exact copy of what should have mapped to the system during a **RealizePalette()** call.

Palette Animation Techniques

Who says application development in 8-bit display mode can't be easy? This next code sample will show that a single function call can make a single graphic image dance. You've seen some of the basics about using palettes (and I *do* mean *some*), enough so that I can show you how to have a little fun with them. Call it an entertaining prelude to the more complicated talks we'll be having later. You can create some pretty interesting effects using palette-related functions: Though it *does* depend on the colors in your bitmap, effects that simulate things like lightning and radiation, or simple color cycling, each example using a single image.

Before I fill your mind with the 'how-to' of each animation, let's review what we should do in preparation for these single-image animations, so there's no mistake about what we've done so far. Here's the step summary:

1. Load an image into memory, along with its color information.
2. Create a logical palette from the color information.
3. Select the logical palette into a memory DC.
4. Realize the palette so the system palette reflects it.
5. Copy the image data (as a DIB using the correct system colors) into the compatible bitmap, and select it into the memory DC.

6 Select the logical palette into the display DC in preparation for blitting to it from the memory DC.

7 Realize the palette so the system palette reflects it before blitting.

8 Blit from memory DC to display DC.

Each time the application window gets a **`Paint`** event, the Blit method of **`clsBmp`** is called. This routine realizes the palette of the display DC, **`picBlit`**, before blitting to repaint the screen display. This ensures that our palette is reflected (hopefully all entries) in the system palette before we display the graphic each time. We do this because we're not sure whether the **`Paint`** event was called after another window was displayed (thus the system palette may not currently reflect ours). Now let's see how the **`AnimatePalette()`** Windows API function works with this methodology of updating the system palette.

AnimatePalette()

When **`RealizePalette()`** updates the system palette with the logical palette specified, messages are sent to other windows telling them to handle the palette change. Since those windows are not topmost, they must accept the new palette entries as is. This is where that chain-reaction of color updating can be triggered, also known as **a palette-shift**. Enter **`AnimatePalette()`**, an alternate method for updating the system palette entries.

The function name **`AnimatePalette()`** is a little misleading. It doesn't, in fact, perform any fantastic feats of animation before our eyes, at least not unless we tell it to, as in this example. What it *does* do is update the system palette directly, bypassing the usual steps through logical palette realization, *immediately* updating all colors in the current display that were pointing to the changed palette entries (see below). To make this call to **`AnimatePalette()`** possible, a few restrictions apply.

Standard Palette Update

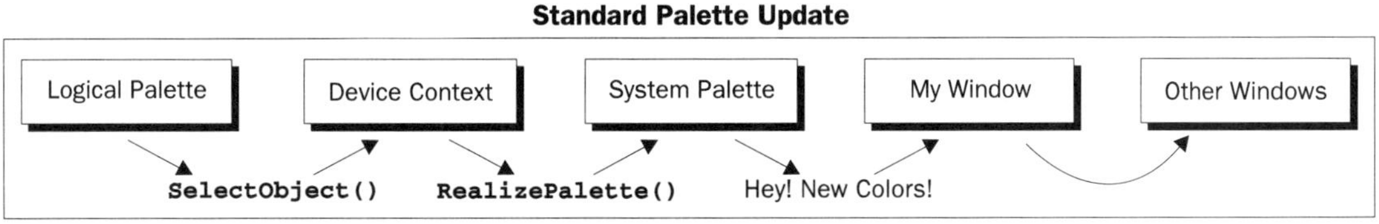

AnimatePalette() Update

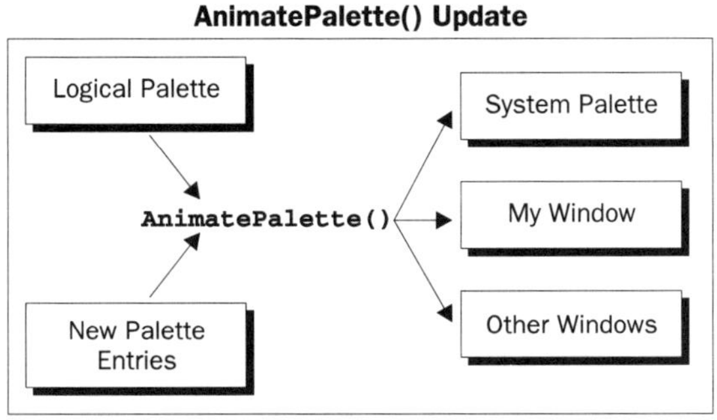

Remember, when the logical palette for this example was first created, each **`peFlag`** element (in the **`PALETTEENTRY`** structure) was initialized to **`PC_RESERVED`**. This flag value signifies that, when linked to a system palette index position, this entry shouldn't be altered by other updates to the system palette. There actually is a point to this restriction. The expectation is that those system palette entries will be altered frequently, which is just what repeated calls to **`AnimatePalette()`** will do. There you have it, just enough information to perform palette animations!

Creating Effects

A single call to **AnimatePalette()** is used for all three animations in this sample. What it does is to take an array of **PALETTEENTRY** structures, with values you set based on what you want to change the current display palette to. It then updates the reserved (**PC_RESERVED** to be exact) palette entries in the logical palette passed to the function. This immediately updates not only the logical palette, but every DC it is selected into and the system palette. Once the system palette has been updated, every color on the screen that is mapped to an index in the system palette will reflect any changes to that system palette entry.

The function is passed a handle to a logical palette that may be selected into several DCs. The second parameter tells the function which palette entry in this logical palette to begin updating palette entries with. The third parameter tells the function how many entries to update, using the array of **PALETTEENTRY** structures passed to the function. The number of palette indexes to update must not exceed the number of entries in the array when added to the starting index. Here's the call that performs this:

```
nRet = AnimatePalette(m_objBmp.hPalette, 0, 256, pal(0))
```

Before the preceding function call is made, the array of **PALETTEENTRY** structures must be filled in with a new set of colors. These entries are filled in, based on the desired result on the display. There are three effects in the sample:

- Lightning
- Radiation
- Color cycling

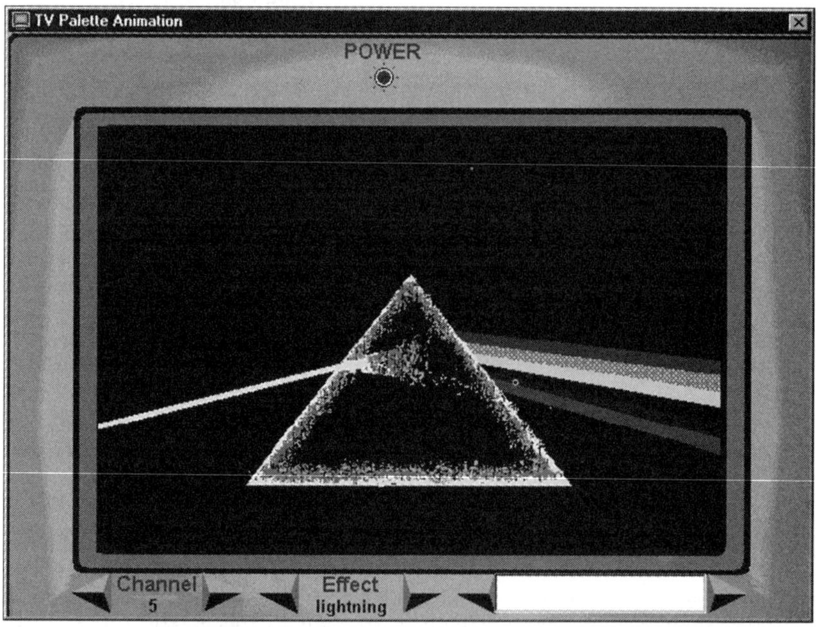

Each of them takes the original palette for the bitmap loaded into the TV display. Depending on the channel selected (this loads one of the five different bitmaps provided with the sample) there will be a different set of colors in the logical palette for the display. No matter what the original palette, the same effects are performed on each bitmap, but you'll notice if you run the sample that the results are very different for each:

When each new bitmap is loaded, its logical palette is backed up into the **PALETTEENTRY** array, **m_palBackup()**, which is defined as an array of 256 items, even if all 256 aren't used. The Windows API call, **GetPaletteEntries()**, is passed the palette handle for the bitmap just loaded and the first item in **m_palBackup()**. This fills in the array and returns the number of palette entries that were in the logical palette in question:

```
nRet = GetPaletteEntries(.hPalette, 0, 255, m_palBackup(0))
```

This array is used as a backup of the original palette, while **AnimatePalette()** is being called which destroys the contents of the original. The reason for this is so that the effects of the animation are not cumulative, which would denigrate the end result. Both the lightning and radiation samples first backup the palette entries to reflect the original palette for the image. I do this because I'm boosting the RGB values, albeit in a random fashion, and without this backup procedure the entire image would eventually be turned to white! Both animations also randomly select an amount to add to the individual RGB values for each entry to be altered. The number of palette entries to alter is determined by the amount specified by the user. Where the two animations differ is in their specification of which palette entry to effect.

In the lightning case, the first *n* number of palette entries, starting at entry 0, is affected:

```
Case FX_LIGHTNING

  ' restore the pal entries to original
  For nColor = 0 To 255
    pal(nColor) = m_palBackup(nColor)
  Next

  For nColor = 0 To m_nAmount - 1
    nAmount = Int(100 * Rnd + 30)

    pal(nColor).peRed = IIf(pal(nColor).peRed + nAmount > 255, 255,
pal(nColor).peRed + nAmount)
      pal(nColor).peGreen = IIf(pal(nColor).peGreen + nAmount > 255, 255,
pal(nColor).peGreen + nAmount)
    pal(nColor).peBlue = IIf(pal(nColor).peBlue + nAmount > 255, 255,
pal(nColor).peBlue + nAmount)
  Next
```

In the radiation case, a random number is selected each time:

```
Case FX_RADIATION
  ' restore the pal entries to original
  For nColor = 0 To 255
    pal(nColor) = m_palBackup(nColor)
  Next

  For nColor = 0 To m_nAmount - 1
    nAmount = Int(100 * Rnd + 30)
    nRndColor = Int(255 * Rnd + 0)

    pal(nRndColor).peRed = IIf(pal(nRndColor).peRed + nAmount > 255, 255,
pal(nRndColor).peRed + nAmount)
     pal(nRndColor).peGreen = IIf(pal(nRndColor).peGreen + nAmount > 255,
255, pal(nRndColor).peGreen + nAmount)
     pal(nRndColor).peBlue = IIf(pal(nRndColor).peBlue + nAmount > 255,        255,
pal(nRndColor).peBlue + nAmount)
  Next
```

I called them *lightning* and *radiation* because of the effects they had on the dark room image. However, you'll notice that when you change the channel, the effects differ per image. In the **COLORCYCLE** sample, the palette entries are only filled with the original palette entries once. From there, the cycling begins and each time through, all palette entries are bumped to the next position, the last one becoming the first. Pretty simple stuff, huh?

```
    Case FX_COLORCYCLE
      If Not flgHasCycled Then
        flgHasCycled = True
        For nColor = 0 To 255
          pal(nColor) = m_palBackup(nColor)
        Next
      End If

      nRed = pal(0).peRed
      nGreen = pal(0).peGreen
      nBlue = pal(0).peBlue
      For nColor = 0 To 254
        pal(nColor).peRed = pal(nColor + 1).peRed
        pal(nColor).peGreen = pal(nColor + 1).peGreen
        pal(nColor).peBlue = pal(nColor + 1).peBlue
      Next
      pal(255).peRed = nRed
      pal(255).peGreen = nGreen
      pal(255).peBlue = nBlue
```

Notice in all samples that it varies per image. Obviously, this type of animation is best performed in controlled environments where you know what the image and/or palette is and what to expect from the alterations. Picture a castle scene, a dark sky and random thunder crackling in the distance as the randomized lightning animation strikes! All with one bitmap!

Summary

You'll be working with palettes again and again throughout the book. Unfortunately, palletized environments are still a very real likelihood that must be addressed in virtually every application environment, especially those that use images. See what other trickery you can achieve by changing the way the palette entries are changed (don't forget to try different graphics). The sky's the limit!

```
rivate Declare Function GlobalFree Lib "kernel32" (ByVal h
rivate Declare Function GlobalLock Lib "kernel32" (ByVal h
rivate Declare Function GlobalUnlock Lib "kernel32" (ByVa
--copying bitmap bits
 copies a global block of data into global memory
rivate Declare Sub CopyMemory Lib "kernel32" Alias "RtlM

--copies global block of data in      B
rivate Declare Function SetDIB        "gdi32" (ByVal m_hd
 ByVal hBitmap As Long, ByVal nStart      As Long, ByV
 ByVal lpBits As Any, lpBI As BITMAPI      ByVal wUsa

--blits DC to DC
rivate Declare Function BitBlt Lib "gdi32" (ByVal hDestDC
rivate Declare Function StretchBlt Lib "gdi32" (ByVal hDes

--palette methods
rivate Declare Function CreatePalett      "gdi32" (lpLogPa
rivate Declare Function SelectPalette      "gdi32" (ByVal m
rivate Declare Function RealizePalette Lib "gdi32" (ByVal r
rivate Declare Sub AnimatePalette Lib "gdi32" (ByVal hPal

--device context methods
rivate Declare Function SelectObject Lib "gdi32" (ByVal m_

rivate Declare Function CreateCompatibleBitmap Lib "gdi32
rivate Declare Function DeleteObject Lib "gdi32" (ByVal hC

rivate Declare Function CreateCompatibleDC Lib "gdi32" (B
```

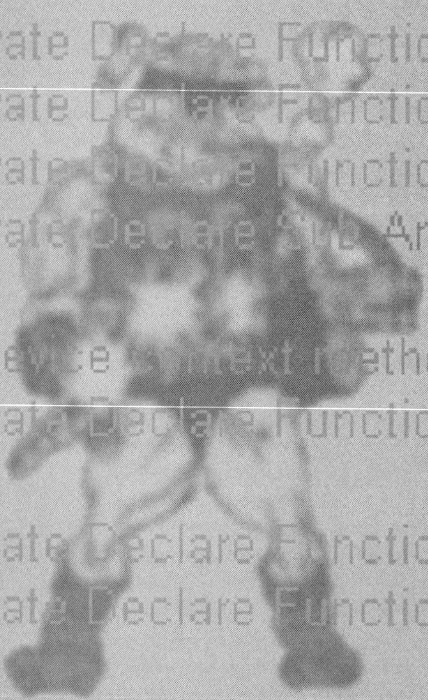

Chapter

4

Graphical Magic

This is where we leave our novice's hat behind and become stud-like VB programmers. The topics I've covered so far should have prepared you for further exploration into each area of animation so that you can create stunning new tricks for your audience. By now you should be comfortable with the following concepts:

- VB4 graphics capabilities
- Using the Windows API
- Bitmap graphics
- Palette basics

So what are we going to do now? I'm glad you asked. For our first actual project, we're going to create a demonstration program. The sample we'll create is a subset of one I wrote for a real project and should serve as a healthy example of how you can use VB to implement a visually-slick graphics presentation for use in advertising tools, tutorials, or for anything else.

In this example, we'll see the main elements of a program that will demonstrate the key capabilities, all with the use of bitmap graphics. In the process, movement, visual transitions and other effects are performed on the graphics to create some stunning results.

The class modules **`clsMem`** and **`clsBmp,`** that we created in preliminary form in previous chapters, are about to become two of the fundamental classes supporting the rest of the book's code samples.

Both of these classes have really been buffed-out since you last saw them in Chapters 2 and 3, so I'll have to walk through their new functionality. Following that, I'll describe some new classes for this chapter's animation techniques:

- **`clsMove`**: sliding movement
- **`clsRectFX`**: transitional rectangles
- **`clsBrushFX`**: dissolving effects

As I lead you through the planning process for this graphical application, I'll point out some of the things to look out for. Then we'll get to the juicy Windows programming, stuff like creating movement, wipes, transitions and special effects. The hot topics we'll cover are:

- Movement algorithms
- Rectangular transitions
- Dissolves using brushes

Oh, and one more thing. I hate to put a damper on the proceedings, but an important part of this project is the discussion of yet another way to handle palettes for an application that uses graphics and requires a variety of colors to be displayed at different times. Not only is there a new palette class, **`clsPalette`**, but there's also a whole thought process involved here that requires careful planning unless you want to spend days on bitmap palettes—uhm, like I did. You'll see how this works by the end of this chapter.

Demo Groundwork

Before I break into the chapter code, you'll need a summary of what this project actually does. Don't overlook the fact that there *is* a planning process for creating *any* application. I'll be walking through the steps that built this code sample, but keep in mind that you can also reuse this planning philosophy for the development of any other type of application.

There were certain assumptions that I was able to make as the programmer on the project and there will always be shortcuts that you'll take to make the development process as fast as possible. In reality, once the first acceptable assumptions are out of the way, you can start coding like crazy, but you'll still be on the lookout for other shortcuts that you can gleefully latch on to as the process continues.

Planning a Script

A demonstration program is a unique application in that it requires a very specific sequence of scripts to portray the information you want to get across. Scene by scene, each script must be laid out, considering restrictions like disk space and available coding methods. Here are the first questions I would ask myself before I started to plan each script in depth:

- What is the programming environment capable of supporting?
- What code have I already written?
- How much time do I have?

Luckily, VB isn't as restrictive as some other environments that support multimedia and graphics programming. VB alone may not have the best graphics support or mathematical speed, but you always have the flexibility to add a DLL call here or there to help out with these requirements. I can't really think of an application that can't be written in VB, so restrictions are more likely to fall under the previously written code and time-constraints heading.

Unless you have some really great sample code, the first time you try a new coding concept, hours can blend into days... weeks... It's very difficult to plan your schedule when you're trying something new. You're almost sure of underestimating the time that you need, but hopefully *your* job will be easier than *mine*—what with all these cool classes in your hands and a detailed description of how they work to boot!

The chapter's sample is condensed, compared to the complete sample which you can see by running **`\Apps\Crimes\Crdemo.exe`**. *Actually, while I was working on the longer version of the demo, I didn't get a chance to include the same number of visual effects that I used for the chapter's code sample–content came first. This is just another example of how the frills get cut when you need something to be done yesterday!*

Making a list of the coding effects you'd *like* to perform on the graphics used can't hurt. Then you can start planning the scenes before you figure out which scene will use which effect, and so on. The demo contains scripts that either describe and summarize main points about the program it's demonstrating, or display scenarios for use within the actual program and results from using the program. In this demo, scenes are assembled from the following components:

- A background display
- A collection of foreground bitmaps
- Instructions coordinating the scene

The background is the stationary area over which the rest of the component display bitmaps are shown. How the components are displayed is the subject of this chapter, be it with movement or transition effects. The demo has two main categories for a background scene. One is the use of a Power Point presentation flare, which is used for those scripts whose content is the main issue of the program. The other category uses the program interface as a background, but scripts that follow each other build on the last script's final display. Since the demo is rather long, a subset of this will be used to demonstrate the code required to implement all of its aspects. Then you can run the finished product to see where it all fits in.

The Sample Demo

Let me give you a quick summary of the content that goes into the sample demo. Though each type of script requires a different activity to be performed on the featured graphic and different functionality to make the script work as planned, there are some common denominators for each. They must both start with a background display that is present before other bitmap activity is implemented, thus demonstrating the animation of graphics. They must both load their respective graphics at the start of the script and then release them at the end.

In this demo, the background display is either initialized by loading a bitmap or is the product of a previous scene's completion. The bitmap background used for the presentation-style scripts is a solid royal-blue bitmap tiled into the display area. On top of this solid display background, other interface graphics are copied to build the program content scripts and, where appropriate, the updated display is copied to memory and stored as the new background scene. In some instances, the background is further altered by a scene and is then used as the backdrop for the next screen, making a previous button not quite worth the trouble.

The following screenshot gives us a peek at the appearance of the presentation scripts in this demo sample:

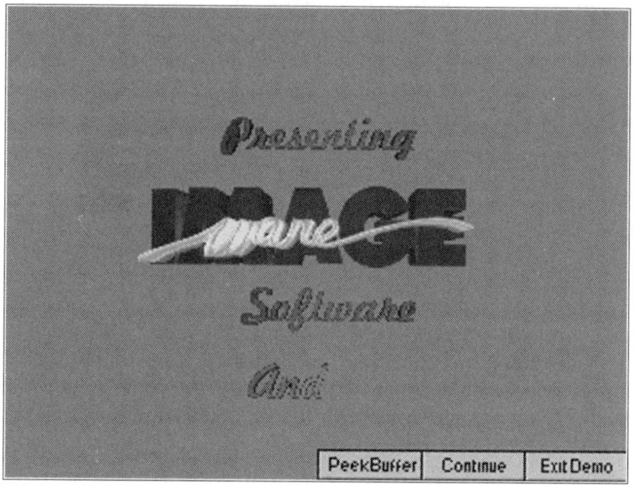

The script graphics used to build the scene are text bitmaps. Using a bitmap rather than printing text to the screen allowed me to use the classes that manipulate bitmap graphics throughout the demo. Furthermore, text created externally with a dedicated drawing program is much more impressive than just a printed font and, although it means using more memory to display the text, 256 color images don't really take up that much space. Besides, VB controls flicker painfully when they're moved across the screen, which forced me to do all graphics work in memory using a double buffer.

This next screenshot shows another scene in the demo. This one displays interface functionality.

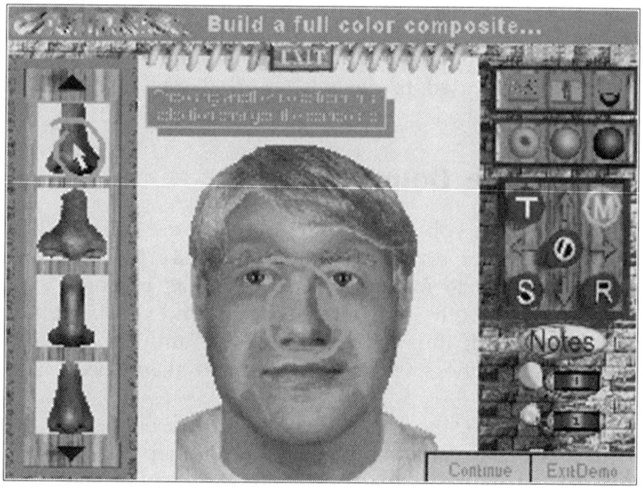

The graphics in this case aren't text but small pieces of the interface that are copied into place when called for. Then there's the bitmap cursor, which demonstrates the cursor movement and also some clicks to lead you through the demonstration.

Each of these sample scenes require different considerations for gathering the graphics and for how they're to be displayed. In the next section, we'll look at the work that went into this part of the planning process.

Gathering Artwork

Having an idea of what can happen to each graphic in a given scene is paramount to creating that graphic. As we discussed in Chapter 1, specifically with the dragon animations, as we create each image, we must consider different issues based on its background, its movement and any other effects to be implemented. Once you have a script and a list of graphics for each scene, you can start to make plans. You'll need to consider the issues of:

- Size
- Background
- Manipulation

The size of the graphic should always represent the content that it has to offer the scene and the smallest bounding rectangle should always be its size. The background of the graphic depends on what it should look like over the scene. Recall from our discussions in Chapter 1 that the bitmap of each dragon frame was either cut from a black background (to match the black background of the scene) or from the castle picture, which meant restricting the dragon frame to a specific position on screen. This leads me to the manipulation of each graphic or, in other words, whether or not it moves over the background.

Take the first screenshot for example. The four bitmap graphics that say *'Presenting Imageware Software and'* are just rectangular graphics:

PRESENT.BMP

IMGWARE.BMP

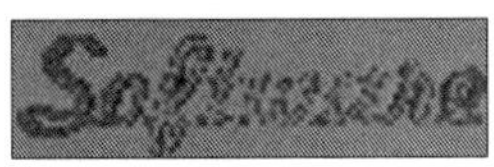
SOFTWARE.BMP

AND.BMP

Notice that the background of each graphic matches the background color of the scene. Remember, if the background of the scene is a solid color, we have more leeway with the foreground graphics. In this first scene, the four bitmaps slide across the screen to their center position, but you can't see the rectangle because the background colors are identical.

Now, let's look at another scene. In the following examples, you see the transition from scenes 1 through 3, the background and display area. By peeking at the buffer (displayed in the top-left and bottom-left of each example), you can see that the background for scene 3 is created from the graphics used in scene 2—but only a portion of them. This means that part way through the script, the display was backed up to represent the background (you'll see the code for this when I describe the new **`clsMem`**).

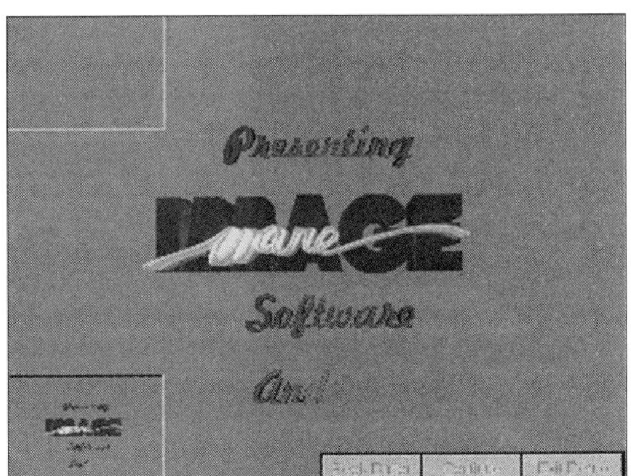

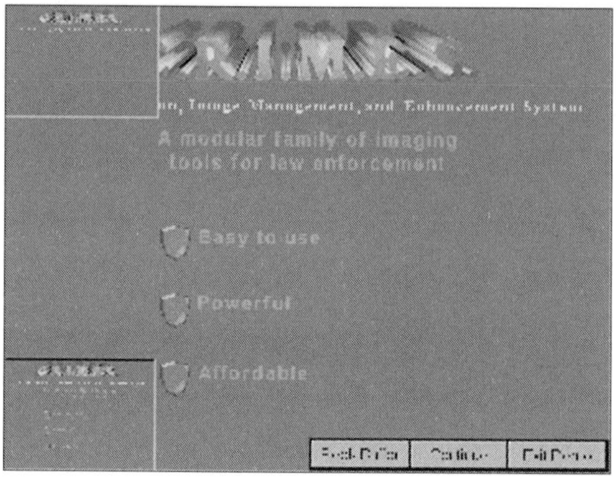

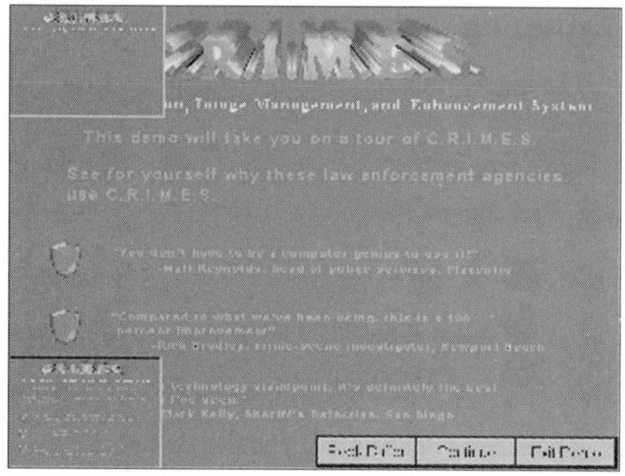

We also took into consideration the exact positioning of graphics on the screen. Here you can see another background that was built from a scene in the demo (**Script_5** in the demo, the functionality of which we'll describe later).

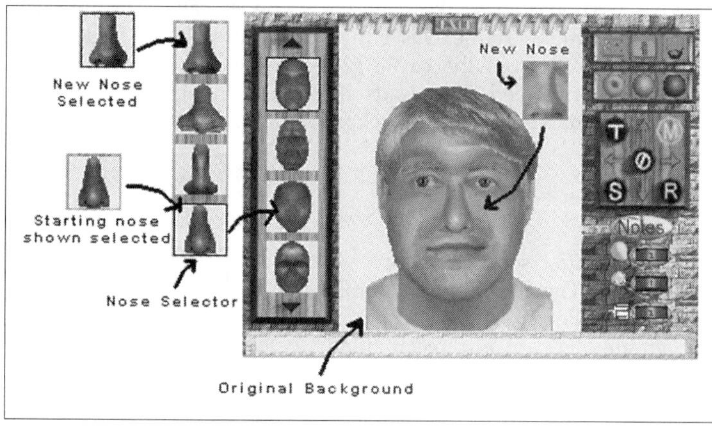

From this, you can see that when the user clicks on a nose on the scroll bar to the left, the face is updated with that nose. The demo does this by replacing the rectangle that represents the nose bitmap on the face. The rectangle must be big enough to cover the nose that was beneath it, which is obviously a hard-coded plan for the demo. So the rectangle that the new nose is cut from is whatever the face is going to be. Since the nose won't be moved, this is better than using a masked bitmap. The trick here was creating the bitmaps. We took a series of screenshots from the actual face image while running the program. This ensures that any new component, when placed over the top of the previous scene's, would always cover the desired area—perfectly.

So, I hear you cry, what about masking techniques? Well, actually, we only need to do this in one area—with the faked cursor bitmap, which we have to move across several scenes in the demo, scenes which don't have a solid color background. The masking capabilities we used in Chapter 2 are easy to implement in this case and you'll be happy to know that the new bitmap class encapsulates the masking of graphics nicely. For all the times I had to look up the raster operations for blitting a transparent graphic, I can (and you can) now rest easy. Here we show the components of one of the scenes that used the moving masked cursor:

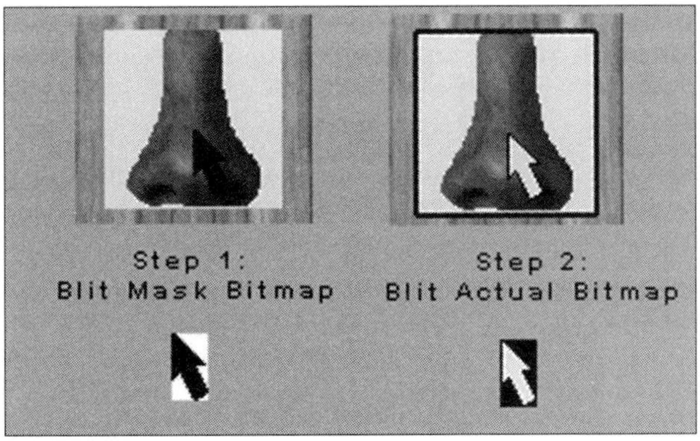

In this section, we've summed up the different graphics methods that are used in the demo, for each bitmap and scene. Now, we'll take a look at the new and updated classes that make the rest happen.

Handling Palettes

After the demo is complete and all the graphics are finalized, we need to step once more into that ugly topic called **palettes**. While you're developing the graphics and planning each scene, it's important to keep palette issues in the back of your mind. In this example, I handle palettes very differently from the previous chapter. In this case, we want the non-dynamic, works every time, palette power, which comes only from finalizing bitmaps in their state and doing some graphic conversions and grouping. We'll cover these techniques:

- Using 256-color bitmaps
- Optimizing palette groups
- Using a master palette with **clsBmp** and **clsMem**

The first issue is how to avoid palette shifts in 8-bit (256 color) environments? Definitely not by using 16-bit (hi color) or 24-bit (full color) graphics. How would you get all those colors into a single palette without completely destroying the wonderful scenes you've created? Not only this, but what about the memory and disk space being consumed if you use images larger than 8 bits per pixel? No matter how you slice it, you need to conserve color and size and the good news is that your application's look and feel doesn't actually have to suffer as much as you may fear. The fact is, unless you're a graphics critic, 256 colors can carry a lot of information. Even 3D rendered text (as I used in some areas of the demo) can look OK. The point is that it must be worth the trade-off, which is space and speed. Using less memory means more memory free and faster graphics transitions. Using less disk space means less time to load the graphics into memory—a positive note on all counts.

OK, what about the palette then? Well, there are several stages in this demo and each requires a wide selection of colors. This makes it rather difficult to assign a common palette of only 256 colors to all of those graphics. You don't have to use the same palette for every graphic if they require very different colors and there are only two restrictions in this respect. The first is that the graphics that appear together on the screen at a single time must be of the same palette. The second is that graphics that are involved in a transition from one screen to another must have colors that exist in the palette used in transition. Both of these restrictions are easy to handle if you plan ahead. Essentially, you could have a different 256-color palette for every scene in the demo. As luck would have it, I didn't need that many, but the demo was broken down into some key sections that required the palette to change. I grouped together those bitmaps and assigned them a common palette.

> **See Appendix C for instructions on assigning a common palette to a large group of bitmaps, using `BitEdit` and `PalEdit`.**

I grouped the graphics for each scene in the demo into a sequential series of scripts that could still keep their integrity while sharing the same palette. For instance, the first scene (**`Script_1`**) uses many pink tones, whereas the script after it uses silvers and grays for the C.R.I.M.E.S. logo and yellows for the shield and text. The graphics for these two scenes can't share palettes and still look OK, especially since the logos were done in a 3D program that uses shading of many similar colors to get the resulting 3D effect. In the sample demo for this chapter, there are three groups of graphics that share a palette among all graphics in their corresponding scenes. The following table shows the grouped scripts and their associated bitmaps:

Script	Associated Bitmap
`Script_1`	**`present.bmp, imgware.bmp, software.bmp, and.bmp`**
`Script_2, Script_3`	**`crlogo.bmp, cracro1.bmp, cracro2.bmp, cracro3.bmp, cracro4.bmp, crinfo0.bmp, crinfo1.bmp, crinfo2.bmp, crinfo3.bmp, sheild.bmp, crcrimes.bmp, creasy.bmp, creasy1.bmp, creasy2.bmp, creasy3.bmp, creasy4.bmp`**
`Script_4, Script_5, Script_6`	**`crlogos.bmp, hdcomp.bmp, demo17.bmp, demo18.bmp, demo19.bmp, demo20.bmp, demo21.bmp, demo22.bmp, demo23.bmp, demo24.bmp, demo15.bmp`**

The bitmaps **`blue.bmp`**, **`cursor.bmp`** and **`cursorm.bmp`** (also used throughout the demo) are not palletized in any of the groups of palettes because their colors are present in all of the palettes used in each grouping.

Once the bitmaps palletized to the same palette for whatever number of scenes require that palette, the only step left is to make sure that the display reflects that palette information. In Chapter 3 there was only one bitmap being displayed at any one time. When the bitmap was read into memory, the memory DC had to reflect the correct palette for the image file and the display DC had to reflect that palette too, before the data was copied from memory to display. In this chapter's sample, two things have changed. First, I don't use the same method for reading the image file into memory—I'm reading the data using the **`LoadPicture`** method of VB into a temporary picture box which is then used to blit into the memory DC for storage. Second, I'm reading in several different bitmaps to be sent to the same display DC (eventually) and they must all reflect the same palette. Each bitmap in a given scene is assigned a palette as per the previous table, or the entire theory is shot.

The new palette class, **`clsPalette`** (described later in this chapter), is used to create each palette used throughout the demo. A procedure called **`Change_Palette`**, private to the form, goes through the steps that implement the use of the new palette. We'll describe this in more detail, but what it essentially does is create a palette from a bitmap, passed as a parameter to the procedure. Rather than using a hard-coded bitmap that uses the desired palette and passing the name of it to the procedure, there are three small bitmaps: **pal1.bmp**, **pal2.bmp**, **pal3.bmp.** Each of these uses the palette for the scenes to follow which, in turn, creates the global palette.

In the **Form_Load**, **pal1.bmp** is created with a call to **SetGlobalPalette** after the double-buffer is created, but before it's initialized with any graphics:

```
SetGlobalPalette "pal1.bmp"
```

In the **Script_Select** procedure, where the next script is chosen, before scripts 2 and 4 (which use a different palette) are called, we make another call to **SetGlobalPalette**:

```
Case 0
    Script_1
  Case 1
    SetGlobalPalette "pal2.bmp"
    Script_2
  Case 2
    Script_3
  Case 3
    SetGlobalPalette "pal3.bmp"
    Script_4
  Case 4
    Script_5
  Case 5
    Script_6
```

Once the palette has been created, before a given scene is played out, that palette is assigned to the memory object so that the double-buffer and display DCs will 'select' and 'realize' *that* palette when appropriate (Chapter 3 covered this, but we'll look at it some more later in this chapter). We also assign this palette to the bitmap objects loaded at the start of every script, rather than letting the bitmap reading code create a new palette object for every bitmap (like the **VBFileIO** code did in Chapter 3). Remember that a palette object can be 'selected' into more than one DC, so we can use it for more than one bitmap at a time.

All of the bitmaps used in **Script_1** use the **pal1.bmp** palette. When **Script_2** is called for, a different palette, **pal2.bmp**, will be ready and waiting in the wings. This transition between the two palettes could cause a palette flash if, as **Script_1** is completed, there are many colors displayed that are also realized into the system palette when the **Script_2** palette is realized. The most graceful way to handle this is to clear the screen to a color that is common to both palettes. Furthermore, if possible, when it's realized to the system palette then the color entry in each palette should be the same entry. When colors are realized into the system palette, the Palette Manager handles the positions of the logical palette entries that are realized. The best way to ensure that this transition is as smooth as possible is to keep the color blue entry (0, 0, 96) as the first entry in both the **pal1.bmp** palette and the **pal2.bmp** palette. This will ensure that the color blue makes it to the system palette. This way, when the new palette is realized to the system, before any new bitmaps are sent to the display that use all those new colors, this common color will simply continue displaying, looking to the same system palette, possibly to a new palette entry position. Once this process is complete, the new palette is ready and waiting for new colors to be sent to the display intact.

You can also follow this process for the steps that lead into **Script_4**, from the **pal2.bmp** palette to the **pal3.bmp** palette, for the same reasons. This will become clearer when we describe the code next, but now at least you know the theory behind it.

New Class Functionality

You've already used some of the classes presented in this chapter, but they still need a formal introduction. You see, when you create a class object, try as you might to think of all the properties and methods you think you want to use with it, there will always be the potential for change when you introduce the class to a more complex project, or the interaction with other classes. The classes that we used in Chapters 2 and 3, **clsMem** and **clsBmp**, are not quite as we need them for the project at hand, and we need to think out the code scenarios to build on each class, which in itself can often be harder than we all think. What you decide on today, you may hate with a passion tomorrow. Then the trade-off simply becomes time. We'll also introduce a new class here—**clsPalette**—which takes some of the functionality from the bitmap class from Chapter 3 and encapsulates it in its own class.

When we need classes to work in conjunction with other classes or with new and ultimately more complex applications, adjustments are inevitable. The memory class (**clsMem**) and the bitmap class (**clsBmp**) were both created for use in very simplistic environments. Now, I'm introducing a real application, one that requires additional functionality, including that already provided by the classes. The adjustments that I made to incorporate them with other classes and with complex application code make them ultimately more reusable, so that I can hope that more adjustments won't be necessary, but this is never a guarantee.

In the next three sections, we'll describe the new palette class, **clsPalette** and summarize upgrades made to **clsMem** and **clsBmp**, describing the reasons for each change. Then, I'll show the link between these classes and the new classes added in this chapter—**clsMove**, **clsRectFX**, and **clsBrushFX**—before I expose their individuality in greater detail.

Class Description: clsPalette

I'll keep this short and sweet, since we covered it in detail during the previous chapter. The following diagram shows the palette class's functionality:

The central method of this new class is **Create**, which is passed a full path to a filename that has a color table from which you want to create a logical palette. This method calls another method, **Read_BitmapInfo**, which verifies that the bitmap is a true bitmap, as we've done before, and reads data into the appropriate structures so that the class will have the information it needs to create the palette:

```
Public Sub Create(sFile As String)
'---Description
' creates a palette from the filename passed
'---
```

```
    ' read bitmap info
    If Read_BitmapInfo(sFile) Then
      ' create palette
      m_hPal = GetDIBPalette()
    End If
End Sub
```

The **Read_BitmapInfo** code is equivalent to the first part of the bitmap class's **ReadImage** method from Chapter 3 (now the **Read_VBFileIO** method):

```
Dim nFile As Long

    Read_BitmapInfo = True

    ' open binary bitmap file
    nFile = FreeFile
    Open sFile For Binary As nFile

    ' read, starting from the first byte, into the BITMAPFILEHEADER structure
    ' check is a valid Windows DIB, signature BM
    Get nFile, 1, m_bmFileHeader
    ' convert first two binary bytes into character values
    ' this must be done one byte at a time to be valid
    sSignature = Chr$(Val(m_bmFileHeader.bfType) And &HFF)
    sSignature = sSignature & Chr$(Val(m_bmFileHeader.bfType And &HFF00&) \ &HFF)
    If UCase$(sSignature) <> "BM" Then
        Read_BitmapInfo = False
        Exit Function
    End If

    ' read after the file header into the BITMAPINFOHEADER structure
    Get nFile, Len(m_bmFileHeader) + 1, m_bmInfo
    Close nFile
```

Once this is done, the call to the **GetDIBPalette** method will have access to all the structure information it needs from the bitmap headers and color table. **GetDIBPalette** is the same as the one used in Chapter 3's **clsBmp**, so it won't be an unfamiliar sight when you look at the code. It still returns a handle to the logical palette created from the bitmap's information. This handle gets assigned to the **m_hPal** variable of the palette class, accessible via the **hPalette** property for external use.

The **FreeResources** method of this class deletes the logical palette object with a call to the Windows API function, **DeleteObject()**:

```
nRet = DeleteObject(m_hPal)
```

The trick here is that, before this method is exercised, we should deselect the palette from any device contexts that it had been previously selected into. You'll see as we get on that the bitmap class (**clsBmp**) and the memory class (**clsMem**) both select this logical palette into memory and display DCs, so it's up to the code to release the palette before deleting the palette object.

Class Description: clsMem

The purpose of **clsMem** is to create and work with the double-buffer components—the display device context and the two memory device contexts for the backup of the display's background and the working area that ultimately gets copied to the display. This class acts as a liaison to the double buffer and there need only be one per project. You saw this class in partial functionality in Chapter 2, but the concept of the double buffer was not entirely encapsulated in the class module. There was only one buffer inside the class—the working buffer—and the background source information came from a **PatBlt()** or bitmap loaded into another picture box.

With this chapter's new **clsMem**, the following improvements and additions are present:

- A fully encapsulated double buffer
- Added double-buffer functionality
- Palette smarts
- Dirty rectangle tracking
- New API 'rectangle selection' functionality
- Memory watching for design time

Let's have a more visual interpretation of these improvements:

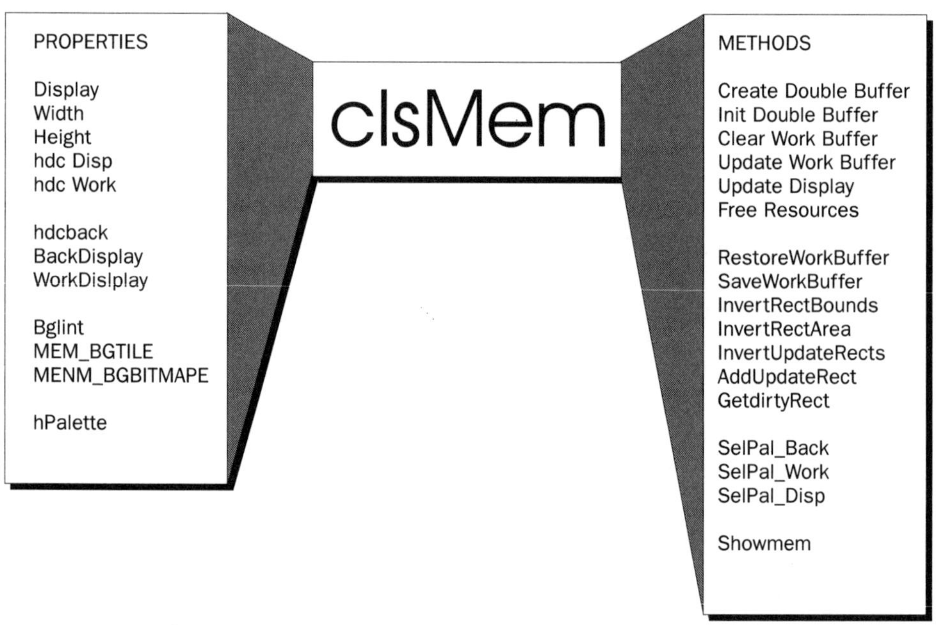

To fully encapsulate the double buffer (see Chapter 2 for more information on double-buffering), we need to connect a background, a working DC and a display DC. To do this, **clsMem** now has two memory DCs and a display DC linked via the property **Display** (a form or picture box) for **clsMem**. The next figure shows the three main physical components (the DCs) used by the class:

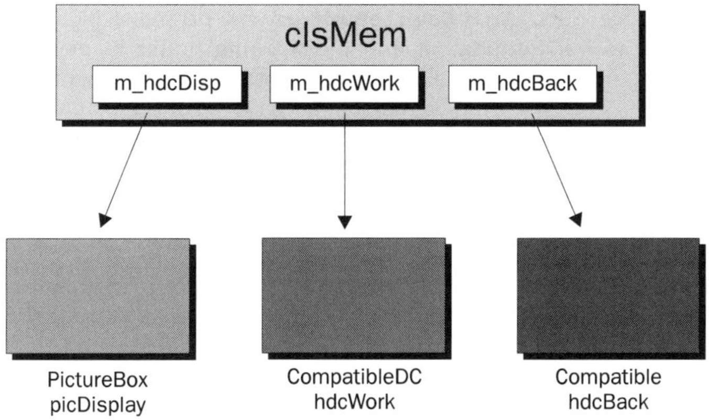

The device context **back** is used to store the original background used by the display, so that we can erase work done in the device context **work** before we copy the new scene to the display. These three DCs share the **Width** and **Height** property of the class, since they're assumed to always be the same size. Properties **hdcBack**, **hdcWork** and **hdcDisp** each point to their respective DC (memory or display) for use with various other classes and Windows API functions, as you'll soon see. The **Display** property is used to create the compatible DCs (same as Chapter 2) for background and working buffer of the display.

Using a picture box rather than a form to display the main components of the interface enables you to handle resolution changes in a slick manner:

Make the picture box 640x480 pixels in size and organize the interface as you would have it.

Write code that maximizes the form and centers the picture box in the form at run time.

Color the form's background or put an appropriate image that stretches to the entire form to appear as a border in resolutions greater than 640x480.

There you have it, free of grief–an interface for all resolutions!

As we did in Chapter 2, to prepare **clsMem** we first need to create the memory DCs and initialize their contents. The **CreateDoubleBuffer** and **InitDoubleBuffer** methods of **clsMem** still take care of that for us, but they've changed a bit. **CreateDoubleBuffer** now creates two compatible DCs using the same methods as before, where a compatible bitmap must be created to the size of the display to fill the DC bitmap area:

```
' Create compatible DCs
m_hdcBack = CreateCompatibleDC(m_hdcDisp)
m_hdcWork = CreateCompatibleDC(m_hdcDisp)

' Initialize area of DCs to match display DC area
' Backup of Background
m_hbmpBack = CreateCompatibleBitmap(m_hdcDisp, m_nDispW, m_nDispH)
m_stbmpBack = SelectObject(m_hdcBack, m_hbmpBack)
' Working Background
m_hbmpWork = CreateCompatibleBitmap(m_hdcDisp, m_nDispW, m_nDispH)
m_stbmpWork = SelectObject(m_hdcWork, m_hbmpWork)
```

In the first version of this class, **InitDoubleBuffer** was passed a picture box control to be used as the DC from which to blit information into the working buffer in memory. Now, the background and working buffer are both memory DCs, so we have to initialize them both in this procedure in the new version of the class. With the advent of the new **clsBmp** that we'll introduce in the next section, there's no need to pass a picture box control, since a bitmap object, using **clsBmp**, will hold the keys to the bitmap to initialize the buffer. This gives the **InitDoubleBuffer** method access to the properties of the entire class, including the DC of the bitmap we want the buffer to be initialized to.

To add a twist, instead of just using **StretchBlt()** to copy a bitmap into the double buffer, an option is created to tile a bitmap into the double buffer as well (I'll get to the reasoning on that soon). The new **InitDoubleBuffer**:

```
Public Sub InitDoubleBuffer(bmp As clsBmp)
'---Description
' initializes the background scene for the
' double buffer, based on the value of m_BgInit
'---
Dim nRet As Long
Dim flgDone As Boolean

  Select Case m_nBgInit
  Case m_BGTILE
    ' tile bitmap into DC area
    ' stretch blit has problems on win 3.1 machine
    With bmp
     SelPal_Back

      flgDone = False
      .SetPosition 0, 0
      Do
        nRet = BitBlt(m_hdcBack, .Left, .Top, .Width, .Height, .hdc, 0, 0,
SRCCOPY)
        If ((.Left + .Width) > m_nDispW) Then
          .SetPosition 0, .Top + .Height
          If .Top > m_nDispH Then flgDone = True
        Else
          .SetPosition .Left + .Width, .Top
        End If
      Loop Until flgDone

    End With
  Case m_BGBITMAP

    If IsMissing(bmp) Then MsgBox "You must pass a bitmap object to copy!"
      SelPal_Back

    ' use bitmap as is, stretch to fit DC area
    nRet = StretchBlt(m_hdcBack, 0, 0, m_nDispW, m_nDispH, bmp.hdc, 0, 0,
bmp.Width, bmp.Height, SRCCOPY)
  End Select

  ' update working buffer with background buffer
  SelPal_Work
  nRet = BitBlt(m_hdcWork, 0, 0, m_nDispW, m_nDispH, m_hdcBack, 0, 0, SRCCOPY)
```

```
    If flgShowMem Then ShowMem

End Sub
```

Notice now that there's a **Select** statement that tests the value of **m_nBgInit** (property **BgInit**) to see whether it's been set to **MEM_BGTILE** or **MEM_BGBITMAP**. In the demo sample, **MEM_BGTILE** is used but, for backwards compatibility of sorts, I've provided for a bitmap to also be stretched into the double buffer. In either case, the work is done to **hdcBack** and then the results are copied pixel-for-pixel to **hdcWork**. Of course, this initialization method does *not* update the display, although it does copy the bitmap accordingly into both the background and working areas. This ensures that they both start off the same.

> *The reason for tiling the blue bitmap, rather than using* **StretchBlt()** *to fill the area is because when this was tested in 16-bit, Windows 3.1 machines seemed to have trouble with* **StretchBlt()** *for such a small bitmap (the size of* **blue.bmp** *is 50x50). This methodology doesn't have trouble with Windows 95, but it was interesting enough to note and keep in this demo example.*

New Palette Functionality

You may also notice that some calls are being made to **SelPal_Back** and **SelPal_Work** in this procedure. These new procedures select and realize the memory class's assigned palette (**hPalette** property) into the corresponding DC before copying information into them (just like we learned to do in Chapter 3). Actually, you'll see in most of the new functionality, that each of the DCs that the memory class works with (**Back**, **Work** and **Disp**) will always be asked to select and realize their palettes before performing a blit of some sort. There is also a **SelPal_Disp** procedure which performs this functionality to the display DC, shown below:

```
Private Sub SelPal_Disp()
Dim nRet

      If m_hOPalDisp = 0 Then
        m_hOPalDisp = SelectPalette(m_hdcDisp, m_hPal, False)
      Else
        nRet = SelectPalette(m_hdcDisp, m_hPal, False)
      End If
      nRet = RealizePalette(m_hdcDisp)

End Sub
```

The new **hPalette** property of **clsMem** is used to set the **m_hPal** variable within the class. This will hold the palette that the memory class is to use for all DCs. The **m_hOPalDisp** variable is meant to hold the previous palette object that the display DC was using before the call to **SelectPalette()** is performed, selecting the palette pointed to by **m_hPal**. This variable should only be set the first time the memory class's palette is selected into the DC, since future calls to **SelectPalette()** would overwrite the value of this original palette with the palette of the memory object. A similar process is performed for the **SelPal_Back** and **SelPal_Work** procedures, but for their corresponding DCs and variables.

When the palette is set for the memory class that is used in these proceedings, it's more than just a logical palette handle passed to the **Property Let** statement. Remember from Chapter 3 that if a palette is selected into a DC that isn't the original stock palette, we can't delete the DC to free Windows resources. The same applies if a logical palette is still selected into a DC. Since deleting any logical palette in the program is part of the palette class which created that palette (as described above), all DCs using it must have their previous palette selected into them before the palette object is deleted. The **hPalette** property takes care of this for the memory class.

```
Public Property Let hPalette(hPal As Long)
'-Description
' set palette handle from a global palette
' or de-select the palette from the bitmap DC
' so it can be deleted
'-
Dim nRet As Long

  If hPal < 0 Then
      nRet = SelectPalette(m_hdcBack, m_hOPalBack, False)
      nRet = SelectPalette(m_hdcWork, m_hOPalWork, False)
nRet = SelectPalette(m_hdcDisp, m_hOPalDisp, False)
  Else
    m_hPal = hPal
  End If
End Property
```

If the **hPalette** property is set to a negative value, the current palette will be selected out of the double buffer and display DCs, otherwise the **m_hPal** variable is set to hold that logical palette handle.

Double-Buffer Functionality

We had to add certain functionalities to **clsMem** to remove the need to use the API functions outside of the class. If you recall Chapter 2's code, the class was not the only place that **BitBlt()** (among other functions) was called to move data both to the screen and to the working buffer. The reason was that the other related classes like **clsBmp** had not yet been introduced and the focus was on double-buffering in general and the use of all the API functions introduced in that chapter.

Now that our classes have grown up, it's time to link them together so that they can have complete encapsulation. There's no need to add public declarations of API functions that belong to the classes, or to move information to the double buffer. You've already seen the first stage of this encapsulation with the passing of the bitmap class to the **InitDoubleBuffer** method. The following methods are also part of this process:

- **UpdateWorkBuffer**
- **ClearWorkBuffer**
- **UpdateDisplay**
- **RestoreWorkBuffer**
- **SaveWorkBuffer**

UpdateWorkBuffer still has the basic functionality as before. It copies a rectangular area of pixels from the DC past the procedure to the specified coordinates on the working buffer DC. The difference here is that we've used **StretchBlt()** instead of **BitBlt()** and, rather than passing the rectangle information individually, class objects of **clsRect** are passed which hold the information needed to specify both a source and destination rectangle. This reduces the number of parameters that we need for this procedure. Another difference is that the **rop** code for the **StretchBlt()** function is no longer assumed to be **SRCCOPY**, since we now have masked bitmaps that require the combination of several **rop** steps for blitting (we demonstrated this with the cursor bitmap earlier in this chapter).

```
Public Sub UpdateWorkBuffer(hdcFrom As Long, rFrom As clsRect, rTo As clsRect, rop
As Long)
Dim nRet  As Long
Dim nToLeft As Long, nToTop As Long, nToWidth As Long, nToHeight As Long
Dim nFromLeft As Long, nFromTop As Long, nFromWidth As Long, nFromHeight As Long

  nToLeft = rTo.Left
  nToTop = rTo.Top
  nToWidth = rTo.Right - nToLeft
  nToHeight = rTo.Bottom - nToTop

  nFromLeft = rFrom.Left
  nFromTop = rFrom.Top
  nFromWidth = rFrom.Right - nFromLeft
  nFromHeight = rFrom.Bottom - nFromTop

  SelPal_Work
  nRet = StretchBlt(m_hdcWork, nToLeft, nToTop, nToWidth, nToHeight,   hdcFrom,
nFromLeft, nFromTop, nFromWidth, nFromHeight, rop)

  Call AddUpdateRect(rTo)

  If flgShowMem Then ShowMem

End Sub
```

The last step in this procedure adds the destination rectangle to a list of rectangles that we have changed in the working buffer. We'll discuss the methodology behind this in Chapter 5, so I won't go into it further for now. Just understand that you don't need to call more than **UpdateDisplay** to send the changed information to the display from the working buffer and that you don't have to track how many changes you've made before updating the information to the display, making decisions about the dirty rectangle. This functionality is now encapsulated into the memory class.

ClearWorkBuffer is now passed a rectangle class object as well, but the source and destination DCs are clearly **hdcBack** and **hdcWork**, so this information is already accessible within **clsMem** and need not be repeated in parameters to the function. Whatever the current state of **hdcWork** is, it will overwrite **hdcBack**.

```
Public Sub ClearWorkBuffer(r As clsRect)
Dim nRet As Long

  SelPal_Work
  nRet = BitBlt(hdcWork, r.Left, r.Top, r.Right - r.Left, r.Bottom - r.Top,
m_hdcBack, r.Left, r.Top, SRCCOPY)
  Call AddUpdateRect(r)

  If flgShowMem Then ShowMem

End Sub
```

This works for erasing the previous frame in a moving animation, before updating the screen with the new frame, which should be copied to the working buffer using **UpdateWorkBuffer**. Notice also that the array of dirty rectangles is updated once again, to keep track of changes made to the working area, for the next time when **UpdateDisplay** is called.

UpdateDisplay used to take parameters that defined the area that should be updated to the display DC. This was rather cumbersome since there could have been several changes since the last update, all which had to be updated at once to prevent an inconsistent screen update. Now, since there is an array of dirty rectangles that gets added to each time any of the **clsMem** procedures change a portion of **hdcWork**, this array can be used to calculate the entire area that should be updated to the display DC. As I said, the how of this method is covered in the next chapter since it's much more dirty rectangle intensive. How the **UpdateDisplay** method looks follows:

```
GetDirtyRect rDirty

SelPal_Disp
nRet = BitBlt(m_hdcDisp, rDirty.Left, rDirty.Top, rDirty.Right - rDirty.Left,
rDirty.Bottom - rDirty.Top, m_hdcWork, rDirty.Left, rDirty.Top, SRCCOPY)
```

Assuming the **GetDirtyRect** procedure does its job, **rDirty** (a **clsRect** object) should be filled with dimensions representing the area that needs to be copied to **hdcDisp**. Now, **BitBlt()** is used rather than **StretchBlt()** since all double-buffer components are created from the same display DC, and should be the same size.

The following figure describes the more global interaction between **hdcWork**, **hdcBack** and **hdcDisp**.

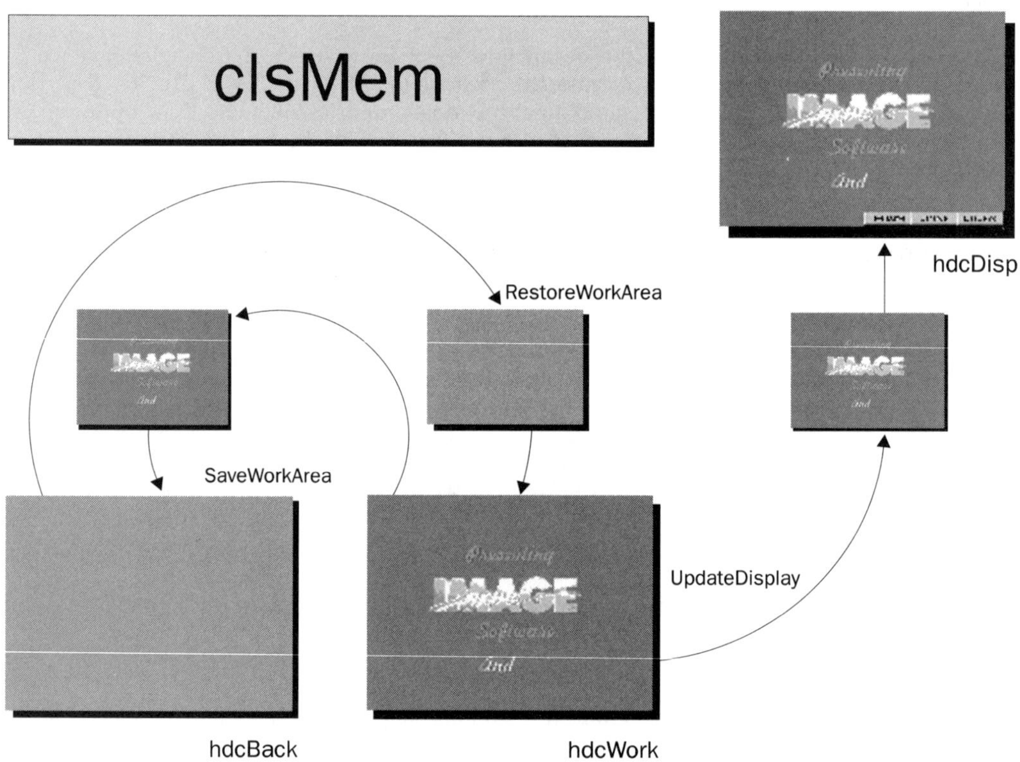

Apart from the individual rectangle changes made to the working buffer, there are two more aspects of **clsMem** that provide movement between the three DCs. You know that the **UpdateDisplay** method copies the contents of **hdcWork** to **hdcDisp**, based on the rectangles that have been changed. **SaveWorkBuffer** is a method that copies the entire work area to the background area. This was the method used to perform the background image update that we saw earlier in the chapter. We can't use this in all applications that use **clsMem**, but I needed it to save on adding background graphics. This instruction acts as an initialization for the background scene which brings the two memory DCs up-to-date (**hdcWork** and **hdcBack**). The opposite of this method, **RestoreWorkBuffer**, copies the background area to the work area, thus erasing all work done in the work area and re-initializing its contents to that of the current background scene. A simple call to **BitBlt()** in either case does the trick:

```
SaveWorkBuffer
nRet = BitBlt(m_hdcBack, 0, 0, m_nDispW, m_nDispH, m_hdcWork, 0, 0, SRCCOPY)
```

```
RestoreWorkBuffer
nRet = BitBlt(m_hdcWork, 0, 0, m_nDispW, m_nDispH, m_hdcBack, 0, 0, SRCCOPY)
```

Once again, **FreeResources** calls the **SelectObject()**, **DeleteObject()** and **DeleteDC()** API functions for their respective compatible DCs and bitmap objects to free Windows memory. From this procedure, the **hPalette** property is set to **-1**, telling the memory class to de-select the current palette from all encapsulated DCs. This method is called by the **Class_Terminate** event, which saves the programmer (i.e. me) from having to remember to clean everything up. That means that all double-buffer components are nicely removed from memory when I kill the memory object variable. We described the three API functions in Chapter 2, so I won't bore you with the gruesome details.

Rectangle Selection

A few new toys have been added to **clsMem** for use with the demo example. Since the demo has sections that are supposed to emulate the use of the actual program it's describing, we need to show the selection of interface components without using extra bitmaps. For instance, when the nose is selected in **Script_5** (described in more detail later), a rectangle shows up around the nose area while the mouse button is down to show that you've selected it. To demonstrate this in the demo, I use the Windows API function, **DrawFocusRect()**.

Since the memory class fully encapsulates the use of the double buffer and all work is normally done to the working buffer first, the method **InvertRectBounds** takes care of calling **DrawFocusRect()**, passing the DC for the working buffer. Then a call is made to add to those dirty rectangles again so that the next **UpdateDisplay** will recognize the change affected by drawing the focus rectangle:

```
' update working buffer and display
  nRet = DrawFocusRect(m_hdcWork, r)
  Call AddUpdateRect(rc)
```

Script_5 uses this method. The effect is:

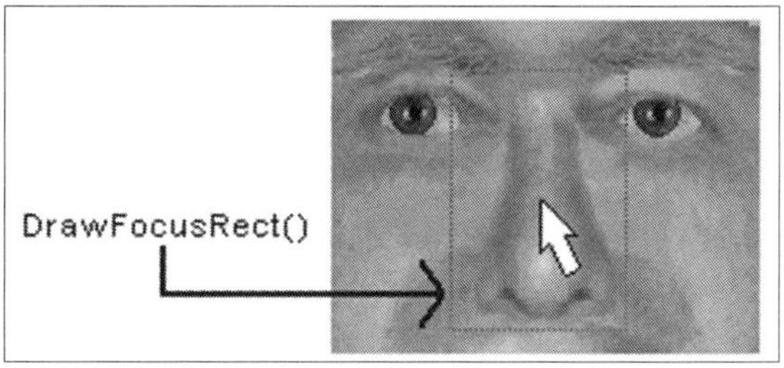

Similar to this, the **InvertRectArea** method serves to show the selection of a graphic button on the same interface. In **Script_6**, when the Size tool is selected (the S to the right of the composite picture), the button is inverted while the mouse button is down to show that it's being selected. This is done using the **InvertRect()** API function, shown here inside the **clsMem** procedure:

```
' update working buffer and display
  nRet = InvertRect(m_hdcWork, r)
  Call AddUpdateRect(rc)
```

Once again, the dirty rectangle array is updated for the next **UpdateDisplay** call. The effect is:

Memory Watching

If you have trouble imagining what's going on behind the scenes with your code, imagine no more! I added some functionality to **clsMem**, just for use at design time. A property of the memory class object, **ShowMem**, is used as a flag to indicate if each of the updates to the working and background buffer should be sent to a display DC, specified by **WorkDisplay** and **BackDisplay** (also properties of the class). Inside the command button **cmdPeek** (stands for memory peek), the following code sets this up:

```
g_objMem.flgShowMem = Not g_objMem.flgShowMem
 picBack.Move 0, 0
 picWork.Move 0, picDisplay.Height - picWork.Height
 picBack.Visible = Not picBack.Visible
 picWork.Visible = Not picWork.Visible
```

This isn't strict code; you can position the display picture boxes wherever you like and call them whatever you like to use this functionality in another application. It really comes in handy with debugging difficult screen updates, where you can see that something is going wrong. This works because all methods of **clsMem** that update the **hdcWork** or **hdcBack** add this line of code to the bottom of the procedure:

```
If flgShowMem Then ShowMem
```

This, in turn, calls the **ShowMem** procedure of the class which uses **StretchBlt()** to copy information from the double buffer to their respective picture box DCs:

```
nRet = StretchBlt(m_hdcWorkDisp, 0, 0, m_nWorkDispW, m_nWorkDispH, m_hdcWork, 0,
0, m_nDispW, m_nDispH, SRCCOPY)
```

```
nRet = StretchBlt(m_hdcBackDisp, 0, 0, m_nBackDispW, m_nBackDispH, m_hdcBack, 0,
0, m_nDispW, m_nDispH, SRCCOPY)
```

To see how it looks, take a look at the demos intro at the start of this chapter, where the top left box is the contents of **hdcBack** and the bottom left is **hdcWork**.

Class Description: clsBmp

The **clsBmp** module that we created in Chapter 3 now needs a small overhaul for it to work with the classes described in this chapter. This is another of the fundamental classes necessary for working with graphics. It contains many necessary properties for describing a bitmap and accessing its image data. I'll go through the new functionality, including that which was moved to the new palette class described earlier.

The following figure shows the current properties and methods for the new and improved bitmap class. The bold items are additions to the class.

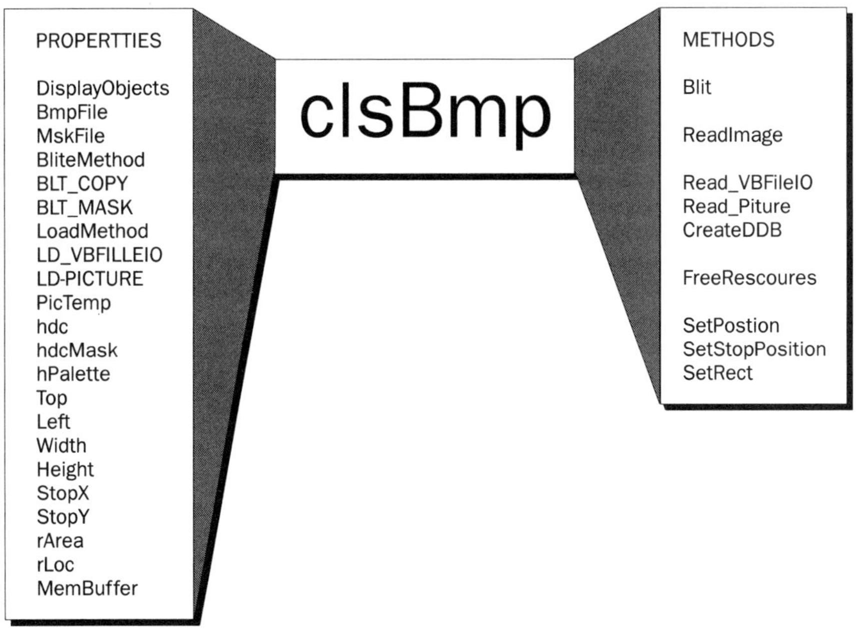

I'm going to spend a little time on this, since, even though existing methods and properties remain, some of their functionality has changed slightly and will require a short description. With a clear description of the reasoning that went into this buffed-out bitmap class, you'll be aware of the thought process that goes into building complex classes that intermingle with one another. The main aspects of the bitmap class that should be outlined here are:

- Reading the bitmap
- Creating the DDB
- Assigning a bitmap palette
- Blitting the bitmap
- Bitmap dimension and location

Reading the Bitmap

The first functionality I'll discuss is the act of reading in the bitmap data. This was already included in the bitmap class from Chapter 3, so you won't be entirely a stranger to it. The first step before using the bitmap class is to set up the name of the file to read. When it's copied to the display, if the bitmap requires a mask (for transparency), we should set up both the **`BmpFile`** and **`MskFile`** properties of the class. Next, we should specify a method for reading in the data. In Chapter 3, I built the bitmap class using **`VBFileIO`** techniques only, so there was only one way to read the bitmap into a memory DC. For convenience, and for another example, I use the picture box control to read the data into memory first, then copy it into a memory DC, thus releasing the picture box of its hold on the image data. The **`LoadMethod`** property can have the two settings of **`LD_PICTURE`** or **`LD_VBFILEIO`**. **`ReadImage`** checks the value of **`LoadMethod`** for one of these values before calling the appropriate read procedure (**`Read_Picture`** or **`Read_VBFileIO`**).

This figure demonstrates the steps that compare **`Read_Picture`** and **`Read_VBFileIO`**:

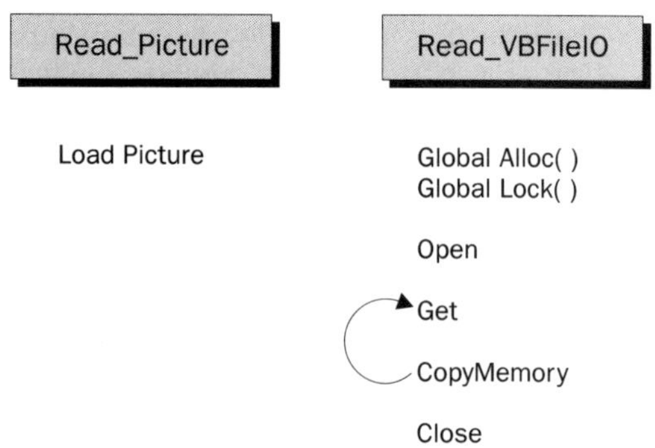

The default method for loading an image in this chapter's sample is **`LD_PICTURE`**, set up in the initialize event for the class along with other default values for the project. This saves a line of code for every bitmap we load throughout the demo (and trust me, there's a lot in the real version), used to set the **`LoadMethod`** property for each bitmap. Notice that there's also a flag passed to **`ReadImage`** now, with its value (**`True`** or **`False`**) representing whether or not the bitmap class is currently reading in the bitmap or its mask (I'll explain that with the blitting discussion):

```
Select Case LoadMethod
  Case LD_PICTURE
    ReadImage = Read_Picture(flgMask)
  Case LD_VBFILEIO
    ReadImage = Read_VBFileIO(flgMask)
  End Select
```

The procedure **`Read_VBFileIO`** is the same code that we used in the previous class' **`ReadImage`** method, which simply reads in the bitmap using **`VBFileIO`** methods using Windows API calls to access global memory and copy the information into a memory DDB. **`Read_Picture`** is the new method used throughout this chapter, which also reads a bitmap into a memory DDB, but I'll get to that soon enough. Since **`Read_VBFileIO`** is a method you've already seen in action, I'll focus on the **`Read_Picture`** method.

Now that you're familiar with how the bitmap's binary data is read into memory and set into a DDB, you'll have more appreciation for what the picture box's **`LoadPicture`** method does for us. Be aware that there are no memory savings in either case. Both the globally allocated memory (using **`VBFileIO`**) and the picture box control (using the **`LoadPicture`** method) are used to store the binary image and both are discarded once the bitmap has been successfully copied into a memory DC's DDB area:

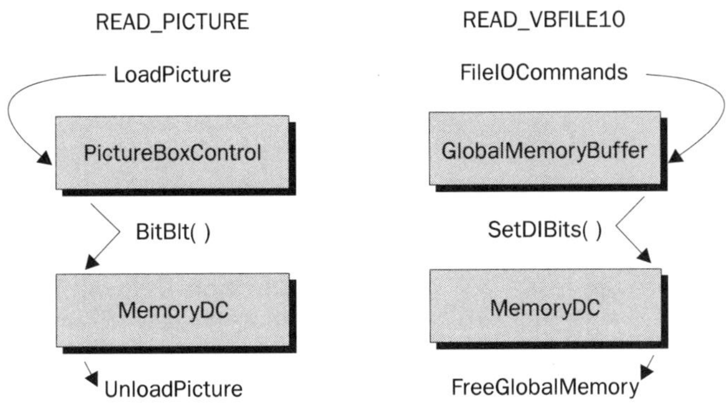

Notice that both methods require roughly the same number of steps. The picture box control doesn't give us access to the bitmap's palette information, so we still need to read that data in via **VBFileIO** if we want the information from the headers. Both methods also require a short period, while the DDB is created, where there are two copies of the image in memory. This doesn't seem terribly efficient, but this is almost always the case with **FileIO**, even with the code behind the picture box controls.

```
Private Function Read_Picture(ByVal flgMask As Boolean) As Boolean
'---Description
' Read bitmap data from the file named in m_sBmpFile
' into a PictureBox control, creating a DDB from the image
' using blitting methods from the PictureBox
'---
  Read_Picture = False

  ' exit if picture control object not set
  If m_picTemp Is Nothing Then MsgBox "Oops...forgot to set picturebox object!":
Exit Function

  ' check if mask bitmap being used
  If flgMask Then
    m_picTemp.Picture = LoadPicture(m_sMskFile)
  Else
    With m_picTemp
      .Picture = LoadPicture(m_sBmpFile)
      .AutoRedraw = True
      .AutoSize = True
      .ScaleMode = 3 'pixels
      m_nWidth = .ScaleWidth
      m_nHeight = .ScaleHeight
    End With 'm_picTemp
  End If

  CreateDDB flgMask
  Set m_picTemp = Nothing
  Read_Picture = True
End Function
```

Once again, the optional parameter (**flgMask**) is checked to see whether we're currently loading the mask image for the main **BmpFile**. (I'll get to that later on.) The main process you see here is loading the image using the picture box control, which first checks that there is a picture control associated with **clsBmp** (**m_picTemp** should be set first), then makes sure the **ScaleMode** for that picture is **Pixels**, so that the **Width** and **Height** properties of the bitmap can be set and will be in that format. We can set these properties at design-time to save overhead. We've simply put this here as a precautionary reminder. (The **Width** and **Height** properties can also be set using the **BITMAPINFOHEADER** as read in by **VBFileIO**.)

Creating the DDB

CreateDDB is called by both the read methods and performs the same function as it did before, with the exception that it now must consider the **LoadMethod** to know how to set the image data into the DDB. Here, there is a difference worth explaining. I'll take a sample from the **CreateDDB** method, excluding the lines that concern the mask bitmap.

First, the memory DC and DDB must be created in preparation for the actual bitmap data that will be stored there once in place. This code is used by both read methods. It's also used in the previous bitmap class to prepare the area in memory to hold the bitmap data.

```
'prepare a memory DC
m_hdc_Mask = CreateCompatibleDC(m_picTemp.hdc)
'prepare a bitmap to hold DDB
m_hBmp_Mask = CreateCompatibleBitmap(m_picTemp.hdc, m_nWidth, m_nHeight)
```

Now we concern ourselves with getting the bitmap into the DDB. In the case of **LD_VBFILEIO**, we used the **CopyMemory()** function to move the binary data into a global area in memory. Since the data that we were copying was in DIB format, we had to set the bits into the DDB (using **SetDIBits()**) after the bitmap's palette was selected into the DC used in the function call, before selecting the DDB into that memory DC. This may look a little different, since the call to the **GetDIBPalette** is no longer there. These steps assume that the **hPalette** property (held in the **m_hPal** variable) has already been set to the bitmap's palette:

```
m_hOldPal = SelectPalette(m_hdc, m_hPal, False)
nRet = RealizePalette(m_hdc)

' bitmap height = number of scan lines
' set bits into DDB
nRet = SetDIBits(m_hdc, m_hBmp, 0, m_bmInfo.bmiHeader.biHeight, m_ptrGlobMem,
m_bmInfo, DIB_RGB_COLORS)

' select DDB into memory DC
m_hStock = SelectObject(m_hdc, m_hBmp)
```

In the case of the picture box method, the image data is already in DDB format, accessible by the **hdc** property of the picture box control. In this case, we must select the compatible bitmap into the memory DC first and, before we copy the data from the picture box DC to the memory DC, select the bitmap's palette into it (assuming once again that it has been properly set). This time, we copy the data using **StretchBlt()** (just in case they were not exactly the same dimension, though they should be) from the picture box into the memory DC's DDB:

```
m_hOldPal = SelectPalette(m_hdc, m_hPal, False)
nRet = RealizePalette(m_hdc)

m_hStock = SelectObject(m_hdc, m_hBmp)

' blit from picture to m_hdc
nRet = StretchBlt(m_hdc, 0, 0, m_nWidth, m_nHeight, m_picTemp.hdc, 0, 0, m_nWidth,
m_nHeight, SRCCOPY)
```

At the end of this process, no matter how the bitmap was read into memory as a DDB, there's an **hdc** property and an accurate **Width** and **Height** for use in Windows API calls and other code that calls for the bitmap information.

Assigning a Palette

In Chapter 3, the bitmap class read a bitmap from memory, reading any palette information first and creating a palette from that information to be used when the DDB was created and when the bitmap was sent to the display. Since so many bitmaps are used in this demo sample and groups of them share a common palette, we can use the same palette for all bitmap memory DCs, as well as the memory class DCs. Rather than the bitmap class reading and creating a new logical palette for every bitmap loaded into memory, the **hPalette** property of the bitmap is set to the logical palette created with **clsPalette**, being used by the current scene:

```
Public Property Let hPalette(hPal As Long)
'---Description
' set palette handle from a global palette
' or de-select the palette from the bitmap DC
' so it can be deleted
'---
Dim nRet As Long

  If hPal < 0 Then
      nRet = SelectPalette(m_hdc, m_hOldPal, False)
      nRet = SelectPalette(m_hdc_Mask, m_hOldPal_Mask, False)
  Else
    m_hPal = hPal
  End If
End Property
```

Since the bitmap class now possibly has two bitmaps associated with it for masking procedures, there is a variable set up to hold the old palette for both of those memory DCs. Just like the memory class did in its **hPalette** property for the **Back**, **Work** and **Disp** DCs, when the **hPal** parameter is passed **-1** to clean up. Otherwise, the **m_hPal** variable is set for the class, for use when we create DDBs from the bitmap files read in.

The **GetDIBPalette** procedure was removed, since the palette class is now taking care of that process (this procedure was used internally when the bitmap data read in by the **ReadImage** procedure read the file from scratch).

Blitting the Bitmap

Once the bitmap class has properly established its bitmap in memory, we can use it to access information about the bitmap, including the DC that is required by other Windows API functions, in order to blit the bitmap to another DC. There are a few special concerns regarding blitting the bitmap information to another DC, which I'll unravel in a few moments.

It makes sense that each bitmap object should have its own **Blit** method, since the blitting functions in the Windows API need the dimension and location information about the bitmap (described next) and the method with which it wants to be copied to the destination DC. In Chapter 3, it was assumed that a bitmap would only be copied to the screen with the **SRCCOPY**. Since there were no transparent graphics in that example, there was no need to expand the bitmap class to include any other flexibility. Now, **clsBmp** lets you have access to both a bitmap and its mask graphic. You can also set some properties of the class to make the process of blitting dynamic, taking the proper raster operations into consideration while blitting to a destination DC.

BlitMethod is used to describe the method that the bitmap needs to be copied. The two possibilities here are **BLT_COPY** or **BLT_MASK**. Using **BLT_COPY**, the default as set in the initialization event for the class, means that the image data is copied, as is, to its destination. **SRCCOPY** is the raster operation used with functions like **BitBlt()** or **StretchBlt()** in this case. If the bitmap requires transparency (covered in Chapter 2) then you need two bitmaps to create this effect. The 'copy' and the 'mask' bitmap. So **BLT_MASK** tells the class that the bitmap should be copied with the methodology of transparent bitmap copying.

The **MemBuffer** property of the bitmap class is linked to the double buffer for the entire project, so that the Blit method can send information directly to the working buffer, never concerned with the update process to the display. **m_nBlitMethod** is used inside this Blit method to perform the accurate blit for the bitmap class:

```
If m_nBlitMethod = m_BLTMASK Then
      m_objMem.UpdateWorkBuffer m_hdc_Mask, m_rArea, m_rLoc, SRCAND
      m_objMem.UpdateWorkBuffer m_hdc, m_rArea, m_rLoc, SRCINVERT
    Else
      m_objMem.UpdateWorkBuffer m_hdc, m_rArea, m_rLoc, SRCCOPY
    End If
```

When **ReadImage** is passed **True** for **flgMask**, it means that the bitmap's mask image is being read in, which means that **MskFile** should be read in and that the **hdcMask** property should be filled, so that there is a DDB in memory for the mask bitmap. The Blit method uses this information with **SRCAND** and **SRCINVERT** to send information to the working buffer, using **clsMem UpdateWorkBuffer**.

The main difference with reading in the mask bitmap is that we don't need to initialize other aspects of the class that should have already been initialized when **BmpFile** was read in. The second filename property for this task is **MskFile**. The assumption is that you won't use a bitmap class without setting up both **BmpFile** and **MskFile** for use if necessary.

Dimension and Location

The last few additional properties and methods for **clsBmp** are for dimensions and location of the bitmap in question. Now it should become apparent why the mask bitmap is included in the same class as the original bitmap. They both reflect the same exact position when copied to the display and move to the same position. As with any bitmap, there are **Top**, **Left**, **Width** and **Height** properties that are filled in when the bitmap is read into memory (only **Width** and **Height** existed in Chapter 3). **SetPosition** is the method that sets up the **Top**, **Left** coordinate, by calling the **SetRect** method of the class. This method does the following:

```
m_rLoc.SetSize m_nLeft, m_nTop, m_nLeft + m_nWidth, m_nTop + m_nHeight
m_rArea.SetSize 0, 0, m_nWidth, m_nHeight
```

The properties **rLoc** and **rArea** (**m_rLoc** and **m_rArea** internally) are declared as rectangle objects using **clsRect** and the **SetSize** method of **clsRect** (not complex enough to describe here—just take a look at it) sets the **Left**, **Top**, **Right**, **Bottom** properties of the class object. These two rectangle objects keep track of the bitmap's dimensions (**rArea**) and location on the display (**rLoc**) to be conveniently passed to other functions and subroutines that require that information—in just one parameter!

One other set of position properties that the bitmap class tracks is a **StopX**, **StopY** coordinate for the purpose of movement. These properties are set by the method **SetStopPosition**.

You'll see how these properties are useful in the actual scripting of the demo. But for now, let's get a peek at how the new classes fit with our new and improved **clsMem** and **clsBmp**.

Class Integration

As with any class modules, their usage and compatibility with other classes depends fully on how the programmer created them. Sometimes, to interact with one another, classes need additional properties and methods, possibly even complete restructuring. The vision of a class is never 100 percent equal in a different programmer's eyes, but, since the classes in this chapter do interact with one another, rather than re-inventing the wheel, I'll explain how I see them fitting together. You may even want to leave them as is for your next project.

It should be fairly obvious that there need only be one memory class to a project. All double-buffering activities should go through that one class which points to the background, the working area and the display. Since the bitmap class is used for all bitmaps throughout the demo, this class requires possibly several per script. In the main module of the project, public variables are declared for the classes that will be constantly in use. Included in these is a single palette object, which is used for the memory class and all bitmaps that are part of those scenes that use that palette.

The next figure nicely connects all of the classes used in this project. I exclude the palette class from this only because the diagram doesn't incorporate the concept of the current scene, but you know from the discussions up to now that the palette is used to set the **hPalette** property of the bitmap and memory classes and that it's not involved in any direct way with the others.

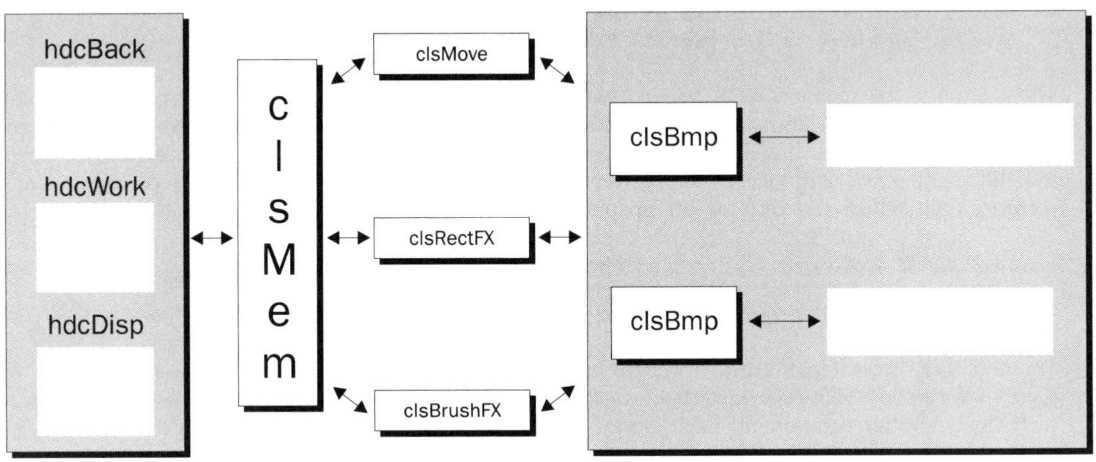

Basically, the memory class points to the double buffer and is capable at a moment's notice to copy from DC to DC, using the methods we described earlier. The bitmap class contains all of the necessary information about each bitmap, like its DC and dimensions and display location. This information is used by each of the animation classes, **clsMove**, **clsRectFX** and **clsBrushFX** to perform the necessary activity unique to the animation class, then pass the results to the memory buffer which can then be copied to the screen.

We'll describe what each class method does further on in this chapter, but next I'll overview the code for **Crdemo_s.vbp**, outlining the initialization of each class in preparation for its use and walking through the basics of each demo script.

Here's a disclaimer on the classes. Any assumptions I make regarding the best property and method setup are just that, my assumptions. There is almost always an argument for other methodology under different circumstances. Feel free to find your ideas for changing classes as better ideas for your next project.

Demo Overview

It would probably help to have some idea of how the demo code was put together, so that it's easier to follow later discussions on how specific portions of the demo worked. Here I'll walk through the process of initializing the demo environment and then talk about the scripts themselves.

Initialization

To start with, each of the class objects that are to be used throughout the demo are dimensioned in the main module:

```
Public g_objMem As New clsMem
Public g_objMove As New clsMove
Public g_objRectFX As New clsRectFX
Public g_objBrushFX As New clsBrushFX

Public g_objBmpScene() As New clsBmp
Public g_objBmpCursor As New clsBmp
Public g_objBmpBlue As New clsBmp
Public g_objPal As New clsPalette
```

There is only one memory class needed, which acts as the double buffer for the project's display work and one of each animation class: **clsMove**, **clsRectFX** and **clsBrushFX**. These are reused with different graphics, but since only one can be functioning at a time, there's no need to keep initializing the class within each script for individual graphics. They each need a connection to the memory class which can then be set up once in the **Form_Load**:

```
Set g_objMove.MemBuffer = g_objMem
Set g_objRectFX.MemBuffer = g_objMem
Set g_objBrushFX.MemBuffer = g_objMem
```

These classes, including the bitmap class, need a connection to the memory class so that they can access information about the dimensions of the display and the handles to the device contexts of each double-buffer component. Each class has a property, called **MemBuffer**, which takes the memory class object as a parameter.

Along with the initialization of the animation classes, the double buffer for **clsMem** is created and initialized (described later) and the display is set up to receive the actions performed in each script. Now let's see how the scripts are called.

Script Selection

A global variable, **m_nCurrScript** is used to track the current script that is playing (or has just played) as the demo proceeds. This isn't a complex feature, since the demo is sequentially played and you can't move forwards and backwards through each demo script. Each time the user clicks the Continue button, **m_nCurrScript** is incremented and **Select_Script** is called.

As you can see from the listing, when the last script is encountered, all but the Exit button are disabled to let the user know that the demo is now over. This is especially useful in this condensed version of the demo, since it's certainly not obvious by the effects on the screen. Run the real demo on the CD, named **Crdemo.exe**, to see what the entire demo looks like and how it finishes.

Script Content

Each script is different in that they all use different graphics and perform varying activities on each graphic. There are, however, several things that the scripts have in common that you can copy as a template from script to script, simply replacing a few things in the code. Using the first script, I'll walk through the similarities of each script, pointing out where they may differ so you can recognize those differences when you get to the code. Then, I'll go into the different activities that take place within each script, to give you an idea of how the code is laid out before we talk about the classes that do the work.

Common Code

Common to all scripts is the process of loading the bitmaps used in the script, setting them up as need be to start the script. Then, at the end of each script, regardless of the actions performed with the graphics, those bitmaps are released from memory.

There were 50 or so scripts in the final demo, so it was important that a common template for each script be formulated to save time on the creation of new scripts as the demo filled out. To make this easier to read, as well as debug, at the top of each script is a series of constants that are numbered starting from 0, representing the array item in that dynamic bitmap object array, **g_objBmpScene()** that will be reinitialized at the start of the script to load each new graphic:

```
Const IDPRESENTING = 0
Const IDIMGWARE = 1
Const IDSOFTWARE = 2
Const IDAND = 3
Const NUMBMPS = 4
```

The constant, **NUMBMPS**, is used to dynamically redimension **g_objBmpScene()** to the number of items this script will require:

```
ReDim g_objBmpScene(NUMBMPS - 1)
```

Then each bitmap needs to be read in. Using the bitmap class, **clsBmp**, several properties and methods must be called to get the bitmap files read from disk into memory. Since this functionality is repeated for so many bitmaps, I created a common procedure that would handle these repeated lines of code, only passing to parameters what is unique to each graphic used in any script. Those unique values are the filename, the top-left position of the bitmap in the memory display and (if applicable) the stop coordinate if the bitmap is being moved to a particular point on the display.

The common procedure is called **BmpDC_LoadNew** and in the first script, **Script_1**, this is how the graphics are loaded:

```
BmpDC_LoadNew g_objBmpScene(IDPRESENTING), "present.bmp", g_objMem.Width, 100
BmpDC_LoadNew g_objBmpScene(IDIMGWARE), "imgware.bmp", g_objMem.Width, 175
BmpDC_LoadNew g_objBmpScene(IDSOFTWARE), "software.bmp", g_objMem.Width, 275
BmpDC_LoadNew g_objBmpScene(IDAND), "and.bmp", g_objMem.Width, 350
```

Notice the memory class, **g_objMem**, dimensions are used to position the graphics offscreen (if you've seen the sample run, you'll know that the graphics in this script are moved onscreen from different directions). The **BmpDC_LoadNew** procedure is shown below. Its parameters for position (**X**, **Y**) and stop position (**nStopX**, **nStopY**) are optional so that the script can set these elsewhere if necessary:

```
Private Sub BmpDC_LoadNew(obj As clsBmp, sFile As String, Optional X, Optional Y,
Optional nStopX, Optional nStopY)
'---Description
' initializes a new bitmap object
' much of this is the same each time
'---

  With obj
    Set .MemBuffer = g_objMem
    .BmpFile = g_sPath & sFile
    .hPalette = g_objPal.hPalette

    Set .PicTemp = picLoad
    .BlitMethod = .BLT_COPY
    .ReadImage False

    If Not IsMissing(X) And Not IsMissing(Y) Then
      .SetPosition X, Y
    Else
      .SetPosition 0, 0
    End If

    If Not IsMissing(nStopX) And Not IsMissing(nStopY) Then
      .SetStopPosition nStopX, nStopY
    End If

  End With

End Sub
```

Here, the memory class is linked to the bitmap class passed in the procedure, the filename is set up using the global path variable and the current script palette, pointed to by **g_objPal**, is assigned. Then, position variables are set up if the information was passed to the appropriate parameters and the image is read in. (We haven't yet described some of these methods, since they are new to the bitmap class. We'll cover them later.)

Once this is done, the bitmap class objects in the array **g_objBmpScene()** are set up and ready to use. At the end of the script, these must be released from memory, since they are no longer needed, which is done with the following code:

```
For nIndex = 0 To NUMBMPS - 1
    Set g_objBmpScene(nIndex) = Nothing
Next nIndex
Erase g_objBmpScene
```

Since a global dynamic array, **g_objBmpScene()** is used and cleared at the end of every demo script, not only could I reuse the lines of code that free the array at the end of each script, but I didn't have to **Dim** the array at the start of each script.

Sequential Script Effects

A script isn't dynamic like a game. A very strict set of instructions is followed to get the intended result on the screen. Each of the animation classes, **clsMove**, **clsRectFX** and **clsBrushFX** are intended to be used, one at a time, on a particular graphic. So let's take into consideration **Script_1**. The instruction set reads something like this:

```
Move IDPRESENT
Move IDIMAGEWARE
Move IDSOFTWARE
Move IDAND
Wait
Erase IDPRESENT
Erase IDIMAGEWARE
Erase IDSOFTWARE
Erase IDAND
```

This is one of the simpler scripts, since it doesn't require tracking what has been backed up to the background buffer, which I'll discuss next.

Script_2 contains two steps. At the beginning, a call is made to another script, **Script_EnterLogo** (this is reused several times in the longer version of this demo, so warranted its own procedure), then a similar set of instructions to **Script_1** are followed, but with different graphics.

Script_EnterLogo works in a similar way to these other scripts in that it loads graphics, works with them, then releases them at the end of the script. It also performs a few additional steps, listed here:

- **Clear Previous Scene with Background Buffer**
- **Move IDCRLOGO**
- **Backup Working Buffer to Background Buffer**
- **Move IDCRACRO1 - IDCRACRO4**
- **Backup Working Buffer to Background Buffer**

These extra steps are provided with the new functionality of **clsMem** (to be discussed). Essentially, this logo is animated into the display, but then becomes part of the background and so must be backed up. Since **IDCRACRO1–IDCRACRO4** are moved into position over top of **CRLOGO**, it must become part of the background buffer, used to assist the movement of those graphics.

Script_2 uses a new effect, along with the movement animation of graphics. Once the logo is safely part of the display, its script flows as follows:

Dissolve-In IDBULLET

Move IDCRINFO1 - IDCRINFO3

Actually, there is one bullet graphic per **CRINFO** graphic, performed in a loop. The dissolve works much like the **Move** and **Erase** in that it works on one bitmap at a time, waiting until it's complete before progressing to the next line of code in the script.

We'll see more on each of these individual effects later but, for now, let's move on to some more complex scripting instructions!

Complex Script Instructions

Not all scripts are as straightforward to implement as those we've just discussed. Calling each of the animation classes one after another looks neat, but isn't really that difficult to script once the code for the actual animation works from within its class code. More difficult to script are those that use the classes with several layers of graphics on the display.

This demo is meant not only to describe key points in the C.R.I.M.E.S. program, but also to give the audience a good idea how the interface of that program works. This means faking the use of the program with hard-coded graphics! Half the work put into the demo was just in grabbing all of the screenshots required to make this work, then taking pieces and parts of those screenshots that could be more efficiently used rather than replacing the entire display each time a change is reflected in the interface of the program.

Let me first outline one of these demonstrative scripts, then explain how this had to be put together to make it work. **Script_4** simply loads the graphics that prepare the background for the scene, which becomes the background buffer for the rest of the scripts related to the interface. **Script_5** instructions, which build on this, are as follows:

- Move the cursor to the nose
- Show the nose selected
- Update the selector to reflect noses (the bottom one is the current nose)
- Move the cursor to select the top nose
- Show the top nose in selector now selected
- Update the nose on the face

We saw the graphical components that make up this script earlier in this chapter. The actual script instructions are a little more complex than this appears. Moving the cursor to the nose coordinate required hard-coding an exact coordinate where the cursor should land on the current display. Showing it selected required the use of the **InvertRectBounds** method of **clsMem**, as we described earlier. These steps are:

```
' CLICK NOSE
Cursor_Move 296, 264 + LOGOHEIGHT

' SHOW SELECTION WITH FOCUS RECTANGLE
.InvertRectBounds 296, 264 + LOGOHEIGHT, 64, 92
.UpdateDisplay
Wait 2
.InvertRectBounds 296, 264 + LOGOHEIGHT, 64, 92
.UpdateDisplay
```

When the nose selector is copied over top of the face selector, it must be backed up to the background buffer so that the cursor can be moved in the next step over top of it without erasing what has been done with the wrong background buffer. Since the **SaveWorkBuffer** method of **clsMem** copies the entire working buffer to the background buffer, this will include the cursor currently positioned over the nose unless we erase it from the working buffer before backing it up. Then the cursor must be blit back to the working buffer, since it's indeed present on the display:

```
' SHOW NEW SCROLL
g_objBmpScene(IDNOSESCR).Blit
.UpdateDisplay

' erase cursor to update background without it
.ClearWorkBuffer g_objBmpCursor.rLoc
.SaveWorkBuffer7
g_objBmpCursor.Blit
Wait 2
```

It can become rather tedious if every script that moves a cursor must remember to erase, backup and recopy the cursor each time something that builds the background is copied to the display. In the real demo, the copying of the cursor as such is 'hacked' in a calculated fashion into the class activity that backs up the working buffer. This isn't appropriate, however, when you intend to reuse the class with other applications that don't use a cursor bitmap, so I removed it for the sample.

As you can see, the code is very specifically tailored to the results expected on the screen and to the results that need to be reflected in the double buffer in preparation for the next step or scene. In this type of scenario, close attention is paid to the current state of the double buffer, so that the background, working and display all reflect the current state they need to. The key is to provide functions in each class and script that precisely handle certain activities so that all you need to is think through what's happening in memory to insure all is well. When in doubt, you can always use the **ShowMemory** option in **clsMem**.

Movement with Class

Since the movement class was the first logical step to creating animation demo-style, I'll use it as an example to describe the issues that surfaced along the way. Most of these points will also relate to the development and use of the other animation classes for this project, but I'll point these out where appropriate. As you read in the previous section, there is a fairly close-knit relationship between the animation classes and **clsMem** and **clsBmp**. No class can be completely stand-alone and without dependencies, unless it wants to remain completely useless to us.

The first thing I'll do here is to describe the use of **clsMove**, whose sole purpose, for now, is to move a bitmap object through repeated iterations.

Using clsMove with clsBmp

As you know, there's only one **clsMove** object variable for this project. It's defined globally so that we don't need to reinitialize it every time a call is made to it. This class also needs to be aware of the memory object, **g_objMem**, and this connection is made once in the **Form_Load**. The assumption is that the memory class remains unchanged throughout the project's run.

Aside from linking the memory object, **clsMove** is also expected to understand the structure of the bitmap object, **clsBmp**. To make applications that work with graphics easier to use, we need to intertwine these classes in some way. Let's see which properties of **clsBmp** relate to the movement object.

First of all, it's important that the starting position for the bitmap is stored before it's told to display or move into place. This way, whether the bitmap object is moved, or simply blit with its own object method, it has already been told where it's located on the display. I had to take on the responsibility for knowing where I want each graphic to start and end up throughout every script of the demo. You saw the use of the **BmpDC_LoadNew** procedure, which is called every time a new script's graphics are to be loaded into memory and which also took a position parameter.

The **SetPosition** method can also be called separate from this generic loading function, as is done in the first script after the graphics are loaded. The following lines of code told two of the graphics to take on a position offscreen to the left. The reason this is called after the bitmap is loaded is because the **Width** property of the bitmap was needed to calculate the correct position:

```
With g_objBmpScene(IDPRESENTING)
    .SetPosition -.Width, .Top
  End With
  With g_objBmpScene(IDSOFTWARE)
    .SetPosition -.Width, .Top
  End With
```

> **You would use SetStopPosition method to set the stop or ending position for a bitmap object. You would only need to do this if the bitmap is to be moved from its current position to another.**

Now we're ready for action—enter the **movDemo** object. You're about to see how easy life becomes once the move class functionality is firmed up! It's amazing. Every script that moves a demo uses the code for preparing the bitmap needs only a few lines of code to make it all happen.

Now you should have a sound understanding of the bitmap preparation for the movement class, but let's see the details behind the scenes of **clsMove** and how it relies on that preparation.

Class Description: clsMove

The beauty of these classes is that they are useful on their own, but much of their data can be used by other classes that understand them. You've seen now that bitmap dimensions and positioning, held by each bitmap object, is useful to the move class. It makes sense that each bitmap has its very own values for these properties, making it so that passing the entire object to another procedure provides access to the entire class's information. Passing a bitmap to **Init_Move** enables **clsMove** to work with the bitmap as movement takes place.

Initializing Movement

Preceding the call to **Init_Move**, the **MoveMode** property should be set to the type of movement calculation that the next movement activity should reflect. The move modes available, as they are accessed as properties of **clsMove**, are:

- **MOV_POINT**
- **MOV_CENTERX**
- **MOV_CENTERY**
- **MOV_CENTER**

In any case, the bitmap's current position needs to reflect where the movement should start from. This is prepared when the graphics are loaded, at the start of each script or, in the case of the cursor bitmap object, starts at a certain coordinate and continues where it was left off in its last movement animation.

The demo code should set up the bitmaps so that their stop coordinates are representative of where the bitmap should end up at the end of the move animation if **MOV_POINT** is the current **MoveMode**. This is because movement is then based on the current position to destination position which must be set for this process to work.

If any of the 'center' options are the current **MoveMode**, the starting position is used as the basis for a parallel movement for **CENTERX** and **CENTERY** and the stop position is set to the center of the display (gathered through the memory class).

The **CalcMovePoints** function is called from **Init_Move** to fill the array of coordinates the bitmap should move along to reach its destination. The following listing shows the contents of the **Init_Move** method for **clsMove**:

```
Public Sub Init_Move(obj As Object)
'---Description
' prepare move activity for a bitmap
' object (clsBmp) initializing path movement
'---
    Set m_objMove = obj

    With m_objMove
      ' find stop position for those requiring calculation
      Select Case m_nMoveMode
        Case m_MOVPOINT
          ' no change, point already set
        Case m_MOVCENTER
          ' find center point
          .SetStopPosition (m_objMem.Width - .Width) / 2, (m_objMem.Height -
.Height) / 2
        Case m_MOVCENTERX
          ' find center X
          .SetStopPosition (m_objMem.Width - .Width) / 2, .Top
        Case m_MOVCENTERY
          ' find center X
          .SetStopPosition .Left, (m_objMem.Height - .Height) / 2
      End Select

      CalcMovePoints .Left, .Top, .StopX, .StopY, m_nSpeed
      m_bComplete = False
    End With 'm_objMove

    ' init point array position
    m_nStep = 0

End Sub
```

Calculating Movement

Horizontal and vertical movement from point to point needs a generic function that can, at all times, come up with the right coordinates for the object to move, based on a movement amount, form start position to destination. This is the function of **CalcMovePoints**, which is our first complex algebraic analysis in this book. This function enables you to pass any coordinates to start and finish at on the display with a speed and come up with a valid set of movement points.

First, let's look at the conceptual conversion that takes place from display coordinates to axis coordinates on the screen. The following figure shows starting point **nX1**, **nY1** and ending point **nX2**, **nY2** and how they appear, after conversion to an axis:

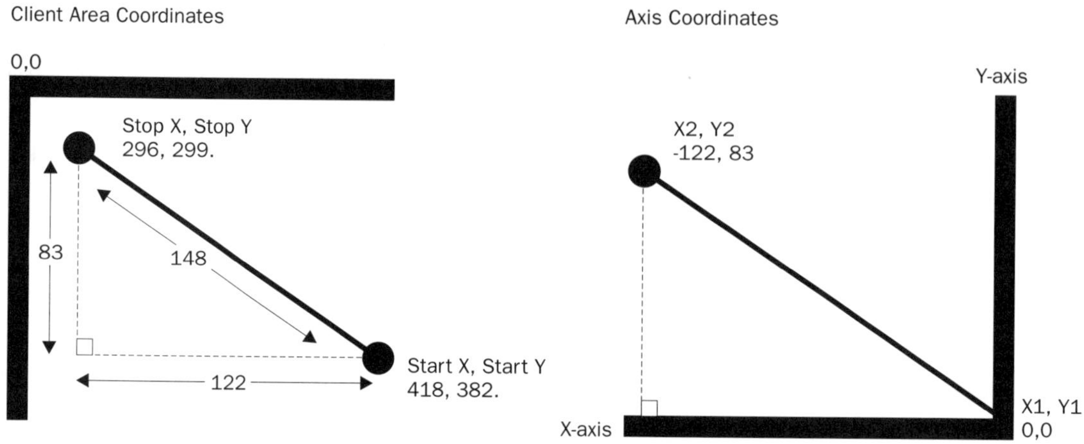

The purpose of the conversion is to make it easier to work with the equations that will calculate the distance along the solid line from point **nX1**, **nY1** to point **nX2**, **nY2** which uses some basic trigonometry and the equations that will calculate the next coordinate in the movement sequence.

CalcMovePoints is passed parameters for the two coordinates, based on their display values, and a speed, which is how far along the solid you want to see the object move. Assume for this discussion that the positions passed through the function are those shown in the previous figure and that the resulting solid line distance is the distance to travel, 148.

The first thing that happens is the coordinates passed to the function are converted and stored in their display variables: **nStartX**, **nStartY**, **nStopX** and **nStopY**:

```
nStartX = nX1: nStartY = nY1
nStopX = nX2: nStopY = nY2
```

These values remain untouched throughout the array calculations, so that they can serve as a backward reference to the intended display coordinates. Then, the distance to move along the X and Y axis are calculated:

```
nDX = nX2 - nX1: nDY = -(nY2 - nY1)
```

Notice that the Y coordinate is inverted from negative to positive, or vice versa, since negative Y is an upward movement in display coordinates, whereas it is positive in axis coordinates.

Now **nX1**, **nY1** and **nX2**, **nY2** variables are converted to axis coordinates. This is done by setting **nX1**, **nY1** to **0**, **0** and **nX2**, **nY2** to the delta movement of **nDX** and **nDY**:

```
nX1 = 0: nY1 = 0
nX2 = nDX: nY2 = nDY
```

Here's where the loop begins, with coordinates that match those of an axis, ready for mathematical calculation. The first line checks the distance from point to point against the speed value for the intended movement. The movement class has a speed setting of 30, so the distance to move must at least be 30 for this loop to be executed. The calculation for the distance from point to point is returned by the square-root of the sum of the squares of the distance along each axis:

```
Do While Sqr(nDX * nDX + nDY * nDY) > nSpeed
```

Huh? Well, if you remember $a^2 + b^2 = c^2$ from algebra class, you know this. This is checked after each coordinate movement is calculated and each time the distance should grow smaller. The first time in, the distance is 148 and the speed of 30 is definitely greater than this value, so we proceed.

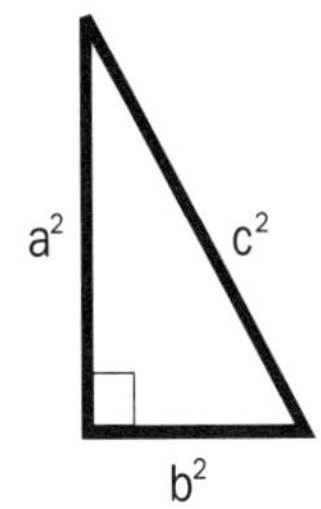

Pythagorean Theory

The sum of the squares of the two right sides of a right-angled triangle equals the square of the hypoteneuse.

$a^2 + b^2 = c^2$

The calculation of the angle for movement in this axis diagram is what helps us to determine the X and Y movement necessary to meet our destination in an even keeled movement. If the X and Y movement was simply 30 and 30 each time (positive or negative, whatever applies), the Y movement would reach its destination faster than the X movement since it's traveling a shorter distance. This is why the complex mess of mathematics is used to make movement smooth and consistent no matter what the distance to travel.

However, these equations aren't perfect for our purposes. Division by 0 doesn't mean 'indeterminate' in VB, it means 'fatal error'. To address this possibility, where there is no Y axis movement, I set the value of the angle to a perfect 360 to make the result indeterminate in our findings:

```
' get angle of movement
If nX2 - nX1 = 0 Then
  'cannot divide by zero
  dAngle = 360
Else
  dAngle = Atn((nY2 - nY1) / (nX2 - nX1))
End If
```

Next, the step is calculated. If you multiply the desired speed by the **Cos** of **dAngle**, you get the X step. Multiplying by the **Sin** of **dAngle** returns the Y step. But this has only number value accuracy; it doesn't take into consideration the quadrants along which movement takes place. We address this by sending **nStepX** and **nStepY** out for fixing to the **CalcQuadrant** procedure, which will make sure they are of the right positive or negative demeanor:

```
' calculate current step along axis
nStepX = nSpeed * Cos(dAngle)
nStepY = nSpeed * Sin(dAngle)
CalcQuadrant nDX, nDY, nStepX, nStepY
```

OK, so now we have a value for the first movement delta, **nStepX** and **nStepY**. We have to do two things with these values. First, we must move X1, Y1 to these values, representing movement along the path specified and thus decreasing the amount of movement left to go for the next iteration of the distance and step calculation. Second these new X1, Y1 values, based on a 0, 0 starting point, now represent the amount of movement that has taken place on the display. The catch that is we must convert them to display coordinates:

```
' move starting xy
nX1 = nX1 + nStepX
nY1 = nY1 + nStepY
' total delta for client starting xy
nPosDX = nX1
nPosDY = -nY1
```

Now, we can redimension the movement array to an additional element and the new position that we assign should be the starting position plus the display converted new X1, Y1 values:

```
' move starting xy
nX1 = nX1 + nStepX
nY1 = nY1 + nStepY
' total delta for client starting xy
nPosDX = nX1
nPosDY = -nY1
```

This is much easier than trying to add to the previous position in the array, the new **nStepX**, **nStepY** values, so it explains why I saved the starting X and Y coordinates in these variables:

```
ReDim Preserve m_ptMovePos(nCount)
m_ptMovePos(nCount).X = nStartX + nPosDX
m_ptMovePos(nCount).Y = nStartY + nPosDY
```

Now we can calculate the new delta, ready for the first line in this loop that checks the distance left against the speed value:

```
nDX = nX2 - nX1: nDY = nY2 - nY1
```

When the speed becomes greater than the amount of movement left, the following code finalizes the movement array to the stop position desired:

```
ReDim Preserve m_ptMovePos(nCount)
m_ptMovePos(nCount).X = nStopX
m_ptMovePos(nCount).Y = nStopY
```

Well, there you have it, an equation that works for every movement you want to pass to it. There are probably more sophisticated mathematical methods that we could use to address the quadrant problem, but that's about as far as I wanted to go into math-land when I wrote this code... and it works. Now let's see how we use this array to perform the actual movement!

Move Method

The bitmap passed to the initialization method, **Init_Move**, is the bitmap about to be moved. The next line, calling **Wait_AnimComplete**, holds processing in a loop where the **Move** method is actually called, until the move class' **Complete** property is set to **True**. Here's the wait loop for movement:

```
.MoveMode = .MOV_CENTERX
.Init_Move g_objBmpScene(IDPRESENTING)
Wait_AnimComplete ID_MOVE
```

The next line calling **Wait_AnimComplete** holds processing in a loop where the **Move** method is actually called, until the move class' **Complete** property is set to **True**. Here's the wait loop for movement:

```
Case ID_MOVE
    tmrWait.Interval = TMR_INTMOVE
    Do While Not g_objMove.Complete
      If Not tmrWait.Enabled Then
        g_objMove.Move
        If tmrWait.Interval <> 0 Then tmrWait.Enabled = True
```

```
        End If
        DoEvents
      Loop
```

The interval of the wait timer is set to some small value, so that the next call to **Move** will not take place so quickly that the object won't even be seen moving across the screen. The speed of this iteration should be about 1/18th of a second, since the **Timer** can't go any faster than this. The loop checks for **Complete** and performs the **Move** until this is **True**.

Inside the **Move** code, the bitmap (set by **Init_Move**) is erased from the display (using **ClearWorkBuffer** and passing the location rectangle of the bitmap), its position values are moved and its Blit method is called to copy the new data to the working buffer. The final call is to **UpdateDisplay**, which sends all these changes to the display. Once again, we need not concern ourselves with the dirty rectangle information for now. Let's have a look at the code:

```
Public Sub Move()
  With m_objMove
    m_objMem.ClearWorkBuffer .rLoc

    SetPosition m_ptMovePos(m_nStep).X, m_ptMovePos(m_nStep).Y

    If m_nStep = UBound(m_ptMovePos) Then
      m_bComplete = True
    Else
      m_nStep = m_nStep + 1
    End If


    .Blit
    m_objMem.UpdateDisplay
End With
End Sub
```

The position that the bitmap is moved to is the next step in the array **m_ptMovePos**, which was filled in by the **CalcMovePoints** procedure. Remember that **m_nStep** is set to 0 when the **Init_Move** method is called, so it can be freely incremented here and tested against the upper bound of the point array until it reaches the last item. At this time, **Complete** is set to **True** and the external code needs to respond to this by stopping the call to the animation.

Class Description: clsRectFX

On to fancier things! One of the things I showed you in Chapter 2 was a transition using a curtain, which either wiped the curtain on or off the display, using **PatBlt()** with black or white as the other part of the transition. This was a very basic to use transition, since we were still introducing the memory class and other issues were more important than the transition itself (like using **BitBlt()** and **PatBlt()**).

Now, with a buffed out memory and bitmap class it's time to address some other ways to implement transitions such as those. Rather than showing you just a simple wipe from left to right, right to left, and so on, I'm going to show you a class (**clsRectFX**) that could include such simpler effects, but shows you a more difficult effect to keep the adrenaline pumping. Once I've described the methodology behind the class, I'll provide a list of possible effects that you may want to try implementing as part of the class later on.

Usage in this Demo

In **Script_1** of the demo, after moving the text *'Presenting ImageWare Software and'* onto the screen, you'll notice that each bitmap is swiftly erased from the display using random rectangle blocks. This is done using a **clsRectFX** object, **g_objRectFX**. Once each bitmap has moved into position, a pause takes place before each one is wiped off by the transition. Each of the transitions is set up tailored to the bitmap to be erased from the display.

If you look at the code inside the first script, you'll see the following code performs the rectangle transition on one the first graphic, 'Presenting':

```
With g_objRectFX
    .Columns = 5
    .Rows = 2
    .Init_RectBlit g_objBmpScene(IDPRESENTING)
    Wait_AnimComplete ID_RECTBLIT
End With
```

The bitmap is divided into rectangle blocks, as shown here:

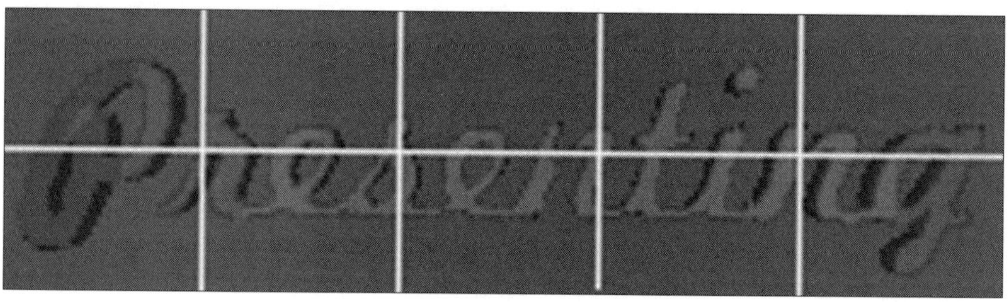

5 Columns
2 Rows

In the case of **IDPRESENTING**, five columns and two rows are specified to divide the graphic into rectangles that will be erased randomly. The call to the **Init_RectBlit** method uses the bitmap class object (**g_objBmpScene(IDPRESENTING)**) passed it to set up the internal parameters necessary for the transition. Remember that the **MemBuffer** property of the class was connected to memory object **g_objMem** in the **Form_Load**, so the double buffer is already available to the class.

Once initialized, **Wait_AnimComplete** is called, passing **ID_RECTBLIT** as a parameter so that the wait procedure will know which timer interval to use for the animation. In this case, the interval constant is set to **0** in the general declarations of the form:

```
Const TMR_INTRECTBLIT = 0
```

It's a **0** interval so that the timer won't be used to perform each call to the **RectBlit** method of the class. It needs to be performed as fast as possible and even a timer interval of **1** slows it down to a rate that makes the transition look clumsy.

What's great about how this transition is set up is that the columns and rows can be changed inside the code and you can visually judge if that breakdown works for the bitmap at hand. Now let's see how this functionality works from within the class.

Initialization

When the **Init_RectBlit** method is called, it's passed a bitmap object. This is used to set the **m_objBmp** bitmap object internally, so that the call to **RectBlit** doesn't require any parameters. Inside this initialization routine, it's expected that **Rows** and **Columns** properties for the class have been set and a precautionary check is made to make sure that at least one row and one column are specified (otherwise, the entire image is copied in one rectangle, rather than a transition).

```
Public Sub Init_RectBlit(obj As Object)
  ' check required properties are set
  Set m_objBmp = obj

  ' setup rectangles for transition
  If m_nRows = 0 Then m_nRows = 1
  If m_nCols = 0 Then m_nCols = 1
  CalcRects

  ' ready to go
  m_nRectCount = 0
  m_bComplete = False
End Sub
```

CalcRects is then called, which fills an array with rectangle information for the transition, based on the number of rows and columns specified. Then, as with most animation classes, the corresponding counter is initialized. In this case, **m_nRectCount**, and **Complete** is set to **False**.

Calculating the Rectangles

CalcRects is a private procedure of **clsRectFX** that sets up the array of rectangles to erase from the bitmap area. For the number of rows and columns, a new rectangle is filled into the array. The bitmap class is used here to define the boundaries, so that the last rectangle of each row and column doesn't go over the size of the bitmap—this could potentially erase other areas of the screen we don't want erased. Of course, this means that the last rectangle could be significantly smaller than the other equally sized rectangles and a fancy algorithm could possibly create more equal rectangles across the board. My thoughts on this? Who really cares! The transition still looks cool and, since it happens so fast, the user won't notice a thing.

Inside **CalcRects**, the first step is to calculate from the rows and columns specified for the bitmap the width and height of each row and column:

```
m_nRowHeight = Int(.Height / m_nRows)
m_nColWidth = Int(.Width / m_nCols)
```

Since this calculation can end up with a width and height for each rectangle that, when multiplied by the number of rows and columns (respectively) may not erase the entire bitmap, a check is performed that will add one more to the number of rows and columns if necessary:

```
If (.Height Mod m_nRows <> 0) Then m_nRows = m_nRows + 1
If (.Width Mod m_nCols <> 0) Then m_nCols = m_nCols + 1
```

Keep in mind that this could mean the last rectangle goes beyond the actual width and height of the bitmap object that we're erasing, which could erase beyond what we want to. This is addressed as the last rectangle dimension is next filled in.

Now, the array of rectangle structures is dimensioned to the number of rectangles that will erase the bitmap. There is a type set up in the general declarations of the class, called **RECTFX**. It includes a rectangle and a flag. A dynamic array of these structures is created, which will be used inside **CalcRects**:

```
Private Type RECTFX
  rBlock As New clsRect
  bFlag As Boolean
End Type
Private m_rfxRects() As RECTFX
```

The flag, **bFlag**, is used to indicate whether the rectangle has been erased during the calls to **RectBlit**. Here, in the loop that generates each rectangle, it's initialized to **False** for each array entry. The rectangle for each entry is filled in, based on its location on the working buffer, so that the appropriate rectangle on the background buffer can be called upon to erase each rectangle, as shown here:

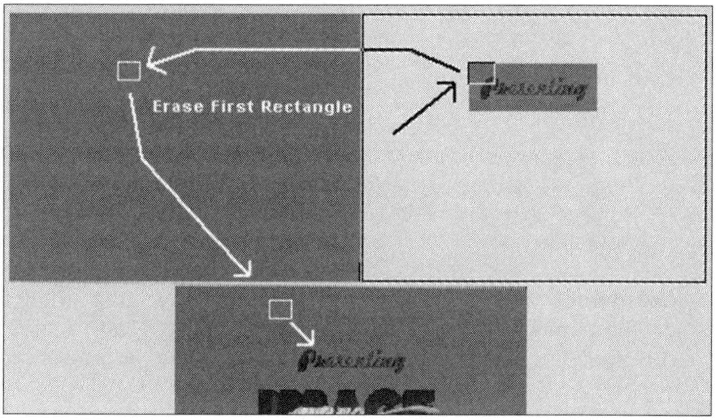

The rectangles, **rBlock**, are filled in for each entry, from left to right, top to bottom. Based on the column and row for the current entry in the loop, the values for **Left**, **Right**, **Top** and **Bottom** are completed.

```
m_nRects = m_nCols * m_nRows
    ReDim m_rfxRects(m_nRects - 1)

    ' fill array of RECTFX structures
    For nRectID = 0 To UBound(m_rfxRects)
      nColIndex = nRectID Mod m_nCols
      nRowIndex = Int(nRectID / m_nCols)

      nLeft = .Left + m_nColWidth * nColIndex
      nTop = .Top + m_nRowHeight * nRowIndex
      nRight = IIf((nLeft + m_nColWidth) > (.Left + .Width), .Left + .Width, nLeft
+ m_nColWidth)
      nBottom = IIf((nTop + m_nRowHeight) > .Top + .Height, .Top + .Height, nTop +
m_nRowHeight)
      m_rfxRects(nRectID).rBlock.SetSize nLeft, nTop, nRight, nBottom

      m_rfxRects(nRectID).bFlag = False
    Next nRectID
```

Notice the **IIf** statement used to set the **Right** and **Bottom** properties of each rectangle. The purpose of this is to trap the last rectangle on each row and column and ensure that the size of it doesn't go beyond the size of the actual area being erased.

RectBlit Method

RectBlit is called repeatedly by the **Wait_AnimComplete** procedure which is called directly after the **Init_RectBlit** method has been called. That part of the wait procedure is shown below:

```
Case ID_RECTBLIT
    tmrWait.Interval = TMR_INTRECTBLIT
    Do While Not g_objRectFX.Complete
      If Not tmrWait.Enabled Then
        g_objRectFX.RectBlit
        If tmrWait.Interval <> 0 Then tmrWait.Enabled = True
      End If
      DoEvents
    Loop
```

Then **RectFX** is called repeatedly until the **Complete** property of **g_objRectFX** is **True**. This is set to **True** by the **RectBlit** procedure when the last rectangle has been erased. Since **TMR_INTRECTBLIT** is equal to **0**, this call to **RectBlit** is repeated as fast as the loop can process. That's why each of the animation wait procedures checks for an interval of **0** before attempting to enable the **timer**, which would then result in the timer never being turned off.

Each time **RectBlit** is called, the first item on the menu is to select a random index from the rectangle array:

```
nRectID = Int((m_nCols * m_nRows - 1) * Rnd + 0)
```

Rather than using this as the rectangle item to erase, a search is performed from that array item forward, searching for the *next* rectangle that has not already been erased (so **bFlag** for that array item will be **False** still):

```
Do
  If nRectID > m_nRects - 2 Then
    nRectID = 0
  Else
    nRectID = nRectID + 1
  End If
Loop Until (m_rfxRects(nRectID).bFlag = False)
```

The reason for this is because without performing a sequential search for the next unerased rectangle, it becomes progressively more difficult to return a random number that lands successfully on an array item that can be erased. This means the rectangle effect slows significantly or can even get lost in an endless loop. This insures that it never happens.

As each rectangle is successfully erased, the rectangle counter, **m_nRectCount**, is incremented and the corresponding **bFlag** element is set to **True** to notify the array of those rectangles that have been selected and erased from display. Finally, the memory class, **clsMem**, is called to update both the working buffer and display. Notice the action here is to erase the rectangle from the working buffer, then update the display, which takes a call to **ClearWorkBuffer** (automatically handling taking the area from the background buffer to the working buffer to perform the erase):

```
m_nRectCount = m_nRectCount + 1
m_rfxRects(nRectID).bFlag = True
```

```
With m_objMem
    .ClearWorkBuffer m_rfxRects(nRectID).rBlock
   .UpdateDisplay
End With
```

Of course, if this class is edited to include copying data in this same manner, some class properties could be defined to determine whether **ClearWorkBuffer** is called, or whether the bitmap object is used to copy the data to the working buffer in this fashion.

Finally, when the last rectangle in the array is copied, **Complete** is set to **True** so that the wait procedure can complete its call to **RectBlit**, and continue to the next line in the script:

```
If m_nRectCount >= m_nRects Then m_bComplete = True
```

Class Description: clsBrushFX

Now that we've seen how to erase and display bitmaps, it's time to discover the magic of dissolve. It's one thing to remove a bitmap from display in bits and pieces, but quite another to blend (fade out) one display into another, like they do in movies at the end of a scene. The same goes for fading-in. The problem is that, as VB programmers, we are quite used to programming square corners. Bitmaps are displayed in picture box controls and they can't retain transparent pixels. There is, unfortunately, no magical 'blend' command that says, "Hey, transition these bitmaps into each other would ya!" So, we turn to the API once again for a helping hand or, in this case, a helping brush.

You need to be very clear on a few things:

- Brushes are bitmaps
- Brushes are Windows objects
- Brushes have many uses

The brush is a very useful object in Windows that, when clearly understood, can give us the power to perform interesting and effective visual effects. Though there are many uses and meanings behind the brush (I'll try to touch on some of them), the focus will be on those things that make our animation adventure more useful. We use the brush to change from one scene to another, presenting a blend effect. Keep in mind that we'll be looking at more transparent pixel effects which require a closer look at the individual pixels of two bitmaps in Chapter 7. We're going to simulate that effect by using the brush object, but first you'll need to know what the brush is and how to create it.

Creating the Brush

A brush is an 8x8 bitmap used by the GDI to fill an area by repeating its pattern. It's a special bitmap object, called the **Brush** object, that we can select into a DC to use for filling specified areas of the DC's drawing area. Once we've selected a brush into a device context, we use it to fill the area in much the same way that we use a **FillColor** property to fill a picture box's area, the difference being that, for example, when simulating a progress bar, the 8x8 square is tiled into the DC. We can use many Windows API function in conjunction with the brush object to create additional effects. **BitBlt()** and **PatBlt()** are just two example functions that are useful for this.

Perhaps you thought that, since we're using the **LoadPicture** method for loading our bitmaps into memory, we're not going to use the bitmap structures in this chapter. Well, we will, but this time we'll be using them to create a bitmap from scratch. Of course, you wouldn't necessarily want to do this with a complex bitmap image, but for brushes this is a perfect use.

A monochrome bitmap uses only a single bit for each pixel. If the bitmap is 8x8, it would surely make sense that the left side of the following figure should visually describe the memory used for a brush bitmap:

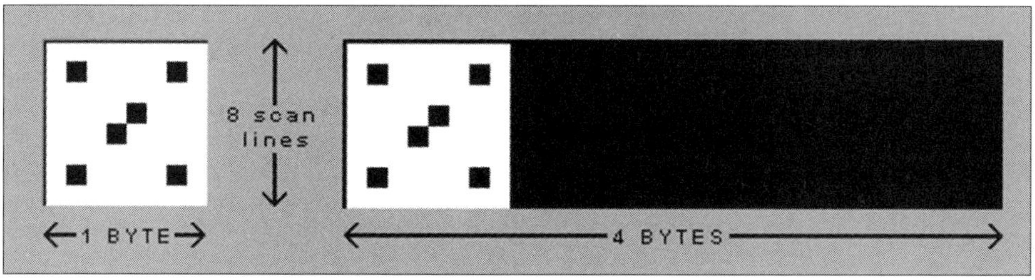

This isn't so. In Chapter 3 I mentioned the byte-alignment requirements of a bitmap. We shouldn't exclude brushes from this ruling, as they are also bitmaps. The right side of the same figure shows the true memory visualization for a brush bitmap. Each scan line read in from a bitmap file on disk must be of a length divisible by four bytes. When we're creating a brush, as if it were read in from a **.bmp** file, we must pad three bytes to the end of each scan line. It doesn't matter what those last three bytes on each line contain. These bytes won't be displayed anyhow, since the only number of bytes that count are those specified in the header when the brush is created.

Let's look at the bitmap structures that describe this brush. Going back to Chapter 3, remember we used the bitmap structures to read a bitmap from disk (as a DIB) and then we created a DDB from that bitmap. A brush has specific bitmap header information too. Our next figure describes the information we need to create a bitmap from scratch, rather than reading in a previously saved bitmap graphic as we did before:

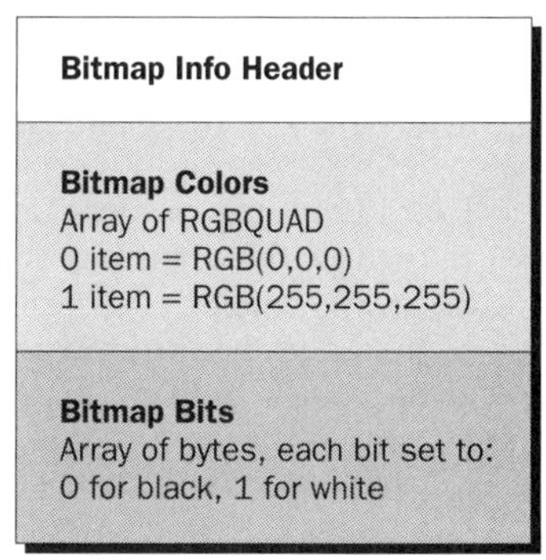

The **BITMAPINFOHEADER** is the main structure required, which includes a copy of the **BITMAPINFO** structure and an array of **RGBQUAD** structures for each pixel's color information. (If you want to refresh yourself of the code, take a quick peek back at Chapter 3.)

Since this brush code is located inside the brush effects class, this is where the brush information is initialized. Common information is used for all brushes, so the details are set up in the class's **Initialize** event, as follows:

```
With m_bmBrushInfo.bmiHeader
    .biSize = 40
    .biWidth = 8
    .biHeight = 8
    .biPlanes = 1
```

```
        .biBitCount = 1
        .biCompression = 0
        .biSizeImage = 0
        .biXPelsPerMeter = 0
        .biYPelsPerMeter = 0
        .biClrUsed = 0
        .biClrImportant = 0
    End With

   With m_bmBrushInfo.bmiColors(0)
        .rgbBlue = 0
        .rgbGreen = 0
        .rgbRed = 0
        .rgbReserved = 0
   End With

   With m_bmBrushInfo.bmiColors(1)
      .rgbBlue = 255
      .rgbGreen = 255
      .rgbRed = 255
      .rgbReserved = 0
   End With
```

The two entries in the **bmiColors()** array show that there are only two possible colors for a brush pixel: black or white. Notice that the **BITMAPINFO** structure has a width and height of 8 pixels and the bit count is set to 1 (1 byte per pixel, that is). So, each brush pixel can point to either index, 0 or 1, in the array of **bmiColors()**. Since a single bit can have a state of 0 or 1, we can describe eight pixels per byte. Keeping in mind the byte-boundary rules, four bytes must reside on each scan line, so you can see that we only need to fill the first byte with values. That means we need a buffer the size of that required by the right side of the brush bitmap figure that we saw a moment ago. But we need only set the first byte in each row to a value that tells each byte which of the eight bits are 0s and which are 1s.

To facilitate this process, another structure was also introduced to aid in the visual representation of each of the eight bits in each brush bitmap row. The array is called **BRUSHBITS** and is simply an array of eight rows, each containing a string of length 8. I used this to set up the 1s and 0s for each row in the **InitBrushData** procedure. Here's how the rows from the brush in the left side of our brush bitmap figure should be described in the code, using the **BRUSHBITS** structure:

```
   Private Type BRUSHBITS
     Row(7) As String * 8
   End Type

   ' BRUSH 1
     sBrush(0).Row(0)  =  "11111111"
     sBrush(0).Row(1)  =  "10111101"
     sBrush(0).Row(2)  =  "11111111"
     sBrush(0).Row(3)  =  "11101111"
     sBrush(0).Row(4)  =  "11110111"
     sBrush(0).Row(5)  =  "11111111"
     sBrush(0).Row(6)  =  "10111101"
     sBrush(0).Row(7)  =  "11111111"
```

If you think in terms of individual pixels pointing to color index 0 or 1, reading the information for each row is much easier. There's one catch, though: the rows are bottom up in this array, so row(0) is actually the 8th row in the brush bitmap and row(7) is the 1st. This row data is just the raw programmer-friendly method I used to visually plan out each brush. This still needs to be converted into a buffer of the same length as the brush: 32 bytes of information. The brush data is stored in a fixed string of that length so that it can be passed to the functions that create the brush. An array of these brush buffers is created and redimensioned, based on the number of brushes used in the dissolve. Then a loop checks each row of the current index of **sBrush** for the bit value. The byte to be set (in our brush bitmap figure, these are the left-most bytes in the diagram that count) is then set to **0**, so all the bits are turned off:

```
    nByteInfo.Value = 0
```

Since the bits are read from right to left, the **For...Next** loop checks the position in the row string, **sBrushRow**, turning the bit on using the same bitmasking procedures from Chapter 2. Since **nPos** is decremented from **8** to **1**, the bit-array index is actually the absolute value of **nPos - 8**:

```
    For nPos = 8 To 1 Step -1
        If Mid$(sBrushRow, nPos, 1) = "1" Then
          ' turn bit on
          nByteInfo.TurnBitsOn nByteInfo.Bit(Abs(nPos - 8))
        End If
      Next nPos
```

The next tricky area comes when we have the value for the byte. How do we get it into the 32 byte length string holding the buffer for the brush data? The byte position is chosen by the line:

```
          nByte = nRow * 4 + 1
```

If **nRow** is **0**, the first byte in the string is set. Every fourth byte is set from there on. This keeps true with the premise that the three final bytes on each row don't actually count for anything, since the first byte holds the eight pixels of color information in its individual bits. The following **Mid$** function sets that byte position to the string return of the numeric value of the eight bits set in **nByteInfo** during the loop for that row of bit information:

```
    Mid$(m_sBrushData(nIndex), nByte, 1) = Chr$(nByteInfo.Value)
```

By the end of the **InitBrushData** procedure, an array of items equaling the number of brushes to use (**NUMBRUSHS** is the constant) is filled with valid data for the entire 32 bytes required for the brush. This information is then used in the function that creates and uses the brushes for the dissolve effect.

Making a Brush

Once again, this class requires a link to the memory buffer and to a bitmap, the reason being that creating a dissolve from one scene to another requires that there be two separate images that are to be combined in some way. More specifically, their DCs are used to do the combining of data.

In Windows terms, what was created in the **Init_BrushData** procedure is an array of DIB information. The bitmap structures were set at the class **Initialization** and are the same for all brush DIBs. The DIB pixel data for each brush is retained in the 32-byte string array, **m_sBrushData()**. To use the brush data, we must convert it from raw data to a bitmap, but we don't need **SetDIBits()** for this as we did in Chapter 3 when creating the bitmap DDB from the read in data. A new Windows API function, **CreateDIBitmap()** will do the trick. The procedure, **GetBrush**, returns a handle to a brush object that can be selected into a device context for the dissolve procedure, using the following lines of code:

```
hBmp = CreateDIBitmap(g_objMem.hdcDisp, m_bmBrushInfo.bmiHeader, CBM_INIT,
m_sBrushData(nStep), m_bmBrushInfo, DIB_RGB_COLORS)
GetBrush = CreatePatternBrush(hBmp)
nRet = DeleteObject(hBmp)
```

Just like **CreateCompatibleBitmap()**, **CreateDIBitmap()** requires a compatible DC to create a bitmap compatible with the current display format. In the case of **CreateCompatibleBitmap()**, we simply created an empty bitmap of a specified width and height. In the case of **CreateDIBitmap()** we're allowed to pass data to the function in the form of a DIB that will be converted to a DDB with the corresponding information passed. The DIB data is the same set of bitmap structures as we read in from a file in Chapter 3. That's why **m_bmBrushInfo** is the data we filled from scratch up to this point, in preparation for this very moment.

The third parameter of **CreateDIBitmap()** is the constant, **CBM_INIT**, which tells the function to read the information inside the second parameter, **m_bmBrushInfo.bmiHeader**, to get the size and dimensions of the bitmap that we're creating.

The array of brush data bytes, held in the **m_sBrushData** array, represents the actual image data that is used to create the bitmap. We didn't look at this data when we read the information from a file in Chapter 3, because we copied it directly to global memory. There was too much information to read into a string variable in that instance. Now, with the brush, we've created the string variable that holds the **1**s and **0**s which are indexes to the color table of the bitmap. We created a color table (**bmiColor()**) of two entries, **0** for black, **1** for white, so each byte in the **m_sBrushData()** entry will be read as either a pixel of black or white when the bitmap is created.

The parameters **m_sBrushData(nStep)**, **m_bmBrushInfo** and **DIB_RGB_COLORS** combined make this possible. **DIB_RGB_COLORS** signifies that the **bmiColors()** information is complete with RGB values rather than the index numbers that point to a palette entry. What's returned is a bitmap handle (a DDB initialized to the brush information as if **SetDIBits()** was called to read the information from a file) that can be used to create the brush we need.

The **CreatePatternBrush()** call is passed our new bitmap and does just what it says. It creates a pattern brush that can, in turn, be selected into a DC for use as the current brush object. Once we've created the brush object, we no longer need the bitmap that was used to create it, and so it's deleted.

Dissolve

When the **Dissolve** is initialized, some miscellaneous settings are prepared, but the main point is that the dissolve step counter be initialized too, so that the first brush in the array will always start the dissolve process. So the purpose of the **Init_Dissolve** method is to assign the bitmap for subsequent calls to **Dissolve** and initializing the step and complete flag:

```
Set m_objBmp = obj

m_bComplete = False
m_nStep = 0
```

As with the other classes, an iteration calls the **Dissolve** method of this class and, each time, the step for the dissolve is incremented by 1. The main difference here is that the **Dissolve** is always complete with the array of brushes that has been cycled through, whereas the **Move** method of **clsMove** could be any number of steps, depending on how far the movement is.

If you've run the code, you'll have seen that the shield bitmap in **Script_2** is used as a bullet for key points that slide across the screen and is dissolved or faded into the display each time. The **Dissolve** function is as follows:

```
Public Sub Dissolve()
'---Description
' using the current step in the dissolve, specified by m_nStep
' select the brush cooresponding to the step into the work DC
' and blit the information for the animation
'---
Dim stBrush As Long
Dim hBrush As Long
Dim nRet As Long

With g_objMem
   ' get next dissolve brush
   hBrush = GetBrush(m_nStep)
   stBrush = SelectObject(.hdcWork, hBrush)

   ' update work buffer
   .UpdateWorkBuffer m_objBmp.hdc, m_objBmp.rArea, m_objBmp.rLoc, MERGEMASK
   .UpdateDisplay

   ' release brush
   nRet = SelectObject(.hdcWork, stBrush)
   nRet = DeleteObject(hBrush)
End With

m_nStep = m_nStep + 1
If m_nStep = NUMBRUSHES Then m_bComplete = True

End Sub
```

First, **GetBrush** is called to get the current dissolve iteration's brush object, based on the array of brushes and the value of **m_nStep**. This figure shows the order in which these brushes will be called:

sBrush(0) *sBrush(1)* *sBrush(2)* *sBrush(3)*

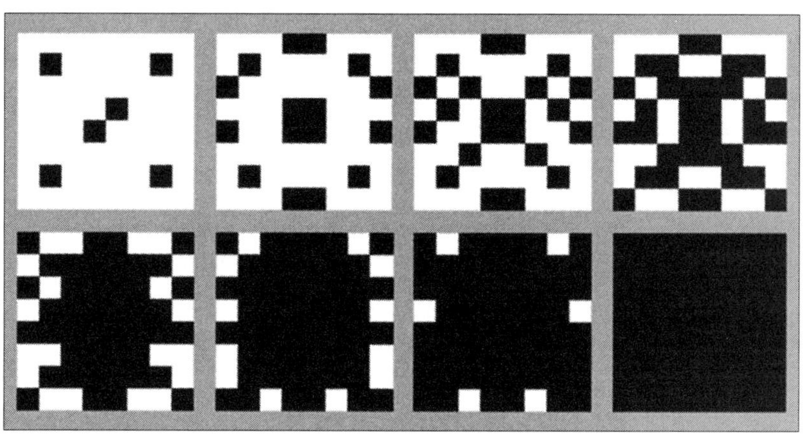

sBrush(4) *sBrush(5)* *sBrush(6)* *sBrush(7)*

The brush object is then selected into the working buffer of the memory class, because this is where the bitmap is going to be copied. Now, the working buffer's DC of **clsMem** has a brush object selected into it, besides the original brush associated with all DCs. This isn't quite enough to effect change on the copying procedure for the bitmap. If the standard raster operation of **SRCCOPY** is used to copy the information to the display, the brush is ignored in the pixel transfer.

A special raster operation code is used to make this possible. This is what combines the brush with the current state of **hdcWork** and the information in the bitmap's **hdc**. The idea is to leave some pixels of the current state of the display, while copying some of the pixels of the bitmap we want to see, in this case the shield. We don't actually want to see the black and white of the brush bitmap at all! Let's walk through the steps:

1. Brush **AND** destination. The brush pixels **AND** the destination pixels will produce black where the brush pixels were black, and will leave untouched those pixels on the destination where the brush pixels were white. We covered this in Chapter 2, but briefly again, **0** (black) **AND** any number will end up **0** (black). **1** (white) and any other number does nothing.

2. **NOT** brush **AND** source. The source pixels that we should copy to the destination are those that are now black on the destination from the previous step. Sounds simple, but how do we copy the source directly to the destination and tell it to ignore non-black pixels? To make those pixels we don't want to copy from the source, black, we **AND** the opposite of the brush with the source.

3. Source **OR** destination. Now that there are black pixels on the source and destination bitmaps the exact opposite of each other, we can do this and get the final result we're looking for. The new source's black pixels will **OR** with the destination pixels that were not changed and will stay black. The new source's unchanged pixels will **OR** with the black pixels of the destination and overwrite them. Now we see no black or white pixels, unless of course they were part of one of the bitmaps involved. The blend is complete!

Is there a faster way? Sure, use the constant that will perform it in one fell swoop, as I do in the function:

```
Const MERGEMASK = &HAC0744
```

The previous figure showed the sequence of brushes used in this sample's dissolve. The first brush has the least number of black pixels, the last is entirely black. Now you can see how the number of black pixels increasing, increases the number of pixels from the source that get copied to the destination in tact. Nice! Go ahead and play with the **1**s and **0**s of the **Init_BrushData** procedure in **clsBrushFX**. See what you can come up with!

Summary

We've introduced many complex topics in the demo sample for this chapter. Several classes now exist that rely on each other in a fairly cohesive manner and some interesting display techniques are encapsulated in **`clsRectFX`** and **`clsBrushFX`** to whet your palette.

We introduced the movement class, **`clsMove`**, which works nicely with the bitmap and memory class to handle movement in a smoothly double-buffered display. The types of movement covered in the movement class are those needed to implement what the sample demo uses, but with this head start, you can probably see how easy it would be to introduce more as you need to. We can also add to the other two effect classes, **`clsRectFX`** and **`clsBrushFX`** by altering the code just slightly. With this framework, all you have to do is play!

Aside from the new classes and techniques, you may have found the demo sample an enlightening new programming idea for future use. But, just in case that wasn't enough to excite you, let's move on and see how a game application might be created using VB and a little help from our API friends!

```
Private Declare Function GlobalFree Lib "kernel32" (ByVal
Private Declare Function GlobalLock Lib "kernel32" (ByVal
Private Declare Function GlobalUnlock Lib "kernel32" (ByV
'--copying bitmap bits
' copies a global block of data into global memory
Private Declare Sub CopyMemory Lib "kernel32" Alias "RtlM

'--copies global block of data into DIB
Private Declare Function SetDIBits Lib "gdi32" (ByVal m_hc
   ByVal hBitmap As Long, ByVal nStartScan As Long, By
   ByVal lpBits As Any, lpBI As BITMAPINFO, ByVal wUsa

'--blits DC to DC
Private Declare Function BitBlt Lib "gdi32" (ByVal hDestDC
Private Declare Function StretchBlt Lib "gdi32" (ByVal hDes

'--palette methods
Private Declare Function CreatePalette Lib "gdi32" (lpLogPa
Private Declare Function SelectPalette Lib "gdi32" (ByVal h
Private Declare Function RealizePalette Lib "gdi32" (ByVal
Private Declare Sub AnimatePalette Lib "gdi32" (ByVal hPa

'--device context methods
Private Declare Function SelectObject Lib "gdi32" (ByVal h

Private Declare Function CreateCompatibleBitmap Lib "gdi3
Private Declare Function DeleteObject Lib "gdi32" (ByVal h

Private Declare Function CreateCompatibleDC Lib "gdi32" (
```

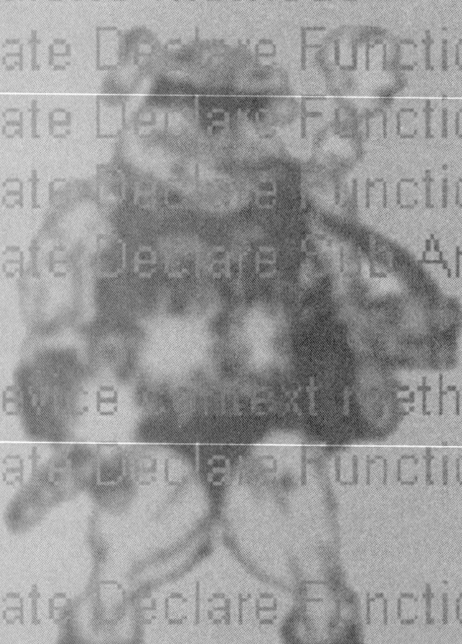

Chapter

5

Fun With Ducks

Just when you thought I might give your brain a break from this fabulous adventure in VB programming techniques, yet another chapter invites you to some light reading. Welcome to Chapter 5. Here's where I start linking some of those useful graphics methods and classes from earlier chapters into game creation. It's not just about copying graphics quickly to the screen, though speedy blitting certainly helps. We must now skillfully place what we've seen in previous chapters into more dynamic situations, ultimately testing their modularity. Let's throw caution (and preplanned scripting) to the wind. Games are of an unpredictable and dynamic nature, requiring more flexible coding practices.

Though modularity is necessary for creating a dynamic game application, there's a trade off for modularity—speed. While attempting to mentally prepare you for some of the trials and tribulations of game programming with VB4, I'll tell you the story of how we created the duck game for this chapter. Be brave, there are tender moments where code had to be stripped and moved and walked through, over and over and over again. It could very well drive you to tears. Don't worry, I'll spare you the really pathetic stuff, so grab a small tissue and read on.

Creating a Game

In Chapter 4, I discussed some planning practices that were necessary to create the demo program. These preparations are useful for developing all applications, but when you're developing a game, you need some additional theory under your belt. The sheer random nature of a game requires careful planning in order to keep the code dynamic and modular (I know, I know, I've said this before, but it's important OK?). Working with reusable code makes it easier to alter a project, introducing some new functionality while editing some older, distinguished methods.

In the following sections, I'll be describing the features of the Fun with Ducks game (I couldn't think of a better title). I'll take you through each level in the game, how it works and what major code components comprise its functionality. Also, as a prelude to the detailed description of each code segment, I'll summarize the significant steps that we followed to build this game. The steps will be in order of those sections of the code that we had to write and perfect first, followed by the new and existing procedures that we needed to add or change as the project grew. This may be your first time programming a game, so stepping through the development process for both levels of Fun with Ducks may lend a hand to your future blockbuster.

Fun with Ducks

Fun with Ducks is a simple game that demonstrates some rudimentary game strategies and coding practices through both of its levels. It also shines a bright light on the drawbacks that VB brings to the table when it comes to game development. I'm not trying to discourage you from writing a game using VB, but there's definitely some craft in keeping the player impressed with speed and slick graphics. Fun with Ducks uses elemental game animation techniques, but should serve as a suitable example when next you embark on a game-building journey using VB, while giving you an insight on some programming paths to avoid.

Level 1, Duck Terminator, begins with a group of ducks flying across the screen, from left to right. The object is to terminate the ducks by clicking them with the left mouse button. Each time you miss a shot, you lose a try. Once all of your tries are gone, it's game over. The animation speed of each duck is only limited to how fast the CPU can process the paint cycle. There are ten ducks to begin with and the catch is that, as you kill off each duck, the remaining ones begin to fly much faster, until there's only one left. Remember, click and miss five times and the ducks aren't terminated—you are!

The main game techniques introduced by Level 1 are:

- Hit testing with mouse clicks
- Efficient repainting for layered objects
- Organizing game loops

When you begin playing Level 1—by clicking the play button when the Level 1 radio button is selected—a number of ducks are immediately generated to fly at random heights from left to right across the screen. These ducks fly at a 'clickable' speed; in other words, since they're not going all that fast, you should have a fairly good chance of popping off at least a few. You should note here that, as you kill more ducks, they begin to fly faster and faster, since there are fewer ducks on screen and fewer paint cycles for the CPU to process (although some would argue that they fly faster because you're getting too good an aim).

Level 2, Lost Duck, repeats some of the basic game functionality of Level 1, but also introduces some new techniques. This time, you're the lost duck and you appear facing to the right in the far left corner of the screen. Your duck can move via the specified keystrokes: *E* moves up, *S* moves left, *L* moves right, and *M* moves down. Other, randomly generated ducks fly in from the right side of the screen at different heights, heading your way. Your duck needs to get to the other side of the screen, without colliding with any of the others. 'Easy' I hear you say. Well, not only do you have to do it once, but for a specified number of times, according to what level you're on. Now it's not so easy, huh!

Level 2 introduces some more techniques:

- Direction and reverse blitting
- Using the keyboard for interaction
- Collision detection

Beyond the specifics for each level, the game also covers other important programming topics, such as:

- Random path movement
- Timing of multiple sprites

Now, for the steps to create the game!

Your First Game

Where do you begin when you're creating your first game? For your first time, you want to start with the small stuff, gradually building up to that wonderful masterpiece that you always knew you could put together. Here's a detailed, bottom-up approach to creating the duck game, which should provide some simple, conceptual steps that make game development easier.

Designing games is a tricky field that relies on a solid understanding of how all types of games work and how they appeal to our senses. What makes a game successful is a very elusive combination of factors and is very much a subjective matter. Check out Appendix E for a full guide to game design resources.

I'll go over Level 1, since this foundation should provide you with sufficient information on how we implemented the game strategies. As I describe each step, I'll mention some notable issues that you need to take into consideration, to give you an idea of the kinds of things that can get in the way if you don't code the game correctly to begin with.

1 Gather existing classes. The classes introduced thus far in the book have been fundamental to several development scenarios. Both the memory and the bitmap class—**`clsMem`** and **`clsBmp`**—are key elements. **`clsMem`** is the memory class for the link to the display and the double buffer area for smooth scene transitions. **`clsBmp`** is the bitmap class for loading and assigning pertinent properties and using standard methods for the each bitmap used throughout. We developed each class with reusability in mind, so should require little change, though some is inevitable when you start introducing game scenarios. As I walk through the process of building up code, I'll point out the changes you need to make and clarify why. Keep in mind that, when you alter them, your classes should still be backwards compatible if possible, though all functionality within the class may not always be used in a given application.

2 Make a duck fly. The best way to start is to ignore things like animation path, timing, or the issue of how each animation is triggered and terminated. Since one of the main components of the game is to make ducks fly across the screen, let's start out by just making one of those duck frames move. First, create a simple loop that gets your new application working with the existing classes and one of the duck bitmaps. This leads to the creation of the sprite class, **`clsSprite`**. You'll see the details of the transition from the bitmap class to the sprite class in another section of this chapter—it essentially reflects much of the bitmap class, with some additional capabilities, like tracking and changing animation frames.

Having moved a single duck frame across the screen and built the sprite class, you can implement a single flying duck across the screen. Once you've done that, we can lead into the next step to game development: generating more sprites.

3 Make more ducks fly. Now that a duck is successfully making its way across an empty sky, let's fill the sky up with some of his friends! Once again, ignoring extraneous issues like timing and quantity, just toss a VB timer control on the main form and generate a new duck every interval. Since the sprite class was used to make the first duck fly, it makes sense that we turn it into a dynamic array to make the rest do the same, right? OK, so a dynamic array it is, currently without a limit. When we add a new duck to the sprite array, a set of starting position coordinates is assigned, along with the necessary frames.

4 Route your ducks. Without introducing any fancy path considerations, when a new duck is created, the least we can do is to generate a different starting position from the last. For now, the actual path along which the ducks fly is parallel to the X axis, which is OK for the purpose of getting this game to work and do its thing. Here we see the territory along the Y axis that the new duck can be told to fly at.

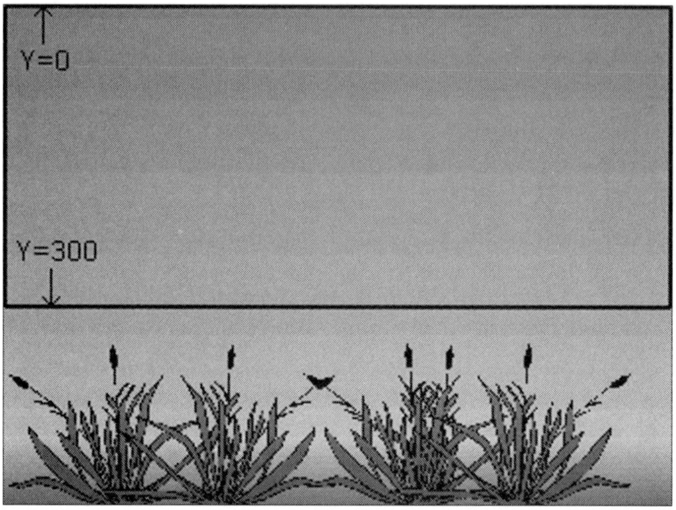

They all start offscreen at stage-left, move right at a set delta movement along the X axis and start again in their original position when they disappear stage-right.

5 Terminate your ducks. Once the ducks are flying happily across the screen, you can implement some code to terminate them. A mouse click that successfully hits a duck is what kicks it out of the scene, so this is the next step. Don't worry just yet about changing the graphic when the duck is hit, just work on how you take the duck out of commission. To implement termination, you must first intercept the **`MouseDown`** event for **`picDisplay`**, using the coordinates passed to determine which ducks, if any, were flying when the user clicked.

When the user clicks the left mouse button, **`L1_HitTest`** is called to perform the hit-testing functionality. A loop through all sprites in the duck array (one good reason for the sprites being a dynamic array), tests the click coordinates against the rectangle coordinates of the sprite (**`clsSprite.rLoc`** property) on the display. When the location of the mouse click is found within a location rectangle of one of the sprites, it's a hit! Once confirmed, that duck in the sprite array item is tagged as hit (the **`clsSprite.Hit`** property), because we don't want to continue moving it across the screen; it should be ignored in the game engine loop.

There's a little more to this topic than just telling that sprite item that it's been hit. We need to make the duck appear to have been hit and then disappear. We also need to do some housekeeping for scoring and the number of tries left. Also, when an item in the array is marked for termination, we can use it for another sprite rather than continuing to add items to the sprite array indefinitely. We'll cover this level of detail in a later section, because, at this point, I'm still just providing an overview of steps.

6 Layer your ducks. What about layers? If more than one duck is flying in the same area of the screen, or their rectangles overlap, how do we decide which duck was hit if a click is successful? By cycling through the duck array from beginning to end, searching for a successful hit, the first rectangle that provides a match will be the one marked as hit. If more than one duck was in the same area, this may not be the duck that was flying in front. Whichever duck is displayed on top should be the one who gets the hit, so, to test for the correct hit, we must add layer information to each.

Layering can become a very complex issue, but to keep things simple here, as each duck is created in the game, the layer value equals the index it appears at, inside the array of duck sprites. This means that if the loop started at the upper bound of the array, stepping backward to the lower bound of the array, the first hit would indeed be the correct layer, since the layer equals the item number. This isn't exactly how the final code works, for reasons which I'll explain, but at the onset this is an easy way to get started.

7 Add some finishing touches. We have implemented the basics of the game now, which makes it ultimately easier to implement more detailed work. Here are the issues that you're faced with at this point:

- A duck isn't hit when the mouse clicks on a transparent pixel within its rectangle.
- When ducks fly over one another, as one is moved, the other is partially erased by the dirty rectangle of the moving sprite.
- When there is just one duck, it seems to fly really fast, but when there are several, they seem to fly a lot slower.

8 Create Level 2! Once you've taken care of these problems, it's time to move to Level 2. Here, your duck flies to the right and the rest fly left, towards you from the right. This is also where you add keyboard control, flip the flying ducks to face left and test for collisions. Once you've implemented Level 1, this isn't such a chore as it may at first seem. The steps are:

- Create your sprite and put in the keyboard code to make it move.
- Create a new sprite from a timer interval, setting its properties to fly backwards (the **`Direction`** property of **`clsSprite`**). Then make the blit code recognize the **`Direction`** property and blit backwards.
- Rather than testing a mouse click within a rectangle, change the code to test for overlapping rectangles with your duck and the backwards ducks in the sprite array.

Class Description: clsSprite

Now that you have an idea of the overall development steps that went into the final game, I can start explaining the code. In this section, I'll explain the creation of the sprite class from the bitmap class, since this is the central class that enables the game to function so smoothly. This includes the purpose of the sprite class, how it handles animating frames and its connection to the bitmap class.

Building clsSprite from clsBmp

First of all, what *is* a sprite? Well, a sprite can come in many shapes and sizes, but essentially it's a graphic that is moved over a complex background, usually of an irregular shape (non-rectangular). This means that it requires some form of transparency to copy the actual sprite data to the screen, without disrupting the background with an ugly rectangular bitmap graphic. This isn't a new topic for us since almost every chapter so far has used some form of transparency for copying graphics.

A sprite can be a single frame (like a ball) that is moved across the screen, but it can also require several frames (like a flying duck). What a coincidence! We use four flying frames to make each of our ducks fly.

duck1.bmp

duck2.bmp

duck3.bmp

duck4.bmp

These frames, shown sequentially, constitute the downward motion of each duck's wings as it flies. This isn't, however, the complete run-cycle for the sprite animation. As each duck flies, it must flap its wings down, then flap them up to prepare for the next flap down, otherwise it falls and dies. I mentioned the concept of the run-cycle in Chapter 1. This is the complete animation cycle that leaves your character in a position where starting at the first frame again won't amount to choppy movement. The following sequence shows the complete flying duck run-cycle:

duck1.bmp

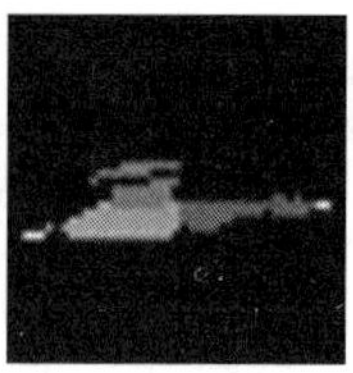

duck2.bmp

duck3.bmp

duck4.bmp

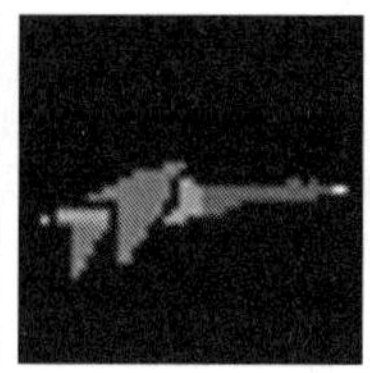

duck3.bmp

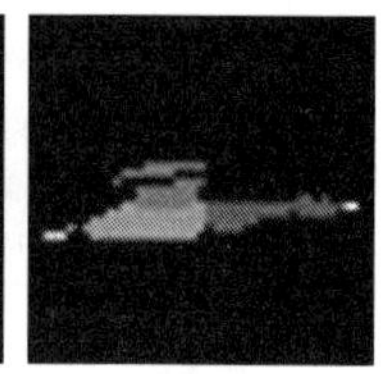

duck2.bmp

The two middle frames are repeated on the way up, but in reverse.

> *On the accompanying CD, we have a selection of over 500 sprites, with a variety of styles, positions and frames to make your mouth water. Hey–if you were worrying about your graphical prowess, like I was with mine, something in this little lot will surely save your bacon! You can find them in* **`\Apps\SpritLib`**, *where they are stored as* **`.bmp`** *graphics files. They are freeware, so if you create a marvel with them, their creator only wishes to receive a credit. You can find further details in the* **`Readme.txt`** *file.*

The Run-cycle of clsSprite

This is where the sprite class comes into play. Here's a visual representation of the link between **`clsBmp`** and **`clsSprite`**, as well as where the actual graphic data is stored:

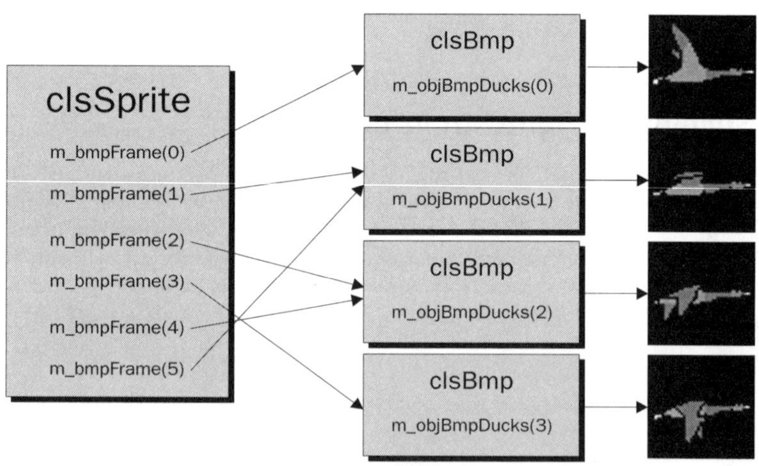

To make them available throughout the game, we don't need to load the four frames more than once, so, as before, we use the bitmap class to read in the bitmap data, place it into a device context in memory and store the dimensions of each bitmap. The duck flying bitmaps are contained in an array of bitmap classes, **`m_bmpDucks()`**. Items 0 through 3 represent each frame.

We then use the sprite class to generate a complete run-cycle. An array of **`clsBmp`** within the **`clsSprite`**, **`m_bmpFrames()`**, is dimensioned to the number of frames in the run-cycle, which is 0 through 5 for duck flight. The sprite class' frame array uses the items in the bitmap array as 0, 1, 2, 3, 2, and 1 to complete the run-cycle. It's important to note that each instance of **`clsSprite`** used for each duck that flies across the screen, does *not* repeat a copy of the actual bitmap in memory which is merely pointed to by the bitmap class **`hdc`** property.

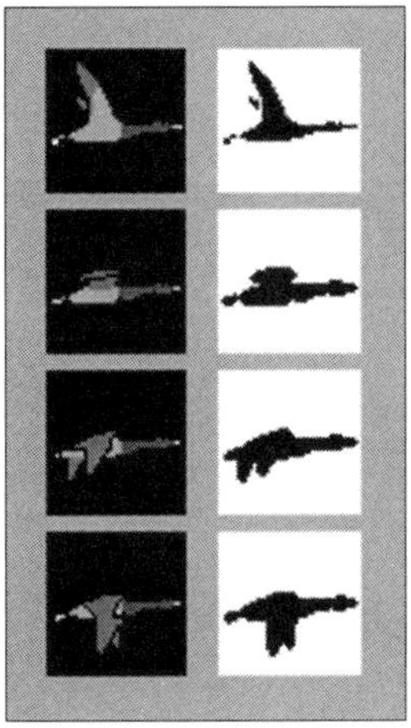

The bitmap class provides a good solid start for developing the sprite class. From the previous chapter, you know that the bitmap class enables transparency by using both the bitmap and its mask bitmap, both pointed to by the same instance of the bitmap class. Each duck frame requires this transparency, so there are two graphics loaded into memory, per **`m_bmpDuck()`** item:

Sprites are moved over complex backgrounds much like the bitmaps were slid across the screen in Chapter 4's demo program. The only difference is, at each interval, not only is the graphic moved, but its appearance is changed to reflect the next frame in the sprite's animation. The sprite class is used to track the cycling of each frame in the animation each time it's told to blit. The fundamental purpose of the sprite class is to organize the frames that make up the animation in a sequence that can be repeated over and over again (the run-cycle) and connect each frame to its corresponding bitmap object, which points to the actual graphic in memory.

Other clsSprite Components

Considering the functionality of the bitmap class, let's think in general terms about what functions the sprite class should perform. As we've said, the bitmap class points to the actual graphics loaded into memory, so the sprite class need not repeat that functionality. However, since the sprite class needs to call for those graphics based on its internal list of run-cycle frames, it needs access to the appropriate bitmap objects for each of them. For this we use an array of **`clsBmp`** (**`m_bmpSprite()`**), dimensioned to the number of frames in the sprite's run-cycle. Another internal class variable (**`m_nCurrFrame`**) tracks the position in the bitmap array of the run-cycle for the current frame being displayed. Each time the sprite is called to be displayed, or blit, the current frame position is bumped to the next frame in the run-cycle, returning to the first position when the run-cycle is complete.

During the transition from **`clsBmp`** to **`clsSprite`**, some central properties and methods in **`clsBmp`** were passed on, some were removed and some added. Let's see how those properties and methods of the sprite class work and how they relate to **`clsBmp`**.

Blitting Using clsSprite and clsBmp

The central functionality of **clsSprite** is as a tracking mechanism for each frame in the run-cycle. When an instance of the sprite class is created, the first property that should be set is the **NumFrames** property, which also dimensions the array of bitmaps to the number of frames for the run-cycle minus 1, and starts the current frame position variable (**m_nCurrFrame**) at the first element in the array:

```
Public Property Let NumFrames(nFrames As Integer)
  m_nNumFrames = nFrames
  ReDim m_bmpFrame(nFrames - 1)
  m_nCurrFrame = 0
End Property
```

Notice that you *don't* use the **Preserve** keyword when you're setting the frame array. It's assumed that, when you're defining a new value for the number of frames in the sprite, you're changing the run-cycle of the sprite animation to a different set of graphics. This means that it's acceptable to reset the array to the appropriate number of frames without preserving the previous frames.

All we have so far is an array of empty bitmap classes and a frame pointer. We must now link each item in the **m_bmpFrame()** to its associated bitmap object. To do this, we'll call the **SetFrame** method of the sprite class with two parameters: an index into the run-cycle array and the corresponding bitmap object:

```
Public Sub SetFrame(nIndex As Integer, bmp As clsBmp)
  Set m_bmpFrame(nIndex) = bmp

  m_nWidth = m_bmpFrame(nIndex).Width
  m_nHeight = m_bmpFrame(nIndex).Height
End Sub
```

Of course, we can assume that the bitmap class will already have loaded the frame in question and that (for this game, anyway) the sprite frames each carry the same dimensions. Though we don't need to set the width and height for the sprite class each time a bitmap frame is set, this was the most appropriate place to put that code, so the last frame you set will define the width and height for the sprite class run-cycle. (When I discuss the use of the sprite class during game play, issues surrounding the retention of certain bitmap properties within the sprite class will become clear.)

As we did with the bitmap class in Chapter 4, we must also set up the sprite with a position, so the **SetPosition** method and the **Top** and **Left** properties have been retained from the bitmap class. **SetStopPosition**, **StopX** and **StopY** are also retained for compatibility and future use, though we don't need them for the duck game. Just as the bitmap class kept track of its position and corresponding rectangle location and area, so does the sprite class using **rArea**, **rLoc** and **rPrevLoc**. These properties are used in exactly the same way that the bitmap class used them, for tracking the rectangular area for any frame in the sprite, along with the rectangular position (the previous position is used if the sprite is moving) where the sprite is located on the display. This way, we always know where the sprite is and its size and we're forced to remember that every frame included in the sprite's array of bitmaps is of equivalent dimensions as the code expects.

Blitting the Sprite

Now that we have a method for accessing each frame and a list of information for the position and dimensions of all run-cycle frames, we need a method of displaying the sprite and cycle through each frame. Whether the sprite is moving or not, each interval of the sprite's animation triggers the display of the next sprite frame. The module level variable, **`m_nCurrFrame`**, is incremented each time the sprite's **`Blit`** method is called, but is sent back to the beginning once the end of the run-cycle is reached.

Though this **`Blit`** method was carried over from the **`clsBmp`**, their functionality is quite different. Betcha thought I'd just repeat all that functionality inside **`clsBmp`**'s **`Blit`** function? No no no! For consistency, we should essentially treat bitmap and sprite objects similarly in code. If Chapter 4's demo moved bitmaps across the screen, at each interval telling the bitmap to blit, then the duck game, which moves sprites across the screen, should tell the sprite to blit. It's encapsulated within the sprite class as to how the graphic is accessed for the actual blitting action. After all, the sprite class contains all the pertinent information about the current frame and the bitmap object that it points to.

The first thing that the sprite's Blit method does is to increment the current frame variable, **`m_nCurrFrame`**, in preparation for the blit:

```
Public Sub Blit()

m_nCurrFrame = IIf(m_nCurrFrame = m_nNumFrames - 1, 0, m_nCurrFrame + 1)

m_bmpFrame(m_nCurrFrame).SetPosition m_rLoc.Left, m_rLoc.Top
m_bmpFrame(m_nCurrFrame).Blit

End Sub
```

We can assume that each time this Blit procedure is called, the next frame is up for display. Then we must set up the position of the bitmap class to match that of the sprite. This is because the sprite is the object being maneuvered on the screen, so *its* position is an accurate reflection of the screen location for the next frame. The bitmap class isn't up-to-date since it's not being moved directly by the game code. Directly before calling the Blit method for the current frame's bitmap object, the **`SetPosition`** method for that object is called, passing the **`Left`** and **`Top`** values for the sprite's current position. Now the bitmap's Blit method will be looking at the correct position. Lastly, the bitmap class' Blit method is called, which performs the same functionality as it always did for any bitmap object. It uses the bitmap's device context information and the API declarations for blitting, with or without transparency:

```
Public Sub Blit()

If m_nBlitMethod = m_blMASK Then
  memGame.UpdateWorkBuffer m_hdc_Mask, m_rArea, m_rLoc, SRCAND
  memGame.UpdateWorkBuffer m_hdc, m_rArea, m_rLoc, SRCINVERT
Else
  m_memGame.UpdateWorkBuffer m_hdc, m_rArea, m_rLoc, SRCCOPY
End If

End Sub
```

Note that both of these listings are simplified from the final Blit methods for each class, since they don't consider the possibility for blitting only a portion of a graphic... I didn't want to scare anybody!

Hit Testing Using clsSprite, clsBmp and clsLocate

The other central purpose of the sprite class is the testing for mouse clicks. The game engine really drives this, but here I can describe how the internals of the function works for each sprite and the relationship between this functionality of **clsSprite** with **clsBmp** and **clsLocate**. Later, when I call the functions described here, you'll know what's going on behind the scenes. I'll be calling methods that belong to **clsLocate**, which has been changed since Chapter 2. Don't panic, though. We'll describe the internals of those class changes later on in this chapter.

The **SpriteHit** method of **clsSprite** is the subject of our conversation now. This is the function that is called when a mouse click is performed in Level 1. As I mentioned in the description of the level, we must test each sprite to see whether its location rectangle (**rLoc**) contains the point that was clicked with the mouse. Below we see the mouse click that generates a call to **SpriteHit**. The dotted line represents the area that the duck bitmap fills.

The function returns **True** if the point coordinates passed are located within the sprite's location coordinates on the screen, **False** if not:

```
Public Function SpriteHit(x, y) As Boolean
Dim locHit As New clsLocate

    SpriteHit = False
           If Not (locHit.PointInRect(CLng(x), CLng(y), m_rLoc)= 0) Then
                 SpriteHit = True
    End If
End Function
```

An instance of the location class (for lack of a better name) is used to call its encapsulated **PtInRect()**, found in the **PointInRect** method of the class. This functionality hasn't changed since you last saw it in Chapter 2. This test will prove insufficient in a short period of time, since sprites aren't actually rectangles but irregularly shaped graphics that require some transparency. I used this test while the rest of the game code was being filled out, but once this hit test was fully debugged, the next step was to create an additional test, asking what the color value was of the pixel beneath the mouse click.

Testing for Transparency

The only way to be sure that a duck was actually hit is to make sure that some other area of the duck's bitmap, besides the duck pixels, were *not* hit. The duck bitmap is made transparent by using a copy of the graphic on a pure black background—RGB 0, 0, 0—and a mask bitmap of that same graphic—the duck filled in with pure black on a pure white background—RGB 255, 255, 255:

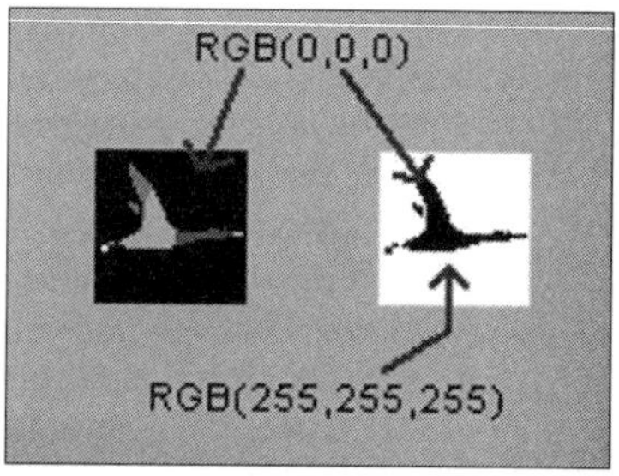

To test for transparency, I had to select the pixel color from either the actual bitmap's DC or the mask DC. If I test the mask DC, I can ask the question "Is the pixel color pure black or pure white?" to determine whether the location was on the sprite area or the transparent area. If I test the sprite bitmap, I'm forced to ask the question "Is the pixel pure black or not?". To keep with what seems to be the standard, the code asks the second question. The reason? As you'll see in Chapter 7, to create transparency in a bitmap's display, we don't always use a mask bitmap. Sometimes a single color (not always pure black) is set aside as the transparent color of the bitmap, then when each pixel is copied to a DC, the transparent pixels are skipped. We can't do this right now for reasons you'll see in Chapter 7, but I'll conform to this theory now by adding a property to the bitmap class, **TransColor**, and initialize it to pure black. This will be my bitmap's transparent color.

In the final version of the **SpriteHit** method of **clsSprite**, once the click coordinate is confirmed to be located within the sprite's location rectangle, the code that tests the pixel color can do its thing. Now the point that was passed to the **SpriteHit** method must be converted into coordinates within the sprite's actual area rectangle. To keep with the example shown in the last two figures, a click at coordinate 300, 70 converts to 20, 20 within the bitmap's device context area:

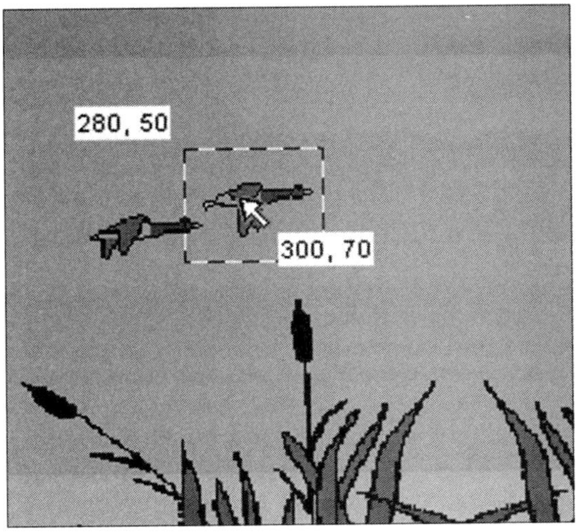

The next step gets us the pixel color from coordinate 20, 20 within the current bitmap frame of the sprite. The Windows API function, **GetPixel()**, returns the RGB color value for a coordinate on a device context's drawing area (or bitmap). The return from this function is compared to the **TransColor** property for that bitmap frame. If there's a match, the click landed on the transparent area of the bitmap so there's no dead duck. Any other color returned is considered part of the actual sprite graphic. The assumption here, of course, is that you won't use the transparent pixel anywhere on the actual sprite. In the case of the duck bitmaps, all areas that appear to be black are RGB values of 3, 3, 3 rather than 0, 0, 0, so that they may look black, but won't match the pure black of the transparent pixels.

Here's the complete version of the **SpriteHit** method:

```
Public Function SpriteHit(x, y) As Boolean
Dim locHit As New clsLocate
Dim nPixColor As Long
Dim nPixX As Long, nPixY As Long

  SpriteHit = False

  If Not (locHit.PointInRect(CLng(x), CLng(y), m_rLoc) = 0) Then
    nPixX = x - m_nLeft
    nPixY = y - m_nTop

    nPixColor = GetPixel(m_bmpFrame(m_nCurrFrame).hdc, nPixX, nPixY)
  If Not (nPixColor = m_bmpFrame(m_nCurrFrame).TransColor) Then
```

```
        SpriteHit = True
      End If
    End If

  End Function
```

The previous sections pretty much sum up the functionality of the sprite class, but now it's time to go over the code that uses this class and see how it's used along with all the other functionality in the game's engine. This is where I can get into other properties of **`clsSprite`** like **`Direction`**, **`Layer`**, and **`Hit`** and how they interact with the code. I'll be referring back to the use of the preceding methods and properties within the class as I go along.

The Game Engine

It's likely that you won't be building a game of any great complexity using VB without the help of DirectDraw methods... *very* likely. However, a simple game like Fun with Ducks (that name really is corny, isn't it?) can be implemented without *too* much agony. All you need is a set of classes taking care of the low-level work of animating, blitting, and moving, and an engine that drives the use of the low-level functionality. Oh, and some graphics, possibly some cleanly written engine code and a good idea (I almost forgot!).

Up to now, you've had a summary of how the duck game works, how we created it and how the sprite engine which drives the animation, works with the bitmap class from earlier projects. To serve our purpose, the game engine will need the components listed below:

- The palette class (**`clsPalette`**) to create a common palette for all graphics loaded for use in the game.
- The memory class (**`clsMem`**) is used to access the display and working buffer, much like it was in previous chapters.
- The bitmap class (**`clsBmp`**) is used to read each bitmap graphic into memory and access them throughout the game.
- The sprite class (**`clsSprite`**) is used to organize complete run-cycles for each duck animation.

Engine Functionality

The game engine drives each of these components, coordinating the interaction between user, hardware and code, all based on the game's specifications. The following figure shows the purpose of the game engine:

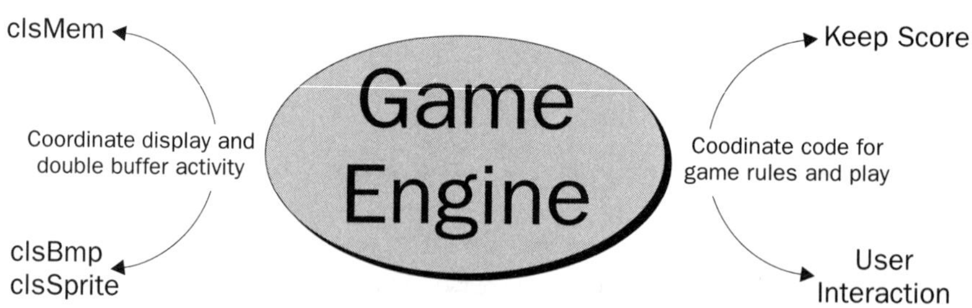

All of this modular coding practice is great, but it comes with a price tag: speed. When a class like **clsMem**, **clsBmp** and **clsSprite** is constantly reused, the trade-off is well worth it. Keep in mind that they may (and did) need a little tweak here and there to improve the speed of their functionality. The idea of compartmentalizing the game module adds yet another layer to accessing code from the main form where the graphics are displayed. Take a look at the following figure which groups the central procedures of the duck game engine. It comes complete with comments on which procedures are used by both levels and which are level-specific.

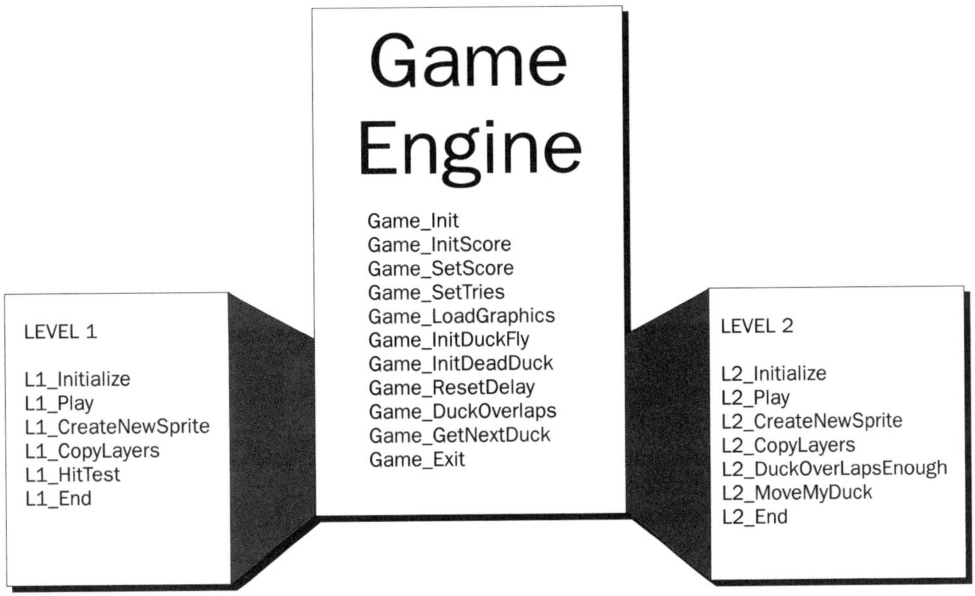

The job of the engine is to implement that which makes the game function properly. It keeps track of the following:

- The animations
- User interaction
- Game start and end
- The present score and number of tries

Essentially, this is the heart of the program which is unlikely to be duplicated for any other game or program. For this reason, it's not much of a loss to keep the game engine inside the form where the scenes are displayed, which also increases the speed of the code. That doesn't mean that there aren't common functionalities that another game might use with slight modifications. As I guide you through the code functionality for each level here, I'll be describing what I consider to be the engine's functionality for each. You'll see then that there is functionality reuse going on, even between the levels of the same game. Let's take a look under the hood.

In preparation for the game, the **Game_Init** procedure is called from **Form_Load**. This procedure, in turn, calls **Game_LoadGraphics** and the **Game_InitScore** procedure. The former repeats functionality that you've seen several times now, whereby the memory class is initialized with a background image and the sprite bitmaps are loaded into their memory DCs, ready for action. The latter procedure initializes the score for the player to 0 and the number of tries they receive to 5. All further preparation for the game is level-specific, so we move now to each level's flow description.

Level 1: Duck Terminator

Simply put, Level 1 consists of a bunch of ducks flying across the display area, dodging mouse clicks. They fly from left to right, disappearing offscreen to the right and reappearing onscreen from the left. Of course, as the code inside the Level 1 game loop would suggest, there's a little more going on than just a bunch of ducks flying.

Level 1 Preparation

Since all of the graphics have been preloaded into memory, we don't need to make many preparations to begin playing on either level. Level 1 has an initialization procedure that contains the following lines of code:

```
m_nHitDuck = -1     '-1 means no duck was hit
m_nDuckCount = 0     'means there are no duck flying
m_nMaxDucks = 6    'maximum number of ducks that should fly at one time

Erase m_sprDucks    'clears any ducks that were left from last play
L1_CreateNewSprite    'creates one duck so the game loop can begin

m_nMaxDelay = 500    'time delay for each loop (described later)

memGame.RestoreWorkArea    'clear screen back to original background
memGame.UpdateDisplay
```

The **L1_CreateNewSprite** procedure is called from the initialization of Level 1, since the game loop will not begin without a duck in existence to begin blitting within the loop. The following lines of code can be found in this procedure:

```
' add or replace duck in sprite array
nIndex = L1_GetNextDuck()
Game_InitFlyDuck m_sprDucks(nIndex)
m_nDuckCount = m_nDuckCount + 1

' setup duck properties
With m_sprDucks(nIndex)
   .SetPosition 0, CInt(300 * Rnd)
   .Direction = .DIR_FORWARD    'facing same direction as the graphic
   .Speed = nRndSpeed
   .Layer = nIndex        'when ducks overlap, layer is required
   .Hit = False        'when duck is hit, this property is True
   .Visible = True        'when duck is terminated, this is False
End With 'm_sprDucks
```

The value of **nIndex** represents the next item in the duck array that is free for use. To be free for use, one of the items in the sprite array must be hit (i.e. terminated), or the item is added to the end of the sprite array (which can't go higher than **m_nMaxDucks**). The **L1_GetNextDuck** function also redimensions the array so that the element exists when we get back to the create procedure. The next line sets the frames for the duck to the flying frames. The **m_nDuckCount** variable always reflects the number of non-hit ducks in the array at a given moment, since the **UBound** of the array will not reflect this. It would if each 'hit' duck was set to nothing (since it's an array of objects) as it was hit, but it complicates the looping issue less if an item in the array, marked as 'hit' is skipped over during playtime.

The properties other than frames are then set for the sprite. Most of them are commented and are self-explanatory so I'll just describe those that I think need some clarification. **`SetPosition`** selects a random number from 0 to 300, which represents the area on the screen (Y coordinate) along which the duck should begin flying. This keeps all ducks from flying at the same height of the screen. We'll discuss speed later in the section on finishing touches. Now you have a duck ready to fly.

Making Ducks Fly

Once we have set preliminary values and created a duck, the game loop for the level is called. This is where the central functionality for the level is coded. The next listing (coming up in a moment) shows the loop in its entirety, but as I refer to specific sections, I'll repeat the lines of code that pertain as I walk through the loop description.

The entire loop cycles through the items in the duck array. This flow chart diagram shows the main components of this loop:

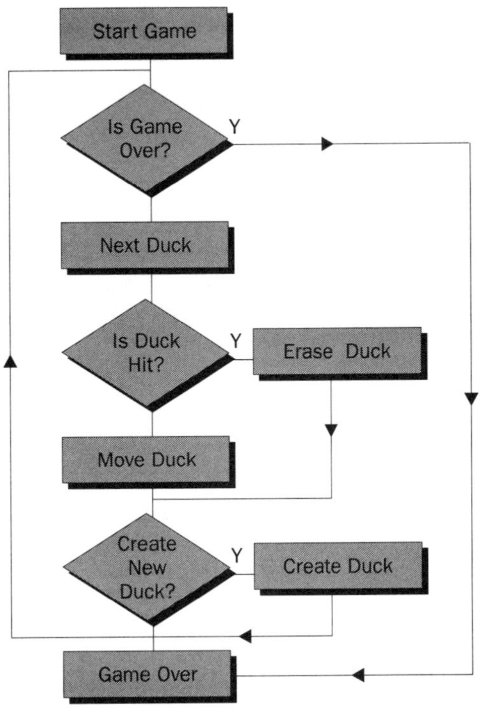

Assuming that no ducks have been hit yet, let me talk about the section that simply flies the ducks for now. To make a duck fly, we have to erase its previous frame, copy its new frame and partially copy any ducks that are overlapping with the area of this duck in their layer order, to keep the screen display undisturbed (this part is more complex and is described in its own section). The only step in the middle here is whether or not the duck is moved before the next frame is copied.

The move class was wellied out for this chapter, since the code that moves the duck didn't really fall in line with the functionality that **`clsMove`** has offered so far. Furthermore, the fewer layers of code called during each iteration, the faster the ducks will fly. There are two parts to the movement of these ducks:

- The **`Speed`** property
- A random Y axis move

You know that the speed is calculated when the duck is created and can be an X axis move ranging from 15 to 30. To make the game more interesting, a random Y axis movement is calculated, within 5 pixels up or down from the duck's current position. This is random and is calculated each time every duck is moved. The only stipulation is that the speed isn't 0, since this indicates that the duck isn't moving. Also, since we know that the ducks are flying from left to right, the ducks are moved to X position 0 if they fly off the screen to the right.

```
Public Sub L1_Play()
Dim nSprite As Integer
Dim timeObj As New clsTime

'—MAIN LOOP: Level 1—'
' continue playing:
' while there are ducks
' while there are tries left
' while player hasn't stopped game

  Do While (m_nDuckCount > 0) And (m_nTries > 0) And (m_flgPlaying)

    nSprite = IIf(nSprite = UBound(m_sprDucks), 0, nSprite + 1)

    With m_sprDucks(nSprite)
      If .Hit and .Visible Then
        ' clear hit frame
        memGame.ClearWorkBuffer m_sprDucks(nSprite).rLoc
        memGame.UpdateDisplay

        ' make hit duck invisible
        m_sprDucks(nSprite).Visible = False
        m_nHitDuck = -1

      Else
        ' only blit visible sprites
        If .Visible And Not .Hit Then

          ' start timer
          m_nStopTime = timeObj.GetTime + m_nDelay

          ' store previous position and erase previous blit
          Set .rPrevLoc = .rLoc
          memGame.ClearWorkBuffer .rLoc

          ' move sprite if applicable
          If .Speed > 0 Then
            Dim nRndVert
            nRndVert = Int((5 + 5 + 1) * Rnd - 5)
            .SetPosition .Left + (.Speed * .Direction), .Top + nRndVert
           If .Left > memGame.Width Then .SetPosition 0
         End If

          ' blit new sprite, considering overlapping ducks
          Game_CopyLayers nSprite

          ' update dirty area to display
          memGame.UpdateDisplay

          ' hold here until set time is passed
```

```
            Do Until timeObj.GetTime >= m_nStopTime
              DoEvents
            Loop
          End If
          DoEvents

        End If
      End With

      ' check for create duck
      If m_flgCreateDuck Then
        m_flgCreateDuck = False
        L1_CreateNewSprite
      End If

    Loop

    ' check how game ended
    L1_End

  End Sub
```

The difference between **L1_CreateNewSprite** and **L2_CreateNewSprite** is in the duck properties. In **L1_CreateNewSprite** all the ducks fly the same way, whereas in **L2_CreateNewSprite** your duck must have different properties because it flies like a duck on speed.

Duck Termination

Each time the loop iterates, a single duck is processed. Without any hits, the duck will simply be reblit to the screen in its new position, if it has one. When a mouse click has been successful in terminating a duck, the **Hit** property is set to **True**. At this point, a new duck frame will be displayed, so the duck isn't invisible quite yet. Several other ducks may be moved before the hit duck is processed, which means that the hit frame will continue to be displayed for those few moments (this is preferable so you can see that it was hit). When the hit duck has run through the loop, it will now be processed by the earlier part of the procedure because **Hit** will be **True**.

At this time, the duck frame is cleared from the buffer but, rather than blitting the next frame, the display is updated to reflect that this duck is no longer visible; its **Visible** property is set to **False** and **m_nHitDuck** is restored to **-1** (no duck is hit). Now, each time the duck is encountered again through this loop (since this duck's array element isn't removed, it's still present in the iteration), neither portion of the loop will paint the duck, since **Visible** is **False**. If the array element is reused when a new duck is created, the properties that are set in **L1_CreateNewSprite** will, of course, set **Hit** to **False**, **Visible** to **True** and change the frames accordingly so that the duck can fly again.

Game Over

The loop continues while the following three conditions are satisfied:

- There are ducks: **m_nDuckCount > 0**
- There are tries left: **m_nTries > 0**
- The user hasn't clicked Exit or Stop: **m_flgPlaying = True**

L1_End is called when any of these conditions become untrue or equal to zero. In this procedure, the message is displayed that tells you either Game Over or Level 1 Complete!, depending on the reason the game loop has ended. I didn't put any fancy code in to move you to a level of greater difficulty, or to automatically start Level 2, since that can overcomplicate things. By selecting the LEVEL 2 radio button and clicking Play, you can move to the next level... no challenge here! (This also allows you to play Level 2 if you can't finish Level 1!!!)

Level 2: Lost Duck

Level 2 adds a few new twists to the game. Now, you're the duck and you're flying in the same direction as the ducks from Level 1 (**DIR_FORWARD**). The rest of the ducks are flying towards you (**DIR_BACKWARD**), which means that they're being blit backwards. Your job is to not get hit and to get across the screen as many times as possible, scoring points as you go. I don't promise that it's impossible to win the game and I don't expect you to get so caught up in it that your boss will look over your shoulder and see ducks flying half the time. The code content is there for you to reuse and make more challenging at your leisure.

Level 2 Preparation

Once again, the graphics have been preloaded into memory when the game was first loaded, so all the graphics used in Level 1 are still available for Level 2. This level's initialization procedure contains the following lines of code:

```
m_nHitDuck = -1
m_nDuckCount = 0
m_nMaxDucks = 6
m_nLapCount = 0     'number of times your duck gets across the screen

Erase m_sprDucks
L2_CreateNewSprite

memGame.RestoreWorkArea
memGame.UpdateDisplay

Me.KeyPreview = True   'so that the keyboard presses can be intercepted
```

Most of the variables shown here serve the same purpose as they did in Level 1. The new variable is **m_nLapCount**, which keeps score of the number of times your duck makes it across the screen (we'll discuss scoring later in this chapter). Note that the **Keypreview** property must be set to **True** so that the **Form_Keydown** event can intercept the key codes that move your duck.

The procedure called from the initialization of Level 2 for creating duck sprites is called **L2_CreateNewSprite**. This uses some of the same functionality as **L1_CreateNewSprite**, but I've kept them separate to make the code easier to follow. The main difference between the two procedures comes after the duck element in the array (**nIndex**) has been selected for the new duck. Then, the following code is run:

```
With m_sprDucks(nIndex)
    If nIndex = MYDUCK Then
      .SetPosition 0, CInt(300 * Rnd)
      .Direction = .DIR_FORWARD
      .Speed = 0
    Else
      ' other ducks
```

```
        .SetPosition memGame.Width, CInt(300 * Rnd)
        .Direction = .DIR_BACKWARD
        .Speed = nRndSpeed
      End If

      .Layer = nIndex
      .Hit = False
      .Visible = True
    End With 'm_sprDucks
```

MYDUCK is a constant that represents array element 0, which is the player's duck. Its **Position**, **Direction** and **Speed** properties are initialized differently than the other ducks that are flying towards it. Since **MYDUCK** is moved by the keyboard (discussed later), as each blit cycle is encountered in the game loop, the duck shouldn't be moved along with the others, so **Speed = 0**, rather than the randomly calculated speed of the other ducks (as in Level 1, 15 – 30 is the range for **nRndSpeed**). Remember that the direction for **MYDUCK** is forward, whereas the others are now flying backwards. So, the start position is at the left side of the display for **MYDUCK**, but the ducks that fly backwards must enter from the right side of the display. Other properties such as **Layer**, **Hit** and **Visible** are common to all the duck sprites.

Colliding Ducks

A lot of the functionality of the game loop for Level 2 is similar to that of Level 1, so once again, I'll just point out the main differences. The flow chart here shows the decision making that goes on inside the **L2_Play** game loop:

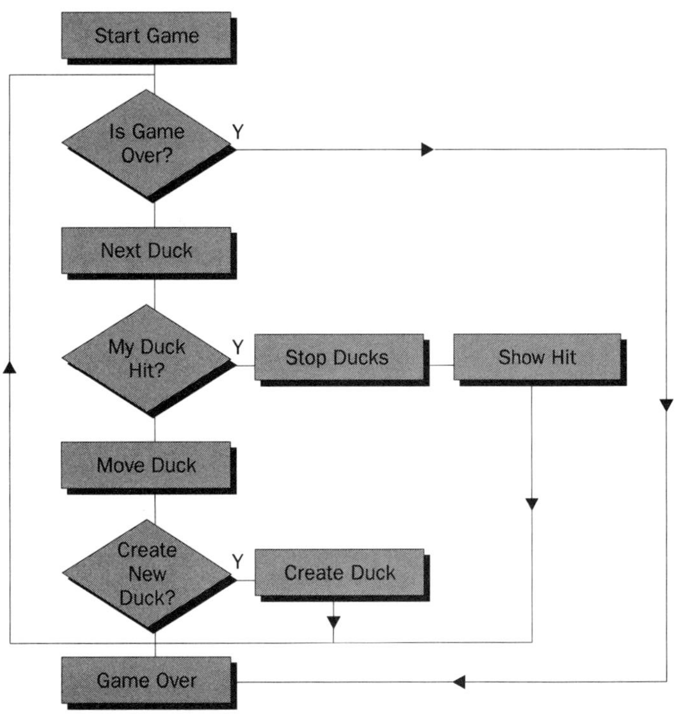

Until there is a collision, each loop iteration simply takes the current sprite and copies its next frame to the screen at the appropriate position (the code that makes it blit backwards is covered later). If it's **MYDUCK**, then there is no movement, otherwise there is. Once again, any overlapping ducks where this duck is being replaced on the screen in its new position, are taken into consideration (also covered later is efficient repainting for layers).

Until there is a collision, each loop iteration simply takes the current sprite and copies its next frame to the screen at the appropriate position (the code that makes it blit backwards is covered later). If it's **MYDUCK** being blit, there is no movement, only frame animation. Once again, any overlapping ducks are taken into consideration (we'll also look later at efficient repainting for layers).

The main difference between Level 1 and Level 2 is in the code that handles the collision of two ducks. Unlike Level 1, where the duck is hit by the click of a mouse (interrupt processing and handle it immediately), now ducks are hit when there is a rectangle overlap. Each loop selects a new duck to blit, possibly in a new position on the screen, so each time this occurs, we must test whether there is an overlap of ducks and whether any of those overlapping ducks happens to be **MYDUCK**. We'll cover the details of this overlap check in greater detail, but, now, you should know that when this overlap of **MYDUCK** is discovered, the **Hit** property for all ducks that overlapped **MYDUCK** is set to **True**.

When the user clicked on a duck on Level 1, right away we could change the frame to the dead duck frame in that event. I knew in that case that the code that copies the layers was definitely not in use, since there're no **DoEvents** during that process within **L1_CopyLayers**. Since **L2_CopyLayers** is the procedure that determines that collision has occurred, it's best to let it run its course, complete the layered copy of the current sprite, but mark the sprites that were hit, as such, to be handled later. The next iteration of the game loop, **m_nHitDuck**, will be equal to **MYDUCK**, so rather than executing the second part of the game loop code, the collision code will be executed.

Since more than one duck can be marked as hit, a loop through all the sprites is performed, searching for those that collided and unblitting their last frame. Along the way, all ducks are set to **Speed = 0** ensure that no more collisions take place while the code plays out the termination of those ducks. Once this is complete, another iteration through the array is performed, this time copying the hit frame to the screen for those ducks that were hit. Then you lose a try and the game starts again, until you run out of tries.

Keyboard Control

All the ducks flying toward you are moved on each iteration of their sprite element in the array, but, as we know, **MYDUCK** isn't moved by code. The following constants list the keys (I tried to make them easy to reach for playing, so the arrow keys just didn't cut it) that move **MYDUCK** in each direction. Change them to your favorites, but these are mine:

```
Const DUCKUP = "E"
Const DUCKDOWN = "M"
Const DUCKLEFT = "S"
Const DUCKRIGHT = "L"
```

Since **Keypreview** is **True**, the **Form_KeyDown** event gets all the keyboard messages first and that's where the code is that moves the duck:

```
Private Sub Form_KeyDown(KeyCode As Integer, Shift As Integer)
Const moveamt = 5
Dim nLeft As Integer
Dim nTop As Integer

  If m_nDuckCount = 0 Then Exit Sub

  With m_sprDucks(0)
```

```
        Select Case UCase(Chr(KeyCode))
          Case DUCKUP
               ' moving up
               nLeft = .Left
               nTop = .Top - moveamt
               nTop = IIf(nTop < 0, 0, nTop)

          Case DUCKDOWN
               ' moving down
               nLeft = .Left
               nTop = .Top + moveamt
               nTop = IIf((nTop > memGame.Height), 0, nTop)

          Case DUCKLEFT
               ' moving left
               nLeft = .Left - moveamt
               nLeft = IIf((nLeft < 0), 0, nLeft)
               nTop = .Top

          Case DUCKRIGHT
               'moving right
               nLeft = .Left + moveamt
               nLeft = IIf((nLeft > memGame.Width), 0, nLeft)
               nTop = .Top
        End Select
     End With
     L2_MoveMyDuck nLeft, nTop
   End Sub
```

Here, a calculation is made for **nLeft** and **nTop**, the new position for **MYDUCK** based on the key being pressed. I hard-coded the amount of movement to be five pixels at a time though, in theory, this could be a game setting that is made elsewhere, based on the level of difficulty. The new position for the duck is passed to the **L2_MoveMyDuck** procedure which clears the previous frame, moves the duck's position and blits the duck to the display. Since there are no **DoEvents** during the processing of another duck in the game loop, I can confidently take care of **MYDUCK** movement independent of that loop, as we've done here:

```
   With m_sprDucks(MYDUCK)
        Set .rPrevLoc = .rLoc
        memGame.ClearWorkBuffer .rLoc
        .SetPosition nLeft, nTop
        .Blit
        memGame.UpdateDisplay
    End With
```

Painting Rectangles

How the game engine interacts with **clsMem**, **clsBmp** and **clsSprite** to maneuver the graphics around the screen is the heart of the game's flow. Now we need to uncover some of the game trickery that's going on underneath the central game loop for each level:

- Using **clsLocate**
- Efficient repainting

- Reverse blitting
- Hits and collisions

Using clsLocate

In Chapter 2, I used a very small class, called **clsLocate**, for checking that a point was within the rectangular area on the screen. I used the API function, **PtInRect()**and created the class to store the **POINTAPI** and **RECT** structures, along with the declaration for **PtInRect()** in one place, where I could use it over and over in new applications. Well, wouldn't ya know, here I am using it again, only this time, I'll be adding some other related intersection-testing functions to the class.

In the General Declarations section of **clsLocate**, there are definitions for the two structures required for the API functions the class uses and the actual declarations for those functions. None of the methods for the class require more than two rectangles, or one point, so you can see there are module-level variables **m_p1**, **m_r1** and **m_r2** declared, private to the class.

```
Private Type RECT
  Left As Long
  Top As Long
  Right As Long
  Bottom As Long
End Type
Private m_r1 As RECT
Private m_r2 As RECT

Private Type POINTAPI
  x As Long
  y As Long
End Type
Private m_p1 As POINTAPI

Private Declare Function PtInRect Lib "user32" (lpRect As RECT, ByVal ptX As Long,
ByVal ptY As Long) As Long

Private Declare Function IntersectRectLib "user32" (lpDestRect As RECT,
lpSrc1Rect As RECT, lpSrc2Rect As RECT) As Long

Private Declare Function UnionRect Lib "user32" (lpDestRect As RECT,
lpSrc1Rect As RECT, lpSrc2Rect As RECT) As Long
```

As I was building the methods for the classes, I had to consider a few things. First of all, throughout the application, there are rectangles keeping track of the position and area of each bitmap/sprite. These rectangles are defined by the class module, **clsRect**, which makes it convenient to simply pass the entire rectangle to the methods that need that information. The problem is, the API functions have trouble with **clsRect** as opposed to passing the buffer held inside the **RECT** structure, so a conversion must take place at some point before the API function is called.

There is a private method to set each of the API-friendly structure components for the class. **SetPoint**, **SetRect1** and **SetRect2** each take the information passed to them and fill the appropriate module-level variables with the information needed. Originally, these three methods were public and called separately, directly before a call to one of the rectangle/point testing methods.

This, however, added unnecessary additional calls to the class, **clsLocate**, before using it to test the results I was looking for at the time. Each call to another class adds some fractional amount of time to the process, but inside an animation loop, this fractional amount can make the difference between a good and bad animation.

The **PointInRect** function is passed an x and y value for the mouse click that generated a hit test in the game and the rectangle of the current sprite being tested. The reason for passing the x and y value rather than creating a **clsPoint** (to be consistent with **clsRect**) is because the effort spent translating the mouse coordinate into a **clsPoint** hardly seems worthwhile. The mouse coordinate passed to the **PointInRect** function would have to be converted into a **POINTAPI** structure, which would simply slow the test procedure down too much.

Remember, an important rule of all graphics programming is saving on speed wherever possible. Graphics slow you down enough as it is.

Passing a **clsRect** object, on the other hand, isn't going to add extra effort, since these are used throughout the code. Inside the function below, you can see that the **SetPoint** and **SetRect1** private methods are called to set up the module-level variables. Then the **PtInRect()** API function is called and its return is passed back with the methods return value.

```
Public Function PointInRect(x As Long, y As Long, r1 As clsRect) As    Long

  SetPoint x, y
  SetRect1 r1
  PointInRect = PtInRect(m_r1, m_p1.x, m_p1.y)

End Function
```

The method **TestRectOverlap** is used for both hit testing and collision testing in this game. First of all, three **clsRect** objects are passed, the last two (**r1** and **r2**) are the rectangle areas to compare for overlap, the first (**rDest**), to be filled with the rectangle representing the overlapping area.

SetRect1 and **SetRect2** are called to convert the **clsRect** object into a **RECT** structure, then the **IntersectRect()** API function is called. **IntersectRect()** does all the work for you. It fills a **RECT** structure (**rFill**) with the intersecting rectangle from two others, returning 0 (false) if there is no intersection. Pretty easy eh? Once an intersection has been determined, the **rDest** object is filled with the appropriate values. Notice I didn't set the return of **TestRectOverlap** with the same return as the function **TestIntersectRect**. That is to insure that a **True** value returned is indeed VB's version of **True**, which is -1. API functions will return a non-zero value, but not necessarily a **-1** as the value for **True**.

```
Public Function TestRectOverlap(rDest As clsRect, r1 As clsRect, r2 As clsRect) As
Long
Dim nRet As Long
Dim rFill As RECT

  TestRectOverlap = False

  SetRect1 r1
  SetRect2 r2
  nRet = TestIntersectRect(rFill, m_r1, m_r2)
  If nRet <> 0 Then
```

```
        TestRectOverlap = True
        With rDest
          .Left = rFill.Left
          .Top = rFill.Top
          .Right = rFill.Right
          .Bottom = rFill.Bottom
        End With
      End If
    End Function
```

Last but not least, a great new addition to my **clsLocate**: **RectUnion**. This method uses the **UnionRect()** API function that actually fills in a **RECT** structure, with the smallest bounding box of two other rectangles. Sounds familiar? How about a great assistant to our **GetDirtyRect** method from **clsMem**. Rather than looping through and tediously testing each component of a **clsRect** object, pass the rectangles here and let 'er rip! Unfortunately, we can only take care of two rectangles at a time, so the **GetDirtyRect** method must still include some logic for iterating through the dirty rectangle array, as we'll see when we open up that section in more detail. The return from **UnionRect()** should, in theory, not matter, since any two valid rectangles should successfully form a union, but, for consistency, since it returns a value then so does the method.

```
    Public Function RectUnion(rDest As clsRect, r1 As clsRect, r2 As clsRect) As Long
    Dim nRet As Long
    Dim rFill As RECT

      RectUnion = False

      SetRect1 r1
      SetRect2 r2
      nRet = UnionRect(rFill, m_r1, m_r2)
      If nRet <> 0 Then
        RectUnion = True
        With rDest
          .Left = rFill.Left
          .Top = rFill.Top
          .Right = rFill.Right
          .Bottom = rFill.Bottom
        End With
      End If

    End Function
```

It's easy to reuse each of these methods contained within **clsLocate** throughout the duck game. The fact that their API declarations and structures are defined within makes this class extremely useful. Now, when the respective areas of the code are covered which use this class, you'll know exactly what its content is and how and why it works.

Efficient Repainting

Level 1 and Level 2 are both driven by their respective play loop as part of the game engine. Though they perform slightly different tasks, each has something in common. They both take one duck at a time for repainting. Both levels use the same array of duck sprites (**m_sprDucks()**) as the only group of graphics to consider for repainting. During an iteration of either level's play loop, each sprite in the array can be in one of four states:

- Moving and flying
- Stationary and flying
- Hit
- Invisible

No matter what the current state is, the loop takes the current sprite in the array that it's working on and, as long as it's not marked as invisible, it paints the duck.

Handling Layers

The process of painting the duck to the screen first involves erasing the current frame, then changing it (if applicable, we move it), and repainting it in its new state. These steps alone would be not unlike what we did in the demo example from Chapter 4, but there's more to consider here. As it flies, each duck has the property to overlap another. This means that any duck in the vicinity of the current duck's dirty rectangle must also be repainted in its appropriate layer with respect to the current duck. Here's where it gets tricky.

If I just moved the duck in question, without considering the others, I could be faced with something like this:

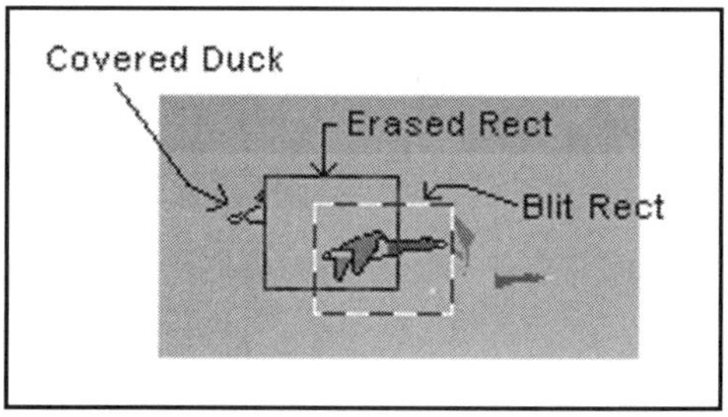

Neighboring ducks get painted over and it looks ugly. Here were my choices:

- Repaint all ducks.
- Repaint intersecting ducks.
- Repaint part of intersecting ducks.

Repainting all the ducks, of course in their layer order, means that the dirty rectangle that I update to the display will always be intact. This is the lazy game programmers way of thinking. The problem is time. If I repaint all the ducks (and there are several), I could be repainting 15 ducks across the working buffer. Even though the screen update only consists of the dirty rectangle, there is still time involved in every work-area blit. If every duck goes through this lengthy process, you'd better believe it'll be obvious. Furthermore, there may not have been any overlapping ducks to blit! Oh, and just one more really horrible caveat. My memory class, **`clsMem`**, keeps track of every blit to the working area, so as soon as every duck is blit to the working area, it's added to the dirty rectangle list and, thus, is tagged for screen update. To avoid this, I would also have to get into the optional flag hack, which tells the memory class to ignore certain blits to the working area and not add them to the dirty rectangle, spoiling an otherwise perfectly modular class. Also not a good thing.

VB game programmers are likely to be better game programmers than some C or DOS nerds. Why? They're forced to reckon with the Windows speed constraints more and thus fix up all their inefficient coding techniques, hoping that cumulatively they will improve the speed of the game. Other game programmers, with super fast video cards and a faster coding environment sometimes tend not to notice any minor lags in game speed.

So there. If you start with VB, you'll be a super stud by the time you get to the lower level, faster development platforms.

The most efficient way of repainting intersecting ducks is to only repaint the part needed to keep the integrity of the layers on the display. This has two bonuses. First, it means that my memory class's dirty rectangle array will never include any rectangles that go outside of the bounds of the intended dirty rectangle (that of the current duck being repainted). Second, it means that there's no danger of recursive intersection checking, since that area of an overlapping duck that doesn't overlap the dirty rectangle of the current duck being repainted won't be disturbed in the working area, or the display. Perfect! Now, how is it done?

Each time a paint operation is called for by a duck sprite on Level 1, its index in the sprite array is passed to a procedure called **L1_CopyLayers**. This procedure loops through the array of duck sprites with the assumption that the index order is the layer order on the screen, checking for overlap with the current sprite (whose index value is held in **nSprite**). To be applicable, the sprite has to be visible, so it can't be the victim of a hit. Each time a sprite that overlaps with the current sprite is encountered, the rectangle that overlaps with the current sprite's dirty rectangle is repainted to the working buffer. This happens in the order they appear in the array, so when the actual sprite is encountered, its entirety is repainted, and the remaining sprites are checked to be copied over the top. Here we see the rectangle outlines for a duck below and a duck over the current duck:

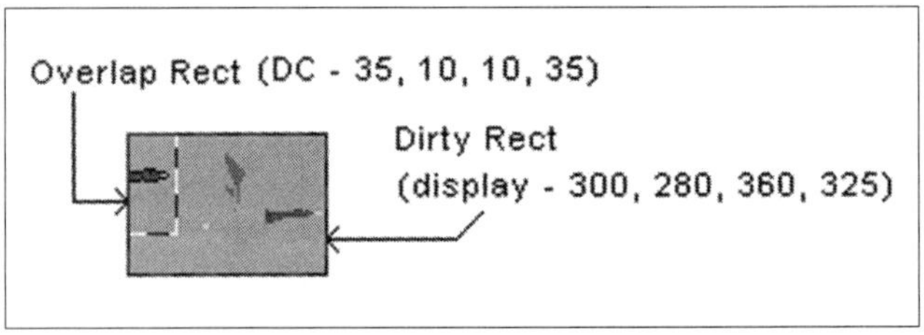

The main functionality of **L1_CopyLayers** loops through the duck array in the order of the array elements, checking for overlap with the current duck. If there is overlap, that portion of the duck that overlaps with the dirty rectangle of the current duck is found and blit to the working buffer. The **Game_DuckOverlaps** function returns **True** if this is the case and fills **rTmp** with the rectangle coordinates of the overlapping area. Somewhere in this loop will be the current duck, which will be blit in its entirety. Then the loop continues blitting any smaller portions of other overlapping ducks above the current duck. Here's the main code for this:

```
For nIndex = LBound(m_sprDucks) To UBound(m_sprDucks)
  If nIndex <> nSprite Then
    If Not m_sprDucks(nIndex).Hit Then
      If Game_DuckOverlaps(nSprite, nIndex, rTmp) Then
      m_sprDucks(nIndex).Blit rTmp
      End If
    End If
  Else
    m_sprDucks(nSprite).Blit
  End If

Next nIndex
If flgHit Then m_nHitDuck = 0
```

The procedure that checks for overlap also returns the overlapping rectangle for the dirty rectangle (**Game_DuckOverlaps**) and is passed the current sprite index and the sprite currently being tested for overlap, along with an empty **clsRect** object to be filled upon the function's return with the overlapping rectangle:

```
Private Function Game_DuckOverlaps(ByVal nSprite As Integer, ByVal nIndex As
Integer, rTmp As clsRect) As Boolean

Dim loc As New clsLocate
Dim rDest As New clsRect

  Game_DuckOverlaps = True

  ' get union of moving duck rectangles
  If loc.RectUnion(rDest, m_sprDucks(nSprite).rPrevLoc,
m_sprDucks(nSprite).rLoc) Then

    ' compare union rect with location of comparing duck
    If Not loc.TestRectOverlap(rTmp, m_sprDucks(nIndex).rLoc, rDest) Then
      Game_DuckOverlaps = False
    End If

  End If
End Function
```

Now that you've read about the functionality of **clsLocate**, you'll find this section pretty easy. First, the union of the previous and current location rectangles of the current sprite (**rPrevLoc** and **rLoc**) are calculated. The **RectUnion** method of **clsLocate** returns this rectangle into **rDest**. (If the sprite didn't move, this will be the same as its current position.) Next, the dirty rectangle (**rDest**) is tested for overlap with the comparing sprite's location rectangle (**rLoc**). Here we're not comparing for overlap of actual sprite pixels that exclude transparency, but for the actual bounding box of each graphic, so we need to do no further testing.

TestRectOverlap returns (using the **IntersectRect()** API) the rectangle in common between the dirty rectangle and the comparing sprite's rectangle on the display. This will be what is blit to the working buffer if the return is **True**.

By the end of the **L1_CopyLayers** procedure, all overlapping rectangles within the bounding box of the current sprite's dirty rectangle are copied in their respective layer order. Seeing what's under the hood here, you can also see what requires careful consideration with speed. For each sprite movement, each sprite object's location rectangle must be considered for overlap and calculations are made for each comparison. Then a small blit is performed if necessary. This is why it's important to call the **clsLocate** from the **Game_DuckOverlaps** procedure only once, with the information that needs to be passed (the rectangles to compare). Each call to another class adds time, since there's another layer to go through and in a simple iteration, where you're only moving one sprite, you want to conserve time wherever possible.

Blitting a DC Fragment

Now that I've addressed the issue of finding rectangular areas of an overlapping duck while blitting the current duck, we'll move on to the other issues to consider. The **Blit** methods of both the sprite class and the bitmap class must now accept a parameter of type **clsRect** and check for its existence before deciding what do to.

With respect to the sprite class, the only issue that we need to address is the changing of frames. If only a portion of a sprite is being copied to the screen, I have to assume that the blit instruction is the result of an overlap, not a command to change the frame of this sprite and blit the entire graphic. The following test handles this issue:

```
If IsMissing(rct) Then
  m_nCurrFrame = IIf(m_nCurrFrame = m_nNumFrames - 1, 0, m_nCurrFrame + 1)
End If
```

The **rct** parameter is passed as optional, so it will only exist in the case where there is a partial blit to perform. Then, the **rct** parameter is in turn passed to the blit method of the bitmap class for further processing. Here, the **rct** parameter is also passed optionally, and only if it exists is the following code. First the rectangle passed is assumed to be the location on the screen to be blit, or the destination rectangle, so **rLoc** is filled in with those values:

```
rLoc.SetSize rct.Left, rct.Top, rct.Right, rct.Bottom
```

Next, the area of the bitmap to be blit is calculated from the location on the screen to be blit. This is done by looking at the location rectangle for this bitmap, applying a little math, as shown below:

```
nLeft = rLoc.Left - m_rLoc.Left
nTop = rLoc.Top - m_rLoc.Top
nRight = nLeft + (rLoc.Right - rLoc.Left)
nBottom = nTop + (rLoc.Bottom - rLoc.Top)

rArea.SetSize nLeft, nTop, nRight, nBottom
```

The rest of the code inside the Blit method is the same as before we addressed the partial rectangle, the only difference being that the rectangle to be blit has shrunk from the entire bitmap to a portion of it and the **UpdateWorkBuffer** method will function just the same, updating its dirty rectangle array with the smaller rectangle.

Flying Backwards

Let me tell you about a little ghost-chasing adventure you might just want to avoid. So far, you have a pretty good idea about the functionality of each level, how the graphics are copied and how each sprite is managed. You've also seen what happens when ducks overlap and how the screen is repainted without resorting to the lazy 'blit the whole screen' method (believe me, even the most professional of C programmers have been known to do this). Everything was going so smoothly until the duck had to fly backwards.

When Level 2 is initialized, only **MYDUCK** is set up with a **Direction** property of **DIR_FORWARD**, as all ducks were in Level 1. The rest of the ducks created are given a **Direction** of **DIR_BACKWARD**. The problem with this, as the figure shows, is that each of the duck sprites in **m_sprDucks()** access the same device contexts that contain the actual graphic. Memory would get pretty sparse and quick if it were any other way.

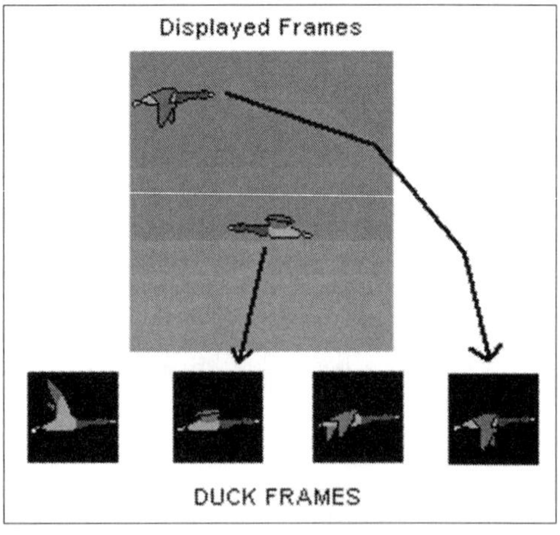

Thankfully, we can instruct the **BitBlt()** function (and related functions like **StretchBlt()**) to blit the contents of a DC backwards. The parameters passed to the **BitBlt()** function include a top-left coordinate and a width and height to blit to the destination DC, shown in bold below:

```
Declare Function BitBlt Lib "gdi32" (ByVal hDestDC As Long, ByVal x As Long, ByVal
y As Long, ByVal nWidth As Long, ByVal nHeight As Long, ByVal hSrcDC As Long,
ByVal xSrc As Long, ByVal ySrc As Long, ByVal dwRop As Long) As Long
```

If a negative value is passed to the **nWidth** parameter, the DC contents are blit vertically flipped and to the **nHeight** parameter, horizontally flipped. Ah, but there's a catch. A funny thing happens when you copy the flipped contents of one device context to another. This figure shows what you would expect a duck frame to copy to the screen during a backward blit and the way it really works.

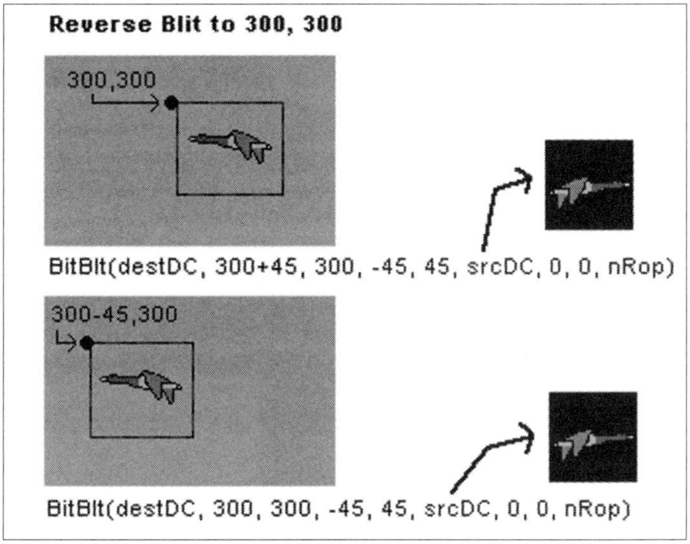

The contents of the DC actually pivot on the specified coordinates for position. This means sending a negative width to the blit function when the destination X is 0, the blit takes place (you guessed it) at an X coordinate equal to the negative width being blit. This actually makes sense if you sit back and think long and hard about it, but it sure messes up a perfectly sound set of classes that handle rectangles and blitting (not to mention I'm not quite sure who the heck would use this functionality).

Now, when you're debugging a new set of animation instructions that suddenly don't appear to be double buffering quite right, the last thing you think to check is the memory class blitting code that has been working for the last three projects you used them in, especially when it appears that the correct rectangle coordinates are being sent to the function. Of course, you won't discover that until you've gone through several painful hours of debugging, when you eventually walk the code down to the lowest level. Finally, just before you crack open another bag of chips to comfort your tormented soul, you find it. How mad are you that the Windows API help on **BitBlt()** doesn't even hint that not only is the graphic reversed with a negative width or height coordinate, but also your destination positioning is altered too?!

But what do you about it? Level 2 requires one duck to fly normally and the rest to fly backward. I could have made a single copy of each duck frame and flipped the copies in memory so that they're ready to roll. This means I'm wasting memory when there's a perfectly good copy of those same frames in memory, just facing in the wrong direction. The alternative? Write some code that addresses the case of reverse flight, managing the destination coordinates accordingly.

The next listing shows the final version of the memory class's **UpdateWorkBuffer** method, which copies a specified rectangle to the working buffer from another DC. An additional optional parameter is now passed to the procedure, **vDir**, which represents either **DIR_FORWARD** (**1**) or

DIR_BACKWARD (**-1**). This is used to differentiate between calls to **StretchBlt()**, where the reverse blit adds the width of the blit back to the left position for the blit. Obviously, this only considers horizontal reversal and any fancier coding would require extra measures to account for further variety. Here I'm using the simplest method for the code at hand. The rest belongs in a book of game algorithms.

```
Public Sub UpdateWorkBuffer(hdcFrom As Long, rFrom As clsRect, rTo As clsRect, rop
As Long, Optional vDir)
'-Description
' called when another DC area should be copied to the work buffer
' rectangle passed is copied, source xy passed this time
'-
Dim nRet  As Long
Dim nToLeft As Long, nToTop As Long, nToWidth As Long, nToHeight As Long
Dim nFromLeft As Long, nFromTop As Long, nFromWidth As Long, nFromHeight As Long

  nToLeft = rTo.Left
  nToTop = rTo.Top
  nToWidth = rTo.Right - nToLeft
  nToHeight = rTo.Bottom - nToTop

  nFromLeft = rFrom.Left
  nFromTop = rFrom.Top
  nFromWidth = rFrom.Right - nFromLeft
  nFromHeight = rFrom.Bottom - nFromTop

  If IsMissing(vDir) Then
    vDir = 1
  End If

  If vDir = -1 Then
    nToLeft = nToLeft + nToWidth
    nToWidth = vDir * nToWidth
  End If

  SelPal_Work
  nRet = StretchBlt(m_hdcWork, nToLeft, nToTop, nToWidth, nToHeight, hdcFrom,
nFromLeft, nFromTop, nFromWidth, nFromHeight, rop)
  Call AddUpdateRect(rTo)

  If flgShowMem Then ShowMem
End Sub
```

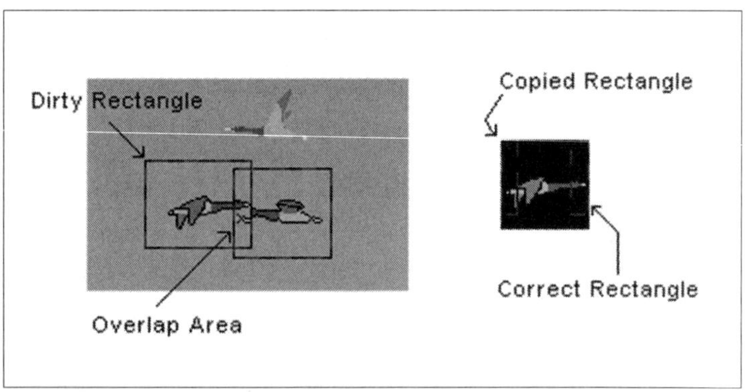

Wait, I'm not done with this subject yet. There is just one more nitty gritty detail that requires immediate attention on the layered blitting front: the partial blit for efficient repainting. This blit in reverse only works if the entire bitmap is blit to the screen. This shows what happens when only the overlapping portion of a backwards duck is sent to the display and what part of the duck that *should* be copied.

It seems a piece of the tail gets copied rather than the beak, which is what we should see. The calculation discussed in the efficient repainting section of this chapter only considers what area of the sprite overlaps with the main sprite being copied at the moment. Whatever that area is, it's taken from the bitmap's DC and copied, but since we're not flipping the entire image, the wrong side of the duck bitmap is copied to the screen in reverse.

To address this issue, before sending the rectangle to be copied to the **UpdateWorkBuffer** procedure, the Blit procedure for the bitmap in question should check to see what part of it should be sent—before reversal is considered within the memory class. The following small alteration to the Blit code for the bitmap class makes a minor adjustment to the area of the bitmap being passed to the **UpdateWorkBuffer**:

```
If m_nDir = m_DIRBACKWARD Then
  nLeft = m_rLoc.Right - rLoc.Right
  nRight = m_rLoc.Right - rLoc.Left
End If
```

If the duck is flying backward, the rectangular area from the graphic to be copied should be taken from the vertical mirror image of the rectangle from that same bitmap.

Hits and Collisions

Firstly, I'll discuss the hit-testing code used on Level 1, and then I'll describe how it relates to the collision-testing that is needed for Level 2. Both of these techniques require careful consideration of issues like:

- Response time
- Target accuracy
- Updating the display
- Removing ducks from play

To keep the details simple, I'll summarize each of these issues as I deal with the intricacies of Level 1.

Response time refers to how fast the code is able to respond to a mouse click while the play loop is going on. As you saw with the description of the play loop for Level 1, there's quite a bit going on during each iteration. With all that happening, how will a click be intercepted fast enough? Well, that's what **DoEvents** is for. There are two moments within each sprite paint where **DoEvents** is called. Once after the paint for this sprite is complete, and once after a new sprite has been created. It's at these two moments that a **MouseDown** event which initiates a hit test is received.

An important thing to note here is why **DoEvents** can't be present during the actual sprite paint. It's very important that nothing interrupt the process within **L1_CopyLayers**, since it's performing a loop through the entire sprite array, searching for overlapping ducks and painting portions of them if they overlap the dirty rectangle of the current sprite. While this is happening, remember that each call to the **Blit** method of the sprite is telling the **MemGame** object to keep track of these blits and their respective rectangles, until the call to **UpdateDisplay** is made. If this is interrupted and all layers have not yet been blit, another call to **UpdateDisplay** will use the dirty rectangles so far sent and the display update may provide unexpected results. We would definitely have a problem if the **L1_CopyLayers** method was too slow, thus delaying the interception of the **MouseDown** event that may have terminated a duck.

Target accuracy becomes an issue once the interception of the **MouseDown** event has called the hit testing method for Level 1, **L1_HitTest**. At the beginning of this procedure, once it has been confirmed that there are still ducks to hit, by checking the value of **m_nDuckCount**, the array of duck sprites is iterated through and a call to the **SpriteHit** method of the sprite class is made to see if this is the sprite that was hit:

```
nLayer = -1
nHitLayer = -1

' test each duck for hit, keep highest layer in nHitLayer
For nIndex = LBound(m_sprDucks) To UBound(m_sprDucks)

  ' test mask hit
  If m_sprDucks(nIndex).SpriteHit(x, y) Then
    ' get layer
    nLayer = m_sprDucks(nIndex).Layer
    ' test with last layer hit
    If Not (nHitLayer > nLayer) Then
      nHitLayer = nLayer
      m_nHitDuck = nIndex
    End If

  End If

Next nIndex
```

The catch here is the order in which each sprite is tested for a successful hit. This is where that layer issue comes into play. The idea is to iterate through the sprite array, checking the topmost layer sprite first, then iterating to the lowermost sprite, exiting the loop once a successful hit is found. If this were done, you can be confident that the first sprite found as a hit will be the topmost rectangle that the mouse coordinate landed on. But knowing that the layer order for each sprite is actually the same as the sprite position in the sprite array is an easy way out of a possibly more complex situation. So, although this is the situation, I still check the **Layer** property of each sprite, just in case down the road my layer logic changed.

What you see in the loop, then, are two variables—**nLayer** for the current sprite in the iteration and **nHitLayer** for the topmost sprite in the iteration—where **nHitLayer** stores the highest layer value as each sprite in the array is tested. By the end of this loop, **nHitLayer** will either still be -1, or will be the index value of the sprite that was within the coordinates of the hit, at the topmost layer.

Updating the display is the next task at hand. This is where a successful hit must be represented on the screen, retaining its layer value, as any other sprite repaint would. A similar set of paint instructions to those for the play loop are used here. But first, the hit duck's frames must be changed to reflect its termination.

Game_InitDeadDuck works much like **Game_InitFlyingDuck** in that it sets up the sprite object passed it with a new set of frames. In this case, there is only one frame being used: termination. As you know from the description of the sprite class, setting the sprite object's **NumFrames** property resets the entire bitmap array for the sprite, so before we do this, we should call the memory object's **ClearWorkBuffer** method in order to erase the latest frame of this same sprite, before we lose its rectangle information to the new sprite frame information to a new set of graphics:

```
      With m_sprDucks(m_nHitDuck)
        ...
       ' erase previous frame
            g_objMem.ClearWorkBuffer .rLoc

            ' show hit frame now
            Game_InitDeadDuck m_sprDucks(m_nHitDuck)
            L1_CopyLayers m_nHitDuck
            g_objMem.UpdateDisplay

          ...
          End With
```

Once the new frames are set up, **Game_CopyLayers** is called again, passing the index of this hit duck, where the overlapping ducks can be considered while the new frame is painted. Then, of course, the display is updated. The sprite class actually makes changing the frames of the duck quite convenient. The rest of the code is already in place for repainting and changing frames within the sprite so no special considerations are required.

Removing the duck from play is the next step. Now we have a sprite that was successfully hit. Its frames have now been changed from flying to the single hit frame:

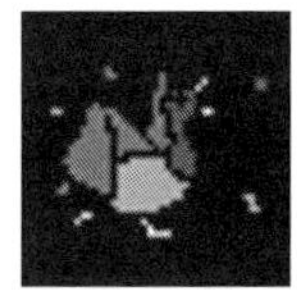

Without you having to do anything else, you'll see the hit frame played repeatedly without moving as the other ducks happily fly past. The layer information is retained as the layer that the duck was when it was hit, since it's still the same sprite object in the array. Referring to the Level 1 play loop, you can see that the first test is whether or not the **m_nHitDuck** variable is equal to the current sprite being painted. If so, this sprite must be removed from sight so that it won't be repainted any longer. A simple call to **ClearWorkBuffer** and some variable and property upkeep and it's done:

```
            'clear from display
            memGame.ClearWorkBuffer m_sprDucks(nSprite).rLoc
            memGame.UpdateDisplay

            'remove that sprite
            m_sprDucks(nSprite).Hit = True
            m_nHitDuck = -1
```

The **Hit** property must be set to **True** and the **m_nHitDuck** variable is set back to **-1**, meaning that no current duck is hit. This will change again once there's another successful **MouseDown** event that lands on another of the duck sprites. As for this dead duck, the **Hit** property set to **True** pretty much removes it from commission until that particular array entry is reused for a new duck (see the description of **L1_CreateNewSprite**).

The Finishing Touches

One, if not *the*, biggest problem areas in creating a good game is speed. I mean it's damn hard trying to make graphics run across the screen at a decent frame rate, especially when you have complex methods that must be performed behind the scenes on an ongoing basis. Each time a graphic is moved, you're no longer considering just the repainting of that one object.

Now you have other graphics to consider that may be partially covering or are being covered by the current graphic. This whole fun with graphics thing becomes a nightmare, mainly because of the fact that Windows-based games don't have the refresh rate of a DOS or direct environment.

Ah, but sometimes this isn't the only problem. You can even have trouble with things moving too fast! In the following sections, I'll address both of these issues as we wrap up game development theory.

Speeding Things Up

It's imperative for a game to function with as little incidental overhead as possible. As we developed the Fun with Ducks game, several things helped:

- Pre-loading graphics
- Cutting down classes
- Using the right timer

Graphics are loaded up from the **`Form_Load`** so that, as each frame is called to the display, it's already loaded into memory. This makes perfect sense, but you must consider the drawbacks to this too. If your graphics are larger, this can be too much for some primitive systems to handle in memory, so you need to make sure the graphics are at least cut down to 256 colors to save on memory usage at run time. Also, if you have a lot of graphics, several levels and different backgrounds in your game, rather than loading them all at the start of the game, it's better to decide at what point those new frame or level graphics need to be loaded.

Class speed is sometimes a must, since VB isn't as fast by itself as a DOS-based game. Rather than putting the level code into a class for each level, which adds a layer to the code called from the form, I kept the game engine inside the form. Also, you probably notice a missing class: the move class. I left this out because the movement was so specific to the game, I saw no point in working it into the movement class at this time. There were only a few short lines of code to write and it just wasn't worth the trouble. Besides, calling each iteration of both level play loops also saved a layer of code.

As you'll see in the next section, we sometimes need a timer to slow things down. However, this can slow things down too much if your accuracy at best is only 1/18 s, as with the VB timer control. When I first implemented the timing to control how fast the game iteration took place when there was just one duck on the screen, I used the VB timer and found it was just too slow when there were several ducks. Timer services through the multimedia DLLs in Windows provided a faster way to slow things down.

Slowing Things Down

The **`timeGetTime()`** API function is part of the multimedia services provided through the **`Mmsystem.dll`** and **`Winmm.dll`** files (for Win32 and Win16, respectively). This function returns the time in milliseconds since Windows was started. Now, this time value may not mean much to us by itself, but if you want a certain number of seconds or milliseconds to elapse before you perform another function in your code, you can check the difference between two times until this difference is equal to or greater than the delay your code requires. This is exactly what I do to try and control the duck movement across the screen when there are fewer ducks.

In the duck game, when there are fewer ducks in the sprite array, the game loop blits the ducks almost too fast. To control this, the loop has to be slowed in order to give the player some chance of hitting a duck or two and, on Level 2, to get out of the way of one. There is a global instance of the time class, **clsTime**, that is used within each level's loop to track that time. Here are the entire contents of the time class used with this code sample:

```
Private Declare Function timeGetTime Lib "winmm.dll" () As Long

Public Function GetTime() As Long
  GetTime = timeGetTime()
End Function
```

As you can see, it's a very lightweight function. You can imagine that it's probably as light as the timer control. I didn't put the test for the delay into the class because I felt it was class method overkill, since the only comparison necessary at this point is to see whether the difference between two returned time values is greater than or equal to another value. It is, however, convenient to at least encapsulate the declaration for the timer function within the class and provide a shorter method name, **GetTime**, that simply returns what **timeGetTime()** would have.

The following variables are used in conjunction with the time class to track the game loop speed:

- **timeObj**: the instance of **clsTime** within each game loop.
- **m_nMaxDelay**: the maximum delay that should ever pass before the next blit.
- **m_nDelay**: the amount of time that should pass before the next blit.
- **m_nStopTime**: stores the time when the next loop is free to proceed.

The maximum delay is set up before the game loop begins. This could be a variable that changes, based on the difficulty level of the game, but this game doesn't include such complex tracking mechanisms since I wanted to keep the code as simple as possible to follow. I set this value to 500 milliseconds. Each time a sprite is created, a call is made to **Game_SetDelay** which sets the **m_nDelay** variable to some percentage of **m_nMaxDelay**. This percentage isn't random by any means. If there are more ducks, I want less delay between cycles so that the ducks can be animated as quickly as possible. If there are fewer ducks in the array, I want to make sure that more time has passed before another duck is animated, or else they'll begin flying much too quickly to click. This is the calculation:

```
m_nDelay = Int((1 / m_nDuckCount) * m_nMaxDelay)
```

The time object has not yet been called. Remember that the value for **m_nDelay** is reused for each game blit cycle as long as the same number of ducks exist in the game for blitting. At the start of a blit cycle, in the section of the game loop where we are about to blit a visible duck sprite, the stop time is set. After this, the current sprite is blit, moved and whatever else must be done with it, but before the loop can proceed to the top once again, a **Do...Until** loop is called until the **GetTi**me method of the time class returns a value greater than or equal to the stop time. The corresponding lines within the game loop code appear below:

```
Start of game loop:

m_nStopTime = timeObj.GetTime + m_nDelay
...
...
```

```
Do Until timeObj.GetTime >= m_nStopTime
  DoEvents
Loop

End of game loop:
```

Summary

OK, so if you've played the game, you've seen a fairly simple example of a game written in VB. It's not at a level of sophistication yet where it hauls you-know-what for speed purposes, but it gives you an idea of the complexity that goes into a game and a starter kit for any VB game you may create.

Remember though, that you can use each of the components that went into this game project elsewhere. There's no reason why a sprite class can't come in handy in an application that uses a small animation. Furthermore, it's not just games that require complex dirty rectangle calculations and ongoing processes that require interaction from the user via keyboard and mouse.

Now, having seen a demo and game sample, both using VB and Windows API techniques, along with interdependent class modules, let's look at another type of animation application: the screensaver. Get ready for a really fun ride and bring your sense of humor along, together with your knowledge from the chapters so far. There are still a few new palette methods and animation techniques to be learned!

```
rivate Declare Function GlobalFree Lib "kernel32" (ByVal h
Private Declare Function GlobalLock Lib "kernel32" (ByVal h
Private Declare Function GlobalUnlock Lib "kernel32" (ByVa
'--copying bitmap bits
' copies a global block of data into global memory
Private Declare Sub CopyMemory Lib "kernel32" Alias "RtlM

'--copies global block of data in      B
Private Declare Function SetDIB      "gdi32" (ByVal m_hd
  ByVal hBitmap As Long, ByVal nStartS      As Long, By
  ByVal lpBits As Any, lpBI As BITMAPI      ByVal wUsa

'--blits DC to DC
Private Declare Function BitBlt Lib "gdi32" (ByVal hDestDC
Private Declare Function StretchBlt Lib "gdi32" (ByVal hDes

'--palette methods
Private Declare Function CreatePalett      "gdi32" (lpLogPa
Private Declare Function SelectPalette      "gdi32" (ByVal m
Private Declare Function RealizePalette Lib "gdi32" (ByVal m
Private Declare Sub AnimatePalette Lib "gdi32" (ByVal hPal

'--device context methods
Private Declare Function SelectObject Lib "gdi32" (ByVal m_

Private Declare Function CreateCompatibleBitmap Lib "gdi32
Private Declare Function DeleteObject Lib "gdi32" (ByVal hO

Private Declare Function CreateCompatibleDC Lib "gdi32" (B
```

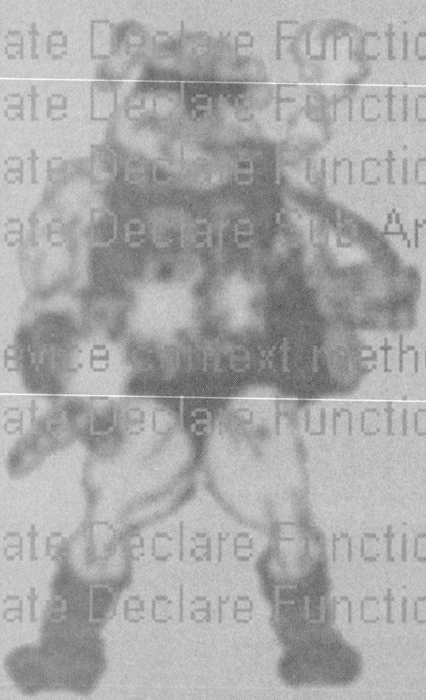

Chapter

6

Paths, Palettes and Whiz

Now this one is gonna be loads of fun! Oh sure, you've read about moving graphics and you've seen some different ways to handle palettes in Chapters 3, 4 and 5. But there's much more to learn. So far, we handled paths completely separately from the animation, so they've been rather simple. The palette issues that we've dealt with so far have also been quite trivial. It's time to batten down those hatches and get ready for some stormy weather as you get into the advanced issues that this chapter will address.

In this chapter, while I rekindle your interest in path movement and palettes, I'll use a curiously interesting screen saver developed at ImageWare to keep the excitement burning. This way, not only will you learn a more complex use for paths and palettes, but you'll also learn how to build your own screen savers to boot and do some nifty screen filtering!

How Screen Savers Work

The character for the screen saver that we'll be building is a dog—bad dog. It runs around your desktop, doingthings that dogs do, like running, scratching, sniffing... and, uhmm, whizzing. Windows 95 introduced screen savers tied to entire themes with the Plus! pack. These themes also change the cursor for the environmental settings in the general Windows display. I won't be going into that level of detail since it would detract from our coverage of the actual animations inside the Bad Dog screen saver.

I *will* be talking about the basics of screen saver development, touching on the extras that aren't covered here so you're aware of what they comprise and that they exist. In the next section, we'll cover how screen savers work in general, along with the various components that comprise a screen saver project and what you need to do to have the system recognize it.

Running a Screen Saver

First thing's first. We need to know how a screen saver comes into existence as an executable and how Windows handles running that executable. The following section sums it up.

The Executable

What makes a program executable a screen saver?

- It must be named with the extension **`.scr`** instead of **`.exe`**.
- This **`.scr`** file should be located in the **`Windows\System`** directory, to be run automatically by the system based on Control Panel timeout settings.
- It should automatically terminate with mouse or keyboard activity.

Of course, you're waiting for me to tell you there's a little more to it than that—and there is. However, building a screen saver application is actually pretty darned straightforward once you know what you need to do.

To demonstrate the basics of the screen saver, I created a test project, **`Tstsaver.vbp`** which isolates some of the basic functionality that must be present for a program to act as a screen saver. This screen saver does nothing but show a black screen, but it reacts as a screen saver should and this is what I'll be talking about first. Once these aspects of the screen saver project are clear, I'll buff out this skeleton code into a much more complicated screen saver, the Bad Dog.

The Control Panel

First off, you select a screen saver through the Display Properties dialog, which is available from the Control Panel. The following figure shows this tab, with some additional comments:

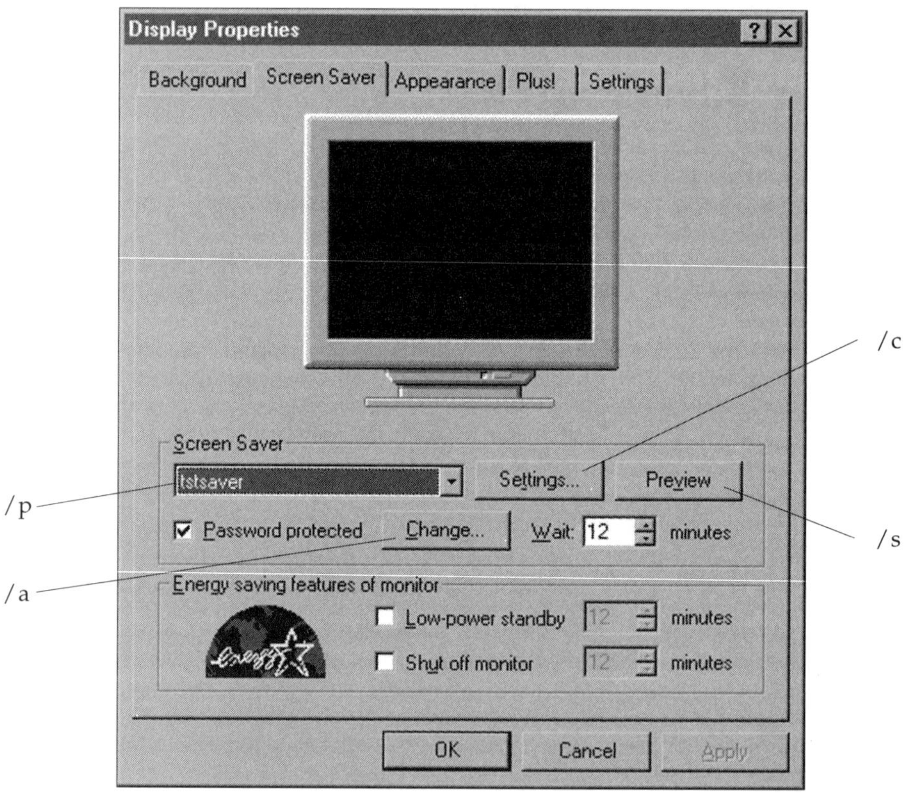

The figure points out the features of the dialog that are worth noting and the command line parameters passed to the **.scr** file when it's called from this dialog in different instances. I'll go through the items in the figure and comment on the command line parameters. The shell procedure in **Tstsaver.scr** that intercepts these parameters is shown here:

```
Private Sub Init_CheckCmdLine()
Dim sCmd As String

  sCmd = UCase$(Trim$(Command$))

  If InStr(sCmd, "/C") Then              '/c passed for configuration
     'show configuration
  ElseIf InStr(sCmd, "/S") Or sCmd$ = "" Then  '/s passed for preview and run
     'run program normally
     frmSaver.Show
  ElseIf InStr(sCmd, "/P") Then   '/p passed for preview window
    'do nothing and see still image
    'OR
    'write code to run program in preview window
  ElseIf InStr(sCmd, "/A") Then   '/a passed for password protection
    'use custom password dialog
      'OR
    'call Windows password dialog
  End If

End Sub
```

The Screen Saver list box shows all screen savers found in the **System** directory. The list is created dynamically when the Display Properties dialog is displayed, based on all the files found with the extension **.scr**. If **Tstsaver.scr** is copied to this directory, you'll see it listed here. As soon as you choose a saver, it's run with the command line parameter **/p**. As you can see from the previous listing, no code is written for this instance and the preview monitor displays the **Tstsaver.scr** window, which amounts to a black screen.

The monitor shows either a screenshot from the selected saver or the actual saver. How does it know what to display? It depends if you include code when the **/p** command line parameter is intercepted. If you don't write code to animate inside that window, you'll just see the window background of your application. **Tstsaver.scr** has a plain black background color, which is what you'll see if you select it.

The Settings button also runs the screen saver, with a command line that starts with **/c**, for configuration. The screen saver code should respond to this with a configuration dialog box, custom to the screen saver. It shouldn't run the screen saver in its normal state in any case. This dialog is where properties for the screen saver can be displayed and edited. It's up to the program to save any changes made from within this configuration dialog, either to registry or a custom **.ini** file where it can be used later, depending on the code you write to save the information. Typically, code specific to your application should still be placed in an **.ini** file for the application, not in the registry, so as not to clutter it up.

If you press the Preview button, the screen saver is run like an executable. The command line parameter **/s** signifies that the saver is to run normally. This parameter is also passed when the screen saver timeout has expired and the saver is run in the usual way. The code that's triggered for this should read any pertinent screen saver initialization data, written by the configuration dialog and then run using those settings. Of course, if there are no settings, like the **Tstsaver.scr** sample, the program can just run as is.

If the Password protected checkbox is selected, the Change button is enabled. Clicking the Change button runs the saver with the parameter **/a**. This is where the screen saver code can respond with a Change Password dialog, enabling the user to change it. The code can supply a customized password dialog, or use the Windows 95 password dialog box. Any password information should be stored where the saver can retrieve it when required. This is when the password must be entered to get back to the Windows environment.

The Wait list box is where the delay timeout is set for the screen saver. Windows monitors keystrokes and mouse movements, starting this screen saver after this period of inactivity. This setting is shown in minutes inside the Screen Saver tab and has little to do with the actual screen saver code, since it's handled by the environment. This information is stored in the Windows Registry.

Setting Information

Now that you've seen the general user's side of things, let's take a look behind the scenes. For instance, where do the selections made inside the display properties dialog get saved? Windows 95 instigates more use of the registry database as an alternative to initialization (**.ini**) files, but not all information is stored there. There are two initialization ingredients to the successful run of a screen saver: the information that the Windows environment expects to be there and the information that your specific screen saver needs. Let's take a peek at the Windows environmental requirements first.

.ini and Registry

The **System.ini** file is still used to tell Windows which is the currently active screen saver. Shown below is the single line beneath the boot section which holds this information:

```
[boot]
SCRNSAVE.EXE=C:\WINDOWS\SYSTEM\TSTSAVER.SCR
```

The rest of the system information that was previously (pre-32-bit) stored inside the Windows **.ini** files, is now located inside the registry database. Here's a screenshot of the registry editor, where the settings for the Screen Saver tab of the Display Properties dialog are stored.

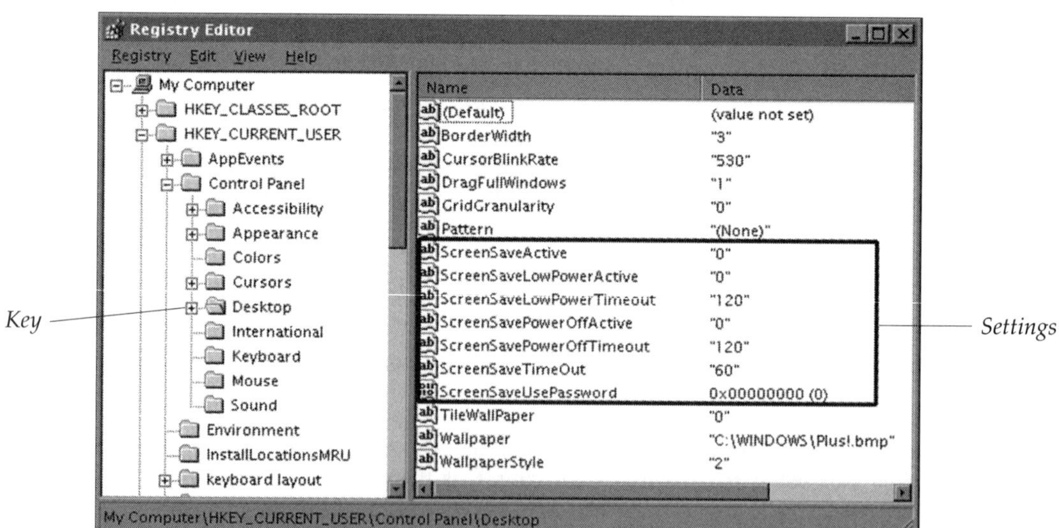

The figure shows the **HKEY_CURRENT_USER** key in the registry with the subkey for Control Panel, and its Desktop subkey open, to display the settings. These are pretty straightforward because they simply record the settings of the Screen Saver tab in the Display Properties dialog. The code for the screen saver doesn't need to concern itself with most of this information, except to respond when the **.scr** file is called and react to the parameters accordingly.

This information would most likely only need to be accessed from an installation program that wants to make the installed screen saver the active one. In this case, the **System.ini** needs to be told of the saver's name and any settings in the registry that need custom attention should be set accordingly. For instance, **ScreenSaveTimeOut** is the key that informs Windows how many seconds of inactivity should elapse before the current screen saver is run and it could be set to a custom value (note that it's in seconds here, but in minutes inside the Control Panel display).

Also, in case a current screen saver isn't set to be active, the **ScreenSaverActiveFlag** should be set to 1, not 0. This ensures that the saver will run after timeout.

Custom Information

Control Panel and system wide settings may not be the only settings required for the screen saver. These are global settings that work for all savers. The Bad Dog screen saver addresses the situation where some custom information is needed, like where graphics are stored and what speed the animation should run at.

When the screen saver is properly set up, there should be a **Baddog_s.ini** file, located in the **Windows\System** directory, along with the screen saver file, **Baddog_s.scr**. This **.ini** file holds this custom information. We'll discuss how this works later in the description of the screen saver class, **clsSaverInfo**.

Execution Particulars

Considering the **Tstsaver.vbp** application, let's go over some of the additional basics that were necessary for this application to become a valid screen saver. The three main questions to answer are:

- How is it started?
- How does it end?
- What about the cursor?

We have already answered the first question. If **Tstsaver.scr** is selected from the Control Panel, after the set timeout delay, the **.scr** file is run with the parameter **/s**. This is the parameter that will run the **.scr** file when Windows instigates the run. Actually, since you may run this as an **.exe** without installing it as a screen saver, we also check for a blank command line, just in case. To run the saver, the main form is shown, since this is the saver's display:

```
ElseIf InStr(sCmd, "/S") Or sCmd = "" Then
frmSaver.Show
```

Now for the next question. Since the form has no interface and no control box, how does it end? I mentioned earlier that screen savers terminate when any mouse movement is detected or when there is keyboard activity. Inside **frmSaver**, the **Form_KeyDown** event calls to the **Saver_Stop** procedure which ends the program. **Form_MouseMove** also calls **Saver_Stop**, but there's a condition that must first be met. Mouse movement can be intercepted even when only a slight jitter of the mouse has taken place. To ensure that the user has moved the mouse intentionally to end the saver, the procedure tests that the mouse has moved five pixels from where it was:

```
Static vLastX As Variant
Static vLastY As Variant

  ' first time in
  If IsEmpty(vLastX) Or IsNull(vLastX) Then
    vLastX = X
    vLastY = Y
  End If

  ' if mouse move at least 5 pixels, end
  If Abs(vLastX - X) > 5 Or Abs(vLastY - Y) > 5 Then
    vLastX = Null
    vLastY = Null
    Saver_Stop
  End If
```

So what about the cursor? As you probably already know, the cursor isn't normally visible during the execution of a screen saver. This is quite easy to address, however, with a simple API call. **ShowCursor()** is part of the **User32** library of functions. Passing zero (**False**) to the **ShowCursor()** function turns off the display of the cursor, while any non-zero value (**True**) turns it on.

When the form is loaded, this indicates that the saver is about to run, so the following line of code hides the cursor:

```
nRet = ShowCursor(False)
```

When **Saver_Stop** is called, the saver is being terminated, so the cursor is shown again, like so:

```
nRet = ShowCursor(True)
```

That about covers the details of the execution of a simple screen saver. Now let's see how some of the command line parameters are handled in a more complex screen saver, not to mention a more exciting display!

About Bad Dog

A screen saver usually contains the following central pieces of code:

- Configuration
- Initialization
- Code content

Settings are specific to the screen saver and are usually customizable from the Control Panel dialog, through a configuration dialog provided by the screen saver itself. When it's initialized, the screen saver should check those settings to determine parameters for run time. Most screen savers offer a password capability so that the user can set a password to terminate the saver. There may not be one, but if there is, the code needs to retrieve this information and handle it.

Let's see how each of the components run within the Bad Dog screen saver.

Configuration

The final version of Bad Dog, which comes on the book's CD, is a little more complex than the sample code I'm describing in this chapter. It was also written in VB3 (as you'll notice), but you should still check it out for interest's sake. To demonstrate some settings from the Control Panel, this example features a simple dialog, called from the panel as described earlier, when the switch **/c** is passed to the **.scr** file.

Information about the screen saver necessary for run time is located in the registry (for 32-bit programs) or in an **.ini** file. This is the information that the code should first retrieve in order to run properly. Some screen savers in Windows 95 seem to toss all their files into the **Windows\System** directory so that when the **.scr** file is run, no information needs to be retrieved regarding location of graphic files, and so on. When the Bad Dog screen saver is installed, the installation directory is saved to an entry in the **Baddog_s.ini** file so that, at run time, the screen saver can retrieve the location of all the graphics without cluttering the **Windows\System** directory.

From the sample code's configuration dialog, you can set the speed for the animation and the installation directory where you can find the dog bitmaps:

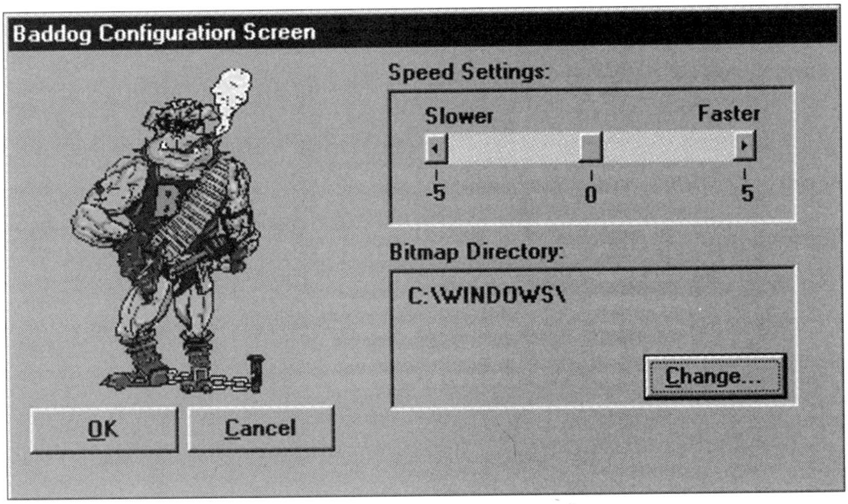

If we used an installation program with this example, the installation directory would reflect wherever the user decided to install. The speed would likely reflect some default value.

When the form is loaded, the scroll bar value is set to the **Speed** property of the saver class (this information will have been filled in when the saver was first run, as you'll see). The installation directory is set to the **InstallDir** property of the same class:

```
With g_objSavInfo
    labDir.Caption = .InstallDir
    scrSpeed.Value = .Speed
End With
```

From the interface, you can move the scroll bar from a value of -5 to 5, where 0 is the default speed for the animation. Once you've run the saver, you decide what best suits your computers capabilities. Changing the installation directory won't move the bitmaps for you because this isn't an installation program. What it will do is let you fix up the **.ini** file to reflect some new directory you may have moved the bitmaps to, without having to edit the **.ini** directly. If you click OK, the following code will save the new information, once again using **clsSavInfo** (which we'll see real soon):

```
With g_objSavInfo
    .InstallDir = labDir.Caption
    .Speed = scrSpeed.Value
    .UpdateSettings
End With
```

Though I didn't write an installation program for this code sample, to get you set up the first time, I *will* give you instructions on how to set up the screen saver so that it will run properly.

Initialization

To understand how the initialization works, it is first important to understand where the information for initialization comes from. Since screen savers are normally installed for us, I'll show you the steps that will ensure you're set up to run this baby at design or run time.

Installation Instructions

For this sample to run properly, you should install it just as it would be by a proper installation program. Here, I'll set you up with the why's and wherefore's that go with Bad Dog. From design time, if you run this from the CD, you should have a directory with the following:

- **Baddog_s.exe**
- **Baddog_s.scr**
- **Baddog_s.ini**
- All the Bad Dog bitmaps
- The Bad Dog source code

The **Baddog_s.ini** looks like this before the saver is properly installed:

```
[Configure]
InstallDir=0
Speed=0
PlaySound=0
Password=0
UsePassword= 0
```

There are some extra settings shown here that aren't used by this sample: PlaySound, Password, UsePassword. *These are placed here in case you ever decide to add further capability to the application.*

As part of a mock installation for this screen saver, you should set the **InstallDir** key in the **.ini** file to the current path where the bitmaps are located. If you put the files on **c:\Baddog_s**, the line should read this way:

```
InstallDir=c:\baddog_s\
```

Now, if you run the **.exe** from this directory, it will run like a screen saver, no problem. When you move the mouse or press a key, it will terminate. If you run the project, using **Vb32.exe** from here, you'll get the same results. If you want to connect it to the Control Panel, where all the other screen savers go, you'll have to follow a few more steps.

Copy **Baddog_s.scr** and **Baddog_s.ini** to the **Windows\System** directory on your machine. Then leave the bitmaps in the directory referenced by the **.ini** file. This is where the program will expect them to reside, and it won't run without finding that directory in the **.ini** file.

That's all you have to do. Now the Control Panel will list this screen saver with the rest!

Class Description: clsSaverInfo

This class is tailored to Bad Dog. It provides some properties and methods that are necessary to retrieve and set the configuration information for the screen saver. The class doesn't have much to it, but this figure sums it up:

When an object variable is created for this class, the initialization event takes care of setting up a few variables that the class will need to function properly. Since the class isn't portable to another screen saver (it merely serves as a foundation for creating a possibly more complex class that handles this type of activity), the **.ini** file that holds the configuration information is hard-coded here. Also, since the **.ini** file is supposed to be located in the same directory from which the saver was run, a path variable is also setup here, based on **AppPath**:

```
m_sAppPath = App.Path
  If Right$(m_sAppPath, 1) <> "\" Then
    m_sAppPath = m_sAppPath & "\"
  End If

  m_sSavINI = "baddog_s.ini"
```

The class can be used in two ways: to get configuration information and fill the class properties, or to set that information after filling in those properties to the corresponding values. The properties for configuration of Bad Dog are **InstallDir** and **Speed**.

To retrieve the configuration settings, the **GetSettings** method should be called. This method is a function that returns **True** or **False**, based on the success of getting those settings. The idea is that if the location of the dog bitmaps isn't set up in the **.ini** file, the saver shouldn't be run.

The first part of **GetSettings** checks to see whether the **Baddog_s.ini** file can be found in the application path. If not, the saver configuration won't be retrievable and the saver shouldn't be run.

```
If Dir$(m_sAppPath & m_sSavINI) = "" Then
  MsgBox m_sSavINI & " file is missing. Cannot run screen saver."
  GetSettings = False
  GoTo endgetsettings
Else
...
```

Once it has been established that the **.ini** is accessible, the two settings are retrieved using the Windows API function **GetPrivateProfileString()**. This function requires the following parameters:

- A section name
- A key name
- A default value
- A buffer for return value
- The length of the buffer
- The full path to the **.ini** file

The return from this function is the number of characters returned into the string buffer. Since the string buffer is initialized to a number of spaces, in order to ensure that there's room for the string to be retrieved (you'll crash if this isn't the case), you use this return to grab only the number of characters that are valid in the return string.

The return from the **InstallDir** key should be the path to the Bad Dog bitmaps. This isn't verified here. A check is made only to make sure that the return isn't the default 0, which would mean that the setting had no value. Otherwise, the **m_nInstDir** variable is set for the class, which is passed to the **InstallDir** property when requested.

```
' get installation directory for graphics
sRetStr = Space$(128)
nRet = GetPrivateProfileString("Configure", "InstallDir", "0", sRetStr,
Len(sRetStr), m_sAppPath & m_sSavINI)
sRetStr = Left$(sRetStr, nRet)
If sRetStr = "0" Then
  MsgBox "Path information is missing. Can't run screen saver."
  GetSettings = False
  GoTo endgetsettings
Else
  If Right$(sRetStr, 1) <> "\" Then sRetStr = sRetStr & "\"
  m_sInstDir = sRetStr
End If
```

The speed settings require the same treatment. Only the default 0 is used if the key name doesn't have a value. Since the **m_nSpeed** variable is a **Long** value, the **Val()** function is used to convert the string into a number value. We can retrieve this value through the **Speed** property of the class:

```
' get speed settings
sRetStr = Space$(128)
nRet = GetPrivateProfileString("Configure", "Speed", "0", sRetStr, Len(sRetStr),
m_sAppPath & m_sSavINI)
sRetStr = Left$(sRetStr, nRet)
m_nSpeed = Val(sRetStr)
```

There are fewer steps with the **UpdateSettings** method for the class since no verification need be done on the information. Since the configuration form, **frmConfig** described earlier, is used to check the information before saving it, the method need only call the **GetPrivateProfileString()** Windows API function once for each setting. The parameters required in this case are:

- A section name
- A key name
- A key value
- The full path to the **.ini** file

The two lines that call this function assume that the properties of **InstallDir** and **Speed** have been updated to their new (and accurate) values, so the **m_sInstDir** and **m_nSpeed** variables are used to set the corresponding keys in the **.ini** file:

```
nRet = WritePrivateProfileString("Configure", "InstallDir", m_sInstDir, m_sAppPath
& m_sSavINI)
nRet = WritePrivateProfileString("Configure", "Speed", CStr(m_nSpeed), m_sAppPath
& m_sSavINI)
```

You've seen already where this is used in the configuration screen for Bad Dog.

Run Preparation

When the saver is first executed, before the parameters passed on the command line are even looked at, the availability of the settings in the **.ini** file is checked. This is done with a call to **GetSettings** as previously described:

```
If Not g_objSavInfo.GetSettings Then End
g_sPath = g_objSavInfo.InstallDir
```

The return from **GetSettings** is **False** if something went wrong while trying to gather the environmental settings for the screen saver. If all goes well, the global path variable for the application may as well be set to the **InstallDir** property of the saver class, since this is where all the bitmaps will be located. I can assume this because I know this is the only way that the path is used in this particular application. Another may require both a bitmap directory and an executable directory. It depends.

Once the environmental aspect of the application has been set up, the call to **Init_CheckCmdLine** is made to decide how the screen saver should be run (as with **Tstsaver.scr** earlier). Similar to the code I demonstrated earlier, a **Select Case** statement is used to check the command line parameter passed:

```
sCmd = UCase$(Trim$(Command$))

If InStr(sCmd, "/C") Then
    frmConfig.Show
ElseIf InStr(sCmd, "/S") Or sCmd = "" Then
    frmSaver.Show
ElseIf InStr(sCmd, "/P") Then
  ' write code here to display saver
  ' actively inside preview window
ElseIf InStr(sCmd, "/A") Then
    ' call password form for changing password
End If
```

This time, if **/C** is passed, **frmConfig** is shown to configure the settings for Bad Dog. The only other parameter that is addressed is **/S**, which runs the saver. The other settings have been left out of this example, seeing as they have little to do with the animation itself.

Code Content

Just like any other application, the screen saver is just an executable. This saver is basically one big animation, so I'll tell you about what you should be seeing on the screen, before I get into the code.

When the screen saver is activated, the bad dog is loaded into memory, but there's a unique background to this application: the desktop. The current display is copied into a buffer in memory and is used as the background image for the animations to follow. In other words, the bad dog does its thing on *your* screen!

The dog animations consist of the following:

- Walking
- Sniffing
- Scratching
- Whizzing
- Turning

The order of these animations is completely random, but movement is kept within reasonable bounds of the screen real estate. A complex gathering of classes and coding techniques makes it possible to coordinate all of these animations, with a twist. You've seen the building of these classes throughout the book so far, so it won't be unfamiliar territory. Beware, though, because one of these animations is *really* bad. That's the one where the dog whizzes all over what you were working on. Remember that old excuse 'the dog ate my homework'? Well, here's a new one for you.

The bulk of this screen saver's code needs lengthy explanation for its individual components. That's the purpose of the next section...

Getting into the Code

Now that you have some idea of what the project is supposed to accomplish as a screen saver and what the animations are, let's see how it all gets put together. Here I'll cover how the dog animation sequences are set up in the code, how the sprite classes are organized to facilitate this complex animation application, the saver animation loop and how it coordinates the ongoing selection of animations is up for discussion.

Grabbing the Screen Display

When the form loads to prepare the screen saver run-time environment, several familiar steps are taken, seen with the same classes as in previous chapters:

- Form size and properties are set
- Memory buffer is created using **clsMem**
- A global palette object is created using **clsPalette**
- Graphics are loaded into bitmap objects using **clsBmp**
- Sprites are created to link to those graphics using **clsSprite**
- The memory buffer is initialized to the background display

These events take place mostly from the **Form_Load** procedure, but **Saver_LoadGraphics** handles loading the bitmaps into memory, creating the sprites and initializing the memory buffer, possibly using one of those loaded bitmaps. Here's where some things have been added to address the use of the current screen display as the backdrop for the animations. I'll cover aspects of each class that work differently than in previous chapters to facilitate this process.

clsMem Additions

Not much has changed with respect to additional properties and methods, as you can see from the class diagram:

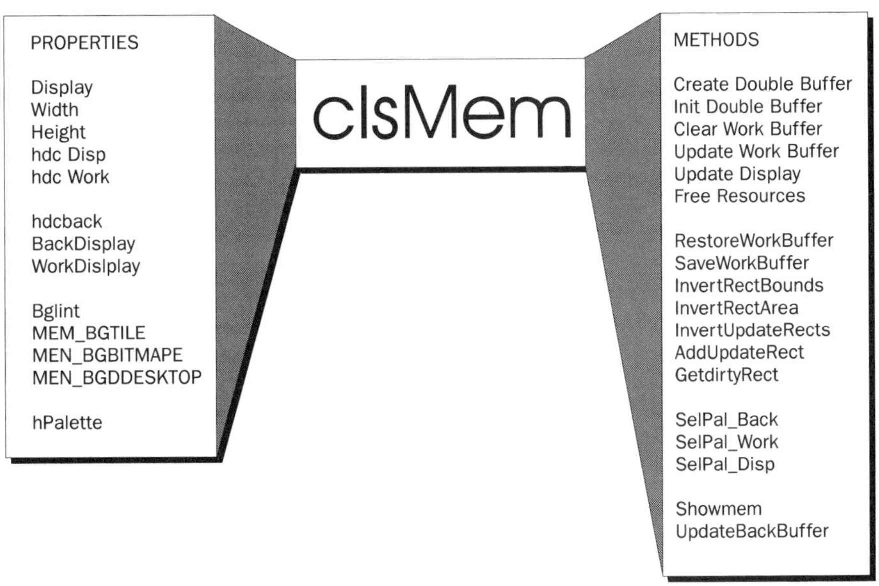

In the Bad Dog screen saver, the current screen display is used as the background bitmap, which means the **InitDoubleBuffer** method of **clsMem** had to be massaged to reflect these changes. First of all, look at the following code where the buffer is initialized:

```
With m_objMem
    .hPalette = g_objPal.hPalette
.BgInit = .MEM_BGDESKTOP
    .InitDoubleBuffer
End With 'm_objMem
```

The palette assignment follows suit with previous chapters where a global animation palette is used. The **BgInit** property now has a new parameter, **MEM_BGDESKTOP**, which is used when **InitDoubleBuffer** is called to signify that a bitmap should be created from the current desktop display, a print screen of sorts, to fill the double buffer. The following lines of code take care of this process:

```
Case MEM_BGDESKTOP

hdcTemp = GetDC(&H0)
nScrHeight = GetDeviceCaps(hdcTemp, VERTRES)
nScrWidth = GetDeviceCaps(hdcTemp, HORZRES)

SelPal_Back
nRet = StretchBlt(m_hdcBack, 0, 0, m_nDispW, m_nDispH, hdcTemp, 0, 0,
                      nScrWidth, nScrHeight, SRCCOPY)

nRet = ReleaseDC(&H0, hdcTemp)
```

The memory buffer is created separate from the code that initializes it with a background display. Considering this, I didn't want to allow the **InitDoubleBuffer** code to count on the size of the memory buffer being that of the desktop. For this reason, I use **GetDeviceCaps()** to give me the accurate resolution of the desktop. **StretchBlt()** then copies the contents of the **hdcTemp** to **hdcBack**. **GetDC()** returns the DC for the desktop into **hdcTemp**, when the hex value **&H0** is passed, which is the screen's window handle. Let's continue and see how this new functionality works.

Using Common DCs

Until now, you've only seen how the **CreateCompatibleDC()** Windows API function is used to create a DC that can later be filled with the bitmap information that we need it to contain. The process includes not only creating a DC, but a bitmap the size of the DC, which then must be selected into the DC. When the DC is no longer needed, the bitmap must be selected out of the DC, followed by a call to **DeleteObject()** to delete the bitmap. Then, **DeleteDC()** must also be called to delete the DC from memory.

Aside from *creating* memory DCs, Windows also offers a collection of common DCs that we may need to get information from. A perfect example, grabbing a copy of the current screen display. Since the screen DC already exists, I can access it by calling the **GetDC()** function as shown above. This returns an already existing handle to a device context, based on the window handle passed it. As we noted earlier, passing a window handle **of &H0** (which is really 0) returns the DC for the screen, which was then used to copy the data from that DC into another memory DC for the memory buffer.

Since getting access to the screen DC through **GetDC()** is done through Windows, as usual, I had to clean up after myself as VB has no idea what I've done here. In this case, the DC I asked for doesn't need to be deleted since it was not created by me, but my link to it must be released and the **ReleaseDC()** function is what does the trick. Notice from the previous code that this function is called directly after the DC information is blitted into the memory buffer DC. At that point, I already got what I wanted—a copy of the DC's contents.

You'll probably notice I interchange 'desktop' with 'current screen display' when referring to the use of current screen display as the background image for this application. In fact, the desktop is a different window handle altogether, and is possibly covered by other application windows. It's easier to refer to the screen display as the desktop, but just bear this in mind.

Creating a Dynamic Palette

Yet another adventure with palettes looms near. There are some interesting things I can point out to you this time around that may even save you some time in the future. Once again, a global palette is being used for all graphics. This really is always the best way to handle graphics for animation purposes. It saves on time in adjusting palettes all over the place, to avoid flicker. If each graphic had a unique palette, screen updates would become difficult to impossible, depending on the programming tools and expertise involved. Imaging programs use complex dithering algorithms to manage screen updates when new colors are dynamically introduced to the display, particularly when filters are applied to an image. Animation graphics can usually be prepared ahead of time, so there's no need to use this technique.

There is a trick used for the palette created in this example to get round a couple of problems I encountered. Since the background used for the animation is the current screen display or desktop, I can't predetermine the palette required for this if need be. Furthermore, I can't feasibly assign a hard-coded bitmap palette to that desktop display, without losing detail and possibly royally messing up the image. Besides, the whole point of this screen saver is to leave you with the impression that the dog is actually running around on your display!

To handle this, some functionality had to be added that would create a palette from the current display. Easy enough, since this is equivalent to the system palette. However, the dog palette colors must also be available in the palette being created or the dog will look messed up. What a dilemma!

Building a Palette

Before I describe the code inside the buffed-out palette class, I'll walk through the theory of what the dynamic palette needs to be and why. First and foremost, the dog bitmaps need their palette to be part of this global palette. Since there are only six palette entries for all of the dog bitmaps, it's not hard to fathom that the six colors can likely be realized to the system palette successfully.

The global palette isn't only used to realize the appropriate palette to the system before blitting to the display from the double buffer. It's also passed to the bitmap classes that read the dog frames into memory device contexts of their own. Since the bitmaps are loaded into a picture box before being blitted to the memory DC, the palette entries of the picture box DC must be reflected in the *same positions* of the memory DC the information is being blit to. Those palette entries are mapped one for one to the destination DC, so if they aren't the same colors, look out!

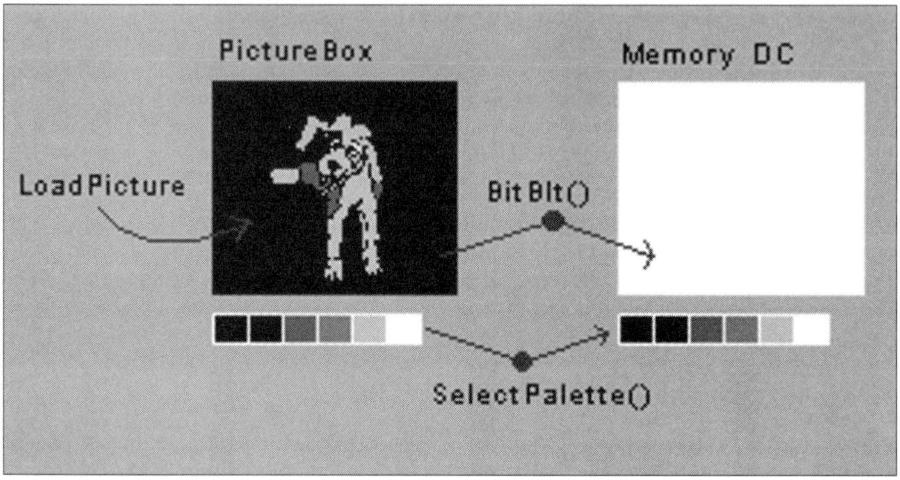

This would be easy if the bitmap color table is made into a palette of its own, selected into the memory DC before the blitting is done from the picture box. Now we have to incorporate the issue of the desktop that is to be our background bitmap.

This bitmap has a palette equivalent to the current system palette. The chance of the first six entries matching the dog bitmap colors is quite slim. What has to be done is a palette created that reflects the first 6 bitmap colors, then the next 230 colors can be the first 230 in the system palette. Actually, the first 10 entries need not be included in this, since once a palette is created and realized into the system palette, the first six entries will remain intact anyway.

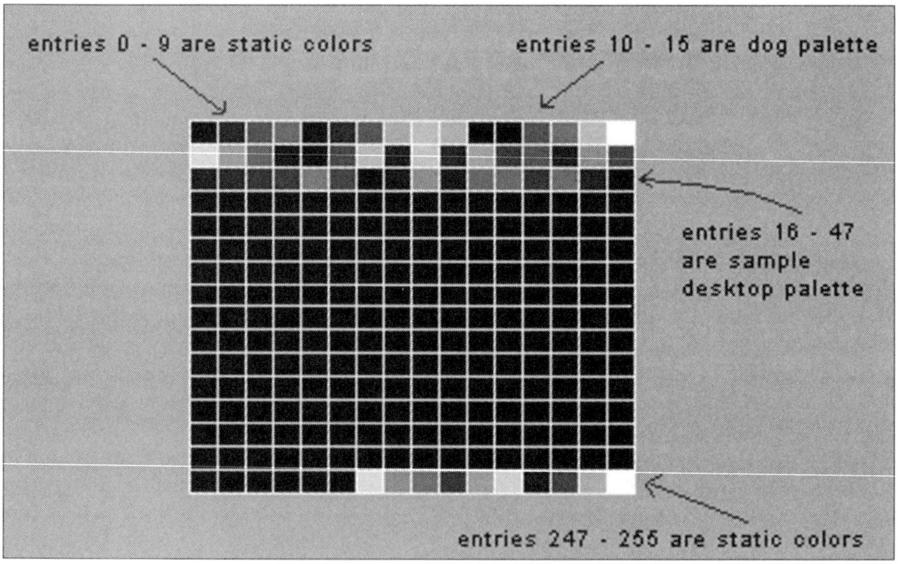

Creating the palette this way ensures that the dog colors will be the first realized to the system palette. Though it's also important that the background bitmap looks as close as possible to the original screen display, it's more important that those six colors are available to the dog bitmaps as they're blitted to the display. When a palette is realized to the system, the first ten system entries remain, the last ten remain and the first 236 colors (assuming that there's room for all of them to be realized) in the logical palette will be placed in the system palette. The worst case scenario, is that the last twenty or so desktop colors don't get realized, but the important colors should be at the beginning of the palette anyway.

Now let's see what the updates to the palette class do to make this possible.

clsPalette Additions

A **CreateMode** property has been added to the class so that, before the call to **Create**, you have told the class object how you want the palette created. The modes provided are:

- Use a bitmap color table
- Use the system palette
- Use both

The first mode, using a bitmap color table, is the method the class has been using up to this point. This is now indicated by the mode **PAL_BMP**. I don't actually use the system palette mode, **PAL_SYSTEM**, in this chapter's sample. This is provided simply for convenience, since I am using a form of system palette in the last mode described. This mode, **PAL_COMBO**, is clearly a method that is tailored to this example. Most of the time, palette work requires a certain level of control, so this isn't entirely unacceptable.

The **Create** method now differentiates between the palette modes and calls the appropriate procedure:

```
Select Case m_nCreateMode
  Case m_PALBMP
    If IsMissing(file) Then
      MsgBox "Must pass a filename when creating a bitmap palette!"
      Exit Sub
    End If
    m_sFile = file
    Create_Bitmap
  Case m_PALSYSTEM
    If IsMissing(hdc) Then
      MsgBox "Must pass a DC when creating a system palette!"
      Exit Sub
    End If
    m_hdc = hdc
    Create_System
  Case m_PALCOMBO
    If IsMissing(hdc) Then
      MsgBox "Must pass a DC when creating a combination bitmap/system palette!"
      Exit Sub
    End If
    If IsMissing(file) Then
      MsgBox "Must pass a filename when creating a bitmap palette!"
      Exit Sub
    End If
    m_hdc = hdc
    m_sFile = file
    Create_Combo
  End Select
```

Two parameters are now passed to this method, both being **optional**. The first is a filename, for use with the **PAL_BMP** and **PAL_COMBO** modes. The second is a handle to a display device context, which is required when requesting the system palette colors, therefore for both the **PAL_SYSTEM** and **PAL_COMBO** modes. Checks are in place to make sure that you pass the appropriate parameters for the mode specified.

Create_Bitmap performs the same functionality as it did before. It creates a logical palette from the bitmap file's color table. **Create_System** creates one from the system palette. Getting the system palette entries doesn't require much work. The Windows API function, **GetSystemPaletteEntries()** does all the work for you. This function requires a display DC handle, then the entry number in the palette that you want to start retrieving from (you don't have to get all the colors if you don't want to), and the number of colors from that entry that you want returned into the array of **PALETTEENTRY** structures, passed to the last parameter.

```
Dim nColors As Long
Dim palSysEntries() As PALETTEENTRY

  nColors = 256
  ReDim palSysEntries(nColors - 1)
  nRet = GetSystemPaletteEntries(frmSaver.hdc, 0, nColors, palSysEntries(0))

  m_hPal = GetPalette(palSysEntries)
```

This method assumes that you want the entire system palette returned into the palette array. **GetDIBPalette** isn't used here, since it uses bitmap information to set up the **LOGPALETTE** structure before creating the palette. Instead, a new method called **GetPalette** is called. This is passed the **PALETTEENTRY** array, in this case **palSysEntries**.

Inside **GetPalette**, a **LOGPALETTE** structure is still set up, but using the palette entries passed instead. Then, the same call to **CreatePalette()** finishes the job and returns the new palette handle:

```
Dim logPal As LOGPALETTE
Dim nIndex As Integer

  logPal.palVersion = &H300
  logPal.palNumEntries = UBound(pal) + 1

  For nIndex = 0 To logPal.palNumEntries - 1
      logPal.palPalEntry(nIndex).peRed = pal(nIndex).peRed
      logPal.palPalEntry(nIndex).peGreen = pal(nIndex).peGreen
      logPal.palPalEntry(nIndex).peBlue = pal(nIndex).peBlue
      logPal.palPalEntry(nIndex).peFlags = 0
  Next nIndex

  GetPalette = CreatePalette(logPal)
```

Create_Combo does a little of both. First, it reads in the bitmap information using the same call that **Create_Bitmap** does (**Read_BitmapInfo**). This simply fills the bitmap structure information for the class with the color table information we need. In this case, the six entries for the dog bitmap passed the function should be read in. A **PALETTEENTRY** array, **palEntries()**, is then redimensioned to fit the colors from this bitmap color table, and the entries are set to these color values.

```
ReDim palEntries(nBmpColors - 1)
  For nIndex = 0 To nBmpColors - 1
    palEntries(nIndex).peRed = m_bmInfo.bmiColors(nIndex).rgbRed
    palEntries(nIndex).peGreen = m_bmInfo.bmiColors(nIndex).rgbGreen
    palEntries(nIndex).peBlue = m_bmInfo.bmiColors(nIndex).rgbBlue
    palEntries(nIndex).peFlags = 0
Next nIndex
```

Recalling the previous discussion about what we want from this palette, this leaves us at the point where the first six **palEntry()** items holds the six dog colors. Now we can work on adding the system palette entries to the end of this **PALETTEENTRY** array. Assuming that we only want the 236 system entries in the middle of the system palette (read earlier), the call to **GetSystemPaletteEntries()** can be passed 10 to the second parameter so that the first non-static color entry is the first entry in **palSysEntries()**. Only 236 colors are requested and the last ten entries are also ignored, as we said previously.

```
ReDim palSysEntries(236 - 1)
nSysColors = GetSystemPaletteEntries(frmSaver.hdc, 10, 236, palSysEntries(0))
```

The last step is to add **palEntries()** which currently contains only the dog colors. The array is redimensioned to hold the six colors plus the number of colors requested from the system palette. **nSysColors** holds this value because the **GetSystemPaletteEntries()** function returns the number of entries successfully returned into the **palSysEntries()** array. These entries are then added to the end of the redimensioned **palEntries()** array.

```
ReDim Preserve palEntries(nBmpColors + nSysColors - 1)
For nIndex = 0 To nSysColors - 1 'nBmpColors To UBound(palEntries)
    palEntries(nBmpColors + nIndex).peRed = palSysEntries(nIndex).peRed
    palEntries(nBmpColors + nIndex).peGreen = palSysEntries(nIndex).peGreen
    palEntries(nBmpColors + nIndex).peBlue = palSysEntries(nIndex).peBlue
    palEntries(nBmpColors + nIndex).peFlags = 0
Next nIndex
```

Now, the palette is complete with dog colors and the system colors for the current screen display. The **GetPalette** method finishes off by creating this palette from **palEntries()**.

```
m_hPal = GetPalette(palEntries)
```

Believe it or not, this works! See for yourself.

Dog Animation Sequences

There are 26 bitmaps used in this screen saver, consisting of all the dog animation frames and their corresponding mask bitmaps, used for transparency. All bitmaps are loaded when the screen saver begins, so that they are available in memory at a moment's notice. The procedure that loads them all, using the same methods as all other chapters, is **Load_SaverGraphics**. They are all 256 color bitmaps, assigned the same palette to help with 256 color displays.

The complicated part comes with grouping the graphics for animating each dog sequence. Remember the five animation sequences that make up the screen saver content?

- Walking, Sniffing, Scratching, Whizzing and Turning

At the end of **Load_SaverGraphics**, once the bitmaps have been safely loaded into memory, a series of calls are made to set up the individual sprite classes that reference these graphics. I'll walk through those in more detail so you're aware of the preparation necessary to work with each sprite sequence. You won't get off scot-free though, I *do* expect that you remember how the sprite class works from Chapter 5. Hee hee.

Walking and Sniffing

The walking and sniffing sequences are the easiest to implement into sprite classes. These two sequences both have a simple run cycle. The dog walking sequence requires five frames:

dogw1.bmp

dogw2.bmp

dogw3.bmp

dogw4.bmp

dogw5.bmp

Saver_InitDogWalk is passed the **DOGWALK** sprite element —**g_sprDogs(DOGWALK)**:

```
.NumFrames = 5
.SetFrame 0, g_bmpDogs(DOGWALK1)
.SetFrame 1, g_bmpDogs(DOGWALK2)
.SetFrame 2, g_bmpDogs(DOGWALK3)
.SetFrame 3, g_bmpDogs(DOGWALK4)
.SetFrame 4, g_bmpDogs(DOGWALK5)
```

The dog sniffing sequence requires four:

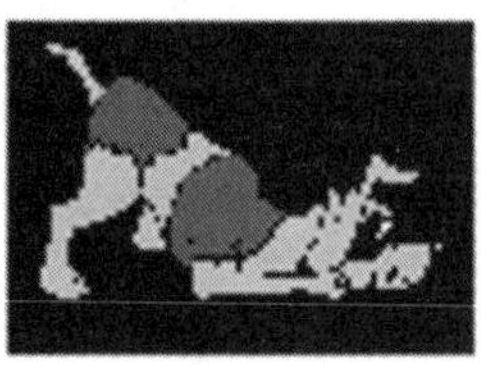
dogsn1.bmp

dogsn2.bmp

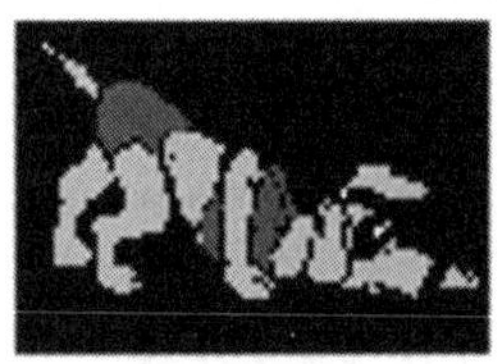
dogsn3.bmp

dogsn4.bmp

Saver_InitDogSniff is passed the **DOGSNIFF** sprite element—**g_sprDogs(DOGSNIFF)**:

```
.NumFrames = 4
.SetFrame 0, g_bmpDogs(DOGSNIFF1)
.SetFrame 1, g_bmpDogs(DOGSNIFF2)
.SetFrame 2, g_bmpDogs(DOGSNIFF3)
.SetFrame 3, g_bmpDogs(DOGSNIFF4)
```

Unlike the duck flying sequences (from Chapter 5) which needed some of the frames to be repeated before the first frame could be played again, these two sequences can go from their last frame to the start of the sequence without any jumps in the animation.

Scratching

As I just mentioned, the duck frames in Chapter 5 required repeated bitmaps to be referenced inside the sprite as additional frames to complete the run cycle. This, in itself, isn't a problem, since the sprite class was created specifically for that purpose. However, it's a problem when there is any random timing involved in smaller parts of the sequence.

As you know, the sprite class is used to access bitmaps in a particular order, based on an appropriate run cycle. The scratching animation sequence requires the same care as the duck flying sprites did. Inside **Saver_InitDogScratch**, the following lines of code turn the five frame animation into ten:

```
.NumFrames = 10
 .SetFrame 0, m_bmpDogs(DOGSCRATCH1)
 .SetFrame 1, m_bmpDogs(DOGSCRATCH2)
 .SetFrame 2, m_bmpDogs(DOGSCRATCH3)
 .SetFrame 3, m_bmpDogs(DOGSCRATCH4)
 .SetFrame 4, m_bmpDogs(DOGSCRATCH5)
 .SetFrame 5, m_bmpDogs(DOGSCRATCH4)
 .SetFrame 6, m_bmpDogs(DOGSCRATCH5)
 .SetFrame 7, m_bmpDogs(DOGSCRATCH4)
 .SetFrame 8, m_bmpDogs(DOGSCRATCH3)
 .SetFrame 9, m_bmpDogs(DOGSCRATCH2)
```

dogsc1.bmp

dogsc2.bmp

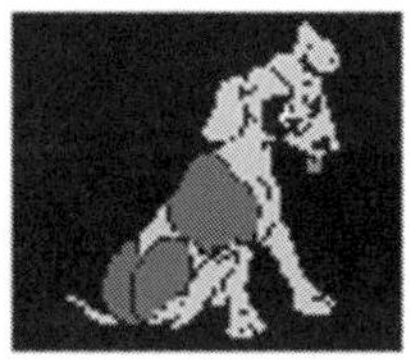
dogsc3.bmp

dogsc4.bmp

dogsc5.bmp

Completing the run cycle this time around wasn't just as simple as repeating some frames on the way back to frame 1. We could have done it this way, but it looks more impressive if the dog lifts his leg to his rear a few times before returning. The sprite class certainly makes this easy to implement by adding items to the sprite's bitmap array and specifying the order they should appear in. In this case, the last two frames where the dog scratches his head are repeated, as shown in the above figure.

Whizzing

For different reasons, both the whizzing and turning sequences needed some special attention. I'll talk about whizzing first, since these are really two different run cycle issues. The whizzing sequence consists of 12 frames and is broken into three parts:

- Movement into whiz position
- Whizzing
- Movement out of whiz position

The first and last of these parts, movement into and out of whizzing position, are almost the reverse of each other.

dogp1.bmp

dogp2.bmp

dogp3.bmp

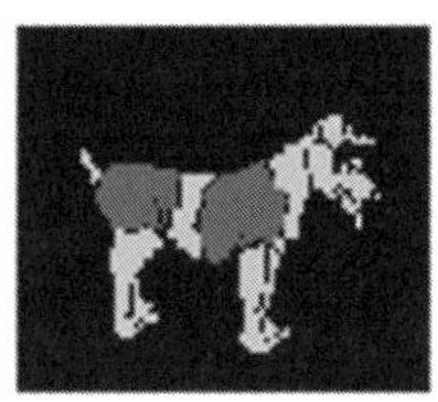
dogp4.bmp

dogp5.bmp

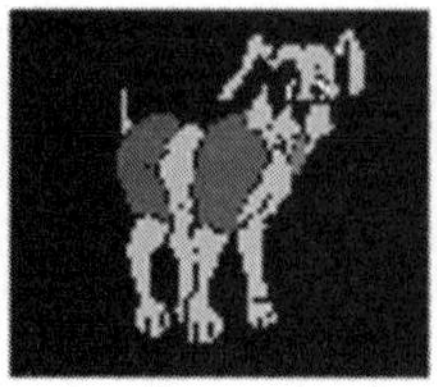
dogp6.bmp

dogp7.bmp

dogp8.bmp

dogp9.bmp

dogp10.bmp

dogp11.bmp

dogp12.bmp

Moving into whiz position includes frame 1 through 10, as shown in the **Saver_InitDogWhizA** procedure:

```
.NumFrames = 10
.SetFrame 0, g_bmpDogs(DOGWHIZ1)
.SetFrame 1, g_bmpDogs(DOGWHIZ2)
.SetFrame 2, g_bmpDogs(DOGWHIZ3)
.SetFrame 3, g_bmpDogs(DOGWHIZ4)
.SetFrame 4, g_bmpDogs(DOGWHIZ5)
.SetFrame 5, g_bmpDogs(DOGWHIZ6)
.SetFrame 6, g_bmpDogs(DOGWHIZ7)
.SetFrame 7, g_bmpDogs(DOGWHIZ8)
.SetFrame 8, g_bmpDogs(DOGWHIZ9)
.SetFrame 9, g_bmpDogs(DOGWHIZ10)
```

This brings the dog from a side view, into a frontal view with his leg partially lifted. The last sequence, moving *out* of whiz position, uses frames 11 backward to frame 3, shown in **Saver_InitDogWhizC**:

```
.NumFrames = 9
.SetFrame 0, g_bmpDogs(DOGWHIZ11)
.SetFrame 1, g_bmpDogs(DOGWHIZ10)
.SetFrame 2, g_bmpDogs(DOGWHIZ9)
.SetFrame 3, g_bmpDogs(DOGWHIZ8)
.SetFrame 4, g_bmpDogs(DOGWHIZ7)
.SetFrame 5, g_bmpDogs(DOGWHIZ6)
.SetFrame 6, g_bmpDogs(DOGWHIZ5)
.SetFrame 7, g_bmpDogs(DOGWHIZ4)
.SetFrame 8, g_bmpDogs(DOGWHIZ3)
```

The idea was to put the dog back into a position where any of the other animations could begin, and frames 1 and 2 were not necessary for this run cycle to make a smooth transition into another.

Now for the middle section, set up in **Saver_InitDogWhizB**, where the dog is actually whizzing:

```
.NumFrames = 2
.SetFrame 0, g_bmpDogs(DOGWHIZ11)
.SetFrame 1, g_bmpDogs(DOGWHIZ12)
```

Frame 11 and 12 comprise this part of the sequence and are repeated over and over again, while the whizzing is taking place. This is the very reason why the sequence had to be broken down into three parts, so that the middle part could be considered a run cycle of its own. This part of the sequence must be called for a number of 'repeats', and I wouldn't have slept a wink had I hard-coded the number of repeats into the sprite class. Since this section ends with frame 12, part C of the sequence must begin with frame 11 for a smooth transition, before continuing back to the start of the run cycle. You'll see why these had to become part of separate sprite objects when I discuss how the code all fits together.

Turning

This sequence comprises part of the whizzing sequence frames, excluding the leg lift, of course. There are two parts to this sequence:

- Movement to face forward
- Movement to face sideways

These two parts are again close to opposites of each other. **Saver_InitDogTurnA** builds the first part of this sequence:

```
.NumFrames = 8
.SetFrame 0, g_bmpDogs(DOGWHIZ1)
.SetFrame 1, g_bmpDogs(DOGWHIZ2)
.SetFrame 2, g_bmpDogs(DOGWHIZ3)
.SetFrame 3, g_bmpDogs(DOGWHIZ4)
.SetFrame 4, g_bmpDogs(DOGWHIZ5)
.SetFrame 5, g_bmpDogs(DOGWHIZ6)
.SetFrame 6, g_bmpDogs(DOGWHIZ7)
.SetFrame 7, g_bmpDogs(DOGWHIZ8)
```

Saver_InitDogTurnB, the second part:

```
.NumFrames = 6
.SetFrame 0, g_bmpDogs(DOGWHIZ8)
.SetFrame 1, g_bmpDogs(DOGWHIZ7)
.SetFrame 2, g_bmpDogs(DOGWHIZ6)
.SetFrame 3, g_bmpDogs(DOGWHIZ5)
.SetFrame 4, g_bmpDogs(DOGWHIZ4)
.SetFrame 5, g_bmpDogs(DOGWHIZ3)
```

dogp1.bmp

dogp2.bmp

dogp3.bmp

dogp4.bmp

dogp5.bmp

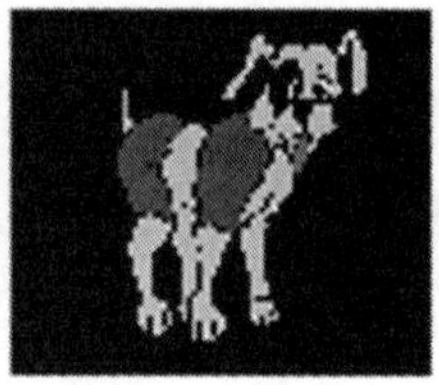
dogp6.bmp

dogp7.bmp

dogp8.bmp

The A sequence calls for frames 1 through 8 of the whiz sequence, and the B sequence calls for frames 8 backward to 3 from the same. This animation isn't broken down into separate sprite objects because of the need for repetition, as with the leg-lifting portion of the whiz animation. The purpose of the turn is to gracefully move the dog to face in the opposite direction. If there were only one sprite object for this part of the sequence, all bitmap frames would be linked to the sprite object. This means that the sprite's run cycle would have to be notified to blit in the opposite direction partway through. Yet another piece of hard-coding I wasn't willing to undertake.

Currently, the sprite object has a **`Direction`** property that is set externally (i.e., not within the sprite class, but via code that sets up the sprite class object). Rather than putting code inside this nicely encapsulated sprite class that can trigger a direction change within the sequence, I broke it into run cycles that the **`Direction`** property could be set for individually. The first part of the sequence is played in the same direction as the last sequence, the second part plays in the opposite direction, thus 'flipping' the dog frames. The logic that calls on each part of the sequence, controlling direction, belongs in the animation loop.

Using Sprite Cycles

Before I can describe the animation loop for this application, you need to understand how each of the dog sprites are used within the application. Some changes were made to **`clsSprite`** to facilitate some new methods that make the dogs work. The figure below highlights the changes and additions made to **`clsSprite`** for this chapter:

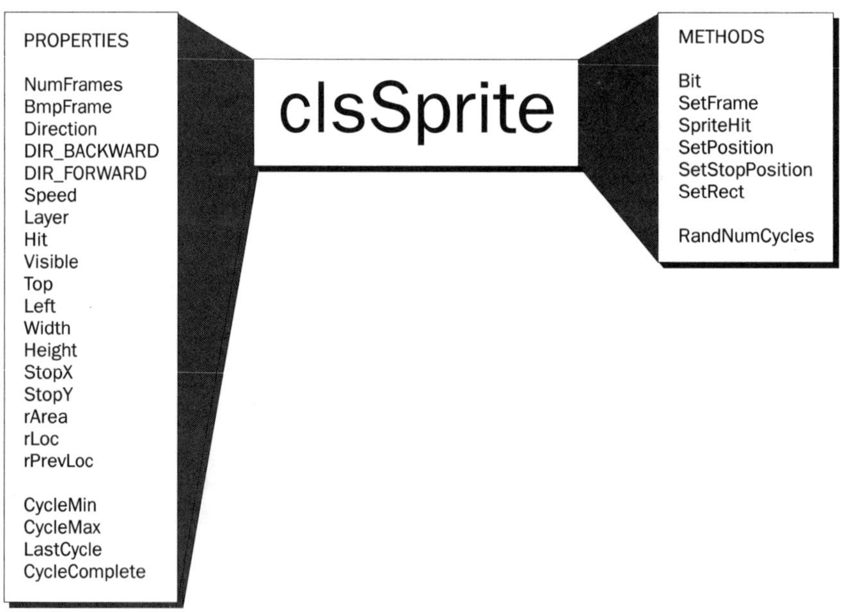

In the previous chapter, the duck sprites continually flew across the screen, unless they were instructed by the program to stop. The same run cycle was used for each duck sprite, until the duck was 'hit'. At this time, a single 'hit' frame was displayed in place of the usual flying frames. A new sprite object couldn't be used in this scenario to show the duck hit frame, since each sprite object contained important layer information about each individual duck. Instead, the same sprite object (say the duck at layer 2 was hit) is altered to reflect a new run cycle, this time of only one frame played over and over again. At this point, the duck sprite is no longer in use, since it was 'hit' so the flying frames for that particular sprite object will not be re-initialized until a new game begins.

In this example, when the dog changes its activities, the current sprite isn't replaced with new frames, since the old frames will be needed again the next time the sequence is called for. At any point in time, the dog can be asked to perform any of the animations available and reloading the images is a precious waste of time.

Instead, there are separate sprites that point to each sequence, or portion of a sequence, as per the previous discussion about sprite organization. When the animation is changed, since all dog sprites are part of an array of sprites (**m_sprDogs()**), an index, **m_nCurrSprite**, is changed to the new sprite that will be used for the animation. This means that the new sprite needs to take on certain properties that the last sprite was set to (this is discussed further on), before continuing.

Since there's no user interaction changing the appearance of the frames, something else triggers the change in dog animation. That 'something' is the completion of some random number of cycles. When a sprite is selected as current, the **RandomNumCycles** method is called, which sets the **m_nNumCycles** variable to reflect a random number from **CycleMin** and **CycleMax**:

```
m_nCurrFrame = -1
m_nNumCycles = Int((m_nCycleMax - m_nCycleMin + 1) * Rnd + m_nCycleMin)
m_bCycleComplete = False
m_bLastCycle = False
```

CycleMin and **CycleMax** are set up for every sprite object, in their respective frame-setting procedures. When the **Saver_InitDogSniff** procedure sets up the dog sniffing sprite (a single sprite works for this animation), the following two values for the sprite's cycle are set:

```
.CycleMin = 1
.CycleMax = 8
```

This means that when the dog sniff animation is selected, it can iterate a sniff run cycle up to eight times before another animation is selected. This is randomly selected so that the animation will not look the same. **Saver_InitDogTurnA**, on the other hand, sets up these values as follows:

```
.CycleMin = 1
.CycleMax = 1
```

This means that there will always be only one cycle for the turn animation. There is a reason for this. Since the act of turning is broken down into two sprites for the purpose of changing direction, I have to make sure that only one iteration of each takes place, then another new animation is selected.

The **Blit** method of the sprite class now has some new considerations that take care of this process. Each time the sprite is blitted, its frame is incremented, as it was in Chapter 5's description of the use of the sprite class. Now, after the blit is complete, the following lines of code track the number of cycles:

```
    ' check run cycle
    If m_nCurrFrame = m_nNumFrames - 1 Then
        ' cycle completed
        m_nNumCycles = m_nNumCycles - 1
        If (m_nNumCycles = 0) Or m_bLastCycle Then
          m_bCycleComplete = True
        End If
    End If
```

If the current frame number is at the end of a frame cycle, one iteration of the sprite's run-cycle has completed. Since there is a variable that is set to the number of cycles that **RandomNumCycles** calculated for the sprite run, this variable, **m_nNumCycles**, is decremented. Without other interference, the only check necessary is that the number of cycles requested are completed, then the **m_bCycleComplete** flag can be set to **True**.

There is one other thing that helps to determine the completion of a cycle. The bad dog is moved from random point to random point, using the move class in a similar way to the move class in Chapter 4's demo. When the destination point is reached, the animation stops moving. This isn't what stops the animation, but it does set the **LastCycle** property of the sprite object to **True**, which should indicate to the **Blit** procedure that the **m_bCycleComplete** flag should also be set to **True**. Notice, this will only happen after a complete run cycle has taken place, which insures that the dog sniff's last frame will always be the last frame displayed before another animation is called for.

Saver Animation Loop

This animation loop is far less complex than that of the duck game. There is no score- keeping involved, nor are there any collisions to detect or any hits to intercept that remove sprites from the loop. These three basic processes take place during each iteration of the saver loop:

- Clear the last sprite's frame
- Move the current sprite's frame
- Update the display

This is a simplification of the loop that doesn't take into account some extra steps that must be taken, specifically for turning and whizzing. The first thing I'll point out is that there's no need to track previous rectangles (**rPrevLoc**), since there's no hit or collision testing involved in the repaint. Simply erase the current location of the current sprite, change sprites if necessary, move the current sprite if necessary, copy the new sprite frame to the working buffer and update the screen.

Here's how the animation loop would look before we introduce the complexity of turning the dog and making the dog whiz:

```
    Do While m_flgSaverRun

         ' erase current sprite
         objMem.ClearWorkBuffer m_sprDogs(m_nCurrSprite).rLoc

         ' check for new animation
         If m_sprDogs(m_nCurrSprite).CycleComplete Then
```

```
         Saver_NewAnim
        End If

        With m_sprDogs(m_nCurrSprite)

           ' move sprite if applicable
           If .Speed <> 0 Then
              If Not objMove.Complete Then
                 objMove.Move m_sprDogs(m_nCurrSprite)
              End If
           End If

           ' blit new sprite
           .Blit

           ' update dirty area to display
           objMem.UpdateDisplay
           DoEvents
       End With
    Loop
```

Notice that the move class is being used differently now. Clearly, this saver loop is doing both the erasing and the blitting of the next frame. The reason for this is because of the fact that the sprite being blitted changes in between erasing and blitting in a new position. Also, not all sprite animations are moved. The dog whizzes, turns and scratches in one place. The move class was updated to include a single flag to notify it if a buffer update should take place. If the **m_bMoveDisplay** flag is set to true when the **Move** method is called, then the standard functionality takes place. Otherwise, the point array is still used to determine the next position for the sprite, and the sprite that was passed as a parameter to **Move_Init** still has its position properties updated:

```
    With m_objMove
      ' find stop position for those requiring calculation
      Select Case m_nMoveMode
      Case m_MOVPOINT
        ' no change, point already set
      Case m_MOVDELTA
        ' no change, point already set
        ' will use delta calculation without stop point concern
      Case m_MOVCENTER
        ' find center point
        .SetStopPosition (m_objMem.Width - .Width) / 2, (m_objMem.Height -
                             .Height) / 2
      Case m_MOVCENTERX
        ' find center X
        .SetStopPosition (m_objMem.Width - .Width) / 2, .Top
      Case m_MOVCENTERY
        ' find center X
        .SetStopPosition .Left, (m_objMem.Height - .Height) / 2
      End Select

      If m_nMoveMode = m_MOVDELTA Then
        CalcMoveDelta .Left, .Top, .StopX, .StopY, .Speed
      Else
        CalcMovePoints .Left, .Top, .StopX, .StopY, .Speed
        m_bComplete = False
```

```
        m_nStep = 0
      End If
    End With 'm_objMove
```

Actually, the **Saver_Run** procedure follows the flow chart in the following figure. For as long as no mouse movement or keyboard activity has taken place (which instantly sets **m_flgSaverRun** to **False** and terminates the loop for cleanup), the first thing it does is to erase the last frame. This is normal for any animation that changes frames or moves. This is done to the current sprite, indicated by **m_nCurrSprite**:

```
    g_objMem.ClearWorkBuffer g_sprDogs(m_nCurrSprite).rLoc
```

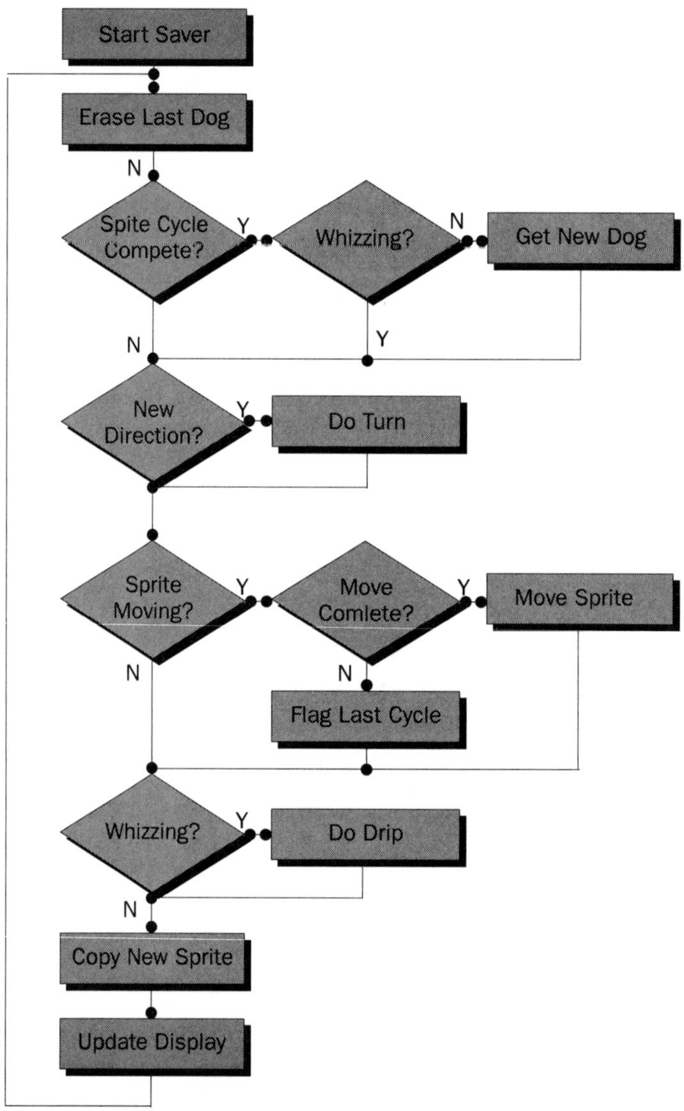

The next step is to check for a new animation before copying and/or moving the next frame to the clear working buffer. The need to get a new animation sequence is triggered by the completion of the random cycles of the current animation. As I explained with the discussion about the sprite cycles, this can be set to complete only when the sprite run-cycle has completed and either the **m_bLastCycle** flag is **True**, or the number of cycles specified for that instance of the sprite animation, has completed (inside the **Blit** method for **clsSprite**).

If **Complete** is **True** for the current sprite, a new animation is selected by calling **Saver_NewAnim**:

```
If  g_sprDogs(m_nCurrSprite).CycleComplete Then
  If Not m_flgWhizzing Then Saver_NewAnim
End If
```

Ignore for the moment that this only happens while the dog isn't whizzing... I'll explain that when I cover how whizzing works. If the cycle isn't complete, the current sprite remains as is and the loop continues. Keep in mind that, at this point, we've erased whatever frame the current sprite had displayed last from the working buffer, so if a new sprite is selected in the previous step, we've already taken care of business with the sprite before it as far as display updates go.

When a new animation is chosen, a new movement is chosen for the dog by selecting a random position on the display (this is discussed next). If the direction of the dog has changed as a result, a flag is set to notify the animation loop that the dog should turn before showing the next sequence:

```
If m_flgTurning Then Saver_Turn g_sprDogs(m_nCurrSprite).Direction
```

Once the turn is complete, after the call to **Saver_Turn**, the loop is returned control at the next line of code, unaware that there have been other screen updates in the meantime, since the state of the display is now, once again, free of the bitmap displayed by the previous sprite sequence. Now, the intended new sprite sequence can be copied to the display. If the current animation has a non-zero speed property, the **Move** method is called as follows:

```
If .Speed <> 0 Then
  If Not g_objMove.Complete Then
    g_objMove.Move
  Else
    .LastCycle = True
  End If
End If
```

The move class's **Complete** flag will have been set after the last move, and if this is true, whatever the current state of the sprite animation, its **LastCycle** property must be turned on so that the rest of the run-cycles won't be executed while the sprite is stationary.

We must do one more thing before we blit the new frame in its (possibly) new position. The question is, is that bad dog whizzing right now? If so, there must be a call to copy the next spray to the screen, before the dog frame is copied over top... more on this later:

```
If m_flgWhizzing Then
  m_flgWhizzing = g_objDrip.WhizDrip(g_sprDogs(DOGWHIZb))
End If
```

Now we blit the next sprite frame and update the display with all of the things we've done to the working buffer. Thank goodness for dirty rectangle code, so we don' t have to track all of this stuff! If you jumped into this chapter without reading about dirty rectangles in Chapter 5, you might want to check it out.

```
.Blit

' update dirty area to display
g_objMem.UpdateDisplay
```

Though many things are going on inside the saver run loop, there is definitely a modular component to this code that makes it much easier to follow. Now that you can see what the overall loop is doing, let's start checking out the side-procedures that make the smaller components happen.

Getting the Next Sequence

One of the processes called by the saver animation loop is getting a new sprite sequence to play. There is more to this than just selecting a sprite index value to set **m_nCurrSprite** to. Some maintenance must take place along the way. How the next animation is chosen has some restrictions and what is done with the new sprite object to set it up requires some attention to detail.

What Animation is Next?

Saver_NewAnim is called from the saver loop, but the first line of code in that procedure backs up the current sprite into **m_nLastSprite**, and calls the function **Saver_GetNextAnim()**, which returns the next sprite index from 0 to 3. This includes all animation sequences (except turning, which I'll discuss separately). Now, I'll describe the call to **Saver_GetNextAnim()** before getting into the setup of the sprite object selected.

The bare bones of the random selection of a new animation should consist of the following lines of code:

```
m_nCurrSprite = Int((3 + 1) * Rnd)

If m_nLastSprite <> m_nCurrSprite Then m_flgNewAnim = True
Saver_GetNextAnim = m_nCurrSprite
```

The first line selects a random animation from 0 to 3, then the **m_flgNewAnim** flag is turned on if the new animation is different from the last. Even though **m_nCurrSprite** is a module level variable, I return it from the function to the calling routine. Since some of the sequences have more than one sprite to them, these three lines of code are not quite enough to handle the selection of the next animation sequence.

This would give us a random sprite index from 0 to 3, exactly what we want, since these are the values for the main sprite indices for walking, sniffing, scratching and whizzing, as described by their sprite index constants:

```
Const DOGWALK = 0
Const DOGSNIFF = 1
Const DOGSCRATCH = 2
Const DOGWHIZa = 3
```

The rest of the constants define the remaining sprites in the sprite array, continuing the rest of the whizzing sprite objects, and the turning sprite objects:

```
Const DOGWHIZb = 4
Const DOGWHIZc = 5
Const DOGTURNa = 6
Const DOGTURNb = 7
```

For this random selection, the first four index values from 0 to 3 are purposely those listed.

The idea is that this function is called when a random number of cycles for the previous animation (this can be just one in several cases) has completed. There are some exceptions to this rule. Here's the actual decision making for getting the next animation:

```
' save last sprite
m_nLastSprite = m_nCurrSprite

' if dog is whizzing there are several steps to animation
Select Case m_nCurrSprite
  Case DOGWHIZa
    ' get next whiz sprite
    m_nCurrSprite = DOGWHIZb
  Case DOGWHIZb
    ' get last whiz sprite
    m_nCurrSprite = DOGWHIZc
  Case Else
    ' select new animation from index 0 - 3
    ' turning is not included in selection since it is triggered
    m_nCurrSprite = Int((3 + 1) * Rnd)
End Select

If m_nLastSprite <> m_nCurrSprite Then m_flgNewAnim = True
Saver_GetNextAnim = m_nCurrSprite
```

The turning sequence is never selected from here, nor will it be in progress when this function is called, since it's handled separately from the rest of the animations. It's actually a transition animation for animations that change direction due to their next random point (more on that later). This leaves only the dog whizzing sprites which need special consideration in the **GetNextAnimation** procedure.

For a random sprite sequence to be selected, as with the simpler example earlier and with the **Case Else** shown above, the current animation can't be in the midst of a dog whizzing sequence. Only the first dog sequence can be selected randomly, as shown by the constant from 0 to 3 earlier (3 selects **DOGWHIZa**), but once the first dog sequence is selected, the next two sequences must follow. That's why, if the current sprite is **DOGWHIZa**, the next sprite must be **DOGWHIZb** (this is the part where the actual whizzing takes place). If the current sprite is **DOGWHIZb**, the next sprite must be **DOGWHIZc**. All other cases, including the end of the dog whiz sprite collection, can generate any of the first four animations in a random fashion.

At the bottom of this procedure, the flag **m_flgNewAnim** is set to **True** if the current sprite is different from the last one. This flag is used elsewhere, as you'll see.

Setting up the New Sprite

Once a new sprite has been selected, even if it's the same sprite animation by chance, there are some preliminary properties that must be set up for the new sprite object. They are:

- **`Position`**
- **`StopPosition`**
- **`Direction`**
- The movement initialization
- The number of cycles to repeat

`Position` is the first item on the list because, no matter what the other parameters of the new sprite object are, this must always be set to the position of the last sprite. Since choosing a new animation doesn't mean replacing the frames of the current sprite object, but switching sprite objects, the new sprite has no other way to be informed of the last position in the display.

```
.SetPosition g_sprDogs(m_nLastSprite).Left, g_sprDogs(m_nLastSprite).Top
```

Only if the new sprite's **`Speed`** property is greater than 0 will the sprite's **`StopPosition`** need to be set up. The only sequences that move are the walking and sniffing animations, and to set their stop position, a random *xy* coordinate is calculated, based on the screen width and height of the desktop (the sprites are allowed to go off screen to the right, to give them more latitude):

```
 ' select random new position
nRandX = Int((g_objMem.Width) * Rnd + 1)
nRandY = Int((g_objMem.Height) * Rnd + 1)
' set stop position
.SetStopPosition nRandX, nRandY
```

If a new **`StopPosition`** was chosen for the current sprite, the **`Direction`** property must be calculated. The direction of the sprite is based on the fact that the dog bitmaps face to the right, so any movement left must reflect a horizontal flip in their display. This is done the same way as with the flying ducks in Level 2 of the duck game, using a direction property of **`-1`** or **`DIR_BACKWARD`** to implement a reverse blit:

```
If .StopX < g_sprDogs(m_nLastSprite).Left Then
   .Direction = .DIR_BACKWARD
Else
   .Direction = .DIR_FORWARD
End If
```

Additionally, since the sprite is being moved, I needed to check whether there was a change in direction from that of the previous sprite, to turn on the turn flag, **`m_flgTurning`**. This isn't done if it's the first time this procedure is called (when **`m_flgSaverRun`** is **`False`**), since that would generate a turn animation as the starting animation sequence:

```
If m_flgSaverRun And (.Direction <> g_sprDogs(m_nLastSprite).Direction) Then
  m_flgTurning = True
End If
```

Next, the move class must be initialized again, to reflect the next plan in movement. Of course, this is based on the fact that the **Speed** property of the current sprite is greater than 0. **MOV_POINT** tells the move class that an array of *xy* coordinates must be generated for the next set of calls to the **Move** method of the class, much like it was used in the demo program from Chapter 4. The **Init_Move** method then takes the current sprite as a parameter to perform those calculations as before:

```
With g_objMove
   .MoveMode = .MOV_POINT
   .Init_Move g_sprDogs(m_nCurrSprite)
End With
```

If the sprite isn't moving, none of the direction or movement code is executed and the following line sets the current sprite's direction to that of the previous sprite, to make sure they are working together. In addition, since I know that the whizzing dog doesn't move, here's where the **Saver_SetupWhiz** procedure is triggered if the current animation is the middle dog whizzing animation, where the actual whizzing begins:

```
.Direction = g_sprDogs(m_nLastSprite).Direction
' is this a whizzing dog?
If m_nCurrSprite = DOGWHIZb Then Saver_SetupWhiz
```

In all cases, a number of cycles is selected for the new sprite, which selects a random number from the sprite class as discussed earlier, to decide how many times this run cycle should iterate. When the sprite is moving, either the completion of the move or the completion of the random cycle iteration can trigger a call to this procedure that selects and prepares for a new sprite:

```
' random number of cycles
.RandNumCycles
```

From this series of steps, the saver loop is returned to, with a new sprite animation that will appear where the last one left off, and, if applicable, in the order that was necessary.

Triggering a Turn

Selecting each of the animations, except for the turn, should be pretty clear at this point. After a set of random cycles are completed, or the dog reaches its random destination, a new animation is requested. Based on the random point chosen for the new animation (only if the sprite selected has its **Speed** property set to some value), the direction for the new sprite sequence is chosen. If this is a new direction from the last sprite, a turn is needed and so a flag is set to notify the saver loop to perform a turn before continuing with the new sprite sequence.

While I was developing the code, I had to think about this, since I wasn't sure whether or not I should just include the turn in the random selection of animations, which could then, in turn, trigger a direction change for all subsequent animations that were also randomly selected (that is, until another turn was selected again). This presented too many other issues. For instance, the selection of a random point on the screen was no longer going to choose the direction, so there could be no random point, just a delta movement until the next turn. Other things, like keeping the dog on screen, also made this seem like a bad idea.

The resulting code suspends the normal proceedings of the saver loop to perform the turn which is located in another procedure, **Saver_Turn**. This procedure is broken down into two parts. The first part of the turn, in the same direction as the last sprite was moving, and the second part, which shows the dog facing the opposite direction. Since the last thing the code did before calling the turn was to erase the last sprite's frame from the working buffer, this code can freely copy a turn frame to the working buffer and update the display without concern.

Here's the first part of the turn. It calls the **RandNumCycles** method, for the sprite, for consistency with all sprites, but the turn sprites were set up with a **CycleMin** and **CycleMax** of 1, so there will only be one iteration:

```
With g_sprDogs(DOGTURNa)
   ' initialize sprite cycles
   .RandNumCycles
   ' set position to that of current sprite
   .SetPosition g_sprDogs(m_nCurrSprite).Left, g_sprDogs(m_nCurrSprite).Top
   ' start from other direction
   .Direction = -nDir
   Do
      .Blit
      g_objMem.UpdateDisplay
      DoEvents

      ' clear for next cycle
      g_objMem.ClearWorkBuffer .rLoc

      If Not m_flgSaverRun Then Saver_Stop
   Loop Until .CycleComplete
End With
```

This sprite wasn't set up with the **Saver_NewAnim** call, so **SetPosition** needs to reflect the last sprite (or the current sprite which has already been set up to reflect the correct values from the call **Saver_NewAnim**). The **Direction** property for the first part of the turn needs to be opposite of the current sprite's **Direction**, which is where the dog is headed via the turn. The **Do...Loop** will iterate through exactly one run cycle for the **DOGTURNa** sprite, exactly what is expected to lead into the **DOGTURNb** sprite sequence. I had to add a test for the termination of the saver, **m_flgSaverRun**, since without it, if the dog is turning while the saver is terminated, the dog will finish turning first... definitely not OK.

Within the same procedure, **Saver_Turn**, the next step is the second part of the turn, which requires a similar loop using **DOGTURNb** as the sprite sequence:

```
With g_sprDogs(DOGTURNb)
   ' initialize sprite cycles
   .RandNumCycles
   ' set position to that of current sprite
   .SetPosition g_sprDogs(m_nCurrSprite).Left, g_sprDogs(m_nCurrSprite).Top
   ' use requested direction
   .Direction = nDir
   Do
      .Blit
      g_objMem.UpdateDisplay
      DoEvents

      ' clear for next cycle
      g_objMem.ClearWorkBuffer .rLoc
```

```
      If Not m_flgSaverRun Then Saver_Stop
    Loop Until .CycleComplete
  End With
```

Here, the **Direction** is that of the current sprite, passed to the procedure as a parameter, but the rest is the same. Notice that the end of the **Do...Loop** is the call to **ClearWorkBuffer**, rather than to **UpdateDisplay**. That's because I left off in the **Saver_Run** procedure with the working buffer freshly erased from the previous sprite. Naturally, since we detoured to perform a move, the first thing that must be done is to blit the new frame of the turning sprite, then update the display. So, the last item in each of the turning loops is always going to be the call to clear the working buffer from the last display update, in preparation for the start of the next loop. That also leaves the working buffer in good form for the continuation to the **Saver_Run** loop which will next be blitting a copy of the intended current sprite that was interrupted by this move.

Oh, but one more thing happens before this procedure is complete. Since the flag to turn was set inside the **Saver_NewAnim** procedure, it must be turned off when the turn is complete so that the turn will not take place again, unless called for by the setup of another new animation that moves in the opposite direction:

```
    m_flgTurning = False
```

Dog Whiz

OK, you got me. The purpose of the application was not just to implement a screen saver. It was to present the kind of sick and twisted animation humor that infests the mind of any decent computer nerd. Using the Bad Dog screen saver you have on the CD as an example (another token of ImageWare's hard work... and play), I've taken the part where the dog whizzes and converted the application to a VB4 sampler, jam-packed with a useful filter class to boot! This section of the animation is quite advanced, since it really gets down and dirty with modular animation programming and interspersing more than just animation frames but also filters on the same display.

The class that performs this functionality, **clsDrip**, is shown here:

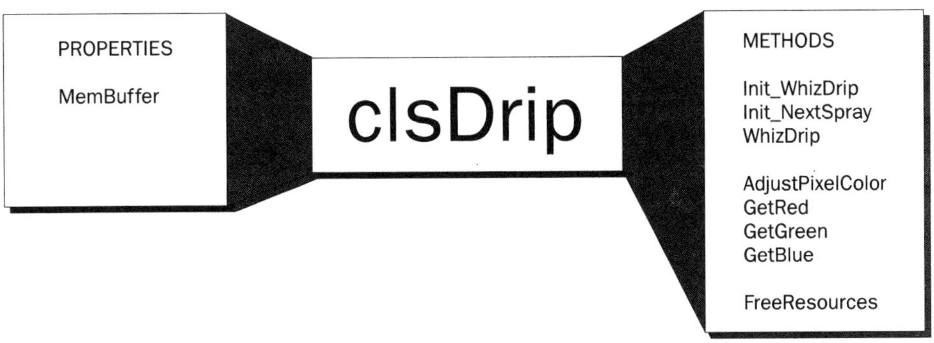

These procedures are few, but several of them need lengthy description and comprehension, so I'll begin with how the whizzing starts, then get into the code behind the class.

Begin Whizzing

As with all other dog animations, the whizzing animation begins with a call to the **Saver_NewAnim** procedure. This is triggered either because the last animation completed its last run cycle, or the destination position was reached and the run cycle in progress has finished. **Saver_GetNextAnim** is called from **Saver_NewAnim**, where a random animation is selected from 0 to 3 (3 being the first part of the whizzing animation). If 3 is selected, the fun begins with the **DOGWHIZa** sprite, where he faces front and lifts his leg up!

This sprite is set up like the rest, taking on the same position as the last sprite, and so on. The entire dog sequence is stationary, so no movement is calculated and the run cycle for this first part of the sequence (**DOGWHIZa**) is executed only once to get the dog facing front with his leg partially lifted.

When the single run cycle of the leg lift is complete, another call to **Saver_NewAnim** is made. This time, when **Saver_GetNextAnim** is called, the current sprite is **DOGWHIZa** which means that a random animation will not be selected. Instead, **DOGWHIZb** is selected:

```
Case DOGWHIZa
  ' get next whiz sprite
  m_nCurrSprite = DOGWHIZb
```

This sprite also must be set up so that the position is that of the last sprite (**DOGWHIZa**), but another special line of code is executed to trigger the whizzing filter. Inside **Saver_NewAnim**, after the new animation is selected, if the current sprite is **DOGWHIZb** (and it is) then the **Saver_SetupWhiz** procedure is called:

```
If m_nCurrSprite = DOGWHIZb Then Saver_SetupWhiz
```

This procedure is shown here:

```
Private Sub Saver_SetupWhiz()
Dim rWhiz As New clsRect

  m_flgWhizzing = True
  With g_sprDogs(m_nCurrSprite)

    ' setup whiz location based on direction
    If .Direction = .DIR_FORWARD Then
        rWhiz.SetSize .rLoc.Left, (.rLoc.Top + .Height / 2) And &HFFFE
    Else
        rWhiz.SetSize (.rLoc.Left + .Width / 2) And &HFFFE, (.rLoc.Top +
                                  .Height / 2) And &HFFFE
    End If
    ' always an 80x80 area for whiz
    rWhiz.SetSize , , rWhiz.Left + 80, rWhiz.Top + 80

    ' initialize the drip class to start whiz
    Set g_objDrip.MemBuffer = g_objMem
    g_objDrip.Init_WhizDrip rWhiz, .Direction
  End With

End Sub
```

In here, the **m_flgWhizzing** flag is set to **True**. If you recall from the **Saver_Run** procedure, this is the flag that is tested to see if the current animation is whizzing or not. I'll go over that again presently. Based on the direction of the current sprite, a rectangular section of the display must be calculated where the whiz will go. The whiz must go underneath the dog's lifted leg, so a portion of the dog bitmap area is set aside. This is hard-coded, since it's purpose is very specific. Here's how it works:

An 80x80 rectangle is the maximum rectangular boundary for the whizzing to take place. The whizzing bitmaps are 148x172 in dimension. It was predetermined that the whiz would begin at the halfway point from the top of the bitmaps that show the leg lifted (frames 11 and 12), so the calculation just has to determine the left coordinate within that bitmap, based on direction. Notice that the rectangle being set, **rWhiz**, will hold the location of the whiz rectangle based on the screen display, not on the smaller, dog bitmap. That's why the **rLoc** property of the sprite class is used, as opposed to **rArea**. This rectangle is passed to the **Init_WhizDrip** method of the drip class (**clsDrip**), along with the sprite's **Direction** property.

I'll get to the whiz code presently, so for now just assume that the whizzing process has been properly initialized for use. Once this is done (remember this was called from the **Saver_NewAnim** procedure) the code makes its way back to the saver loop. In there, until the **m_flgWhizzing** flag is turned off, the second sprite sequence belonging to the dog animation will be repeated. In between erasing the previous leg-lift frame of this run cycle, and blitting the new one, the following code is called:

```
If m_flgWhizzing Then
  m_flgWhizzing = g_objDrip.WhizDrip(g_sprDogs(DOGWHIZb))
End If
```

Each time the **WhizDrip** method is called, a larger area of whiz is 'sprayed' and copied to the working buffer. This gets copied to the display with the same call to **UpdateDisplay** that updates the new frame (once again, thank goodness for dirty rectangle code!). This next figure shows what a series of calls to **WhizDrip** looks like after the display has been updated:

The two dog frames that belong to **DOGWHIZb** are interchanged each time the loop is repeated.

Remember that the random number of cycles for the dog whiz frames can only be 1. This means that after the first run cycle of this leg-lift is complete, the **CycleComplete** *property will be* **True** *for the sprite. This is precisely why there is a condition to getting a new animation, which is, don't do it if the dog is in the middle of a whiz. This is part of the* **Saver_Run** *code:*

```
If g_sprDogs(m_nCurrSprite).CycleComplete Then
        If Not m_flgWhizzing Then Saver_NewAnim
End If
```

Normally, when work is done in the double buffer, **hdcWork** is used to build the next display update, and **hdcBack** is used as a backup of the original background. This is used to erase previous frames before new frames are copied for a smooth update. In this case, the background should reflect the whizzing unless we don't want the whiz sprays to accumulate on the display. In this case, we do.

To handle this, each **WhizDrip** is called, and the working DC is updated with the whiz before each display update with the new dog frame. At the end of the whizzing process, the background DC is updated with the entire whizzed-on area, thus becoming part of the background. Here's the final state of the whizzing:

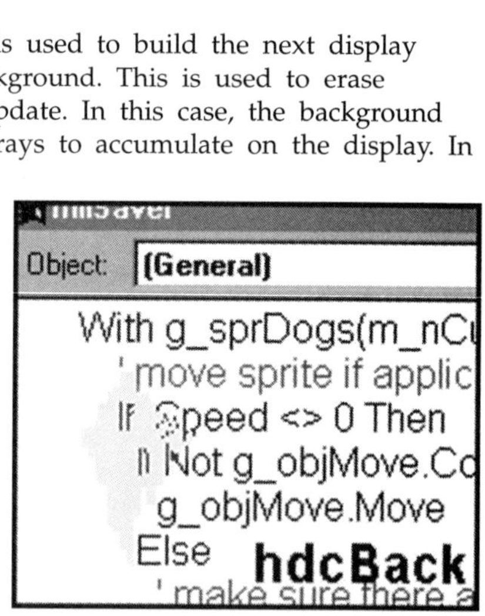

Once whizzing is complete and **m_flgWhizzing** is set to **False**, the **Saver_NewAnim** procedure will be called to select a new animation, which will be the final whiz sequence, **DOGWHIZc**. This returns the dog from leg-lift position to a side view where another animation can then pick up, without disrupting the smoothness of the dog's movement.

Initializing the Drip

The preparation of the whiz dripping process is paramount to the functionality of whizzing. There's a whole diagrammatic theory behind the drip that drives each whiz 'spray' in a slightly random fashion. First, let's understand what happens when the **Init_WhizDrip** method is called, with the help of several diagrams.

This procedure is passed a rectangle, which is a representation of the area of the background to be whizzed upon and the direction that the dog sprite is facing. When the direction of the dog changes, so does the orientation of the whiz. You can already see that this drip class isn't intended to be a portable class for other applications since it was prepared specifically for the dog whizzing sequence. And so what? It's still a foundation that can be changed later.

Startup Variables

At the start of **Init_WhizDrip**, the class's drip array is initialized to its first entry and several other class variables are initialized to their starting values. Included is the number of drips, which will be set in this procedure, and the number of sprays, which will be incremented as the **WhizDrip** method is called from **Saver_Run**. The number of sprays starts at 0. Also, the direction parameter is stored for future use, and the **Complete** flag (**m_bComplete**) is turned off.

```
ReDim m_Drip(0)
m_nNumDrips = 0
m_nSprayCount = 0
m_nDir = nDir
m_bComplete = False
```

Next, the dimension variables of the class for the **WhizDrip** are set up. Just like any other bitmap or sprite, the whiz area needs a location rectangle, an area rectangle and dimension variables. These are all set based on the **rDrip** rectangle object passed as a parameter to the initialization procedure:

```
m_nWidth = rDrip.Right - rDrip.Left
m_nHeight = rDrip.Bottom - rDrip.Top
m_rWhizLoc.SetSize rDrip.Left, rDrip.Top, rDrip.Right, rDrip.Bottom
m_rWhizArea.SetSize 0, 0, m_nWidth, m_nHeight
```

Remember that the rectangle passed to this procedure was based on the location rectangle (**rLoc**) of one of the whiz frames. That means that its dimensions are based on the location of the whiz on the double buffer area, not within the bitmap frames to be blit.

Using the location rectangle (**m_rWhizLoc**) a temporary memory DC will be created representing the whiz area. The reason for this is because we don't want to work on the background buffer. The functions that create this temporary device context should look familiar:

```
m_hdcDrip = CreateCompatibleDC(m_objMem.hdcDisp)
m_hbmpDrip = CreateCompatibleBitmap(m_objMem.hdcDisp, m_nWidth, m_nHeight)
m_stbmpDrip = SelectObject(m_hdcDrip, m_hbmpDrip)
```

```
nRet = BitBlt(m_hdcDrip, 0, 0, m_nWidth, m_nHeight, m_objMem.hdcBack,
m_rWhizLoc.Left, m_rWhizLoc.Top, SRCCOPY)
```

Once this is done, there should be a new memory DC that holds the contents of the background buffer:

The Drip Structure

Now the drip is set up. This requires some explanation of what the drip structure is and how it's used in the code. Then I can walk through the code that builds this drip structure. There is an actual user-defined type, **DripFilter**, that is part of the drip class. This structure is used to organize the individual whiz drips. The **DRIPFILTER** structure holds information for an individual drip, so a dynamic array of these structures is required to begin. An initialization procedure redimensions the array of drips, and fills in the data for each drip. The **DRIPFILTER** structure is shown below:

```
Private Type DRIPFILTER
    Width As Integer
    Start As Integer
    Up As Integer
    Down As Integer
End Type
Private m_Drip() As DRIPFILTER
```

This figure shows the appearance in diagram format of the array of drip structures:

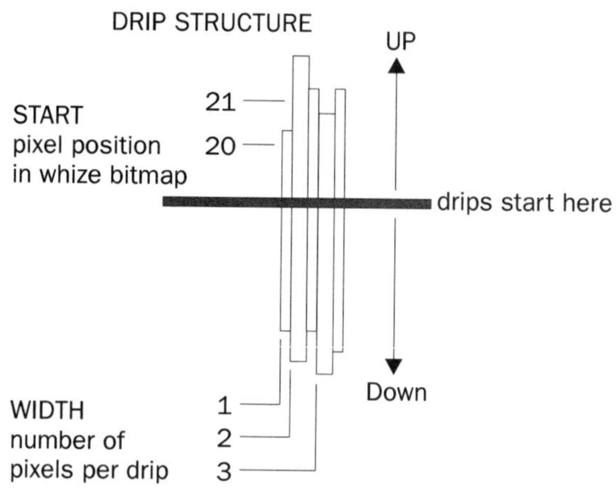

First of all, each drip has a width measured in pixels ranging from a width of 1 to 3 pixels. When the array of drips is filled in, a random width is selected so the drips will vary each time the whizzing animation is called. The **Start** position reflects the pixel location, in the whiz area (using **m_rWhizArea** not **m_rWhizLoc**) where each drip begins. This means the first drip starts at a leftmost pixel of 1 and subsequent drips will start at the next pixel where the previous drip left off, depending on its width.

The actual dripping process moves in both an upward and downward motion for each drip. All drips are initialized to start at a specified *y* coordinate within the **m_rWhizArea**. This *y* coordinate is the value that the up and down elements are set to for *all* drips in the array. They all start from about 35% of the way down the drip area, shown set in the **Init_WhizDrip** method by the following line of code:

```
nHorzStart = m_nHeight * 0.35
```

This, again, is hard-coded for the whizzing animation, just so you know. Though the up and down elements for each drip are initialized to **nHorzStart**, these elements are used to track drip movement as **WhizDrip** is called. Each drip continues along its upward and downward path, storing the next up and down position to drip from at the end of each spray. Every drip drips in both directions starting from the original *y* coordinate. Since this is whiz and all, it makes sense that more drips go down rather than up, which is why the horizontal position was above the halfway point in the height of the whiz area.

Filling in the Drips

To setup individual drip information, a loop is performed from the first drip pixel possible in the area, to the last pixel in the area. If all drips were 1 pixel wide, there would always be the same number of drips as there are pixels in the width of the whiz area (**m_nWidth**).

The loop that fills each drip assumes an iteration from the first pixel to the width of the area, but it exits when the width of the last drip reaches that width.

```
nHorzPos = 0
For nCount = 1 To m_nWidth
  m_nNumDrips = m_nNumDrips + 1
  ReDim Preserve m_Drip(m_nNumDrips)

  m_Drip(m_nNumDrips).Start = nHorzPos

  ' set drip width
  nRandWidth = Int(3 * Rnd + 1)
  If nHorzPos + nRandWidth > m_nWidth + 1 Then
    ' last drip, width is covered
    m_Drip(m_nNumDrips).Width = m_nWidth + 1 - nHorzPos
    Exit For
  End If

  ' start coordinate for drip
  m_Drip(m_nNumDrips).Down = nHorzStart
  m_Drip(m_nNumDrips).Up = nHorzStart
  m_Drip(m_nNumDrips).Width = nRandWidth

 ' sum so drips dont go over end of bmp
  nHorzPos = nHorzPos + nRandWidth

Next nCount
```

The variable that keeps track of the number of drips we have to work with, **m_nNumDrips**, is incremented as each drip is filled in. The drip array, **m_Drip**, is redimensioned each time, starting with the first drip at item 0. The starting index position of the drip is the left position in the whiz area where the first pixel in the first drip begins, as shown in the earlier diagram. This index begins at 0.

Then, **nRandWidth** is set to a random drip width of 1 to 3 pixels, used in setting the Width element for the current drip in this loop iteration. Before using the returned value, the position of this index is tested to make sure that adding it to the last pixel of the last drip doesn't go over the width of the whiz area. If it does, the width is set to whatever value doesn't exceed this area, and the drips are complete so the loop is exited. At this point, the width of the whiz area has been covered by the series of drips in the **m_Drip()** array. The number of drips in the array is held in the **m_nNumDrips** variable. To make sure that each drip starts at the next available *x* coordinate in the area, each iteration increments the **nHorzPos** value by the width of the drip just filled and the next drip's start position is set to this value.

Drip Indents

There's still one last bit of information that the **WhizDrip** method will need prepared before the first iteration. That is the indents from the left and right of the whiz area bitmap where the dripping should start and stop. Here, we demonstrate the purpose of these settings.

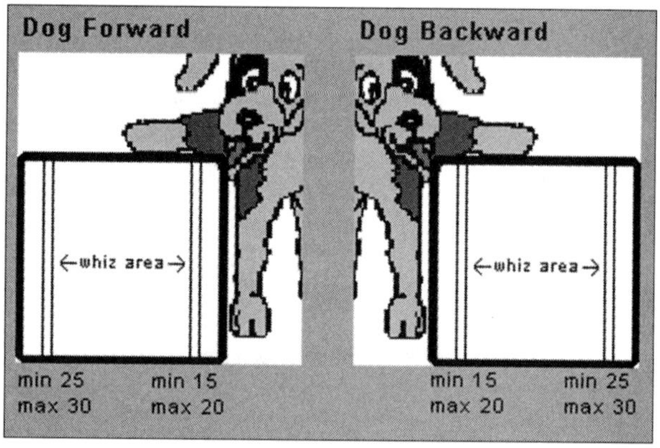

Just because a drip array has been prepared that covers the entire area of the drip about to happen, doesn't mean that the drip should be the same size every time the drip function is called. After all, this could get boring after a while.

To address this possibility, a random range of left and right indents—again, hard-coded based on the dog animations—is set up. These differ, based on the direction of the dog animation, shown in the previous diagram. A random value from each of the min/max combinations is put into the **m_nLeftIndent** and **m_nRightIndent** class variables, so that they are accessible to the animation:

```
    If m_nDir = m_DIRFORWARD Then
        nLeftMax = 30
        nLeftMin = 25
        nRightMax = 20
        nRightMin = 15
      Else
        nLeftMax = 20
        nLeftMin = 15
        nRightMax = 30
        nRightMin = 25
```

```
End If

' setup random indent values for start of drip
m_nLeftIndent = Int((nLeftMax - nLeftMin + 1) * Rnd + nLeftMin)
m_nRightIndent = Int((nRightMax - nRightMin + 1) * Rnd + nRightMin)
```

We'll see how this is used when we get to the **DripWhiz** code coming right up.

Spraying Whiz Drips

At this point, the drip array has been set up and all of the variables that needed to be initialized, have been. This is the function that is called when the whizzing flag, **m_flgWhizzing**, is turned on during the saver loop. It returns **True** until the whiz is complete, which is when the first drip hits the bottom of the whiz area. Based on the current settings for **m_nLeftIndent** and **m_nRightIndent**, only part of the drip array is cycled through to perform a drip. Each drip is dripped both up and down, by some random value and continues where it left off last time when the function is called again.

Every call to **WhizDrip** cycles through all of the drips in **m_nDrip()**, dripping each one a little more upward and a little more downward. The indentation randomizes the width of the current drip. A 'spray' is a single call to **WhizDrip**. For every spray, each drip within the random indentation should be dripped.

Cycling through each drip in a given spray starts with this **For...Next** loop:

```
For nDripIndex = m_nLeftIndent + 1 To m_nNumDrips - m_nRightIndent
```

The next step is to select a random number of pixels to drip up and down for the current drip pixels:

```
nDripDown = Int(4 * Rnd + 1)
nDripUp = Int(2 * Rnd + 1)
```

As is expected from the start position, there is more dripping downward than upward, so the random possibilities are 4 and 2, respectively. These are the numbers, **nDripDown** and **nDripUp**, that will be used to decide how many pixels the current drip will drip downward and upward.

Now, each pixel in the width of this current drip should be iterated through as follows:

- Get the pixel color value of the up and down pixels
- Tint the down pixel color yellow
- Copy that new color value down **nPixDown** pixels
- Tint the up pixel color yellow
- Copy that new color value up **nPixUp** pixels
- Set the next up and down pixel position for this drip

Updating Pixels

Two pixel values are retrieved and altered for every drip. The color value at the current up location of the current drip is returned to the variable **nPixUp**. The color value at the current down location of the current drip is returned to the variable **nPixDown**. Both colors are taken from the corresponding coordinate on the background buffer using the **GetPixel()** API function introduced in Chapter 5:

```
nPixDown = GetPixel(m_objMem.hdcBack, nVertPos + m_rWhizLoc.Left,
m_Drip(nDripIndex).Down + m_rWhizLoc.Top)

nPixUp = GetPixel(m_objMem.hdcBack, nVertPos + m_rWhizLoc.Left,
m_Drip(nDripIndex).Up + m_rWhizLoc.Top)
```

Now, each of these **Long** color values can be converted into individual RGB intensity values (0 to 255), and each intensity put into a **COLORREF** structure (discussed in Chapter 3) for easy manipulation. Here's a reminder of the **COLORREF** structure:

```
Private Type COLORREF
    crRed As Long
    crGreen As Long
    crBlue As Long
End Type
```

Since the Long value will appear rather cryptic, the following three custom functions use hex methods to convert the colors to their individual RGB values. Here are the lines that convert the Long value into separate RGB values of the variable **colPixel**:

```
colPixel.crRed = GetRed(nPixDown)
colPixel.crGreen = GetGreen(nPixDown)
colPixel.crBlue = GetBlue(nPixDown)
```

Next, the **AdjustPixelColor** function is passed this color reference for tinting. The **colPixel** value comes back with a new RGB value which is used to update the **nPixDown** variable in preparation for subsequent calls to **SetPixel()** which will do the opposite of **GetPixel()** by setting a pixel at a specified coordinate to a new color value.

```
AdjustPixelColor colPixel
nPixDown = RGB(colPixel.crRed, colPixel.crGreen, colPixel.crBlue)
```

The same actions are performed for the **nPixUp**. Now I'll describe how the dripping is done.

Dripping Up and Down

To explain the dripping process, I'll use the drip down pixel, **nPixDown** as an example. To get the 'drip' effect on the background image, the new down pixel color is copied to not only the pixel it came from, but also to a random number of other pixels in the downward direction. Assuming that **nPixDown** has been set to its new tinted value, the following loop will drip that pixel for the random number of pixels specified earlier for this drip item:

```
If Not m_bComplete Then
  For nHorzPos = m_Drip(nDripIndex).Down To (m_Drip(nDripIndex).Down +
nDripDown)
    If nHorzPos > m_nHeight Then
```

```
        ' when first drips hits bottom of drip area, drip is complete
        m_bComplete = True
        Exit For
      End If
        nPixDown = SetPixel(m_hdcDrip, nVertPos, nHorzPos, nPixDown)
     Next nHorzPos
   End If
```

For the current down pixel position (in **m_rWhizArea**), to the number of random down pixels requested for this drip (**nDripDown**), this new pixel color is copied to the whiz buffer. A check is put here to see if this pixel reaches the bottom of the whiz area, and if it does, the drip class's complete flag, **m_bComplete**, is turned on. Dripping up need not perform this test:

```
For nHorzPos = m_Drip(nDripIndex).Up To (m_Drip(nDripIndex).Up - nDripUp)
Step -1
  If nHorzPos > 0 Then
    nPixUp = SetPixel(m_hdcDrip, nVertPos, nHorzPos, nPixUp)
  End If
Next nHorzPos
```

It does, however, check that the pixel drip doesn't go higher than the first pixel in the area, since this would be futile.

At the end of the up and down dripping process, the current drip's up and down elements are decremented and incremented, respectively, by the number of random pixels each was dripped, adding one each way to insure that the next pixel selected for dripping (next time **WhizDrip** is called) is a new pixel, not a tinted one:

```
m_Drip(nDripIndex).Down = m_Drip(nDripIndex).Down + nDripDown + 1
m_Drip(nDripIndex).Up = m_Drip(nDripIndex).Up - nDripUp - 1
```

Then we move on to the next drip, and so on. This process is repeated until the last drip in the cycle is reached.

Pixel Tinting

In **clsDrip**, when the **MemBuffer** object is set up, a few more steps are executed. Not only does this class need to access the double buffer provided by the applications global memory class, but it needs information about the current is play mode. We then use the **GetDeviceCaps()** API function, used in several other chapters already, to return information about the number of bits per pixel the display is using and the number of planes. Technically, planes are usually 1, so this is just a formality. Multiplying the number of bits per pixel by the number of planes yields the color mode for the current device. This is calculated in the **MemBuffer** property **Set** procedure, using the memory class's display device as the DC passed to **GetDeviceCaps()**.

```
nBits = GetDeviceCaps(m_objMem.hdcDisp, BITSPIXEL)
nPlanes = GetDeviceCaps(m_objMem.hdcDisp, PLANES)
m_nColorMode = nBits * nPlanes
```

The **m_nColorMode** variable is used in the **AdjustPixelColor** method of the class, where the tinting of each pixel is performed.

I'm using the word *tinting* here loosely, since I'm not using a complicated tinting algorithm like you would find in an imaging program. What I'm doing is taking the pixel color's individual RGB values and editing them based on a few parameters. The result should be a more 'yellow' color, unless the color is too dark to tint. This way, the background is still distinguishable and clearly looks like something was poured (or sprayed) on it.

This process that determines a new, tinted value for a pixel, is different for 8-bit environments than it is for hi-color or better, the reason being that there are fewer new colors to choose from in a palletized environment. The **AdjustPixelColor** method first checks the value of **m_nColorMode**, to determine the method for tinting the color value passed to the procedure.

```
If the current display mode is hi-color or better, the following code is executed
to tint the color value:If (colPixel.crRed > 140 Or colPixel.crGreen > 140 Or
colPixel.crBlue >        140) Then
  If colPixel.crBlue > 50 Then colPixel.crBlue = colPixel.crBlue - 50
Else
  If colPixel.crRed < 205 Then colPixel.crRed = colPixel.crRed + 50
  If colPixel.crGreen < 205 Then colPixel.crGreen = colPixel.crGreen + 50
End If
```

The first test is to see whether any of the RGB values are greater than 140. The reason for this is because the intensity of the color as a whole will be higher and the goal will be to remove some blue from that color value (red and green make yellow). Since we're dealing in a hi-color environment, the subtlety of this change is noticeable but not unrealistic for a tint value.

The darker the color value (the first condition unsatisfied where one value at least is > 140 intensity) the less likely that a yellow tint would be noticeable. In this scenario, boosting the red and green by an equal amount of 50 will make the darker color more yellow, but possibly not yellow at all. The test for a value of < 205 is just to ensure that the red and green intensity are not set to a number greater than 255, since that's the limit.

Now, working in a palletized environment is another story altogether. The following code determines the new RGB values for an 8-bit display mode:

```
If (colPixel.crRed > 230 And colPixel.crGreen > 230 And colPixel.crBlue >
230) Then
  colPixel.crBlue = 0
  colPixel.crRed = 255
  colPixel.crGreen = 255
ElseIf (colPixel.crBlue > 100) Then
  colPixel.crBlue = colPixel.crBlue - 60
ElseIf colPixel.crRed < 60 And colPixel.crGreen < 60 And colPixel.crBlue <
60 Then
  colPixel.crRed = colPixel.crRed + 100
  colPixel.crGreen = colPixel.crGreen + 100
End If
```

In this scenario, there is a realized palette for the current display and the dog colors. There is surely a pure yellow among the static system palette colors, but any other yellow-tinted value calculated here will have to be looked up in the system palette for a closest match.

If all of the RGB values are greater than 230 intensity, the color is changed to pure yellow (255, 255, 0). This means the original color was a fairly light color in the first place, which means that the strongest tint would be realized anyway (the lighter the color, the more likely that the color can be tinted). Otherwise, if the blue value is greater than 100, it is decreased by 60 to leave a more yellow color. Keep in mind that this new color needs to be looked up in the current system palette for a closest match. If neither of these cases are true, if the color is very dark (all RGB values are < 60) then the red and green are increased by 100 each, for a more drastic yellowing effect. Again, this new color must be looked up for a closest match in the current system palette.

Running in a 256 environment puts out pretty good results for this tinting work, but it can be unpredictable since you're also relying on the work of **SetPixel()** to do the lookup, and RGB to find a closest match. You take your chances. The alternative would be to make the entire whiz pure yellow, but that would take away the fun of dripping the desktop display!

Wrapping up the Spray

After the spray is complete, there are a few things to do before going back to blit the next dog whizzing frame. First, the spray count must be incremented, and the indentation must be updated. These two tasks are accomplished by the **Init_NextSpray** procedure:

```
m_nSprayCount = m_nSprayCount + 1

If m_nSprayCount > 5 And m_nSprayCount Mod 2 = 0 Then
  If m_nDir = m_DIRFORWARD Then
    m_nLeftIndent = IIf(m_nLeftIndent > 0, m_nLeftIndent - 1, 0)
    m_nRightIndent = IIf((m_nNumDrips - m_nRightIndent) < (m_nWidth - 1),
m_nRightIndent - 2, 0)
  Else
    m_nLeftIndent = IIf(m_nLeftIndent > 1, m_nLeftIndent - 2, 0)
    m_nRightIndent = IIf((m_nNumDrips - m_nRightIndent) < m_nWidth,
m_nRightIndent - 1, 0)
  End If
End If
If m_nRightIndent < 0 Then m_nRightIndent = 0
```

The **m_nSprayCount** variable is incremented each time the **WhizDrip** is called. This provides a method to further randomize the indentation changes for the entire spray. You see, the indentation affects the width of the spray, which you probably noticed spreads upwards, downwards and outwards. The outwards portion of this is related to the indentation, which affects the number of drips, width wise, that are cycled through each spray.

Ahh, now it's all coming together. So the indentation needs to slowly be released to become less on either side, based still on the direction of the dog as you can see from the previous code snippet. The logic is, after 5 sprays, the indentation can be released from both sides, every other spray. The outer edge of the spray is to release faster so you can see that the indentation is either decremented by 1 or 2 according to direction and side.

The other issue that must be put to rest is updating the changes to the working buffer and the background buffer. When this function returns, the next dog frame is scheduled to be blitted to the working buffer, and the display subsequently updated. Before this happens, the current whiz buffer should be sent to its position in the working buffer:

```
m_objMem.UpdateWorkBuffer m_hdcDrip, m_rWhizArea, m_rWhizLoc, SRCCOPY
```

Next, in order to figure out if the whizzing is complete, the **m_bComplete** value is tested (remember that this is set when any drip reaches the bottom of the whiz area).

```
If m_bComplete Then
  m_objMem.UpdateWorkBuffer m_hdcDrip, m_rWhizArea, m_rWhizLoc, SRCCOPY
```

```
    m_objMem.UpdateBackBuffer m_hdcDrip, m_rWhizArea, m_rWhizLoc, SRCCOPY
    FreeResources
  End If
  ' return false if drip is complete
  WhizDrip = Not m_bComplete
```

At this time, the temporary whiz device context is copied to the background buffer so that the whizzed area will become part of the background. This is a new function that mimics the **UpdateWorkBuffer** method of the memory class, only copying the information to **hdcBack** instead of **hdcWork**.

Resources are freed when the whizzing is over, in preparation for the next call to **Init_WhizDrip** which will set this all up again. Here, the temporary buffer is deleted:

```
  nRet = SelectObject(m_hdcDrip, m_stbmpDrip)
  nRet = DeleteObject(m_hbmpDrip)
  nRet = DeleteDC(m_hdcDrip)
```

Each time **WhizDrip** returns (since it's a function not a subroutine) it returns the opposite of the **m_bComplete** flag. So, when **m_bComplete** is **True, WhizDrip** returns **False**. The **m_flgWhizzing** flag gets the return, so it will become **False** when **m_bComplete** is **True**.

Summary

This chapter certainly offers a new twist on animation programming. We've covered an entertaining subject with some solid coding content, including:

- Grabbing the desktop
- Creating a dynamic palette
- Filtering the display
- Coordinating complicated animation sequences

Not bad. Now for a few tips on the content covered. First of all, the palette creation code. Notice that the **peFlags** element for the **PALETTEENTRY** arrays is always set to 0. We set it to **PC_ANIMATE** in Chapter 3 which caused the palette entries (once realized to the system) to be locked so that other applications couldn't realize their palettes to those entries. It also enabled us to perform some palette animation techniques since the call to **AnimatePalette()** required that the palette entries be flagged this way.

Without setting the flag to a value, the palette realizing should look for a closest palette entry to the color requested. This works for our purposes. Try setting the flags to **PC_NOCOLLAPSE** and watch what happens to the animations. The dog no longer seems to be able to find his colors! That's because the **NO_COLLAPSE** flag tells the system to look for an available entry first, which means that the dogs colors that are expected to be in the first 6 non-static entries, may not go there at all! Just a little tidbit for you there!

So on to bigger and better things. The next and final chapter will compete against the filtering 'hack' that made the dog whiz possible, and show you how real imaging programs do pixel color alteration. This will be a fun finale that will really open your eyes to how those programs work, maybe even entice to try some more filters in your not-so-spare time!

The only question left for this chapter is: how'd the whiz go?

```
rivate Declare Function GlobalFree Lib "kernel32" (ByVal h
rivate Declare Function GlobalLock Lib "kernel32" (ByVal h
rivate Declare Function GlobalUnlock Lib "kernel32" (ByVa
'--copying bitmap bits
' copies a global block of data into global memory
rivate Declare Sub CopyMemory Lib "kernel32" Alias "RtlM

'--copies global block of data in       IB
rivate Declare Function SetDIB        "gdi32" (ByVal m_hd
 ByVal hBitmap As Long, ByVal nStartS     As Long, By
 ByVal lpBits As Any, lpBI As BITMAPI       ByVal wUsa

'--blits DC to DC
rivate Declare Function BitBlt Lib "gdi32" (ByVal hDestDC
rivate Declare Function StretchBlt Lib "gdi32" (ByVal hDes

'--palette methods
rivate Declare Function CreatePalett      "gdi32" (lpLogPa
rivate Declare Function SelectPalette     "gdi32" (ByVal m
rivate Declare Function RealizePalette Lib "gdi32" (ByVal r
rivate Declare Sub AnimatePalette Lib "gdi32" (ByVal hPal

'--device context methods
rivate Declare Function SelectObject Lib "gdi32" (ByVal m_

rivate Declare Function CreateCompatibleBitmap Lib "gdi32
rivate Declare Function DeleteObject Lib "gdi32" (ByVal hO

rivate Declare Function CreateCompatibleDC Lib "gdi32" (B
```

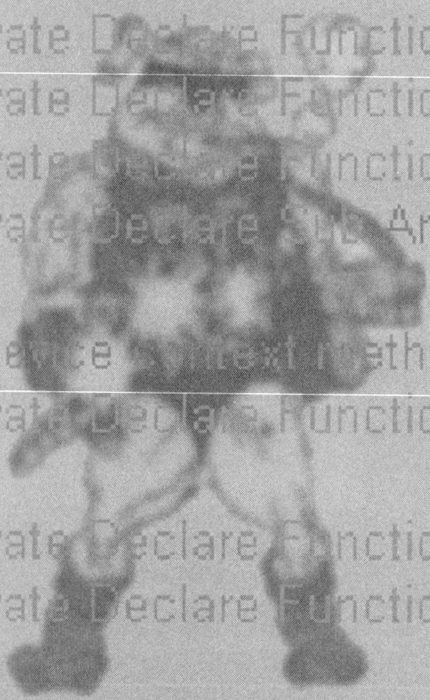

Chapter

7

Real Imaging Techniques

So far in this book, we've built every animation sample using VB as the central application environment, using the Windows API when VB couldn't cut the mustard. If you haven't been exposed to the Windows API in a previous life, this has probably opened some interesting doors to application development with VB. Perhaps you've found that you can do things either that you thought were impossible or that you never even thought of doing. The fact is, using external functionality, like that available with the Windows API, truly makes all VB applications more powerful. So now that you've got a solid grip on *that* reality, it's time to start you on a *new* learning experience: graphics manipulation.

In this chapter, I'm going to show you where the Windows API stops and where custom DLLs start, with respect to graphics. I'll introduce to you a non-API DLL that addresses some of the functionality that the API isn't capable of offering us through VB directly, due to limitations with the programming language. The custom DLL provided, **`Dibsect.dll`**, exposes functionality to your VB code. This means that not all of the work is going to be done in VB, but if you've got a DLL to do it with one function call, why not use it? Using imaging techniques that might otherwise be found in a graphics manipulation program, I'll show you animation techniques that use this DLL and teach you a thing or two about graphics programming.

Introducing DIBSection

A DIBSection is a 32-bit device-independent bitmap object that lets you perform GDI methods on a device-independent bitmap (DIB) rather than the former device-dependent bitmap (DDB) restriction in 16-bit environments. In this section, I'll try to enlighten you to the reasons behind the DIBSection, how it came to be, why you'd want to use it and when you definitely wouldn't. This will be a theoretical discussion, with coding details to follow. I'll summarize the differences between the GDI, WinG and DIBSection, explaining the maturation of DIBSection from the other two graphics methods. We discussed these things in Chapter 3, but the review should help refresh your memory. Then, I'll get into the uses for DIBSection and how it compares with the GDI, ignoring WinG, which isn't necessary in a 32-bit environment (the code in this book is pure 32-bit only).

GDI, WinG and DIBSection again

The fastest way to manipulate graphics data is to go right to the video card, like DOS programmers have always done. There's one catch, though: you have to have access to it directly, which means that, like DOS programmers, you have to write a device driver for each type of video card and call functions that manipulate the display data. Another way to speed up the manipulation of graphics data is to access the raw bitmap data directly, as opposed to going through a device-context. Before I explain what I mean by all of this, let's review the ways you can access bitmap data and why you might do so. Then, I'll get into what we'll be doing with respect to these topics in this chapter.

Comparing Pixel Access

This is really a quick summary of what you can do with graphics data, as we've already covered it in Chapter 3. As you've seen throughout the book's code samples, the GDI provides access to pixel data through the device context. When you copy image data to the display, you use **`BitBlt()`** which requires a handle to a DC. When you ask for the color value of a pixel, you use **`GetPixel()`** which also requires a handle to a DC. The catch is that, to get an image from disk (a device-independent graphic) into a DC for using GDI functions, you have to convert it to the current graphics display mode (color format, more specifically).

When the GDI was created, the Windows platform became the interface to the same display data that DOS programmers had written custom code to reach. So what the GDI gives us is a method to quickly move data, with limited manipulation capabilities as per the examples throughout the book. It's the device context that GDI functions interact with directly in order to have changes reflected by the display device. Of course, for memory DCs to transfer data *quickly* to the display DCs that update the video card's display data, they too had to be compatible with the current display driver (i.e. both 256 color, both hi-color...).

All of the bit-block transfer functions we've used like **`BitBlt()`** and **`PatBlt()`**, and the palette functions, font functions, and so forth, are core Windows functions. The blitting functions are particularly fast ways to alter and move data from one DC to another, since no color conversions take place on the way to each DC. In most cases, the faster the display is updated, the better the reaction from your users. This is especially true with animation and game programming.

Something was missing with the DDB-dependent GDI methodology: the direct manipulation of each pixel of bitmap data. When we read an image into memory, remember that the data is at first accessed via a global pointer to memory, which contains a series of bytes (actually, an array of pixel data). We can look at each byte individually by moving the pointer one byte at a time (done by adding to the pointer value). Once we've moved the data into a DDB (or, attached it to a DC), the only way to access the bitmap is to use the handle to the DC and whatever GDI functions are provided to manipulate that data.

This is great if you just want to copy rectangular data from one DC to another, possibly using brushes and raster operations to make things more interesting or to get the result you want. But this doesn't cut it if you want to change the value of the data pixel for pixel, say, to tint a rectangular area green, or use other imaging techniques. The GDI doesn't provide a 'TintToGreen' function, just a few pixel getting and setting functions that I'll demonstrate in this chapter's code samples. We can certainly use these to change the value of each pixel, based on some coded rules, but you'll see that this isn't exactly the speediest way to perform this type of manipulation. You'll see soon that, to change an image, pixel for pixel, with any speed, the raw bitmap data must remain in the global memory allocation created when it was first read from disk. This requires a little outside assistance beyond the Windows API, which we'll unveil presently.

Comparing Translation and Speed

Given that we can only do certain things through direct pixel access, the ideal scenario would be to have access to the raw bitmap data (the pointer to some global memory) as needed, but still be able to use the data through a device context (after the **`SelectObject()`** function is called) for things like fast pixel copying using **`BitBlt()`**, which requires the DC handle, not the raw data pointer. Regardless of the reasons why we want to use bitmap data both from a DC and from its raw state in memory, the ultimate goal is almost always to copy information to the display. We can do this by combining information into one working buffer (a DC or raw bitmap buffer), then copying the data to the display DC, or by copying each display component from their respective memory locations and formats directly to the display DC.

> *Remember that when we're reading in an image from disk, it always starts out as a DIB, so we must convert it to a DDB at some point, either by a call to* **`SetDIBits()`**, *as we did in Chapter 3 originally, or by the* **`LoadPicture`** *method, which takes care of this for us while creating the DDB associated to the* **`PictureBox`** *control.*

This figure shows the conceptual movement of the same graphical data, one stored as a DDB, the other as a DIB, on its way to the screen from disk.

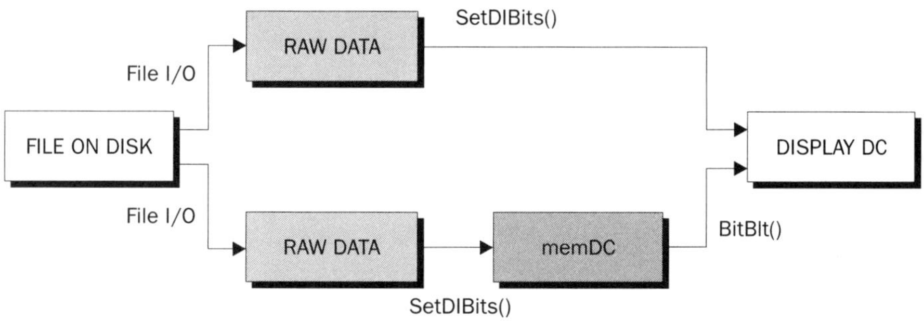

Copying raw bitmap data to the display using **`SetDIBits()`**, actually appears to be one less step doesn't it? Well, sure, if all you were doing is copying the data directly to the display, this would be one less step, since the memory DC must subsequently be blitted to the display. However, images stored in memory are normally used for more than just one simple copy to the display. When a sprite is copied to the display (or working buffer more likely) during an animation, it's combined with the destination device context using raster operations to get a transparent effect. Also, sometimes, work is done on graphics in between screen updates, on an ongoing basis (as you'll see in this chapter) which means that a **`SetDIBits()`** call would have to be recalled each time the raw bits were changed.

Here's where it gets complicated. As you know, the **`SetDIBits()`** call converts the DIB into a DDB in the format of the destination device context. This conversion requires that each pixel value is looked up in a table and mapped to the table (or logical palette) belonging to the destination. If this is a 1:1 mapping (when you take the color information directly from the DIB, create a logical palette from it and select it into the destination DC first), the call works faster. However, if there are differences, this process is slower. Frankly, even when the color mapping is identical, **`BitBlt()`** is still faster. So what's better? Several calls to **`SetDIBits()`** each time the raw data is changed, or one call to **`SetDIBits()`** when the image data is first read in, which converts it to a DDB right up front and leaves all subsequent work to what the GDI has to offer?

Now *there's* a good question, but a few pointers will help you to decide which data movement method is best for the situation:

- Are you directly manipulating pixels in the bitmap data?
- Are you doing this repeatedly?

You'll probably notice that most animations are performed using static graphics, which are images that won't change at run time, like the frames of each animation in previous chapters of this book. One of the main requirements of animation, transparency, is handled just fine through the GDI using bitmasking with **BitBlt()** raster operation codes and static bitmaps. However, if your application performs any image manipulation methods, as this chapter's does, you must do this by accessing the raw bitmap data. Any time pixels are being altered (i.e. more than one in a single pass), the process can take some time. Worse, if this process is done repeatedly, like in an animation loop, that time weighs heavy on application performance. What you're actually doing to alter the pixels is irrelevant (that varies with the application) but the point is that individual pixels need to be looked at and their color value or index possibly changed. The problem with this is that, every time a change is made to the raw data, a slower bit-transfer method like **SetDIBits()** *must* be called to convert the data to a DDB, either to the display DC or to one of the memory DCs on its way.

Comparing Pixel Data Storage

You knew I was leading to something, right? I mentioned the use of the GDI, WinG and DIBSection as possible uses for graphics data. You should remember from Chapter 3 that each of these methods provides slightly different access to the data and slightly different manipulation capabilities. I'm not going to say that one is better than the other, since it really depends on the circumstances. The progression from the GDI to WinG to DIBSection was certainly an attempt at providing more functionality for circumstances that required it, so my goal here is simply to clarify the transition, now that you've seen what we can and can't do.

The following table shows a short list of the main points of interest for the three graphics methods:

Method	Points
Standard GDI	16-bit only **hDC** for GDI methods **hBmp** for compatible bitmap attached to **hDC** Full access to 16-bit GDI functionality Fast bit-transfer methods
WinG	16-bit or 32-bit **hWingDC** for WinG methods **hWingBmp** for WinG DIB attached to **hWingDC** Partial access to 16-bit GDI functionality through WinG library Full access to 32-bit WinG library Fast bit-transfer methods with access to raw data
DIBSection	32-bit only **hDC** for GDI methods **hBmp** for DIBSection DIB attached to **hDC** full access to 32-bit GDI functionality Fast bit-transfer methods with access to raw data

The standard GDI was the original set of 16-bit functions that made it possible to work with image data in the quickest way possible, as a DDB. This meant that data was converted instantly to DDB format for compatibility with the display and with the GDI's expectations. As I've mentioned, this wasn't without limitations; faster direct pixel manipulation methods were not available. All access to bitmap data was provided through the use of the DC, right down to the individual pixels.

Beyond the GDI, a new method was necessary to address the point I keep making about accessing raw bitmap data. Available direct pixel manipulation methods, used with functions like **SetDIBits()** to get the information to a DC, didn't provide a quick enough blit from a DIB. That's how WinG came into being. The WinG device context supports DIBs in that its bitmap object is a DIB created by special WinG functions. This DIB's data isn't only available through the handle to the WinGDC (as we're accustomed to with the GDI's DC handle), but also through a pointer to the raw bitmap data. So now, performing bit-level manipulation is fast (you'll see how this works when I discuss accessing raw data through code), and a fast blit is available to move the DIB, rather than a DDB, to other DCs.

The catch here is that the function calls are part of the WinG library of functions, not part of the GDI. That means that only the functions that the WinG library cared to duplicate for the purpose of using them with this special device context, are available. Mind you, the main graphics functionality is there, but in some scenarios there's a lack of flexibility. This sacrifice was particularly worthwhile when you wanted to write code that could run on 16-bit and 32-bit environments. The WinG library of functions automatically accessed the appropriate WinG or DIBSection (soon to be explained) functions, depending on the environment the code is run in. Certainly, this flexibility provided some relief for the sacrifices (which may even seem minute to some programmers) made from the GDI to WinG.

DIBSection introduced the 'real' WinG of the 32-bit environment (*only* available in a 32-bit environment), but while providing access to raw bitmap data, let you keep the functionality of the GDI. In this chapter, we'll compare this methodology in detail with GDI methods. Clearly, there are still pros and cons to the use of both, so you must be very clear on what you're signing up for before you take the DIBSection plunge.

DIBSection and Dibsect.dll

Before I go any further, let's be really clear on something. The GDI is *still* the fastest way to manipulate graphics in the Windows environment, no exceptions, but there are some things that the GDI just *can't* do. The thing is, there are special circumstances that require access to raw data, that overrides any other loss of functionality or speed. In other words, read the rest of this chapter keeping in mind that just because DIBSection is cool and new, doesn't mean that it's the best animation methodology—it's just another option. Now that you know this, try things out for yourself and decide.

To make use of DIBSection, VB requires a helping hand from a custom DLL (this will be described shortly). That said, let me explain how a DIBSection is created and what its structures are. Then, I'll gently describe the process of reading pixel data in its raw form, discussing the role of pointers. Of course, this will lead me to the custom **Dibsect.dll**'s functionality in all of this.

Creating a DIBSection

Some of the necessary Windows API functions that create a DIBSection require some funky parameters, like pointers to pointers... well, this isn't something VB can support (and I won't even get into what those are used for in C, just in case you were wondering). The bottom line is that this is one of the factors introducing the need for a custom DLL to create the DIBSection. The **Dibsect.dll** (described in full, later) provides a function called **LoadCreateDIBSection()** which performs the steps I'll outline below. First, I'm going to cover the steps that create the DIBSection, explaining what API structures are used. Although this file IO process is encapsulated within the DLL, since you've already done some file IO, I can just step through the process explaining the structures and comparing it to what we started in Chapter 3 within the bitmap class.

Reading in DIBSection Data

You know by now that the process by which data is read from an image file into memory varies. If you use the picture box, what happens is transparent to you as the programmer, but from our current bitmap class, **clsBmp**, you know the file I/O involved in this process. Depending on their file format, all DIBs are organized in a strict structure so that the code that reads in the data can support it in memory so that other functions understand it. So far in this book (why not stick with a good thing) I've only read in the Windows DIB file format, better known as a **bmp**. They've all been 256 color bitmaps too, which will change in this chapter.

The function **LoadCreateDIBSect()** does the work of reading the image data into the appropriate Windows API structures, using similar methods that the bitmap class uses in its **Read_VBFileIO** method. This figure compares the three, now present, methods that I've exposed throughout this book for performing file I/O.

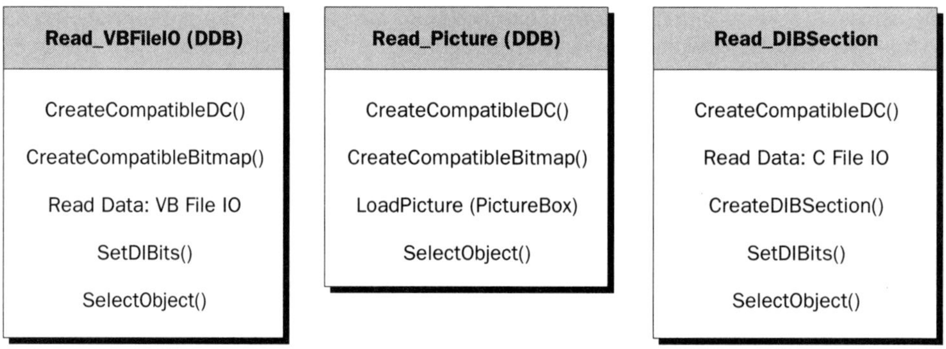

The main differences between reading data into a DDB and reading data into a DIB are as follows:

- **CreateCompatibleBitmap()** versus **CreateDIBSection()**
- DDB structures versus DIB structures

The call to **CreateCompatibleBitmap()** creates an empty DDB, compatible with the current device, which has its pixel data set by a call to **SetDIBits()** in the previous file I/O examples. This uses a pointer to some bitmap data and the color information supplied with the bitmap header information to set the device-dependent bits of the DDB. The call to **CreateDIBSection()** creates an empty DIB, which isn't needed to be compatible with the current device. The following figure shows the comparison.

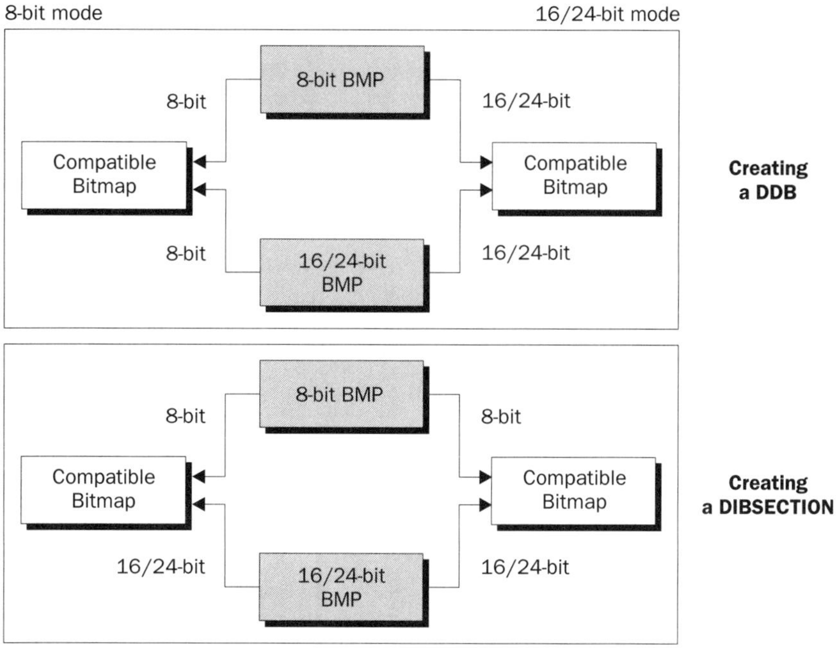

Notice that using a DDB, the bitmap data is stored in the DC in the same color format as the display device! So an 8-bit image that is supposed to save on memory during use is actually being converted to a 24-bit image if that's the current display driver in use. A DIB, on the other hand, stores its data in the same format as the file was on disk. In 256 colors, this causes some problems with speed, as you'll see when I get to the code samples, but the image data remains as it was on disk.

LoadCreateDIBSect()

`LoadCreateDIBSect()` is a function provided by **`Dibsect.dll`** to perform the file I/O on reading in a DIBSection bitmap. The call to **`CreateDIBSection()`**, a Windows API call, is one of the final steps in this procedure, so I'll walk through the entire process, pointing out comparisons where appropriate. Put your Chapter 3 hat on, because I won't be repeating what you should already know from our original file I/O endeavour.

First, the **`BITMAPFILEHEADER`** is read in, which is used to check the type of file, exactly the same way as the **`Read_VBFileIO`** example does. Before continuing, the function will verify that it understands the format for the data about to be read in. For our purposes, only the Windows DIB, or **`BMP`**, will be used.

Next, **`BITMAPINFO`** is read in, which includes color format information for the file. Here, information about the number of colors the bitmap uses, which means whether or not there is a palette, is read to decide whether a palette should be created. This also tells the function where the bitmap data starts in the file (remember, headers, then colors, then bits), so that the read pointer for the data can be positioned accordingly. If a color table exists, the next step is to create a logical palette that reflects the bitmap data's requirements.

Remember, the **BITMAPINFO** *structure is broken down into the* **BITMAPINFOHEADER** *structure and the color table if there is one. However the pixel information is stored (in 1 or 3 bytes of information per pixel), the bitmap data follows the size of this structure. The array of* **RGBQUAD** *should be ignored if there isn't a color table, though. In the example below, the array has 256 items in it:*

```
Private Type BITMAPINFO
    bmiHeader As BITMAPINFOHEADER
    bmiColors(0 To 255) As RGBQUAD
End Type
```

When this header and color table information was read in using the **Read_VBFileIO** method of the bitmap class, the header and palette information was read directly into variables of the appropriate data type and the **GlobalAlloc()** function created space for the image data in memory (space required equal to the size of the image without it's headers). This DLL function works a little differently. **GlobalAlloc()** is used to allocate space first for the header information that has been read in so far. Without getting into the details of C programming, what this means is that the contents of the variables that held the header information in our example are actually moved into globally allocated memory and pointed to with a pointer variable. The allocated memory looks like the this:

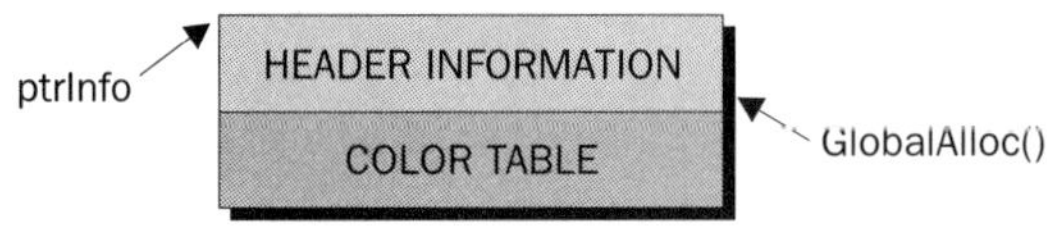

When this function proceeds to read in the pixel information for the image, since there's already a pointer to the header information of the image, the pixel information is tacked on to the end of that global allocation. In this case, the global memory allocation isn't only going to hold the image data, but preceding it will be the entire DIB's information, including the header and any color information. Using an API function called **GlobalReAlloc()**—I won't get into this in detail, this is just in case you try stepping through the C code—that same allocation is increased in size to hold the rest of the image data as shown here:

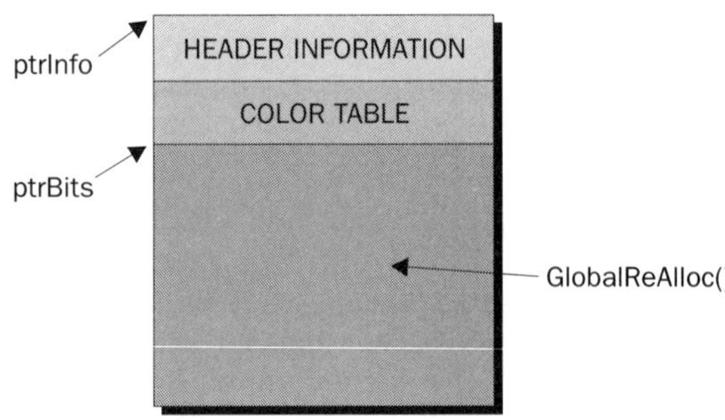

Now it's time to create the DIBSection. The call to the **CreateDIBSection()** API function takes the following parameters:

- A handle to a DC
- **BITMAPINFO** structure
- Color usage flags
- A pointer to a pointer to data bits in memory
- A file mapping object
- An offset within file mapping object to bits

You can go ahead and ignore the last two parameters, since we don't need to do anything with them here and you won't likely be needing this from VB in the near future, especially with a nice little DLL that does the work for you.

The palette, created from the bitmap data, should be selected into a temporary device context because the call to **`CreateDIBSection()`** uses it as a reference for color information. **`CreateDIBSection()`** returns a handle (that Windows object pointer thingy) to a DIBSection object that is made up of the following new API structures:

```
Type BITMAP '14 bytes
        bmType As Long
        bmWidth As Long
        bmHeight As Long
        bmWidthBytes As Long
        bmPlanes As Integer
        bmBitsPixel As Integer
        bmBits As Long
End Type
```

```
Type DIBSECTION
        dsBm As BITMAP
        dsBmih As BITMAPINFOHEADER
        dsBitfields(3) As Long
        dshSection As Long
        dsOffset As Long
End Type
```

If the palette entries of the logical palette selected into that DC are identical to those of the DIB that was read in, the mapping process is faster when **`SetDIBits()`** is called (you'll see that call further on).

`BITMAPINFO` is the same structure used by the **`Read_VBFileIO`** method that supplies information about the DIB, before it becomes device-dependent. In this case, the DIB will remain a DIB and the **`BITMAPINFO`** structure will remain part of the DIBSection, as you can see by the **`DIBSECTION`** structure.

The third parameter, color usage flags, is used the same way as **`SetDIBits()`** uses them. It tells the function whether the palette selected into the DC is to be used as the lookup for each color in the DIB. The fourth parameter is supposed to receive a pointer to the pointer to the bitmap's bit values. Since there's already an allocated area in memory with the bits read into it and a pointer to that area, we don't use this variable in this scenario.

To complete this process, the handle returned from the call to **`CreateDIBSection()`**, or the handle to the new DIBSection object, is selected into a temporary device context, after the bitmap's palette has also been selected into that DC. This works in a similar way to the scenario you saw where the handle to the DDB, returned by **`CreateCompatibleBitmap()`**, was selected into a DC. This had provided an empty DDB bitmap, ready for a call to **`SetDIBits()`** to move the DIB information into the DDB area, thus converting it to a DDB. In this case, there's now an empty DIBSection bitmap, joined to a device context, waiting for the bits that had been read into memory to be moved to the new DIBSection. To do this, **`SetDIBitsToDevice()`** is used.

This next figure shows the difference between the process of moving the bitmap data into a bitmap object, using **`SetDIBits()`**, and moving the bitmap data into a device context's area, using **`SetDIBitsToDevice()`**.

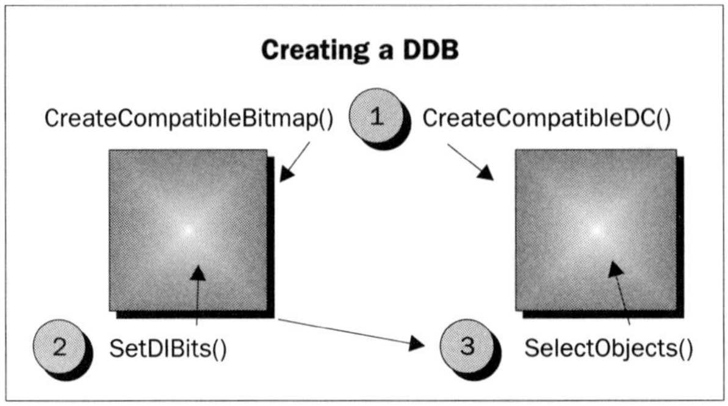

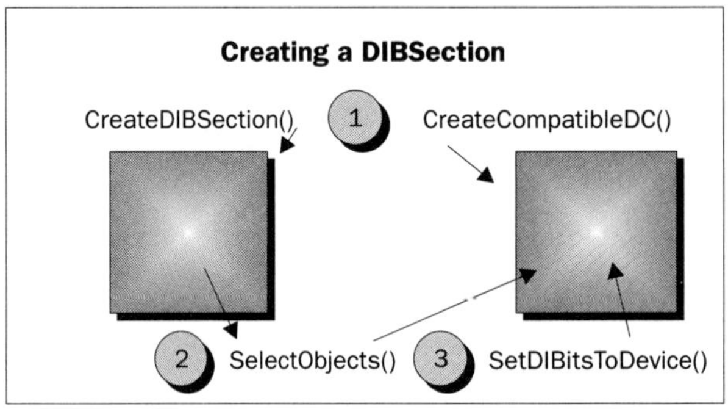

SetDIBits() was used to convert the bitmap data into a DDB, *before* selecting the bitmap into a device context. Since DC's support DIBSection bitmaps in 32-bit environments and the data is to remain in DIB format, **SetDIBitsToDevice()** facilitates copying the data to a device context, regardless of whether the DC has a DIBSection or DDB selected into it. The beauty is that once this process is complete, the DIBSection bitmap can be selected out of the temporary DC, but it now has all the bitmap data successfully pointed to by the DIBSection elements and it's still a DIB.

This entire process is performed in the **LoadCreateDIBSection()** function, provided by **Dibsect.dll**. When the function returns, it brings with it a handle to the DIB's palette, *and* a handle to the DIBSection bitmap. You'll notice in the code that an API function, **GetObject()**, is used to fill the structures shown above that describe the DIBSection. You'll see just when this is necessary when the actual code is described and at that time I'll explain how the function works.

Before I walk through a summary of the **Dibsect.dll**, which provides DIBSection functionality to our VB code, I'd like to explain a little more about how this new DIBSection data is accessed. Now you'll have that long-awaited introduction to C programming techniques, without the discomfort of having to read the code behind it.

Data in the Raw

Now, before the rest of the functionality of the **Dibsect.dll** is unveiled, I'd like to give you a little vision into the storage of bits in memory, the way that C programmers see it. If you consider our original file I/O introduction, with the **GlobalAlloc()** and **CopyMemory()** functions inside **Read_VBFileIO**, you can imagine the data stored in a memory block, accessible through a pointer to global memory. It's from here that data is raw and from here that the following discussion commences. Now, it's time to dig into a little low-level understanding of how addressing works in Windows, good experience even on a bad hair day.

Raw Bits and Data Pointers

You have a pointer variable, **ptrData**, that contains some number that makes sense to Windows, as far as what byte position in its memory the data begins. The way C programming works, image data is stored in a memory block as an array of bytes. You can see from this diagram that **ptrData**, let's just say it pointed to an address of 100 in memory, points to the same data as **ptrData[0]**, which show the pointer referencing the data block as an array.

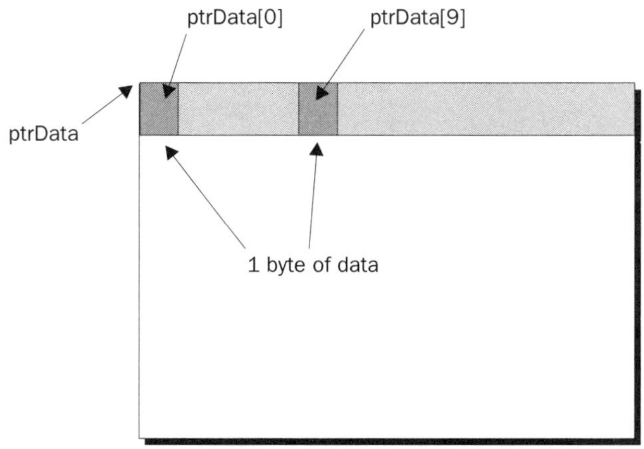

If I wanted to find out the contents of the 10th byte of data in the block, I would used **ptrData[9]**. If VB could hold an array big enough for a 100x100 bitmap image, it could store the data like this:

```
Dim sBytes(1 to 10000) as String * 1

sBytes(1) => palette index for pixel 1 in row 1
sBytes(2) => palette index for pixel 2 in row 2
...
sBytes(10000) => palette index for pixel 100 in row 100
```

The actual data in the file would be stored in binary, so there would be a conversion necessary if we wanted to read the palette index values that filled each byte. I'm assuming here that each byte is a palette index and the image data comes from an 8-bit image, so 1 byte or 8 bits-per-pixel are used. If this were a full color image, the data would be stored as full RGB values per pixel, which means that three bytes are taken for each pixel and the data would have to be read that way. Note also that this increases the size of the array by three times.

Reading from each item in the array will return a single byte string for each item. Arrays in VB are not the same as those in C programming environments. Without getting into C coding practices in too much detail, let me demonstrate, theoretically, how such an array of bits would be accessed using C. This should facilitate an understanding of why it's faster to access bits this way rather than using GDI methods through a device context.

In the VB example of an array of image byte data, to move to the next pixel of information you would increment the element index for the array. How this differs from C programming techniques is that the pointer, **ptrData**, is used with the appropriate functions to tell Windows what byte address in memory (therefore, what element in the byte array) to look at. From the previous figure you can see that **ptrData** is the master pointer to the start of the bits, or, the first byte of data at that memory address. If you wanted to put the index value of pixel 1 into a byte variable in VB, you would do the following:

```
Dim nByte as Byte

nByte = Val(sBytes(1))
```

Keep in mind that when I use examples from VB to describe accessing raw bitmap data using C techniques, it is theoretical. There are binary to string or numeric data conversions that may be necessary in the process. Look back at Chapter 3, where I discussed reading in the **`bmType`** *element of a bitmap using file IO for an example of a necessary conversion from binary data.*

To get the same information in C a different methodology is used. Where **`nByte`** was used in the VB version of accessing a pixel above, a pointer to a byte would be defined in C. Since **`ptrData`** is a pointer to a byte in memory, adding 1 to the pointer moves it to the next byte of data in memory. If the pointer was another variable type, then adding one would move the pointer by *that* variable size.

Put another way, adding 1 to a pointer variable, mathematically speaking, doesn't add a digital 1 to the binary contents of the pointer, but adds to the position of the pointer, by an amount reflective of the type of pointer it is (just like a variable type, a pointer is told what kind of data it points to). To look at the next byte then, a byte pointer can be incremented by one byte, or it can be treated like an array. Referring (once more) back to the previous figure, **`ptrData`** starts at 100. To look at byte 109, the following can happen:

```
ptrData = ptrData + 9      'moves the actual pointer
or
ptrTemp = ptrData[9]      'creates a new temporary pointer
```

Reading Raw Pixel Data

You've had it pretty easy so far, using functions like **`GetPixel()`** and **`SetPixel()`** get the RGB value that a specified coordinate uses. However, inside those functions is another set of functions that reads the raw bitmap data behind the scenes. It's high time that I unravelled how all that works. Even though the C DLL in this chapter handles the rough stuff for you, you may need to look at that code some day, or have a better understanding of how the data is accessed.

Now, let's carry the previous discussion into what happens when you try to get at pixel data in the DIB. The information, as it's stored in memory, is just a sequence of bytes, one after another. Each byte represents an index position in the color table (from 0–255) or each 3 bytes represents a value for red, green, then blue (each can have a value from 0–255). The pointer to the data, or the byte pointer, is how you can look at the value for each byte. As long as you know how the bitmap data is stored (thus, a purpose for header information unfolds) you know what each byte is supposed to mean. That's how the code decides which way to interpret the data.

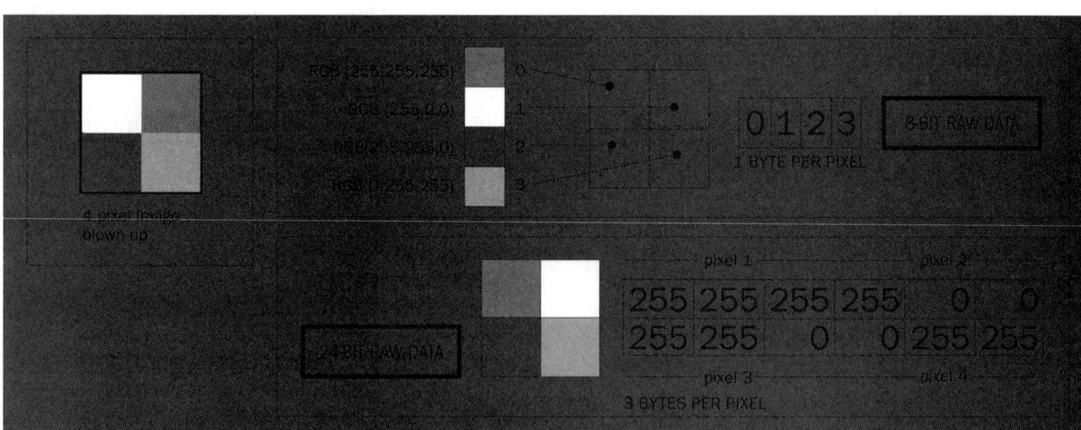

If the image data is 8-bit, each byte is read individually for its palette index, which means to get a pixel value in RGB, the palette index must in turn be looked up in the color table for the DIB. If the image is 24-bit, there are three bytes per pixel, not to be confused with the color table's **RGBQUAD** structure, which is four bytes per color reference. Reading each individual byte in order means that a count of three bytes brings you to the start of the next pixel.

To get at pixel data in the middle of the bitmap, imagining it as a 2-dimensional object, means calculating what byte that pixels *x,y* coordinate maps out to in memory:

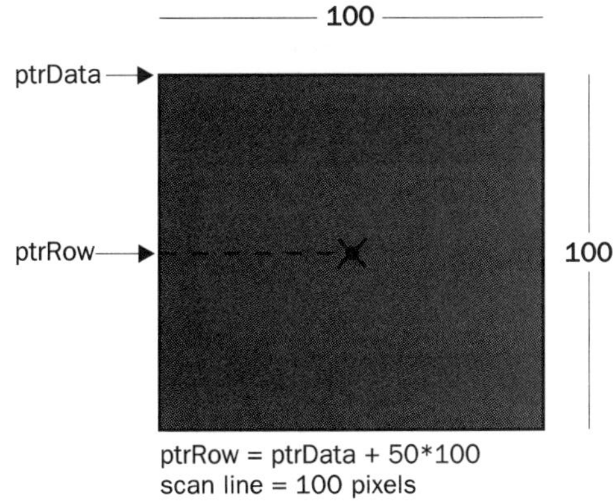

The information in memory about the DIB includes width and height. The *y* coordinate of the pixel color requested, multiplied by the width of each scan line, puts the pointer at the start of the row where the *x* coordinate is located. Notice that the row pointer, **ptrRow**, is set to **ptrData**[width * y], which means that width * y is the item in the byte array that **ptrRow** looks to (this assumes each byte is a palette index, not one of the RGB values). Now, to get to the byte (pixel) on that row that was requested by the x coordinate x bytes from **ptrRow** is what we want, so **ptrRow**[x] will return that byte of information. That is the byte that would be set if there were a change in index value.

Now let's compare this pixel accessing process with the DDB. When a bitmap is selected into a device context, it becomes a two-dimensional object, which means we can ask for pixel data by x, y coordinate. In a sense, DIB data isn't stored like DDB data at all, so some of the diagrams up to now are a little misleading. This figure shows the 2D view of the a 2x2 image, as shown an earlier diagram, and that same image, represented as a DIB, as stored in memory (one pixel after another, one dimension).

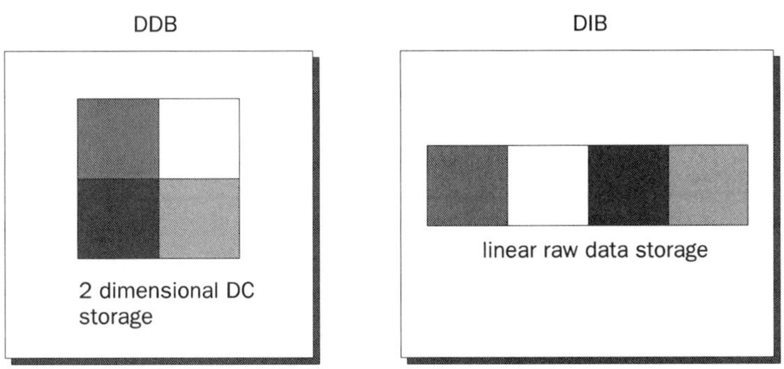

That's why the previous discussion makes pixels seem so linear, by having to calculate a coordinate by y value and row width and then adding x to the end.

This certainly sheds some light on the work that is being done inside the **`GetPixel()`** and **`SetPixel()`** functions supplied by the Windows API. It also makes sense that this must also be done within the DLL, for every function that looks at individual pixel values to alter them. Keep this conversation in mind when I go through the individual functions, and what they do to access the raw bitmap data.

Dibsect.dll Overview

Beware: you can use the DLL in its current state. C source-browsing isn't recommended for scared victims of a sheltered VB existence.

So, now you know more than you want to about C programming concepts regarding graphics. You also know how a DIBSection is created, which is just another way to store bitmap data, available in 32-bit environments. The fact that this data is also compatible with GDI functionality, just like you are accustomed to with compatible bitmaps, is a bonus. In addition, DIBSection bitmaps have a pointer to their raw data and even though they can be selected into a device context, other functions provided by the **`Dibsect.dll`** will be able to perform some neat tricks on the image data directly. **`Dibsect.dll`** exports the following functions:

- **`LoadCreateDibSection()`**
- **`GetOurPixel()`**
- **`PutOurPixel()`**
- **`TransparentBufferCopy()`**
- **`AdjBitmapTransparency()`**
- **`AdjBitmapColor()`**

`LoadCreateDIBSection()` performs file I/O on the image file, returning information about the created bitmap object in memory. This function is called from the **`Read_DIBSection`** method of **`clsBmp`** and it returns a handle to the bitmap object it creates. Like **`CreateCompatibleBitmap()`**, only the data is filled into this bitmap object:

```
m_hDIB = LoadCreateDibSection(m_sBmpFile, m_objMem.hdcDisp, m_hPal)
```

The first parameter is the name of the file to read, the second a display DC used as a compatible DC by the function and the last is a variable that will be filled in with the handle to the associated palette for the DIB (if the DIB is 8-bit). That means, from VB there will be a handle to the DIBSection (I'll get to its use), and a logical palette for the bitmap, which we normally create ourselves with the VB code.

`GetOurPixel()` and **`PutOurPixel()`** are similar functions to the GDI's **`GetPixel()`** and **`SetPixel()`**—really. The difference is that the GDI functions are passed a handle to a device context that has a bitmap selected into it and the **`Dibsect.dll`** functions are passed a DIBSection. Also, since the bitmap isn't a DDB, associated with a device context and logical palette, the palette for the DIB information must be passed to the function. If the DIBSection is stored as an 8-bit DIB, those palette entries must be looked up in the original palette for the DIB when it was read from disk. Compare the following functions.

```
nPixel = GetPixel(.hdcWork, nPosX, nPosY)
GetPixelValue = GetOurPixel(m_dibsect, nPosX, nPosY, m_hPal)
```

```
nRet = SetPixel(.hdcWork, nPosX, nPosY, nPixel)
PutOurPixel m_dibsect, nPosX, nPosY, nPixel, m_hPal
```

All that talk about pointers and raw data should now become useful, since that's what is happening inside these DLL functions. The DIBSection structure, passed to the **`GetOurPixel()`** and **`PutOutPixel()`** functions, has an element that points to the memory address where the bits are for the bitmap. Inside each function, they check whether or not the pixels are stored as 1 byte or 3 byte pixels (8-bit or 24-bit) and from there, the C code steps through, looking for the pixel requested and changing its setting to the appropriate value. Compare the speed of the two processes in the **`Dibtest.vbp`** code discussed in this chapter and you'll find the results very interesting!

`TransparentBufferCopy()` is used as an alternative method to bitmasking with the GDI, to gain non-rectangular blitting effects. We've used this throughout the book in every animation sample and, in **`Dibtest.vbp`**, you can compare the GDI and DIBSection methods side-by-side. What the function does is copy the data, pointed to by the DIBSection structure passed it, to a destination DIBSection (also passed). But the copy procedure must go through each row and column of color information, skipping over pixels that equal the color value passed as the transparent color:

```
TransparentBufferCopy dsBall, 0, 0, dsBg, .Left, .Top, .TransCol
```

You see, instead of using two bitmaps to create the transparent effect, if you know which color is transparent, that pixel can conveniently not be copied to the destination bitmap. There's a little more to how this fits in with the VB code that has been built on through each chapter, so stay tuned.

`AdjBitmapTransparency()` is where we start getting into imaging techniques. This function, like **`TransparentBufferCopy()`**, copies one DIBSection bitmap to another, blending the pixels of the destination with the source based on a blend factor (we'll cover the details later). It also takes into consideration a transparent color value for the source bitmap, since it may be a sprite that requires a non-rectangular copy. The DIB's logical palette is also passed to this function, so that any adjustments to color can be looked up in the color table if necessary:

```
AdjBitmapTransparency dsBall, rArea, dsBg, rLoc, .hPalette, nGlowAmt, .TransCol
```

`AdjBitmapColor()` takes a single DIBSection and adjusts the color value of a specified rectangle of the bitmap, by a specified amount for each RGB value. It also must know the transparent color of the bitmap, so that the transparent pixels aren't altered by this function, rendering it non-transparent for future use. The DIB's palette is also passed to this function, since color values are being altered and they may need to be looked up:

```
AdjBitmapColor dsBall, .hPalette, rArea, nColorBoost, .TransCol
```

That pretty much sums up the **`Dibsect.dll`**'s functionality. Now you just need to know how and where I used it, so let's go!

Windows API DLLs are located in the **`Windows\System`** *directory, so you can take for granted that they are in the path. When using custom DLLs, since the* **`Declare Function/Sub`** *statement doesn't take a full path to that DLL, they* must *be located in the path. But, if the custom DLL isn't a shared DLL, needn't reside in the* **`Windows\System`** *directory and can be placed in the same directory as the* **`.exe`**.

The problem is, when running in design time, your current directory may not be the same as the **App.Path**, *if the VBP wasn't double-clicked to open up the VB environment. To insure your code will always work from design time, put the following code in the* **Sub Main()**:

```
If Left$(App.Path, 1) <> Left$(CurDir, 1) Then
     ChDrive Left$(App.Path, 1)
     ChDir App.Path
End If
```

Dibsect.dll vs GDI

Dibtest.vbp is the first project that uses the custom **Dibsect.dll** in an attempt to compare the use of our already familiar VB classes with the standard GDI methods used so far, and the new methods introduced with the custom DLL. I'll explain a little about how the code works and what changes need to be made to the existing classes used throughout this book.

Dibtest.vbp

There are three tests being performed in this project. One demonstrates how individual pixels can be altered using DDBs and DIBs, the other how the GDI uses DDBs to generate a non-rectangular blit and how DIBSection uses DIBs to do the same. This figure shows the interface that is provided for each of these tests:

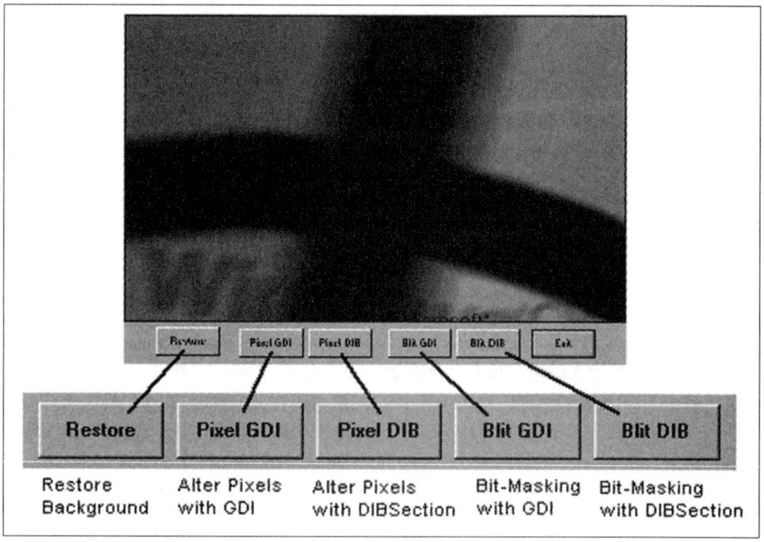

The button that restores the background is used to refresh the double buffer with the original background graphic, after work has been done by the other button selections. The first two button selections compare the GDI and DIBSection pixel boosting procedures, and the last two compare the GDI and DIBSection transparent copying procedures. I'll explain these in the sections to follow.

The graphics used consist of a background and a bulls-eye ball that will be bounced around the background are:

The bulls-eye has a copy and mask graphic, set up just as we've seen in previous chapters. You'll see that not all examples to follow will require the mask bitmap to perform transparent copying of the bulls-eye when I compare transparent copying methods of the GDI and DIBSection.

Initialization

The usual initialization procedures are executed when the program starts. When the form loads, the memory object (**g_objMem**) is initialized with the usual GDI buffers using **clsMem**. Before the contents of that double buffer are initialized, the bitmaps are loaded into their respective bitmap classes. As you can see below, I've added a few new procedures to the form that set up generic bitmap classes. Previously, there was a procedure for the actual bitmap file for the class, then one for the mask portion of the class. These procedures were created for convenience and were especially useful when there were several bitmaps being loaded in a project. Using **BmpDC_LoadNew** and **BmpDC_LoadMask**, the parameters that needed to be set up for every bitmap class could be done in one place. Now, **DIBDC_LoadNew** performs the same functionality for DIBs:

```
DIBDC_LoadNew g_objDIBBg, "back.bmp", False
DIBDC_LoadNew g_objDIBBall, "ball256.bmp", True

BmpDC_LoadNew g_objBmpBg, "back.bmp"
BmpDC_LoadNew g_objBmpBall, "ball256.bmp"
BmpDC_LoadMask g_objBmpBall, "ball256m.bmp"
```

The only real difference here is that there is no mask bitmap necessary for the DIBSection ball, even though it's being read in as a sprite that requires transparency. In the **DIBDC_LoadNew** procedure an additional parameter was added to address this issue, in order to set the **BlitMethod** to the appropriate setting of **BLT_COPY** or **BLT_MASK**. Whatever is passed to the **flgMask** parameter is how the DIB is considered during blitting procedures. Using a DDB, the **BmpDC_LoadMask** procedure handles this. What is in memory at the end of this process is shown on the following page.

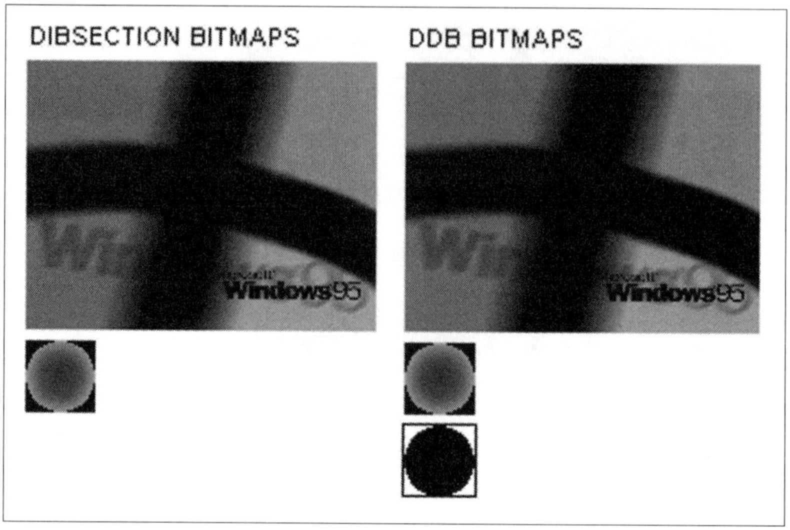

A copy of the background is loaded in as a DDB and as a DIB. A copy of the bulls-eye ball is loaded in as a DIB and a copy of the same ball and its mask bitmap are loaded in as DDBs. Then, there's the double buffer created by **clsMem**, which has space the size of the background bitmap for both the background DC and the working DC which are filled in with the bitmap using **BitBlt()**. Of course, the **hBmp** of **g_objBmpBg**, or the **hDIB** of **g_objDIBBg**, could have been selected into the double-buffer's device context, rather than being contained in device context's of their own, but for simplicity and lack of regard for memory usage at run time, I'm keeping the DIBs and DDBs in their own bitmap class and blitting to the double buffer as we are accustomed at this point.

Changes to clsBmp

To accommodate the new DIB format, there were some additions and changes made to the bitmap class. Since the DIB doesn't require a mask bitmap for transparency, due to the fact that the DIBSection bitmap is tightly linked to the **Dibsect.dll**, there are no considerations made for the mask bitmap that would normally be a possibility with standard bitmaps. Here's a diagram of the new functionality added to **clsBmp** to support DIBSection:

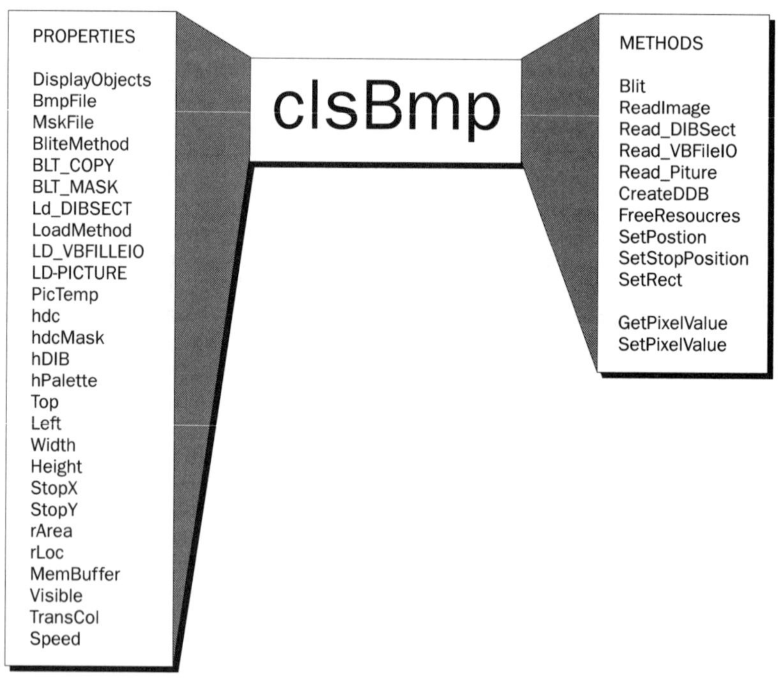

The **ReadImage** method of **clsBmp** contains the following additional lines of code:

```
Case m_LDDIBSECT
    m_nBitmapType = m_BMPDIB
    ReadImage = Read_DIBSect
```

This sets **m_nBitmapType**, to **m_BMPDIB**, to indicate that it's a DIBSection bitmap object, not the standard GDI type that we've been using thus far throughout the book. Then, the new **Read_DIBSect** method is called to read in the DIBSection:

```
Public Function Read_DIBSect() As Boolean
'-Description
' uses custom dll, dibsect.dll, to read in the bitmap data
' into a DIBSection structure read to select into a DC
'-
    Read_DIBSect = True

  ' open binary bitmap file
  nFile = FreeFile
  Open m_sBmpFile For Binary As nFile

  ' read, starting from the first byte, into the BITMAPFILEHEADER structure
  ' check is a valid Windows DIB, signature BM
  Get nFile, 1, m_bmFileHeader
  ' convert first two binary bytes into character values
  ' this must be done one byte at a time to be valid
  sSignature = Chr$(Val(m_bmFileHeader.bfType) And &HFF)
  sSignature = sSignature & Chr$(Val(m_bmFileHeader.bfType And &HFF00&) \ &HFF)
  If UCase$(sSignature) <> "BM" Then
    GoTo eh
  End If

  ' read after the file header into the BITMAPINFOHEADER structure
  Get nFile, Len(m_bmFileHeader) + 1, m_bmInfo
  Close nFile

   m_hDIB = LoadCreateDibSection(m_sBmpFile, m_objMem.hdcDisp, m_hPal)

    ' set data into DDB bitmap for manipulation
  m_nWidth = m_bmInfo.bmiHeader.biWidth
  m_nHeight = m_bmInfo.bmiHeader.biHeight

  CreateDDB False

eh:
End Function
```

This time, the DLL does most of the file I/O work for us, but the **BITMAPFILEHEADER** must be read in so that the width and height information for the bitmap can be used to set the width and height properties of the class. Since this is normally done before the **CreateDDB** call, for consistency it's done here in this procedure as well. For consistency, the signature of the file is checked first, to ensure that a true bitmap (**"BM"**) is being read in, so that the width and height properties are sure to be accurate.

The call to **LoadCreateDIBSection()** returns the handle to the DIB into the **m_hDIB** property of the class, which is similar to the **m_hBmp** property normally returned when the bitmap is read in as a DDB. This takes the file I/O a step further than we normally get with the other two methods that this class provides, so when we get to the **CreateDDB** method, this must be considered. The palette for the bitmap, **m_hPal**, is filled in by the call to **LoadCreateDIBSection()** as well.

In the **Dibtest.vbp** *sample, a palette class is still required since other file IO methods are also used for the GDI examples. In the* **Dibanim.vbp** *sample, there are only DIBSection bitmaps, so no palette class need be included in the project.*

CreateDDB now has to consider the DIBSection option. The first step in this procedure normally creates the memory DDB and DC for copying the image data from memory or the picture box, depending on the method used to read in the image data. Now, there's a condition to the creation of the compatible bitmap, which is not to create it if this is a DIBSection:

```
If m_nLoadMethod <> m_LDDIBSECT Then m_hBmp =
CreateCompatibleBitmap(m_objMem.hdcDisp, m_nWidth, m_nHeight)
```

Next, we added the following lines of code to the method:

```
Case m_LDDIBSECT
      m_hOldPal = SelectPalette(m_hdc, m_hPal, False)
      nRet = RealizePalette(m_hdc)

      m_hStock = SelectObject(m_hdc, m_hDIB)
      ' fill in DIBSection structure
      nRet = GetObject(m_hDIB, Len(m_dibsect), m_dibsect)
```

The creation of the palette for the DIB is skipped since the palette has already been created through the DLL function and returned into the **hPalette** property in the **Read_DIBSect** method. Now, the DC that will have the DIB selected into it will need its palette (remember that if the palette handle is 0, nothing happens), before the call to **SelectObject()**. This time, **SelectObject()** is passed a handle to a DIB, through the **m_hDIB** variable, rather than the handle to a DDB, through the **m_hBmp** variable.

The last step is a new one, which calls the **GetObject()** API function. The call to **LoadCreateDIBSection()** returned a handle to the DIBSection without the rest of the DIBSection's information, which was originally read in by the DLL function and no longer accessible to us from VB. To fill the bitmap class structures (**DIBSECTION**, **BITMAPINFO**) with the DIB's information, for use with function calls that need it, the **GetObject()** function is called. This function returns the corresponding information for the object handle (in this case, a handle to a DIBSection) passed it. The structure supplied in the last parameter must correspond to the information that the object handle points to and the length of the structure must be the length of that structure (buffer) to be filled. Windows does the rest.

This is how the DIB's information is accessed from within the bitmap class. Actually, since classes can't return user-defined types to properties or procedures, nor use them for parameters, it's best to encapsulate all functionality that requires the use of the bitmap structures in **clsBmp** (including those belonging to DDBs), within the class. You'll see why that wasn't possible in all scenarios of this project, but two additional methods to **clsBmp** that exemplify this are **GetPixelValue** and **SetPixelValue**. They were both created to encapsulate changing the pixel value of the DIB.

GetPixelValue calls the **GetOurPixel()** function supplied by **Dibsect.dll** which requires that a DIBSection structure is passed along with the *x, y* coordinate of the pixel value requested:

```
If m_nBitmapType = m_BMPDIB Then
    GetPixelValue = GetOurPixel(m_dibsect, nPosX, nPosY)
End If
```

Since the **m_dibsect** structure was filled in with the call to **GetObject()** when the DIBSection was created, this information is ready to be used. Notice that a test is put in here to check for the type of bitmap this class object is, just to make sure that only a valid DIBSection is sent to the **GetOurPixel** function. Otherwise, **GetPixel()**, the GDI function should be used, but I didn't put it in here for other reasons.

SetPixelValue code follows the same layout:

```
If m_nBitmapType = m_BMPDIB Then
    PutOurPixel m_dibsect, nPosX, nPosY, nPixel
End If
```

Changes to clsMem

For consistency, a new diagram for **clsMem** is:

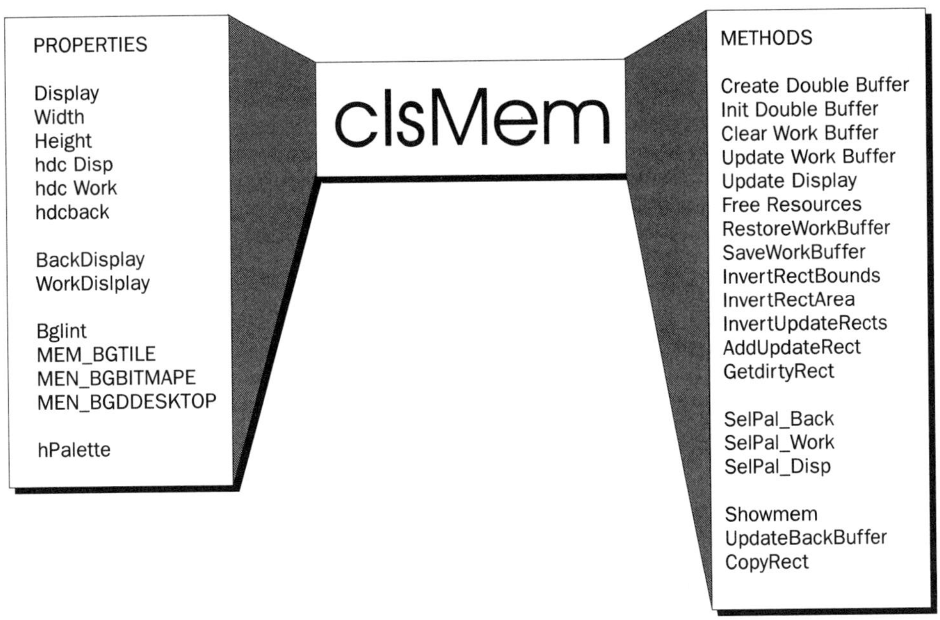

As you can see, few changes have been made, since this class isn't really (nor should it be) directly related to the use of a DIBSection or a DDB. There is, however, some tailoring that could have been done, to accommodate the use of the double buffer with the functions provided in **Dibsect.dll** (you'll see why as I get there). To make sure that the code was easy to follow, the new part to this chapter, I kept it separate from complicated class upgrades that may have been more appropriate for encapsulation purposes.

The reason for these changes to **clsMem** will become more apparent in the code that pertains to them. First of all, I added a method to allow blitting a rectangle from one DC to another. This enabled me to use the memory class's rectangle tracking capabilities to update the display in the right place, without having to use the strict functions that expect bitmap objects passed them, rather than DC handles. Here's what the code looks like in **CopyRect**:

```
nRet = StretchBlt(hdcDest, rDest.Left, rDest.Top, rDest.Right - rDest.Left,
rDest.Bottom - rDest.Top, hdcSrc, rSrc.Left, rSrc.Top, rSrc.Right - rSrc.Left,
rSrc.Bottom - rSrc.Top, SRCCOPY)
```

Basically, a set of rectangles is passed, along with a set of source and destination DCs for those rectangles, and a copy is performed. Well, that was painless—next?

Getting and Setting Pixels

Using **`BitBlt()`** or other like functions is the quickest and easiest way to change the pixel data of a DDB—note I said DDB. The reason these types of functions are so quick is precisely because they work with like data. Moving a rectangular block of pixel data from one DC to another requires no translation whatsoever to place the new pixel values onto the corresponding destination DC. If the current display mode is 8-bit, all DCs, display or compatible, will be created based on that current mode, so will be the same color mode. That means that an exact pixel match is performed, since each pixel takes up the same amount of space to hold its data.

Now for the tough part. What if you want to set individual pixels, not copying from another DC but actually affecting a DC's bitmap object directly? Next, I'm going to compare the process of getting and setting pixel data, without using one of the bit-block transfer methods and we'll see how the methods rate against each other. First, the DDB way, then the DIB way. Why would you want to do this? Assuming that the bitmap is a DDB, selected into a DC, you can move this data to any location you want. What you can't do is tell it to brighten its pixels or blend its pixels with another bitmap (unless you rely on one of the raster operations handling the exact blend you're looking for between the two DDBs). So far in this book, the focus has been on preparing any graphical data used by an application, so that it need not be affected in any way, except for the use of transparency and some other neat affects that used brushes and so forth. All of these operations were performed quite nicely using the bit-block transfer functions like **`BitBlt()`** and **`StretchBlt()`**.

What we haven't talked about is altering a graphic in memory dynamically, without copying the data to another DC to do so. If you run the sample **`Dibtest.vbp`**, you'll see that there's a button called Pixel GDI and one called Pixel DIB. These call functions which alter individual pixels of a DDB and a DIB, respectively.

GetPixel() and SetPixel()

These are two functions provided with the Windows API—**`GetPixel()`** and **`SetPixel()`**—the purpose of which is to get and set pixels on an individual basis when you don't want to do a block transfer. The **`SetPixel_GDI`** procedure contains the following code which loops through the entire working buffer, accessed conveniently through the memory class object and brightens each of the pixel's RGB values by 10 (in other words, brightens the entire image by an intensity of 10):

```
With g_objMem
      ' loop through each Y pixel
      For nPosY = 1 To .Height
        ' loop through each X pixel
        For nPosX = 1 To .Width
          ' get pixel value, boost by 10 each color
          nPixel = GetPixel(.hdcWork, nPosX, nPosY)
          nRet = SetPixel(.hdcWork, nPosX, nPosY, nPixel + &H101010)
        Next nPosX
      Next nPosY
```

```
        ' copy results to the display
        .UpdateDisplay
    End With
```

Here's a 'before and after' shot of our background:

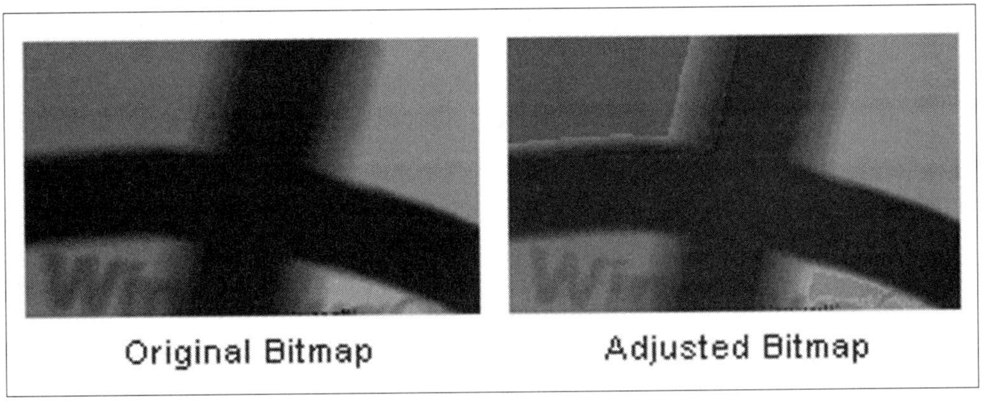

GetPixel() and **SetPixel()** are part of the GDI library. **GetPixel()** retrieves the color value for a pixel at a given *x, y* coordinate on the specified DC. Remember that with DDB bitmaps, their format inside the device context matches the current display mode. If the current display mode is 8-bit, the *x,y* coordinate on the 2D memory device context will return a palette index, into the device context's logical palette. That means a lookup must be performed to get the actual RGB value when **GetPixel()** is called, to return the color value.

SetPixel(), sets the value for a pixel for a given *x, y* coordinate on a specified DC. Once again, if the bitmap is stored in 8-bit, the 'setting' process needs to write a palette index to that position in the memory device context. This means that from the color value passed to **SetPixel()**, the closest match is looked up in the DC's logical palette, and the corresponding palette index is written to the bitmap coordinate. What's going on behind the scenes during this process will be apparent when I explain. Of course, if the DDB is in 8-bit format, the functions still return and accept color values, since the function is internally taking care of the actual bitmap bits, setting their values accordingly. This will make more sense when I explain how the **Dibsect.dll** handles the identical scenario.

The use of **GetPixel()** and **SetPixel()** is more efficient in situations where the bitmap area is very small, or only sparse pixels are being retrieved and set. In the Fun with Ducks game, checking a single pixel value for a hit test was trivial. In the Bad Dog screen saver, getting and setting a small area of pixels was unnoticeable. But here, we're pushing the envelope! Brightening the pixels of an entire bitmap's area is a lengthy process. That's where you really need to get into some raw data access, which is exactly what we're gonna do.

GetOurPixel() and SetOurPixel()

These two functions reside in the **Dibsect.dll** and are similar to the previously discussed GDI functions. The difference is that they work with DIBSection rather than DDBs. The following code performs the same pixel alteration as that described using GDI methods, located inside the **SetPixel_DIBSect** procedure:

```
With g_objMem

        ' boost all pixel values by 10
        For nPosY = 0 To .Height
          For nPosX = 0 To .Width
            nPixel = g_objDIBBg.GetPixelValue(nPosX, nPosY)
            g_objDIBBg.SetPixelValue nPosX, nPosY, nPixel + &H101010
          Next nPosX
        Next nPosY

        ' copy results to working buffer before copying to display
        g_objDIBBg.Blit
        .UpdateDisplay
End With
```

Again, each pixel in the background bitmap is iterated through, only this time, instead of using the working buffer of the memory class, which is a DDB, the copy of that background bitmap in DIBSection format is used (**g_objDIBBg**). This is done using the additional methods inside the bitmap class, **GetPixelValue** and **SetPixelValue**, which call **Dibsect.dll** as long as the **m_nBitmapType** variable is set to **m_BMPDIB**.

Within the DLL procedures for **GetOurPixel()** and **SetOurPixel()**, some detailed checking is going on to see if the DIB is stored as an 8-bit or 24-bit DIB. Both functions are passed and return an actual pixel value for the coordinate, but internally the functions treat this information differently. I described the meat of this process earlier when I discussed the process of reading pixel data as a single byte that specified an index to a color table, or a set of three bytes in a row, per pixel, that stored RGB information for the pixel. Either way, the end result is a change in the pixel's color value, or an accurate color value return, just like the GDI functions do. Now compare this function with the GDI method. It performs the same pixel brightness alteration in half the speed! Well, almost always.

What you'll notice is that there is a difference in speed when the DIB is a 24-bit and an 8-bit image. Remember that the DIB is stored as its original image was in memory, not as per the current device mode. That means, the palette index lookup doesn't happen when the image is 24-bit, even if the display mode is! So, the speed of the pixel alteration is slower when the image is 8-bit, since the palette index lookup must be performed every time a pixel is altered. Conversely, the alteration screams by comparison if the image is 24-bit. This may seem strange, since the image takes up more memory in 24-bit, but I'll enlighten you later on the possible fixes for this. It's a little (OK, a lot) beyond the scope of this book. As I've said more than once, direct pixel access is faster than using the GDI any day.

There are many permutations to this getting and setting of pixels, based on the current display mode (8-bit or higher color), but the focus of this comparison is the speed with which a change can be made to a pixel value, going through a DC versus going directly to the bitmap's bits. The DLL's functionality matches that of the GDI get and set methods and so the comparison is on equal grounds.

Transparent Blitting Methods

From VB alone, there's really only one way to create a transparent effect with bitmaps, which is to use the masking process and one of the bit-transfer methods that support this methodology. Now, I'm going to show you another way to get transparency out of a sprite like the bulls-eye ball. The button selections on the interface for **Dibtest.dll**, Blit GDI and Blit DIBSection, compare the process of bouncing the bulls-eye ball around the background, with transparency in both methods.

GDI uses both the **Ball256.bmp** and the **Ball256m.bmp**, where DIBSection requires only the **Ball256.bmp**. Of course, a DLL is required to perform the DIBSection example, because of the access to raw data being performed. Luckily, **Dibsect.dll** has been provided for that exact purpose.

Bitmasking with the GDI

Using the GDI way, a slick combination of raster operations and bitmaps makes a graphic transparent. I probably don't need to summarize this process, seeing as we've used it in almost every chapter in this book so far. We have to do some work up front for this to be possible, using a copy and a mask version of the same bitmap. From there, the bitmap class nicely encapsulates the copy and mask bitmap and the blitting calls made to the working buffer where the bitmap object is require a mask for transparency.

Inside the **Blit_GDI** procedure, the standard animation blitting code is part of the animation loop. None of this stuff is new, so I won't describe it again for you and the animation is simple. The move class is used to perform the erasing, moving and blitting of the bitmap, as we've done so many times before. The GDI may be slow with individual pixel manipulation, but loses no speed when it comes to blitting bitmaps, with or without transparency.

I'll show you the central part of the loop in the GDI procedure, for comparison with the DIBSection example:

```
With g_objBmpBall
  nStart = objTime.GetTime
  If g_objMove.Complete Then
    nRandX = Int((g_objMem.Width) * Rnd + 1)
    nRandY = Int((g_objMem.Height) * Rnd + 1)

    .SetStopPosition nRandX, nRandY
    g_objMove.Init_Move g_objBmpBall
  End If

  g_objMove.Move
  nCount = nCount + 1
End With 'g_objBmpBall
```

If we really wanted to, the Blit method of the bitmap class could use its **TransCol** (transparent color) property, and perform a pixel for pixel copy to the double buffer, skipping those pixels that match the **TransCol** value. Hmm... now that wouldn't be any extra work would it? Well, this is the work that the next function performs, only on raw data. In this case, you'll see that it's very necessary to get the job done.

TransparentBufferCopy()

The DIBSection way to perform a transparent copy is using the **TransparentBufferCopy()** function from the **Dibsect.dll**, provided for this chapter. It copies the pixels of a source DIBSection, starting at a specified point, to the destination DIBSection, starting at a specified point. While doing so, it refrains from copying pixels that match the transparent color value passed the function.

The following list are the parameters passed to this custom function:

- Destination **DIBSECTION**
- Destination **X**
- Destination **Y**
- Source **DIBSECTION**
- Source **X**
- Source **Y**
- Transparent **COLORREF**

We could alter this function to look more like **StretchBlt()**, where a width and height are also passed for the destination and source, but for simplicity, this sample assumes that your source is an animation bitmap, like one of the screen saver dogs (or the ball in this sample) where you want the entire source copied to the destination, with transparency. Keep this in mind if you use the function in another application somewhere.

Once again, this function cycles through each pixel of image data, setting the corresponding pixel data of the destination to the same value it came across in the source. Now, I'll show you the code that does it.

The movement class is initialized with the DIB version of the ball sprite, **g_objDIBBall**, rather than the **g_objBmpBall** object used in the GDI example. Notice that this works painlessly as if there were no differences (thank goodness for classes):

```
' initialize movement
With g_objMove
   .MoveDisplay = False
   .MoveMode = .MOV_POINT
   .Init_Move g_objDIBBall
End With
```

In this case, **MoveDisplay** is set to **False**, so that the **Move** method will not take care of blitting the sprite to the working buffer. This is because the copying of that data will be done using the **TransparentBufferCopy()** function in the **Dibsect.dll**, which will require a source and destination DIB for the raw data work to be done. You'll see.

Before the loop begins, the **GetObject()** API function must be called, for each of the DIBs to be used in this loop. This is because the function requires the use of two DIBSections and to access each bitmap object's **DIBSECTION** structure information, you must define a variable of type **DIBSECTION** and call **GetObject()** to fill them up. There's that lack of inheritance with VB classes again. I can't use the DIBSection information from the individual classes, outside of the class, without setting individual property procedures for each element in the structure... not in your dreams can you make a single function call and be done with it! Structures can't be returned from or passed to class procedures. So, there are some duplicate structures defined in the **modMain** module (for **DIBSECTION** and **BITMAP**), where this code resides:

```
Dim dsBg As DIBSECTION
Dim dsBall As DIBSECTION
```

```
    nRet = GetObject(g_objDIBBg.hDIB, Len(dsBg), dsBg)
    nRet = GetObject(.hDIB, Len(dsBall), dsBall)
```

When the move is complete, some of the same old initialization processes are performed inside the loop, to select another set of movement points for the DIB. The **ClearWorkBuffer** method is called using the location of the DIB object, **g_objDIBBall**. Nothing new here. Ahh, but the next line calling **CopyRect**, that new method supplied by the memory class, is called to copy the same rectangle from the background DC for the double buffer (**hdcBack**) to the background DIB object, **g_objDIBBg**.

The call to **TransparentBufferCopy()** needs to do the destination work on the background DIB, not on the working buffer of the memory class. As a result, any changes that we want reflected to the double buffer, so that the other useful aspects of these classes can still be used, should be copied directly to the appropriate location. That means changes made to the background DC of the double buffer must be also copied to the background DIB, and vice versa.

Transparent Copying with DIBSection

Here's the main loop using **TransparentBufferCopy()**, as compared to the loop shown earlier that uses GDI methods:

```
With g_objDIBBall
  nStart = objTime.GetTime
  If g_objMove.Complete Then
    nRandX = Int((g_objMem.Width) * Rnd + 1)
    nRandY = Int((g_objMem.Height) * Rnd + 1)

    .SetStopPosition nRandX, nRandY
    g_objMove.Init_Move g_objDIBBall
  End If

  ' clear working buffer and DIB background
  g_objMem.ClearWorkBuffer .rLoc
  g_objMem.CopyRect g_objDIBBg.hdc, g_objMem.hdcBack, .rLoc, .rLoc
  ' move ball
  g_objMove.Move

  ' use dibs to do transparent copy to dib background
  TransparentBufferCopy dsBall, 0, 0, dsBg, .Left, .Top, .TransCol
  ' copy ball location of background dib using blit method
  g_objDIBBg.Blit .rLoc
  g_objMem.UpdateDisplay
End With 'g_objDIBBall
```

The main difference between this animation loop and the earlier example (using GDI masking methods) is in the use of the **clsMove** object, **g_objMove**. In the GDI example, the Move method took care of erasing the previous frame of the ball, moving the bitmap object's position, and copying the new frame in its new position to the working buffer. In this example, the Move method (which handles GDI only) can't be used in its entirety. Since the **TransparentBufferCopy()** function is used to copy the bulls-eye DIB to the background DIB, in order to get the transparent sprite effect, the Move class call to the bitmap object's Blit method can't be used. The **MoveUpdate** property of **clsMove** is set to false, so that the Move method will only change the bitmap to its new position in the animation, without updating the double buffer in any way.

The **ClearWorkBuffer** method is called from the animation loop, before the Move method, to erase the previous position of the bulls-eye DIB from the working buffer. Since this doesn't clear the same area of background DIB (**ClearWorkBuffer** clears the double buffer DDB only) the memory class's new **CopyRect** method is required. This method copies a rectangular block of data from one DC to another, regardless of DIB or DDB selected into it. The DIBSection background bitmap (**g_objDIBBg**) is the one that is used as the background to copy the DIBSection ball bitmap to (**g_objDIBBall**) with transparency. It's after this process is completed with the DIBSection bitmaps that the background DIBSection is copied using **BitBlt()** to the working buffer of **clsMem**. This extra step is necessary, only because the DIBSection version of the background wasn't selected into the working device context of the memory class object. The process is summarized here:

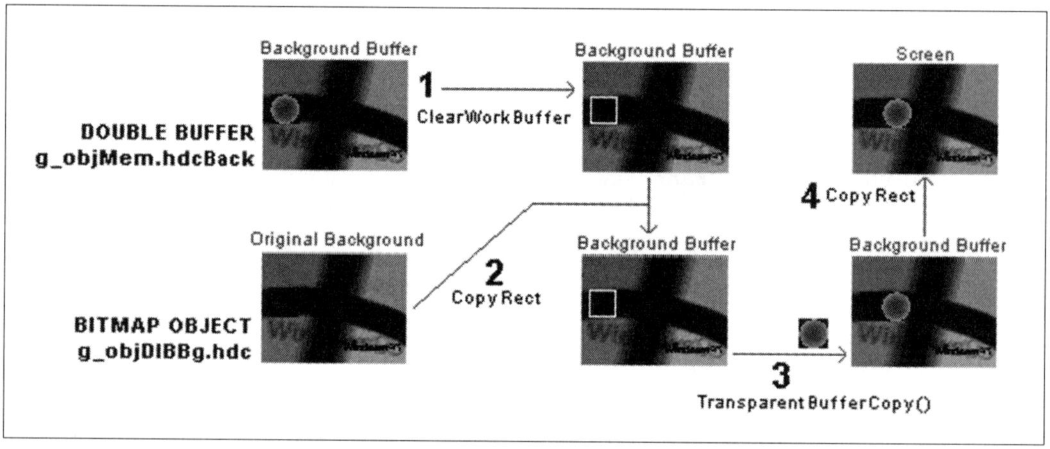

In this case, rather than blitting the sprite bitmap, **g_objDIBBall**, to the working buffer using our regular Blit method of the bitmap class, the background bitmap, **g_objDIBBg**, is blitted. Of course, the **rLoc** rectangle of the actual bitmap is passed to the Blit method of the background bitmap, so that only that updated area will be blitted to the working buffer. The difference is, the transparency has already been taken care of when the **TransparentBufferCopy()** was called, and the background bitmap doesn't have the **Blit** method of **BLT_MASK** so the raster operation of **SRCCOPY** is used when the double buffer is blitted to. This work-around facilitates using the classes to move the data to the working buffer and updating the dirty rectangles of the memory class that are so nicely encapsulated by these methods. Keep in mind that the DIBSection is the last new topic covered in this book, and that the classes used up to this point have been altered as little as possible so as not to confuse the functionality you've probably grown accustomed to. If you were to build a full application on DIBSection, you would likely want to encapsulate its functionality a little more into some new classes or some different memory and bitmap classes, to skip some of the extra steps performed here.

In the case of transparent copying methods, the comparison is not one of speed but of technique. There's no reason to use the **TransparentBufferCopy()** method to attain transparency with a sprite, unless your intention is to use the raw data of the graphics involved in the application, as you're about to see.

Image Manipulation Techniques

There are plenty of software packages out there that include capabilities which alter the pixels of an image to filter it in various ways. Things like tinting, changing the image to grayscale, and posterization are among the typical capabilities of such a program. All of this processing data is done with the original image in memory, by accessing its raw bitmap data. Imagine how slow image processing applications would perform if they used GDI methods, as in the comparative example earlier.

Without exploring the entire set of image processing techniques that many programs use, from the sample animation in this chapter I'm going to go through the different imaging techniques used to put it together. You've already had a peek under the hood of the **Dibsect.dll** and so now I'll describe the integration of that with the sample animation.

Dibanim.vbp

OK, now for the fun stuff. Now you know what a DIBSection is, how our classes have been updated to accommodate the DIBSection object, and you've seen the practical comparisons between the GDI and DIBSection methods. The only thing left is using DIBSection for those things that we couldn't have done before, which is having some fun and frolics at the pixel level!

Initialization

This simple animation uses the same graphics already described for the **Dibtest.vbp** example. This time, the only graphics read into memory are one copy of the background and one of the ball, in DIBSection format. Actually, there's one catch this time, which is that there's a choice of what color format you want the background and ball bitmap to be read in as. Since DIBSection bitmaps are not stored in the same format as the current display driver, but in the format that the bitmap is saved, a choice is given at the start of running the sample, asking if you would like to load 256 color graphics or not. If you answer yes to this dialog, the 256 color versions of each graphic are loaded. Select no to load 24-bit graphics of the same. Of course, 256 color graphics are easier on memory usage, but there is an interesting speed difference between using 256 color and full color bitmaps. Here's the small section in the **Form_Load** that takes care of this process:

```
If vbYes = MsgBox("Load 256 color graphics?", vbYesNo + vbQuestion, "Select a
graphics color format") Then
    ' load 256 color graphics
    DIBDC_LoadNew g_objDIBBg, "back256.bmp", False
    DIBDC_LoadNew g_objDIBBall, "ball256.bmp", True
Else
    ' load full color graphics
    DIBDC_LoadNew g_objDIBBg, "back24.bmp", False
    DIBDC_LoadNew g_objDIBBall, "ball24.bmp", True
End If
```

The interface for this sample is shown on the following page.

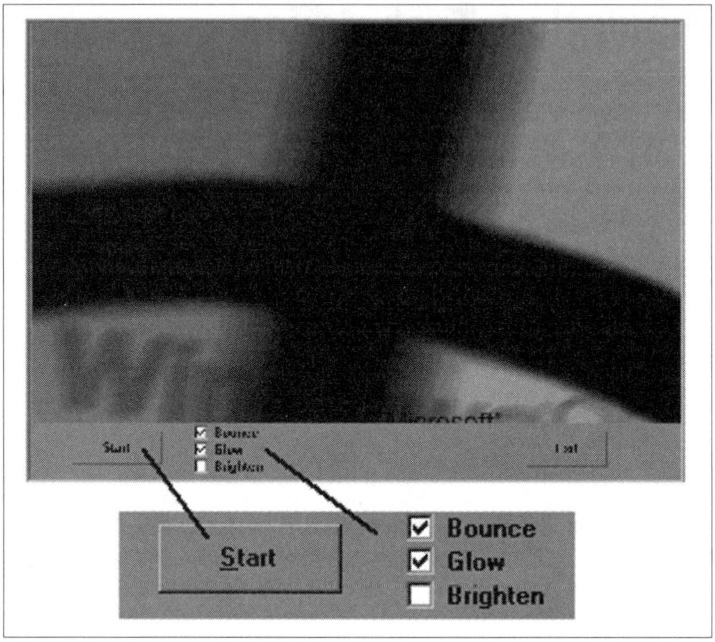

The background bitmap is copied to the display at start up but the animation doesn't begin until you hit the Start button. This button toggles between Start and Stop so that you can do so at any point in the animation. The three check boxes turn on and off the following aspects of the animation:

- Bounce: the ball bounces from random point to random point.
- Glow: the ball's transparency level is adjusted, rendering it from opaque to transparent.
- Brighten: the ball's color values are brightened.

Select one or all of the check boxes to vary the activity going on with the ball as the animation continues. The individual effects are described in the next sections, since they are performed with the other functions provided with the **`Dibsect.dll.`** They're performed by manipulating the bitmap data directly which, as we've already discussed, couldn't be done with any speed using the GDI. What you're about to learn is a snippet of what goes on behind the scenes in a real-live imaging program, so if image processing has ever stumped you, this will be enlightening!

DIBAnimate

The actual animation loop is contained in the DIBAnimate procedure in **`modMain`**. Most of the procedure is similar to the **`Dibtest.vbp`** animation, where the ball bounces around the display, from random point to random point. At the start of the actual animation loop, two calls to **`GetObject()`** are made to fill the local DIBSection structures, **`dsBall`** and **`dsBg`**. Within the animation loop these steps are followed:

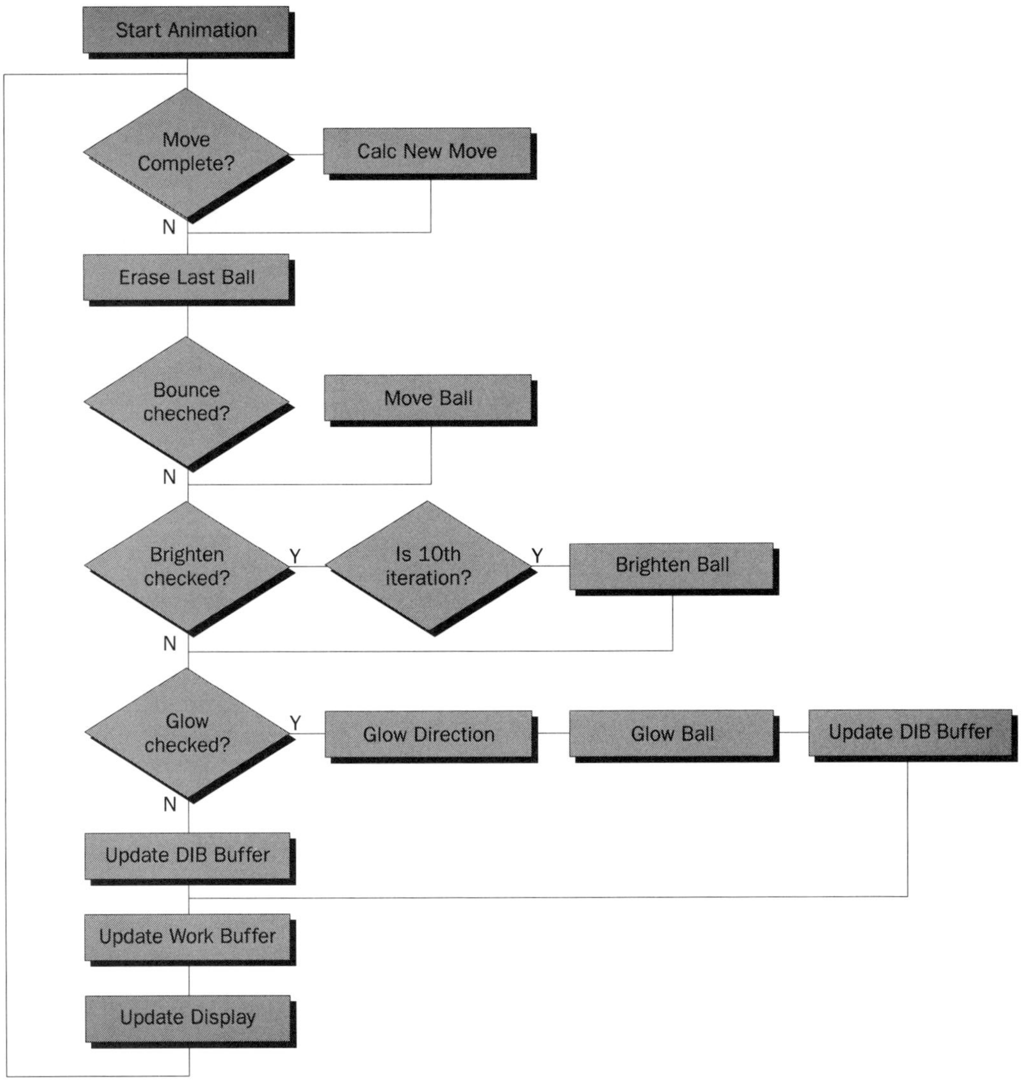

First, the previous location of the ball is erased from both the working buffer, and the background DIBSection, **dsBg**. Once again, the move class is not used to do the erasing since the processes involve DIBSection bitmaps rather than the standard double buffer work using bit-transfer methods. Then each of the components of the animation—bounce, glow and brighten—are performed if they are turned on. The move class is used for the bounce option, but is not updated to the display until the rest of the options have been tested. Something you'll notice in the movement option is that a **RECT** structure is updated, **rLoc**, to hold the **rLoc** elements of the ball bitmap class object. This is because the **Dibsect.dll** functions require that a rectangle structure is passed, not a VB rectangle class. This way, the rectangle is always up-to-date.

The process of copying the ball DIBSection bitmap with transparency has already been discussed with the **Dibtest.vbp** example earlier. The process of brightening the ball bitmap's pixels is performed first, then either the transparency adjustment or the transparent copy function is exercised based on the selections in the check box. The reason for this is because the **AdjBitmapTransparency()** function also copies the source DIBSection to the destination DIBSection. You'll see how this works shortly. Now, the color and transparency adjustment of the ball, as it's copied to the background, will be discussed in the following two sections.

Brightening Pixels

Even though you may already be aware of the process behind brightening an image, I'll explain the process. It consists of taking the RGB value of each pixel in an image, and increasing the intensity of each color to create a brighter version of the original color value. If you were to do the opposite, decreasing the intensity of each color in a pixel by an equal amount, the image would become darker. The key is to change each value by an equal amount, so that the actual color value doesn't change, just the intensity of the same color.

The section in the animation loop that calls **AdjBitmapColor()** is only performed if the corresponding check box is selected. So that the brightening doesn't take place too quickly to follow, a counter, **nCount**, is used to brighten only if the counter has a value of 10. For each loop, **nCount** is incremented to 10 and started over at 0 again:

```
If frmDibAnim.chkBrighten Then
  If nCount = 10 Then
    AdjBitmapColor dsBall, .hPalette, rArea, nColorBoost, .TransCol
  End If
End If
```

After the bitmap color has been adjusted, it still needs to be copied to the display, but this is taken care of in the last step of the loop, using either the **AdjBitmapTransparency()** or the **TransparentBufferCopy()** function, both of which copy the ball to a destination DIBSection. This function only updates a single DIBSection bitmap.

AdjBitmapColor()

The **AdjBitmapColor()** function takes the following parameters:

- A **DIBSECTION**
- A handle to a logical palette
- A **RECT** structure
- The amount to brighten
- A transparent color value

What happens in this function is that the DIBSection object, in this case the bulls-eye ball, is altered directly at the pixel level. Each pixel is examined from left to right, top to bottom and is individually brightened by the amount specified in the fourth parameter. Keeping in mind that pixels have three components that make up their color value—red, green and blue—and that their value can be anything from 0 to 255, you want to select an amount to brighten that will reflect the results you're looking for. In this sample, the variable **nColorBoost** is set to a value of 10, before the animation loop commences:

```
nColorBoost = 10
```

In looking at each pixel in the DIBSection passed to the function, the **RECT** passed is the area affected on the bitmap. This way, the function isn't restricted to always affecting the entire DIBSection bitmap passed to it. In this example, I always pass the entire rectangle of the ball bitmap. This is set at the initialization into a local **RECT** variable, **rArea**. Since the **rArea** property of the bitmap class is a rectangle class, it's not a structure that the DLL will understand when passed on the stack.

The other thing to be considered is the possible color that the bitmap uses for transparency. The reason for this should be clear, since if the call to **TransparentBufferCopy()** is made after the bitmap is brightened, the expected transparent pixels (RGB value 0, 0, 0) will be no longer considered transparent with their brightened value (RGB value 10, 10, 10 after one pass to **AdjBitmapColor()**). As each pixel is brightened, its color value is compared against the transparent color passed to the function, and if there's a match, the pixel is not brightened.

The second parameter is the bitmap's palette, which is used to look up the closest match to the newly brightened color if the bitmap is an 8-bit DIBSection.

8-bit and 24-bit Adjustments

When we discussed how the bitmap bits were stored earlier in this chapter, I explained that each pixel may have 1 byte assigned it, for a palette index, or 3 bytes, one for each RGB value. When we're calculating a new pixel value during the brighten bitmap function, we first have to find the pixel value. This is a quick process when the DIBSection is stored as 24-bit, since the raw data has a byte for each RGB value, ready and waiting. When it's stored as 8-bit, we must do lookup to the palette passed to the function (I have to assume that you have saved the palette for the DIB when the DIBSection was created). This, in itself doesn't add much hit time to the procedure, but the next step will.

You'll see if you run this sample loading 256 color bitmaps, rather than full color bitmaps, that the animation moves much slower. Regardless of the current display mode, there is work to be done behind the scenes for the color format of the DIB itself. What takes all the extra time in 256 color is not the look up to the palette for the pixel's color value, but what happens after the new pixel color has been calculated according to the requested color boost. Since the DIBSection data points to indexes in this fixed palette, rather than holding individual bitmap colors, the new color's closest match in the palette must be found, so *that* new color index can be set into the current byte for that pixel.

The **GetNearestPaletteIndex()** API function is the culprit. Doing this on an incidental basis may not be a big deal, but for every pixel in a bitmap it really slows things down. The return from the function is the palette index for a logical palette passed it, that most resembles the RGB value also passed, like so:

```
nNewIndex = GetNearestPaletteIndex(hPal, RGB(R, G, B))
```

What the really slick imaging programmers will do is come up with some functionality that performs a mathematical calculation on the pixel color to be used (this is known as a dithering function), so that the speed difference is not noticeable. Uhm, don't worry I won't even think of going in there.

Adjusting Pixel Transparency

The process of adjusting transparency can take place only when there's more than one bitmap involved. What transparency refers to in this case is whether or not a foreground bitmap (or sprite) is see-through over the background bitmap it's copied to. The results of copying the ball bitmap to the background with 0, 100 and 50 percent transparency, are shown here:

The amount of background to show through will depend on the level of transparency of the foreground bitmap.

In the animation loop, the check box that refers to the transparency level is called Glow, since the effect looks more like the ball is glowing over the background. A variable, **nGlowAmt**, holds the level of glow for the bitmap, and starts at 100 percent:

```
nGlowAmt = 100
```

This means that 100 percent of the ball should be shown, therefore it's opaque. The other variable that helps to track the glow of the ball is **nGlowDir**, which starts of at -10, meaning that **nGlowAmt** will now be decremented by 10 each loop:

```
nGlowDir = -10
```

If the Glow check box is selected, this code is executed:

```
If nGlowAmt = 100 Then
  nGlowDir = -10
ElseIf nGlowAmt = 0 Then
  nGlowDir = 10
End If
nGlowAmt = nGlowAmt + nGlowDir

AdjBitmapTransparency dsBall, rArea, dsBg, rLoc, .hPalette, nGlowAmt, .TransCol
```

When 0 or 100 is reached, the increment/decrement of the glow amount is reversed, which is what makes the ball appear to glow. Then, the **AdjBitmapTransparency()** function is called, passing the current glow amount along with the other required parameters.

AdjBitmapTransparency()

The **AdjBitmapTransparency()** function takes the following parameters:

- A source **DIBSECTION**
- A source **RECT**
- A destination **DIBSECTION**
- A destination **RECT**
- A logical palette
- A transparency level
- A transparent color value

The use of the source and destination **DIBSECTION** and **RECT** is obvious here:

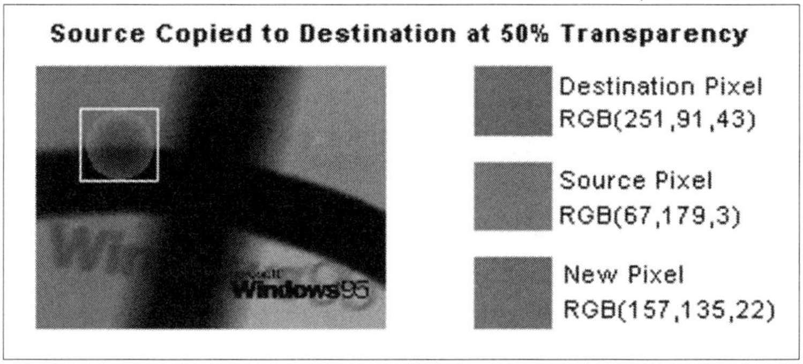

The size of the two rectangles should be the same for the function to perform accurately. For instance, if the ball was being copied to 0, 0 as shown in the diagram, then the source and destination rectangles should be the same. Each pixel of the source is compared with the same relative pixel of the destination and the transparency level is taken into consideration to determine what color this destination pixel should become.

If the source were to be copied with full opaqueness, a transparency level of 100, the pixels from the source should be copied in their current color. If they were to be copied with full transparency, a level of 0, the pixel color of the background should show through completely. Any other level of transparency requires a closer look at the source and destination pixels, which I'll describe in the next section. Once again, the palette must be passed to the function so that the resultant pixel can be looked up in the color table for the DIBSection, if the DIBSection is indeed in 8-bit format.

Finally, the transparent color, not to be confused with the actual transparency, is passed to the function. This is so that as each color is compared, pixel by pixel, if the source pixel is a designated transparent pixel, it's treated as non-existent (a transparency level of 0). In the diagram the bulls-eye is copied with 50% transparency, so the new pixel is a color value exactly between the source and destination color.

Pixel Blending Math

Just as with the **AdjBitmapColor()** function, when a new pixel color is to be calculated for a blend value, we first have to consider the issue of color format. Since two DIBSection bitmaps are passed to this function, both DIBSection's pixels must be looked up, pixel for pixel, then a new pixel value calculated. If either DIBSection is stored as 24-bit, there is no extra step involved in getting the color value for each pixel, but if the DIBSection is stored as 8-bit, the steps described earlier for brightening a bitmap's pixels should be followed.

In either case, once the source and destination RGB values are available, the math for calculating the blended pixel value must be performed. There are a few rules to follow that I'll describe. First of all, there must always be a foreground and background bitmap to perform any transparency calculations. Second, it's the foreground bitmap that is transparent, thus showing through the pixels beneath it on the background bitmap. Given this, some blend of the pixel color beneath shows through the pixel color in front of the background or destination. Having said that, in VB code, I'll walk through the code that determines the blend of each individual pixel.

Each RGB color component is first tested to see which of the source or destination pixels has a darker value of that component. If the source pixel has a darker red intensity, for instance, the resulting red value should be either the same (if the transparency level, amount, is 0), or less than it's current state, by some percentage closer to the destination's red intensity. If the destination pixel has a darker red intensity, the destination red should end up brighter, based on adding to the intensity of the source, using the transparency factor. The equation, written out the long way for simplicity, would look like this:

```
If (srcR > dstR)
  dstR = srcR - (((srcR - dstR) * amount)/100)
Else
  dstR = srcR + (((dstR - srcR) * amount)/100)
End If
```

Let's assume that the source red is of a higher intensity than the destination red. If the amount was 0, the source red intensity, **srcR**, would end up as the destination red intensity. If the amount was 100, the source red would subtract the entire difference between the source and destination red intensity, which ends up being the destination intensity. Any amount in between 0 and 100 ends up subtracting from the more intense source red intensity, some fraction of the difference between source and destination red intensity. The end result is that the less amount of the source that is requested to show through, results in a darker or less intense red.

If the destination is more intense than the source, the opposite is true. The end result should be that the destination red intensity becomes more intense, so is added to by some percentage of the amount of transparency.

The same is done for all color components, for every pixel in the source and destination rectangles that line up:

```
If (srcG > dstG)
  dstG = srcG - (((srcG - dstG) * amount)/100)
Else
  dstG = srcG + (((dstG - srcG) * amount)/100)
End If
If (srcB > dstB)
  dstB = srcB - (((srcB - dstB) * amount)/100)
Else
  dstB = srcB + (((dstB - srcB) * amount)/100)
End If
```

At the end of this process, the resulting destination pixel RGB must be written to the destination DIBSection. This destination DIBSection acts as the working buffer for this process. If the destination bitmap is stored in 8-bit, the resulting blended pixel value must be looked up in the palette passed to the function for a closest match, so that the index into the palette can be set to the corresponding pixel's.

When you're planning any application's display bitmaps, (if all the graphics are 256 color) you can assume that they're assigned the same palette. There's no point in confusing the code to calculate the same palette for these graphics. It would be completely unnecessary extra work.

Summary

So there you have it. A touch of imaging and animation in one! Of course, the imaging techniques used here are provided as a lesson in what you can do with graphics, that goes a little beyond your standard animation. Where you would apply these techniques depends on the results you're looking for. Regardless, being aware of what you can do with graphics is the first step in creating new and exiting applications. Often, what limits us as VB programmers is the lack of awareness of what goes on with the bits and bytes, since we're sheltered from this by the development environment. But it's amazing how easy it is to understand what's happening behind the scenes once you're introduced to it in a smaller venue than the C development environment (that is, if you're not familiar with it yet). It also makes experimentation with the Windows API much easier when you know what's happening behind the scenes.

We have covered the foundation for animation as each chapter unfolded throughout this book. We started with some simple animations, using VB and what needed improvement because of the limitations of VB graphics capabilities. The use of the Windows API along with double-buffering and creating transparent graphics, started you on your way to a smoother and better animation. Then, we introduced palettes, never to be left out of the conversation again, since they are paramount to the portability of any application, especially animations which rely heavily on graphics.

After covering these fundamental topics at an introductory level, I showed you some real applications that put those techniques to use, using animation in various venues. The demo, duck game and screen saver all demonstrated animation techniques. Each example introduced something new and interesting to the code. After this chapter, you're left to explore each of these topics further, adding imaging techniques to the list of subjects to dive into.

Now you can see that there's no reason that VB can't do almost anything you want it to. You just have to part your hair on the other side for a moment and take VB on an off-roading adventure!

```
rivate Declare Function GlobalFree Lib "kernel32" (ByVal h
rivate Declare Function GlobalLock Lib "kernel32" (ByVal h
rivate Declare Function GlobalUnlock Lib "kernel32" (ByVa
--copying bitmap bits
 copies a global block of data into global memory
rivate Declare Sub CopyMemory Lib "kernel32" Alias "RtlM

--copies global block of data in   B
rivate Declare Function SetDIB      "gdi32" (ByVal m_hd
 ByVal hBitmap As Long, ByVal nStartS     As Long, ByV
 ByVal lpBits As Any, lpBI As BITMAPI     ByVal wUsa

--blits DC to DC
rivate Declare Function BitBlt Lib "gdi32" (ByVal hDestDC
rivate Declare Function StretchBlt Lib "gdi32" (ByVal hDes

--palette methods
rivate Declare Function CreatePalett     "gdi32" (lpLogPa
rivate Declare Function SelectPalette     "gdi32" (ByVal m
rivate Declare Function RealizePalette Lib "gdi32" (ByVal m
rivate Declare Sub AnimatePalette Lib "gdi32" (ByVal hPal

--device context methods
rivate Declare Function SelectObject Lib "gdi32" (ByVal m_

rivate Declare Function CreateCompatibleBitmap Lib "gdi32
rivate Declare Function DeleteObject Lib "gdi32" (ByVal hO

rivate Declare Function CreateCompatibleDC Lib "gdi32" (B
```

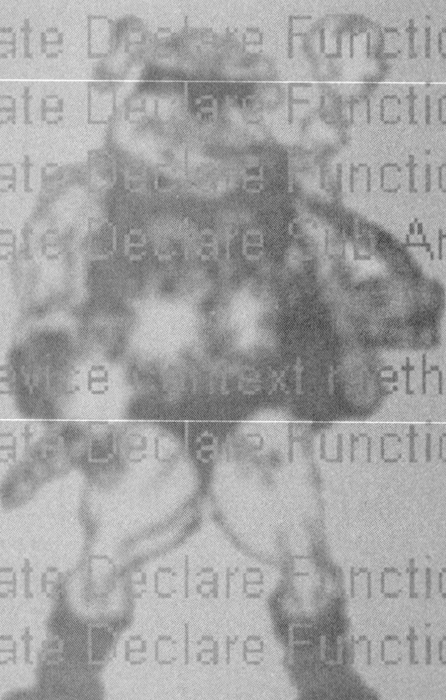

INSTANT

VB Animation

Appendix A

Buffing Out VB

The first area of dynamic linked libraries or DLLs is of such importance that I decided to give them an Appendix of their own. The reason? Well, you simply can't live without them. They give you the power to completely customize your applications. The Window API DLLs play an extremely important role in a polished VB program, especially when you're talking graphics and effects. In no time, you'll have your VB applications swelling with capabilities that you didn't know existed! What's more, you won't have to bulk up your installation using the Windows API. They're part and parcel of the Windows operating system.

What are DLLs?

DLLs have a lot in common with EXEs. I'll summarize the EXE first, for a point of reference. A typical Windows executable can have these components:

- A startup function
- A user interface
- A place where messages are evaluated
- Numerous other functions and subroutines

Although there doesn't *have* to be a visible window sporting an interface, this is standard. The startup function in VB, **`Sub Main()`**, sets up the interface and prepares the program's environment. In every Windows program, there's something called a **window procedure** which acts as a message-handling center. It's called each time a message is sent to the program. From this central location, other functions and subroutines are called to execute the appropriate process based on the message received. VB houses this message hub for us and takes care of calling the appropriate event procedure, that is, if we've written code for it.

A DLL is, in actuality, *also* an executable. What's special about it is that it can 'export' any number of its functions and, in doing so, makes them available to other running applications. It's the nature of a file that exports one or more functions that makes it a DLL, but EXEs and OCXs can be considered *types* of DLLs when they export some form of functionality. In doing so, they are considered to have DLL properties.

How are the functions made available? When a DLL is created, the programmer specifies which functions should be exported. These are the functions that can be accessed by other applications. I won't go into detail about the C side of things, but it helps to be able to picture what makes DLL functions available to other applications, where the code resides, and so on. A C DLL has a project file, similar to our VBP file, known as a definition file (**.def**). This is where information about the project is located, though not in the same format as VB's. The **Dibsect.dll**, a custom DLL used and discussed in Chapter 7, exports six functions, named in the **.def** file under the heading **EXPORTS**, where functions are explicitly exported. The **Dibsect.cpp** file contains the exported functions, but there is also a **Dib.cpp** file that contains other functions, referenced internally. When the DLL is compiled, it creates the file so that those functions listed under **EXPORTS** can be found by Windows when the DLL is loaded into memory.

```
LIBRARY       DIBSECT.DLL

DESCRIPTION  'Dib Section Utility Windows Dynamic Link Library'

EXPORTS
    ; Explicit exports can go here
      TransparentBufferCopy    @1
      LoadCreateDibSection     @2
      AdjBitmapColor           @3
      AdjBitmapTransparency    @4
      GetOurPixel              @5
      PutOurPixel              @6
```

```
DIBSECT.CPP
...
...
HANDLE __declspec(dllexport) __stdcall LoadCreateDibSection(LPSTR fname, HDC hDC,
HPALETTE *hPalette)
{
       return (OpenDIB(fname, hDC, hPalette));
}
...
...
```

In the following figure, you can see how DLL functions interact with other running applications. Notice that there can also be functions within it that are only accessible internally (by the DLL itself) because they are not specifically 'exported'. Those functions that *were* exported by a DLL will appear to the calling program as though they were a function inside that program. For instance, **LoadCreateDIBSection** (which reads a bitmap from disk into memory, including any palette information) actually calls another function called **OpenDIB** which isn't exported. Now let's see how linking takes place for the DLL call to be possible.

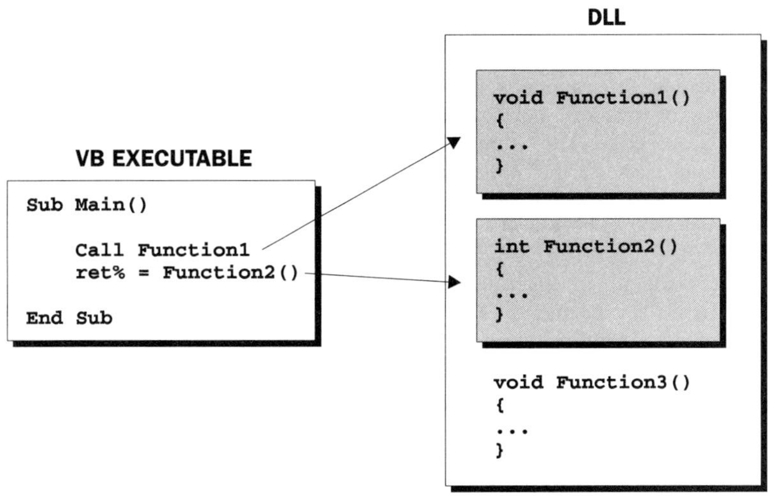

How DLLs Work

When we create a VB program, we use **Declare Function** statements to describe any external procedures that the program will need to use, along with the library or DLL they are located in. The following example declares the **TextOut** function (used in Chapter 2) located in the DLL **Gdi32.dll**:

```
Declare Function TextOut Lib "gdi32" (ByVal hdc As Long, ByVal x As Long, ByVal y
As Long, ByVal lpString As String, ByVal nCount As Long) As Long
```

This function returns a **Long** value (defined at the end of the statement **"As Long"**) and passes five parameters (more details to come on DLL declarations and variables). For now, know that there could be several **Declare** statements, each defining a unique procedure located either in the same DLL (**Gdi32.dll**) or in another DLL's library of functions. VB loads all of the necessary DLLs, defined in these declarations, when the VB application is first executed. Though the library itself may be referenced in more than one declaration, only one physical instance of the DLL is loaded into memory. That's the whole purpose of using them, so that one library of functions can be used by many programs. The details of the declared procedures are not used when the library is loaded, but when the actual function is called in your VB code.

So, VB gets the DLL into memory for us. In fact, another DLL function is used to load these DLLs! As you'll see when you read further about the Windows API, there are DLLs that are already available in memory just by running Windows. Every Windows executable can use the exported functions in these preloaded DLLs. When VB encounters a declare statement that points to a DLL that's already in memory, it doesn't attempt to load it again.

How are the DLL functions accessed? When a library is loaded into memory, Windows keeps track of the place (address) in memory where it can be found. At this time, Windows also fills its address book with a list of memory addresses, each one pointing to an exported DLL's function. This is what makes those procedures readily accessible as they are called. Now, how these memory locations are actually accessed is beyond the scope of our required knowledge—whew!—since Windows handles *that* one for us.

The Windows API

API stands for **Application Programmer's Interface**. An *interface* is anything that invites interaction between two processes or systems. For example, programs usually provide a 'user' interface for users to interact with our code. They don't call our functions by name, but, essentially, that's what they're doing when they click on the Quit button and the code calls the **End** function for them. Windows API doesn't quite soften the blow as much for us to use *its* functionality. We have to know **where** the function can be found, its **name** *and* its expected **parameters** and **returns**.

The Windows API is made up of several DLLs that expose functions for use with Windows programs. These DLLs go by the names **KERNEL, USER** and **GDI**. We must load them into memory for the Windows operating system to run, since they house almost all of Windows' functionality. This is much the same as VB applications need to load the appropriate runtime DLL (**VB40016** or **VB40032**) to access all of the VB function calls that we make throughout our VB applications.

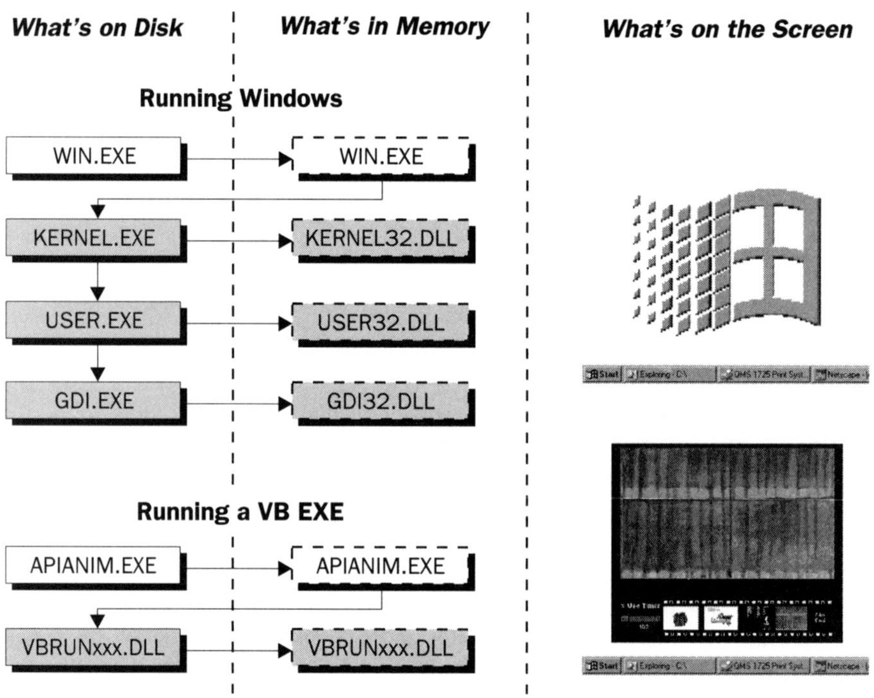

Each of the Windows DLLs were components of the original Windows 3.x environments. In Windows 95, this functionality was upgraded to support 32-bit applications, so there are now two versions for each of these files:

- **Kernel.exe, Kernel32.dll**
- **User.exe, User32.dll**
- **Gdi.exe, Gdi32.dll**

Note that some have an **.exe** extension, but they are not application executable's with a user interface and so forth. The original Windows DLLs were named as EXEs, and the 32-bit equivalents are 32-bit versions of the same functionality, plus some new functionality to boot. These DLLs supply over 1000 functions for external use by any running Windows application. The table below describes the functionality each Windows API DLL supports:

DLLs	Supported Functionality
KERNEL	System issues like message delegation and queuing, communication, memory management and general issues for running applications.
USER	User interface, including windows, dialogs and menus.
GDI	Graphics capabilities, like line drawing, icons, bitmap images or the fun stuff!

Let's look at how the Windows API and other DLLs are used by a Visual Basic application.

Select Your Function

I've spoken briefly of what DLLs are, how their functions are exported for use by other applications and how VB declares these functions in order to use them freely throughout program code. Before you can introduce any extensibility to a VB application through DLLs, you first need to find the right DLL that will do what you're looking for. You'll need to:

- Find useful DLLs.
- Define areas where a DLL can augment your program's capabilities.
- Locate procedures to facilitate this improvement.
- Learn all the new theories that circle those new procedures, so you don't miss something!

Most often, the Windows API is the first place you will look to for enhancing VB's functionality. After all, these DLLs provide virtually all the standard Windows programming capabilities, some of which VB doesn't provide, and they're resident on everyone's Windows machine so you don't have to distribute them. Other software development kits—specifically kits providing highly specialized functionality like compression or live video-capture—usually provide DLLs for use by Windows programs written in either C or Pascal. In fact, they'll often provide special DLLs or OCXs for VB use. This is because not all DLLs are defined so that VB can access exported functions—certain types of parameters that DLL functions expect may require the use of pointers in such a way the VB can't handle the conversion properly when calling the function. An alternative is creating home-grown DLLs to perform specific tasks not provided elsewhere.

Where you enhance VB's capabilities is an individual decision. The answer lies in whether or not VB is performing all of the necessary functionality that your program needs. If it is, there's obviously no need to pursue further help. If it isn't, knowing where you can find help is the first step, the second is finding the appropriate method of help and implementing it, hopefully without biting off more than you can chew! We'll start off with a few basic API calls that improve VB's animation methods, but throughout the book you'll find many of the advanced techniques need *mucho* assistance (oh, that means 'a lot') and you'll see what to do about it.

Having defined an area of code requiring improvement and having decided that there *are* DLL functions available to assist, you'll need to locate the source DLL and look for the desired function's description and prototype. The description is what will tell you if the function indeed provides the means to an end. The function prototype becomes the next step to making your VB declarations—this comprises the name of the function and DLL, the expected parameters and the return type if applicable. Of course, if the DLL is home-grown, you won't need documentation to tell you any of this information—you probably designed it yourself!

Windows API DLLs are described in the **API32.hlp**file provided with the CD. This is where you'll look to see what each API function does to decide if it is useful to you. There's just one catch: it doesn't tell you *which* DLL to find it in! Thus, your next stop, is VB4's **API Text Viewer**. Once you know the API functions you want to use and have seen the constants it may require as parameters or returns, you can easily copy the function and constant declarations into your VB code by way of VB's **API Text Viewer**. This will include the library name for your convenience. For the most part, this means you don't really have to understand the translation of the function prototype into VB terms, i.e. how the string variable passed to this function and so forth.

This isn't to say that you shouldn't be aware of the methods that VB should follow to pass a parameter of a specific type to a DLL function. We *will* come across some instances throughout this book where the prototype needs a little massaging for it to work with VB. Also, other third-party DLLs, though they provide their own documentation and a prototype, don't always provide the actual VB declarations. In these instances, you must make sure the parameters you are passing match the correct protocol, practice makes perfect.

DLL Declarations

Now you must declare the list of external DLL procedures that you want to call from your VB. **Declare Function** and **Declare Sub** are two statements in VB that describe external procedures. Here are two example declarations:

```
Declare Sub GetSystemTime Lib "kernel32" (lpSystemTime As SYSTEMTIME)

Declare Function PtInRect Lib "user32" (lpRect As RECT, ByVal ptX&, ByVal ptY&) As
Long
```

Declare Sub is used to define procedures that don't return a value, like a VB subroutine. There are very few API calls that don't return a value, which gives the somewhat oddball example used here, **GetSystemTime()**. **Declare Function** is used to define procedures that *do* return a value, like a VB function. The **PtInRect()** example above demonstrates a function that returns a **Long** value. An alternative method to describe a **Long** value return from a DLL function is by using the type-declaration character for **Long** (**&**) in the declaration, after the function name, in this case **PtInRect()**, rather than at the end of the declaration:

```
Declare Function PtInRect& Lib "user32" Alias "PtInRectA" (lpRect As RECT, ByVal
ptX&, ByVal ptY&)
```

To describe other return types, you would use their type-declaration instead, like integers (**%**) or strings (**$**).

From the same two sample declarations, you can see that the function or subroutine name is stated after **Declare Function** or **Declare Sub**. This function name must match with the name as it appears in the DLL's prototype. After the procedure's name, the location is stated in quotes after the keyword **Lib**. In our example, **User32.dll** is the library and it doesn't require that we type in the full name and extension of the file. Normally, with other DLLs you would include the extension **.dll** within the quotes.

The **PtInRect()** function is one of those special cases where the API Text Viewer's declaration doesn't work if it's used as is. Here's how it's declared:

Declare Function PtInRect Lib "user32" Alias "PtInRect" (lpRect As RECT, pt As POINTAPI) As Long

The **RECT** structure and **POINTAPI** structure are commonly used custom types that define a rectangle or a point. These are defined as follows in the Windows API definitions:

```
Type RECT
     Left as Long
   Top as Long
   Right as Long
   Bottom as Long
End Type
```

```
Type POINTAPI
    ptX as Long
    ptY as Long
End Type
```

This makes sense because the function tests whether a point is inside the specified rectangle. Quick and easy.

The **RECT** structure parameter is expected as an address to that rectangle information, which works fine from VB if you pass the structure by reference. The problem is with the **POINT** structure, which is expected to be passed as the collective point information, which means it should be passed by value, using the **ByVal** keyword. This doesn't work from VB, so the only way to 'fool' the DLL into thinking it was passed two **Long** values **ByVal**, is to pass two **Long** values **ByVal**! On the VB side, we're actually adding a parameter to the declaration that isn't there and it works! This is how the code looks that calls the function:

```
Dim rectstruct as RECT
Dim ptstruct as POINTAPI

nRet = PtInRect(rectstruct, ptstruct.ptX, ptstruct.ptY)
```

Another example function that uses the **POINTAPI** structure as a parameter is the **GetCursorPos()** function. Rather than sending the data, this function is also expecting to receive new data into the structure. Since the point is expected to be filled in, it's expected to be passed by reference and the declaration can safely use the API Text Viewer's version of it, like so:

Declare Function GetCursorPos Lib "user32" Alias "GetCursorPos" (lpPoint As POINTAPI) As Long

One thing to note about declarations is that, sometimes, an alias (an alternative procedure name) is the internal name for the function or procedure. We truly need the API Text Viewer to supply us with this information, since, from any API help file, all you can see is the external name for the procedure. An example is the procedure **PtInRect()**. As you can see from the earlier declaration for the function, the alias is **PtInRectA** and, if this were not there, the function call would fail.

Looking back at our two sample declarations **GetSystemTime()** and **PtInRect()**, you can see that the former requires that a structure called **SYSTEMTIME** is passed to the DLL. This is passed without the keyword **ByRef**, as is the **RECT** structure to the **PtInRect()** function, because that is the default. **ByRef** means that the variable (or, in this case, an entire structure) that is passed, can be altered or sometimes filled in by the function. When your code calls the subroutine **GetSystemTime**, though it's not a function returning a value, upon its return there will be current values inside the **SYSTEMTIME** structure. Conversely, variables passed **ByVal** can't be altered because only the actual value of the variable passed is received by the DLL, not the address in memory where the variable information is stored. Unless, of course, the variable is a string. (You knew things couldn't be straight forward in *every* case didn't you?)

> **Note that ByRef passes the address of a variable, so the called function can *look* at this address and read the value or change it, whereas ByVal passes only the value of the variable and doesn't say where it's stored.**

The string variable defies the theory of passing by value and by reference. Generally, strings are always passed **ByVal** but they can still be altered when this is done. This is due to the fact that VB does not support pointers to memory addresses and so to alter a string's contents, the whole buffer must be passed anyways, pre-filled to the length of the string that the DLL can write to it. If you don't pre-fill it, look out! The function will try to write information to a location that has not been allocated yet!

The most important and sometimes tricky part of these declarations is the parameters that need to be passed to the function. If the parameters are not declared *exactly* as the DLL expects—ssssseeeeee ya, the program can crash.

The GPF Lives On

It used to be, pre-Windows 95, that a GPF (General Protection Fault) was an ugly, non-explanatory white dialog box. You knew hitting one of the dialog's buttons would send you out of your program and sometimes, for the jackpot crash, right back to DOS. Now, there's a more appealing looking dialog, still with no enlightening news about the crash and you don't have to reboot afterwards but you still lose the culprit program's instance.

A GPF is still about as annoying as it was before, because you're still left on your own to investigate the cause. The worst thing about it is... it's your fault!

```
rivate Declare Function GlobalLock Lib "kernel32" (ByVal h
rivate Declare Function GlobalUnlock Lib "kernel32" (ByVa
-copying bitmap bits
 copies a global block of data into global memory
rivate Declare Sub CopyMemory Lib "kernel32" Alias "RtlM

-copies global block of data in
rivate Declare Function SetDIB           "gdi32" (ByVal m_hd
 ByVal hBitmap As Long, ByVal nStartS      As Long, By
 ByVal lpBits As Any, lpBI As BITMAPI      ByVal wUsa
```

```
-blits DC to DC
rivate Declare Function BitBlt Lib "gdi32" (ByVal hDestDC
rivate Declare Function StretchBlt Lib "gdi32" (ByVal hDes

-palette methods
rivate Declare Function CreatePalett      "gdi32" (lpLogPal
rivate Declare Function SelectPalette      "gdi32" (ByVal m
rivate Declare Function RealizePalette Lib "gdi32" (ByVal m
rivate Declare Sub AnimatePalette Lib "gdi32" (ByVal hPal

-device context methods
rivate Declare Function SelectObject Lib "gdi32" (ByVal m_

rivate Declare Function CreateCompatibleBitmap Lib "gdi32
rivate Declare Function DeleteObject Lib "gdi32" (ByVal hO

rivate Declare Function CreateCompatibleDC Lib "gdi32" (B
```

Appendix B

The Easy Route to Understanding Computer Math

Tricky Methods

There comes a time in every programmer's life where he or she must take a short detour to the wonderful world of computer math. It must be said that a little mathematical involvement is unavoidable when you're coding in the world of animation and games, but I don't want you getting worried now—this won't hurt a bit!

About Bits and Bytes

Right around the time you thought you had basic mathematics down, along came bits and bytes. Here's where we vigorously rip apart decimal numbers, transforming them into these bits and bytes. A number can be represented differently by changing its number base or **notation**. See how the decimal value of 49 is displayed here in octal, hexadecimal and binary notation:

Number Base	Value (Decimal 49)
Decimal = base 10	49
Octal = base 8	61
Hexadecimal = base 16	31
Binary = base 2	110001

All numbers are inevitably converted into binary for the computer to discern and manipulate them. In the next figure, we show the binary representation of the decimal number 49, bit by bit. Using binary notation, the result is calculated by adding together all of the 'on' bits' actual values. Each bit can be either 0 or 1, but the value is calculated by the bit's position (starting from the right at 0) where the position represents the exponent to which the base is raised. In decimal, the value 49 is calculated this way:

4 * (10 ^ 1) + 9 * (10 ^ 0) = 49

The only difference with binary is that the base changes to 2, shown from right to left here up to the last 'on' bit,

1 * (2 ^ 5) + 1 * (2 ^ 4) + 0 * (2 ^ 3) + 0 * (2 ^ 2) + 0 * (2 ^ 1) + 1 * (2 ^ 0) = 49

or, reading each bit's value based on its binary representation:

32 + 16 + 0 + 0 + 0 + 1 = binary 110001 = 49

Instead of using a separate binary number for every flag your program requires, you can use each individual bit position as a flag. If the bit is on, the bit value is 1, if it's off, the bit value is 0. This means explicitly turning bits on and off and ignoring the decimal value altogether. So the 16-bit number in the following figure can hold up to 16 different Boolean answers (true or false) represented by 1 or 0. Starting from the rightmost bit, the decimal value 49, shown here, currently has 3 flags of the 16 turned on (those in positions 0, 4, and 5) while the rest are off:

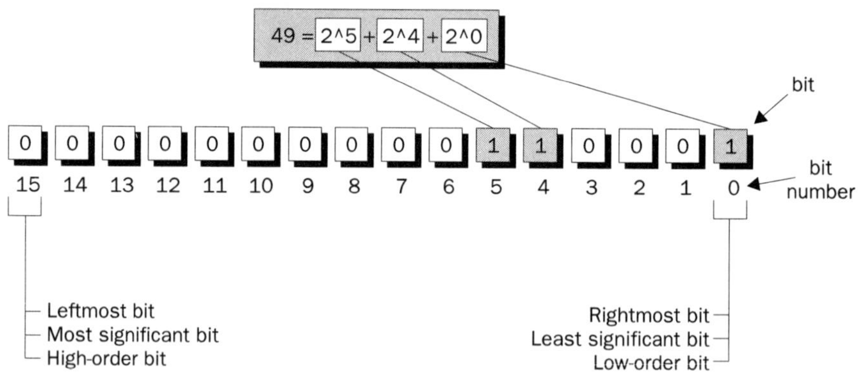

What this means to a given program is up to the programmer. You decide which position means what.

Once again, there's a distinction between VB and C. We can't specify VB's numeric data types as 'unsigned'. The high-order bit (15th position) is used to identify a number as positive or negative when it's read as a decimal value. This means that a VB integer can only create a decimal value up to 32767 (only 15 bits count) rather than 65535 (all 16 bits count). If you're using the integer to toggle bits on and off, the high-order bit being turned on would simply indicate that the 16th flag is on. Just remember that, in decimal terms, if that bit is 'on', the number is negative. When you're manipulating bits, if you need a value that represents 'all bits off', that value is 0. Some programmers use -1 as an 'invalid' value that they *think* won't turn any bits on. In fact, the value -1 is represented by *all* bits being turned on:

1111 1111 1111 1111 = -1

Twiddling Bits

Here's where the fun begins. Twiddling is the actual act of manipulating the individual bits of a numeric value. There are several things you can do:

- Turn a single bit on or off
- Turn a group of bits on or off at one time
- Check to see whether an individual bit is on or off
- Check to see whether a group of bits are on or off

You do this using bit operators. You may have actually been using this method for some time, using the operators supplied with VB. See the effects of each of them in the following table:

Operator	Example	Operator	Example
OR	1101 1000 1101	**AND**	1101 1000 1000
XOR	1101 1000 0101	**NOT**	1101 0010

Bitwise operations compare bits in identical positions in two numbers, using the operator as the basis of comparison. You can see from the table the results from each operation when two bits are on, one bit is on or both are off. **NOT** is a special operator that uses a single number's bits and 'flips' or inverts each bit to the opposite value.

Manipulating individual bits, turning them on or off, or checking their value, is where it gets tricky. First, you need to find the bit position. You do this by comparing the value of the byte before and after the bit is turned on. Using the first figure as an example, to turn the second bit on, you need to take the number value and use a comparison that would turn bit position 1 on, leaving the rest as they are. We know from the previous table that using the **OR** operator if one or both bits are 1s, gives the result 1. The two 0s result in 0. So, **OR**-ing 49 with 2 ^ 1 will result in the number 51, which turns on bit 1 (the second bit).

You can see the result of **OR**-ing decimal 49's bits with decimal 2's bits opposite. Decimal 2 is the value of only the second bit turned on in an integer (2 ^ 1). This results in the second bit being turned on and the decimal value becomes 51:

0000 0000 0011 0001 **OR**
0000 0000 0000 0010
0000 0000 0011 0011

Any time you want to turn a single bit on, you simply need **OR** with a value representing all the bits off, except for those you want turned on. Now, turning bit 1 off again requires a clever move. To do this, you need to **AND** with all the bits on except for the one we wish to turn off! This is where the **NOT** operator saves the day.

Using **AND** without **NOT** will turn all bits off:

0000 0000 0011 0011 **AND**
0000 0000 0000 0010
0000 0000 0000 0010

0000 0000 0011 0011 **AND**

Using **AND** with **NOT** on the second value: 0000 0000 0000 0010 **NOT** 1111 1111 1111 1101

0000 0000 0011 0001

This way, any bit that is on in the first value will stay on when it encounters a 1 in that position in the second value. All bits are 1s, except the one that is to be turned off. The 0 bit(s) in the second number will turn the same bit position off in the first number, regardless of whether it's on or off already. So to turn a bit off, you need to **AND** the value that contains the bit you want turned off, with all the bits on *except* the one you want turned off. Then all the bits that were on will stay on, *but,* the bit in question will get toggled.

An Easier Way

Seeing how decimal values compute into binary bits is important in understanding how the individual bits of a decimal number can mean something, even when the number doesn't! However, you'll be glad to know that there's an easier way to follow the turning on and off of bit values.

Consider the next diagram, which uses the number 49's bits and shows what decimal numbers need to be used to **OR** with the value 49 to turn on the specified bits:

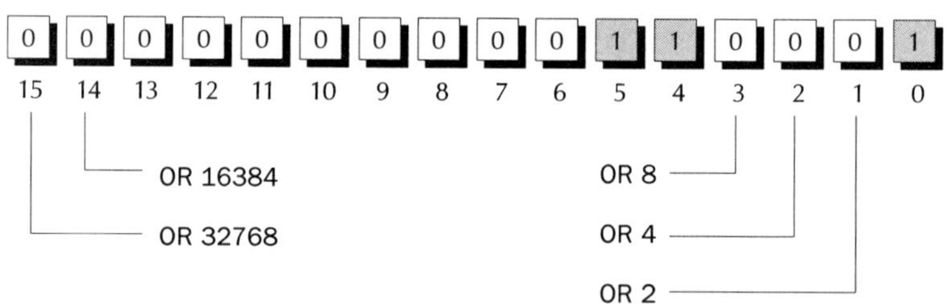

For turning bits 1, 2 and 3 on, it's easy to remember that decimal values 2, 4 and 8, respectively, turn those bits on when the two values (49 and the bit value) are combined with the **OR** operator. When you get to turning higher bit positions in, you need a really good memory. Notice the numbers required to turn bit 14 and 15 on are 16384 and 32768, respectively.

Now for the easy way. In Chapter 2, we described a bit-masking class which includes an array of numbers that each represent a numeric value for a single bit being turned on. The value corresponds to it's element index in the array, such that the first item in the array (item 0) holds the value 1, which is the decimal value for only bit 0 turned on. If the array has 16 items, index 15 would be set to 32768, which is the value for only bit 15 turned on.

OK, so an array is useful, since you don't have to remember the values for each bit position, except for when you initialize the array for the first time. Aha, but there's a way to easily remember the bit values too! Using hexadecimal notation, this is a piece of cake. Here's a snippet of array initialization using hexadecimal values, with comments of the more difficult to remember decimal equivalent:

```
m_nBit(0)  = &H1       '1
m_nBit(1)  = &H2       '2
m_nBit(2)  = &H4       '4
m_nBit(3)  = &H8       '8
m_nBit(4)  = &H10      '16
m_nBit(5)  = &H20      '32
m_nBit(6)  = &H40      '64
m_nBit(7)  = &H80      '128
m_nBit(8)  = &H100     '256
m_nBit(9)  = &H200     '512
m_nBit(10)  = &H400    '1024
m_nBit(11)  = &H800    '2048
m_nBit(12)  = &H1000   '4096
m_nBit(13)  = &H2000   '8192
m_nBit(14)  = &H4000   '16384
m_nBit(15)  = &H8000   '32768
```

See how easy it is! All you have to remember is that each byte (4 bits a peice) adds a 0 to the end of the hex value. The rest is just knowing which bit position you want to work on, which conveniently matches the array index. The use of this in the bitmask class, **clsBitMask**, is described in Chapter 2. Now that didn't hurt a bit, did it? You can see how this is used in the bit-masking class described in Chapter 2.

```
rivate Declare Function GlobalLock Lib "kernel32" (ByVal h
rivate Declare Function GlobalUnlock Lib "kernel32" (ByVa
--copying bitmap bits
 copies a global block of data into global memory
rivate Declare Sub CopyMemory Lib "kernel32" Alias "RtlM

--copies global block of data in[illegible]IB
rivate Declare Function SetDIB[illegible] "gdi32" (ByVal m_hd
 ByVal hBitmap As Long, ByVal nStartS[illegible]As Long, ByV
 ByVal lpBits As Any, lpBI As BITMAPI[illegible]ByVal wUsa

-blits DC to DC
rivate Declare Function BitBlt Lib "gdi32" (ByVal hDestDC
rivate Declare Function StretchBlt Lib "gdi32" (ByVal hDest

-palette methods
rivate Declare Function CreatePalett[illegible] "gdi32" (lpLogPal
rivate Declare Function SelectPalette [illegible] "gdi32" (ByVal m_
rivate Declare Function RealizePalette Lib "gdi32" (ByVal m
rivate Declare Sub AnimatePalette Lib "gdi32" (ByVal hPale

-device context methods
rivate Declare Function SelectObject Lib "gdi32" (ByVal m_

rivate Declare Function CreateCompatibleBitmap Lib "gdi32
rivate Declare Function DeleteObject Lib "gdi32" (ByVal hO

rivate Declare Function CreateCompatibleDC Lib "gdi32" (B
```

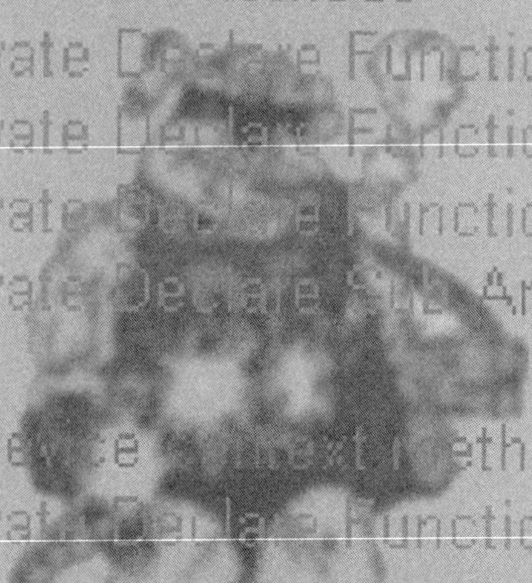

INSTANT

VB Animation

Appendix C

Using Tools to Prepare Your Graphics

Using BITEDIT and PALEDIT

These two programs combined provide the standard tools you need to alter any bitmap's image specifications. We've provided an installation for both programs on the accompanying CD. I used them to assign the appropriate palettes to bitmaps used throughout the book. This would entail building a palette from each of the images so that at least some colors from each image were included, thus not causing severe image degradation as the new palette is assigned. In this case, it was easy. I started with **`\Code\Chapter2\Apianim\Cmdfilm1.bmp`** which is the film strip image that combines screen shots of all three sample animation displays and the curtain as well:

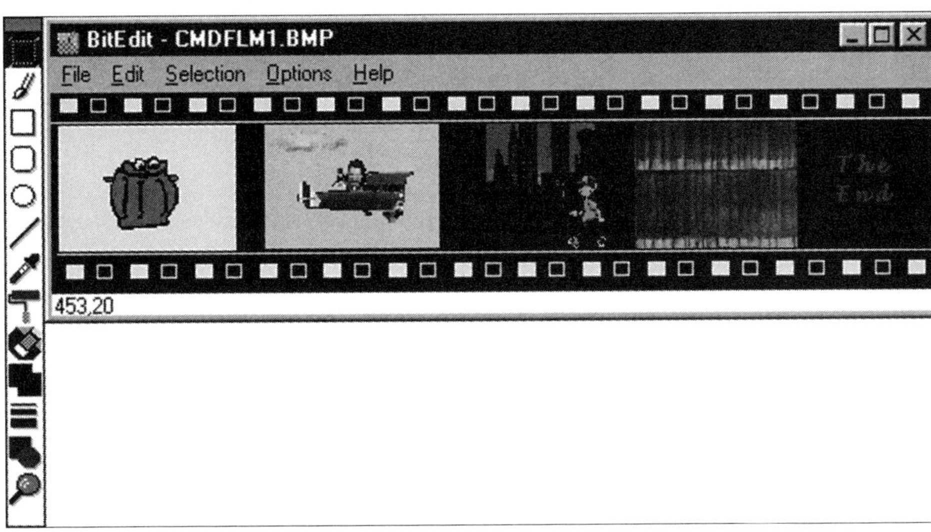

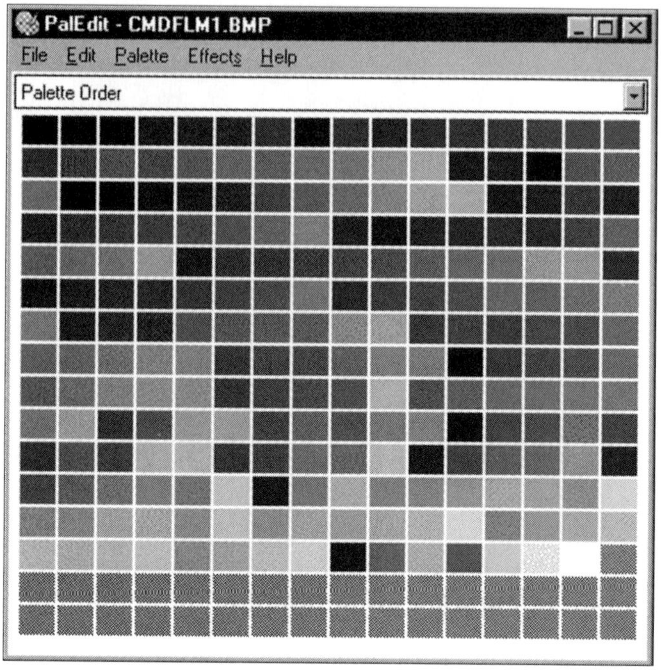

To load a bitmap into **Bitedit**, which you can find in **\Code\AppendixC**, you simply choose Open from the File menu and select the bitmap of your choice. Here's the palette, shown by selecting Show Palette from the Options menu in **Bitedit**:

You can't tell this from the figure, but the palette contains a combination of colors from each of the animation bitmaps, since each frame in the film strip is a sample from each animation. The first step to assigning this palette to the other bitmaps is to save the palette from the **Cmdfilm1** bitmap:

1 In **Bitedit** load the bitmap, **Cmdfilm1.bmp**, by choosing Open from the File menu.

2 Choose Show Palette from the Options menu. This will bring up the **Paledit** interface and displays all the colors used in the bitmap.

3 Choose Select Unused Colors from the Edit menu. This will highlight the palette entries that are duplicate colors or are unused in this bitmap.

4 Choose Delete from the Edit menu. This will remove those superfluous entries, leaving room to add more colors if we need to, later on.

5 Choose Save to File from the File menu. This lets you save the palette entries currently displayed to a file with the extension **.pal**. I named it **Apianim.pal**, in keeping with the convention of the chapter's project.

Now, to assign this new palette to another other image. For each image used in Chapter 2's sample code, load the image into **Bitedit** and display the bitmap's palette as previously instructed (steps 1 and 2). Then you assign the saved palette as follows:

1 From the **Paledit** interface choose Apply from File from the File menu. This presents an open file dialog where you'll choose the **.pal** file we previously saved. The new palette will display, the bitmaps colors will be mapped to the new palette.

2 Exit the **Paledit** program.

3 From the **Bitedit** interface choose Save from the File menu. This will save the bitmap, including the changes made by assigning the new palette.

Pretty easy stuff! You'll notice that when you apply the palette from a file, a message is displayed asking if you're sure you want to change the current bitmap's palette, warning you that palette entries may be lost. This is because what **Paledit** will do is find the closest RGB match for each color in the bitmap's current palette, in the palette we are assigning it. If it doesn't find a suitable match, some strange color may be assigned causing significant alteration to the bitmap's appearance. We can rest assured in this case since the palette we are using also includes at least a few shades of each color required by each animation sample. A convenient coincidence? I think not.

Things to watch out for!

We're not quite done with this palette preparation thing yet. An additional step is necessary to insure that there are no colors missing from the palette before assigning it to all the other graphics. There was one color missing from the saved palette from **Cmdfilm1.bmp** that caused each animation to have a flaw. We can't have that. The culprit, pure white. Take a look at this figure for the before and after of resolving this missing palette entry after being assigned the original **Apianim.pal**.

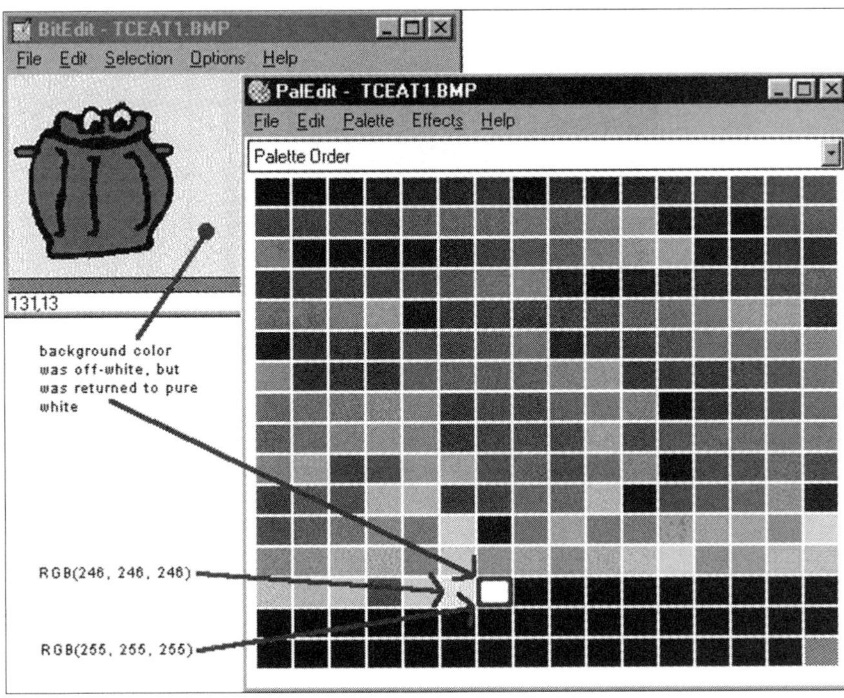

The trashcan bitmaps no longer had a pure white background, so you see the rectangle of each animation frame in an off-white shade. Also, the pilot and kid frames didn't quite mask the way they should have (masking is explained in the chapter), thus providing a not-so-transparent effect as each moved across the screen — a subtle difference, but none-the-less incorrect.

To fix this, I had to add pure white to one of the available palette slots, then (oh no) re-save this new palette and re-assign it to each and every bitmap. What a drag! That's why if you know that certain colors need to be present, it's a good idea to check this before going through the palette assignment steps. Things like solid background animations like the trashcan example, and required mask colors like pure black and pure white, are first on the checklist. Here's how to add to the palette:

1 Load the first bitmap, **`Cmdfilm1.bmp`** and show its palette like before.

2 From the **`Paledit`** interface choose Add Color from the Palette menu. You're given an Add Color interface, where you can choose a color using the color gradient area, the intensity scroller, or by entering exact RGB values and levels of hue, saturation and lightness. In this case, for pure white I simply scrolled the red, green and blue values to the max, for a value of 255 in each.

3 Click the Add button, then the Close button.

4 Save the palette again, overwriting our previous **`Apianim.pal`**.

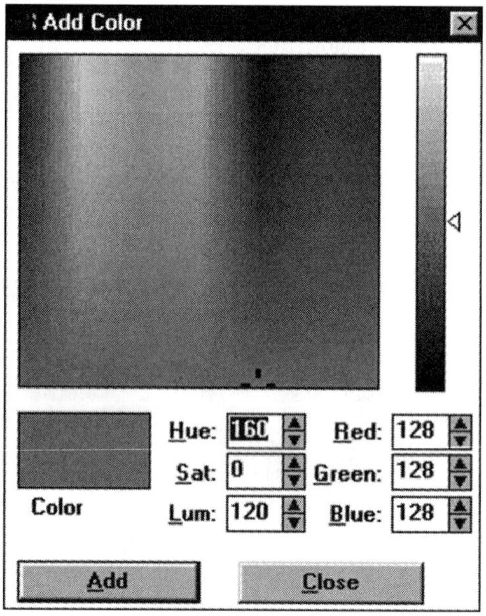

In the case of adding a new color there's one additional step to perform while re-assigning the new palette to each bitmap. Adding pure white to the bitmap's palette doesn't update that off-white color in the actual bitmap to its desired, pure white state. Let's do an example with one of the pilot mask bitmaps so you can see how its done:

1 Open up one of the pilot mask bmp's in **`Bitedit`**.

Click on the Current Color Tool and select the last color in the displayed palette.

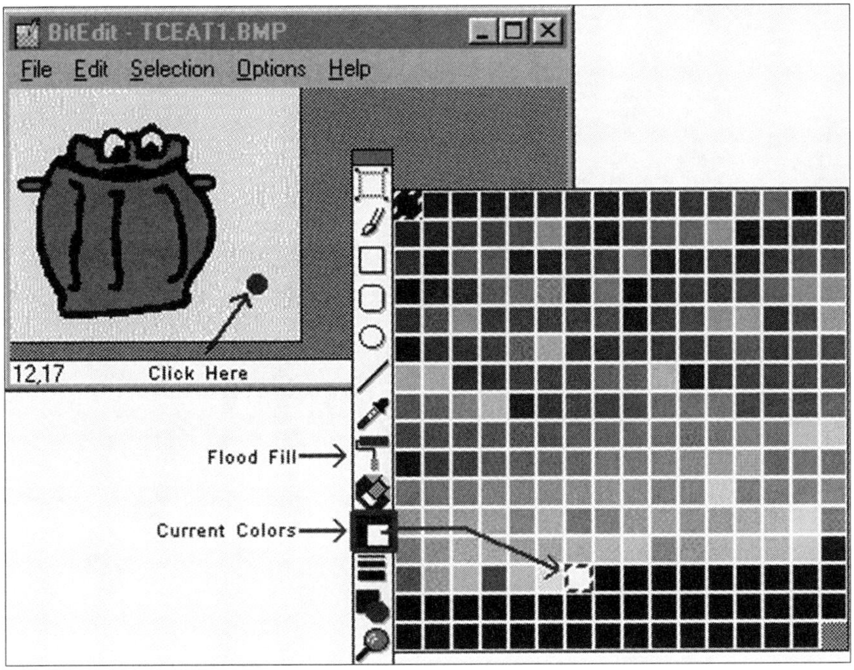

This will make the current color our new pure white addition to the bitmap's palette.

2 Click on the Flood Fill Tool. The next place in the current bitmap display that you click, will flood fill with the current color. Flood fill works only on adjacent colors of the same value.

3 Click on an area in the image that you want filled with the current color. Clicking on the off-white area, will change the entire off-white area to pure white, which is the current color.

4 Re-save the bitmap.

If you double-click on a palette entry from the paledit display, the same dialog is displayed with RGB values representing *that* entry's color value. This way, you can double check if an entry is the color value you're expecting. If you change the color in the dialog, the bitmap pixels that point to *that* entry will automatically change to reflect the new value.

Repeat this process for all images that need palette alterations, only performing the last set of steps to those that need an off-white conversion to pure white, and you're done! Of course, there are many more uses for **`Bitedit`** and **`Paledit`**, but the main steps I've demonstrated here are those necessary to get the results you need, as were used for the graphics in each of the book's samples.

```
rivate Declare Function GlobalFree Lib "kernel32" (ByVal h
rivate Declare Function GlobalLock Lib "kernel32" (ByVal H
rivate Declare Function GlobalUnlock Lib "kernel32" (ByVa
--copying bitmap bits
 copies a global block of data into global memory
rivate Declare Sub CopyMemory Lib "kernel32" Alias "RtlM

--copies global block of data into DIB
rivate Declare Function SetDIBits Lib "gdi32" (ByVal m_hd
 ByVal hBitmap As Long, ByVal nStartScan As Long, By
 ByVal lpBits As Any, lpBI As BITMAPINFO, ByVal wUsa

--blits DC to DC
rivate Declare Function BitBlt Lib "gdi32" (ByVal hDestDC
rivate Declare Function StretchBlt Lib "gdi32" (ByVal hDes

--palette methods
rivate Declare Function CreatePalette Lib "gdi32" (lpLogPal
rivate Declare Function SelectPalette Lib "gdi32" (ByVal m
rivate Declare Function RealizePalette Lib "gdi32" (ByVal r
rivate Declare Sub AnimatePalette Lib "gdi32" (ByVal hPal

--device context methods
rivate Declare Function SelectObject Lib "gdi32" (ByVal m_

rivate Declare Function CreateCompatibleBitmap Lib "gdi32
rivate Declare Function DeleteObject Lib "gdi32" (ByVal hC

rivate Declare Function CreateCompatibleDC Lib "gdi32" (B
```

INSTANT

VB Animation

Appendix D

Windows API Functions Used throughout the Book

AnimatePalette()	Rapidly updates the display with new colors assigned to a logical palette associated with that display.
BitBlt()	Transfers a specified block of bitmap data from one device context to another, using the specified raster operation.
CopyMemory()	Used to copy data from one place in memory to another.
CreateCompatibleBitmap()	Creates a bitmap object of a specified width and height, compatible with the device context specified.
CreateCompatibleDC()	Creates a memory device context compatible with the device context specified.
CreateDIBitmap()	Creates a device-dependent bitmap based on a device-independent bitmap.
CreateFontIndirect()	Creates a logical font with characteristics that match the information passed.
CreatePalette()	Creates a logical palette from the color values passed.
CreatePatternBrush()	Creates a logical brush using a bitmap pattern from a device-dependent bitmap.
DeleteDC()	Deletes the device context specified.
DeleteObject()	Deletes a windows object freeing associated system resources.
DrawFocusRect()	Draws a focus rectangle on a device context. The rectangle is drawn using the exclusive-or operation in the style used to indicate the focus (typically a dotted line).
GetDC()	Retrieves a to the device context for the client area of the specified window.
GetDeviceCaps()	Retrieves device context information about a specified device.

GetNearestPaletteIndex()	Returns an index position in a specified logical palette that is the closest match to a given color value.
GetObject()	Returns information about a graphics object. The returned information varies based on the object requested.
GetPaletteEntries()	Fills a **PALETTEENTRY** array with a range of palette entries from a logical palette.
GetPixel()	Retrieves the RGB value of a pixel in the specified device context.
GetPrivateProfileString()	Returns the string value for an entry in an initialization file.
GetSystemPaletteEntries()	Fills a **PALETTEENTRY** array with a range of palette entries from the system palette associated with the specified device context.
GlobalAlloc()	Allocates a block of global memory for the number of bytes specified.
GlobalFree()	Frees the specified global memory object.
GlobalLock()	Locks a global memory object returning a pointer to the first byte in the memory block. The address will remain valid until the memory block is unlocked using the **GlobalUnlock()** function.
GlobalUnlock()	Unlocks the specified memory block that had been previously locked using the **GlobalLock()** function.
IntersectRect()	Fills a destination rectangle with the intersecting rectangle of 2 source rectangles. This means that the destination rectangle includes all points that are common to both source rectangles.
InvertRect()	Inverts the specified rectangle on a device context by inverting the value of each pixel.
PatBlt()	Paints a rectangle to a device context using the brush object of that device and the raster operation specified.
PtInRect()	Determines if a specified point lies within a specified rectangle.
RealizePalette()	Maps logical palette entries selected into a device context to the system palette.
ReleaseDC()	Releases the specified device context previously obtained through calls to **GetDC()** or **GetWindowDC()**.
SelectPalette()	Selects a logical palette into a device context. This replaces the previous logical palette the device was using.
SelectObject()	Selects a windows object into a device context replacing the previous object of that type.
SetDIBits()	Sets the pixels in a device-dependent bitmap with data from a device-independent bitmap.

SetPaletteEntries()	Uses a **PALETTEENTRY** array to update entries in a logical palette.
SetPixel()	Sets the RGB value of a pixel in the specified device context.
ShowCursor()	Controls the visibility of the cursor.
StretchBlt()	Transfers a specified block of bitmap data from one device context to another, stretching or compressing the bitmap to fit the destination rectangle.
TextOut()	Prints a text string to a device context at specific coordinates using the device context's current font object.
timeGetTime()	Returns the system time (time elapsed since Windows was started) in milliseconds.
UnionRect()	Fills a destination rectangle with a rectangle that encompasses 2 source rectangles.
WritePrivateProfileString()	Writes a string value into the specified section of an initialization file.

```
rivate Declare Function GlobalFree Lib "kernel32" (ByVal h
rivate Declare Function GlobalLock Lib "kernel32" (ByVal h
rivate Declare Function GlobalUnlock Lib "kernel32" (ByVa
--copying bitmap bits
 copies a global block of data into global memory
rivate Declare Sub CopyMemory Lib "kernel32" Alias "RtlM

--copies global block of data in    B
rivate Declare Function SetDIB      "gdi32" (ByVal m_hd
 ByVal hBitmap As Long, ByVal nStartS    As Long, By
 ByVal lpBits As Any, lpBI As BITMAPI     ByVal wUsa

--blits DC to DC
rivate Declare Function BitBlt Lib "gdi32" (ByVal hDestDC
rivate Declare Function StretchBlt Lib "gdi32" (ByVal hDes

--palette methods
rivate Declare Function CreatePalett     "gdi32" (lpLogPa
rivate Declare Function SelectPalette    "gdi32" (ByVal m
rivate Declare Function RealizePalette Lib "gdi32" (ByVal r
rivate Declare Sub AnimatePalette Lib "gdi32" (ByVal hPal

--device context methods
rivate Declare Function SelectObject Lib "gdi32" (ByVal m_

rivate Declare Function CreateCompatibleBitmap Lib "gdi32
rivate Declare Function DeleteObject Lib "gdi32" (ByVal hC

rivate Declare Function CreateCompatibleDC Lib "gdi32" (
```

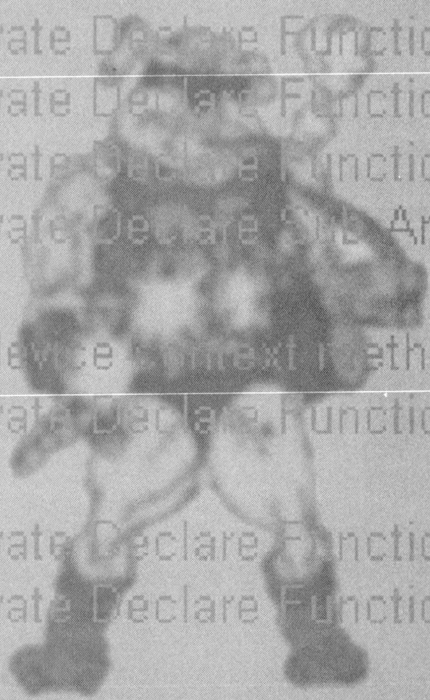

Appendix E

Visual Basic Animation Resource

Although we have tried to include as much information, help and support as possible, there are always parts of software development that you can't cover in a book. This appendix is a comprehensive road map to those places that may be of further help to the student of Visual Basic Animation. Here, we'll list web pages, magazines and other books that will give you a helping hand as to where you can go next.

You can also find these resources updated frequently, with a more comprehensive list, on the Instant Visual Basic Animation Web Pages. Point your browser at:

`http://www.wrox.com/books/ivba0788/ivba0788.htm`

Please drop by and make your own suggestions to these resources.

Books

If you're still eager for more reading, check out the following recommended texts. The first in invaluable to every serious Visual Basic developer:

Visual Basic Programmer's Guide to the Win32 API, Daniel Appleman, ZD Press, ISBN: 1-56276-287-7

This is a truly great reference, but for a well-rounded tutorial, take a gander at:

The Revolutionary Guide to Visual Basic 4 Professional, Larry Roof, Wrox Press, ISBN: 1-874416-37-0

If you want to read about writing games for VB, look no further than:

Black Art of Visual Basic Game Programming, Mark Pruett, The Waite Group, ISBN: 1-57169-005-0

It's written for VB3 but does include some good code and nice games. For a guide to bitmaps, graphics and multimedia techniques I recommend:

The Revolutionary Guide to Bitmapped Graphics, Control Zed, Wrox Press, ISBN: 1-874416-31-1

Magazines

An extremely popular source for technical Visual Basic information and one of Michele's popular haunting grounds is:

Visual Basic Developer, Pinnacle Publishing Inc., 18000 72nd Avenue South, Suite 217, Kent, WA 98032, monthly, mail order.

A more glossy Visual Basic magazine that's a necessity is:

Visual Basic Programmers Journal, Fawcette Technical Publications, 209 Hamilton Avenue, Palo Alto, CA 94301-2500, monthly, news-stand.

Newsgroups

The newsgroups are a free for all, global, question and answer session. There are many dedicated to Visual Basic:

comp.lang.basic.visual
comp.lang.basic.visual.3rdparty
comp.lang.basic.visual.announce
comp.lang.basic.visual.database
comp.lang.basic.visual.misc

and there are a few that deal with animation, multimedia and game development:

comp.graphics.animation
rec.games.programmer
rec.games.design

but unfortunately, there isn't one that deals with both multimedia and Visual Basic together.

WWW Pages

There are many, many good Visual Basic web pages and most are listed here at Yahoo's index to Visual Basic pages:

http://www.yahoo.com/Computers_and_Internet/Programming_Languages/Visual_Basic/

Probably the best Visual Basic page, though, is Carl & Gary's Visual Basic Home Page which you can find here:

http://www.apexsc.com/vb/

As well as being full of juicy links, book reviews, articles and useful information, this page misses absolutely nothing. Another great Visual Basic page is the one run by The VB Pro at:

http://www.inquiry.com/techtips/thevbpro/

As well as answering a whole hog of nasty coding questions, he maintains loads of supporting material, like a mailing list, help groups and VB script demonstrations. But for a site that covers Visual Basic *and* animation, look no further than Powermedia's Multimedia Resource Center:

http://www.omnisoft.com/~omnisoft/mmrs.html

For information about sprite manipulation and creation, look no further than Ari Feldman's web site:

http://www.walrus.com/~ari/spritlib.htm

From the creator of the Sprite Library that you can find on the CD, you can find everything you need to know about sprites here. You can find the ultimate page for animation resources here:

http://www.isisnet.com/dayglo/anim.html

The number and quality of links and information is unsurpassed.

Using OmniSoft's PowerMedia

Programming Animation Made Simple

If you're a regular Visual Basic programmer, you'll know how simple it is to create powerful programs, with minimal effort. The same is true for programming animation in Visual Basic—using **PowerMedia** by **OmniSoft**. Just follow these steps and you'll soon be on your way to creating eye-grabbing programs with animation that literally jumps of the screen.

Installation

1 From the CD, run the PowerMedia setup program **`D:\Apps\PMedia\SETUP.EXE`**.

2 After PowerMedia is installed, you will be informed that the Autodesk Animation Player Setup will be run. Make sure that you check *all* of the setup option boxes.

Note: It's best not to change the default directory that Setup offers, if possible.

Running PowerMedia

Visual Basic 3.0 users click the Load PowerMedia Controls for VB3 icon in the PowerMedia Windows Group. Visual Basic 4.0 users click the Load PowerMedia Controls for VB4 icon in the PowerMedia Windows Group.

Neither of the above will work if you have the PowerMedia directory on a drive other than C. If your PowerMedia directory is on a B or D drive, manually load the controls as outlined here:

Visual Basic 3.0 users start Visual Basic. Then from the menus: File...Add File, select the PowerMedia VBX's from your PowerMedia directory: **`Poweranm.vbx`**, **`Powerbac.vbx`**, **`Powermus.vbx`**, **`Powersnd.vbx`** and **`Powervid.vbx`**.

Visual Basic 4.0 users start Visual Basic. Then from the menus: Tools...Custom Controls. Click the browse button. Select the PowerMedia VBX's from your PowerMedia directory: **`Poweranm.vbx`**, **`Powerbac.vbx`**, **`Powermus.vbx`**, **`Powersnd.vbx`** and **`Powervid.vbx`**.

Using PowerAnimation

1 Double-click the Slides button. A PowerAnimation control will appear in the center of your window.

2 Click on the PowerAnimation control.

3 Hit F4 for properties.

4 Move to the MultimediaFile property and double-click on it. A File Open dialog box will be opened.

5 Choose an animation (**.fli**, **.flc**) file from the resource flow directory installed by PowerMedia by default: **c:\Powermed\Resflow** directory.

6 Click OK, then close the Properties Box.

7 Start the application (F5).

8 Click on PowerAnimation and enjoy the show!

Tips for PowerAnimation

Invisible at Run Time

If you want the animation to play without the user clicking on it, set the **PowerAnimation Visible** property to false. Then in the **Form_Load** procedure insert the following code:

```
PowerAnimation1.action  =  "play"
```

Loop the Animation

If you want the animation to play continuously, set the **PowerAnimation Loop** property to **True**.

> **For more information and help on PowerAnimation, please consult the PowerMedia Help Online.**

Other Controls

After trying PowerAnimation, please feel free to use the other controls which make it easy to add sound, music, video, and backdrops to your program. For additional help, please consult the PowerMedia Help Online.

Purchase

If you are finding that you're using PowerMedia and/or are distributing applications with PowerMedia, you must order the licensed copy:

NAME:____
ADDRESS: ____
____
____
____
PHONE NUMBER: ______________________________________
FAX NUMBER: ____
EMAIL ADDRESS: _____________________________________

POWERMEDIA (single user)- $79	________
Sales Tax: 7.75% (CA residents)- $6.12	________
Shipping and Handling-Continental US- $4	________
Shipping and Handling-Outside US- $11	________
TOTAL:	________

Please send this form along with a check payable to **Omnisoft** to:

OMNISOFT
1723 WESTBROOK AVENUE
LOS ALTOS, CA 94024

E-mail: bchandra@omnisoft.com
Sales/Technical: (415) 917-1395 Fax: (415) 917-1345

```
rivate Declare Function GlobalFree Lib "kernel32" (ByVal h
rivate Declare Function GlobalLock Lib "kernel32" (ByVal h
rivate Declare Function GlobalUnlock Lib "kernel32" (ByVa
--copying bitmap bits
 copies a global block of data into global memory
rivate Declare Sub CopyMemory Lib "kernel32" Alias "RtlM

--copies global block of data in  B
rivate Declare Function SetDIB     "gdi32" (ByVal m_hd
 ByVal hBitmap As Long, ByVal nStartS   As Long, By
 ByVal lpBits As Any, lpBI As BITMAPI    ByVal wUsa

--blits DC to DC
rivate Declare Function BitBlt Lib "gdi32" (ByVal hDestDC
rivate Declare Function StretchBlt Lib "gdi32" (ByVal hDes

--palette methods
rivate Declare Function CreatePalett    "gdi32" (lpLogPa
rivate Declare Function SelectPalette    "gdi32" (ByVal m
rivate Declare Function RealizePalette Lib "gdi32" (ByVal 
rivate Declare     AnimatePalette Lib "gdi32" (ByVal hPa

--device context methods
rivate Declare Function SelectObject Lib "gdi32" (ByVal m

rivate Declare Function CreateCompatibleBitmap Lib "gdi3
rivate Declare Function DeleteObject Lib "gdi32" (ByVal h

rivate Declare Function CreateCompatibleDC Lib "gdi32" (
```

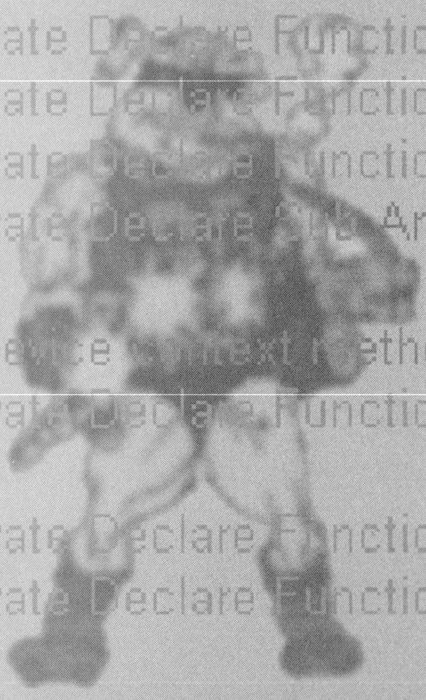

INSTANT

VB Animation

Index

Symbols

A

B

C

D

E

F

R

S

T

U

V

W

X

```
rivate Declare Function GlobalFree Lib "kernel32" (ByVal h
rivate Declare Function GlobalLock Lib "kernel32" (ByVal h
rivate Declare Function GlobalUnlock Lib "kernel32" (ByVa
-copying bitmap bits
 copies a global block of data into global memory
rivate Declare Sub CopyMemory Lib "kernel32" Alias "RtlM
```

```
-copies global block of data into DIB
rivate Declare Function SetDIB... "gdi32" (ByVal m_hd
 ByVal hBitmap As Long, ByVal nStartS... As Long, ByV
 ByVal lpBits As Any, lpBI As BITMAPI... ByVal wUsa
```

```
-blits DC to DC
rivate Declare Function BitBlt Lib "gdi32" (ByVal hDestDC
rivate Declare Function StretchBlt Lib "gdi32" (ByVal hDes
```

```
-palette methods
rivate Declare Function CreatePalett... "gdi32" (lpLogPal
rivate Declare Function SelectPalette ... "gdi32" (ByVal m
rivate Declare Function RealizePalette Lib "gdi32" (ByVal m
rivate Declare Sub AnimatePalette Lib "gdi32" (ByVal hPal
```

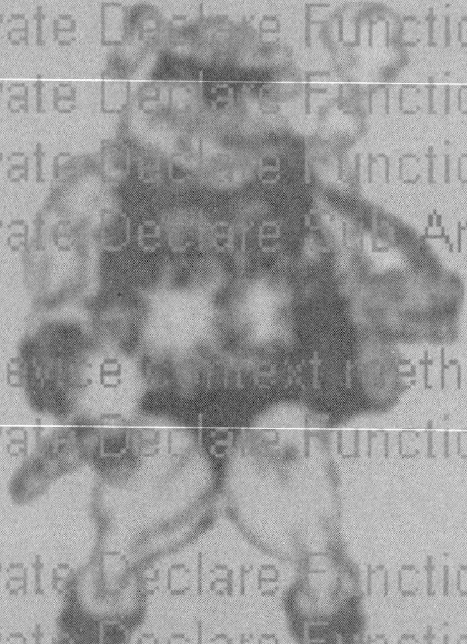

```
-device context methods
rivate Declare Function SelectObject Lib "gdi32" (ByVal m_

rivate Declare Function CreateCompatibleBitmap Lib "gdi32
rivate Declare Function DeleteObject Lib "gdi32" (ByVal hC

rivate Declare Function CreateCompatibleDC Lib "gdi32" (B
```

WROX

Register Instant VB Animation and sign up for a free subscription to The Developer's Journal.

A bi-monthly magazine for software developers, The Wrox Press Developer's Journal features in-depth articles, news and help for everyone in the software development industry. Each issue includes extracts from our latest titles and is crammed full of practical insights into coding techniques, tricks and research.

Fill in and return the card below to receive a free subscription to the Wrox Press Developer's Journal.

Instant VB Animation Registration Card

Name ______

Address ______

______

______

______

City ______ State/Region ______

Country ______ Postcode/Zip ______

E-mail ______

Occupation ______

How did you hear about this book? ______

- ☐ Book review (name) ______
- ☐ Advertisement (name) ______
- ☐ Recommendation ______
- ☐ Catalog ______
- ☐ Other ______

Where did you buy this book? ______

- ☐ Bookstore (name) ______ City ______
- ☐ Computer Store (name) ______
- ☐ Mail Order ______
- ☐ Other ______

What influenced you in the purchase of this book?

- ☐ Cover Design
- ☐ Contents
- ☐ Other (please specify) ______

How did you rate the overall contents of this book?

- ☐ Excellent
- ☐ Good
- ☐ Average
- ☐ Poor

______

What did you find most useful about this book? ______

______

What did you find least useful about this book? ______

______

Please add any additional comments. ______

______

What other subjects will you buy a computer book on soon? ______

______

What is the best computer book you have used this year?

______

Note: This information will only be used to keep you updated about new Wrox Press titles and will not be used for any other purpose or passed to any other third party.

 Check here if you don't want a subscription to The Developer's Journal or to recieve further support for this book. ☐

Free phone in USA 800-USE-WROX
Fax (312) 465 4063

Compuserve 100063,2152.
UK Tel. (44121) 706 6826 Fax (44121) 706 2967